EFFECTIVE COACHING

A PSYCHOLOGICAL APPROACH

DONALD E. FUOSS, ED.D.

Professor of Physical Education
California State University, Sacramento
Sacramento, California

ROBERT J. TROPPMANN, M.A.

Head Football Coach
College of Marin
Kentfield, California

Director of Physical Education
Redwood High School
Larkspur, California

JOHN WILEY & SONS
New York • Chichester • Brisbane • Toronto

Library of Congress Cataloging in Publication Data:

Fuoss, Donald E.
  Effective coaching.

  Includes index.
  1. Coaching (Athletics)   2. Sports—Psychological aspects.   3. Coaching (Athletics)—Psychological aspects.   4. Motivation (Psychology) 5. Learning, Psychology of.   I. Troppmann, Robert.
II. Title.
GV711.F87   796'.07'7   81-7624
ISBN 0-471-03233-6   AACR2

Printed in the United States of America

10 9 8 7 6 5 4 3 2 1

PREFACE

Effective Coaching: A Psychological Approach is written by two authors whose combined coaching experience exceeds 50 years. This book may be used by the in-service coach, as well as the preprofessional student at the undergraduate or graduate level who is enrolled in psychology of coaching, psychology of sport, or general coaching courses. This book also covers all sports and should be beneficial to all regardless of the sport one coaches.

Written from the perspective of coaches, and not individuals formally educated and trained in psychology, this book deals in detail with psychological concepts, theories, and principles, drawn from an extensive survey of the research that has been termed "classic," as well as more current and relevant literature on psychology and sport psychology. We have also included the literature from several different disciplines, but only where it was of a less technical and more practical nature.

The typical coach is not likely to be aware of the diverse background and expertise of today's sport psychologists. There are clinical, educational, and research psychologists, psychiatrists, physiologists, physicists, physical educationalists, and others, all working within an area generally called sport psychology. The unique principle these diverse individuals share in common is a conviction that one's maximum athletic performance is affected by one's psychological makeup, as well as by one's physical attributes and skills.

Where possible we have attempted to cut away and minimize much of the psychological jargon and language, without giving the appearance of writing off the top of our heads, so that the reader can see not only the psychological theories being presented but more importantly the application to coaching. In the study of psychological conceptualizations and theories there are few simple answers, and perhaps no "right" ones. Thus, our strategy has been to present the topical subject historically, many times introducing the early research first—the "classic" work—and then including more up-to-date research examples throughout the discussion to clarify the theories; we usually follow this with a section on the implications for coaching, or how coaches might apply this information. Each chapter concludes with a brief Summary, to tie together the salient points, and numerous References and at least several additional "Selected Readings." In most instances the "Selected Readings" are different from those used as References, and the serious-minded "student," whether he or she be athlete, coach, or would-be coach, may wish to delve deeper into the subject.

For the most part, today's athlete is likely to be stronger, bigger, faster, more agile, healthier, better fed, and more knowledgeable about his or her participation in sports, as compared to his or her parents and grandparents. Furthermore, today's athlete has better facilities and equipment and is exposed to better training techniques and coaching methods than those used in the past.

All coaches should be interested in how psychology and sport psychologists can help them and their athletes. A more important question, however, is—How can a coach know and learn about psychology and its application to coaching without the availability of a sport psychologist? We attempt here to humanize the coaching process in a systematic way. There has been much study on how to improve athlete performance, but a systematic approach to the psychological aspects of a person in terms of improving maximum athletic performance has not been attempted. Many times athletes are well-prepared physically for competition, but their psychological preparation is lacking and inadequate or, on occasion, practically nonexistent. When there is a lack of integration of mind and body, this is reflected in an athlete's ultimate performance. Interest in the psychology of sport is not something new; it has been with us for many years. Coaches have always been interested in the psychological factors that affect their players and in how to get them ''up'' for a competitive game. Our intent is to provide useful information that can be applied to athletic coaching.

A coach's experience often enables him or her to formulate ideas about personality, motivation, leadership, team cohesion, and numerous other topics that are discussed in this book. Unfortunately, one's conclusions are not always accurate. While coaching experience is invaluable and is a good teacher in terms of the learning process, on occasion, the experience gained is costly in terms of mistakes, errors, and time lost. This book will make it possible for coaches and students of sport psychology to expand on their understanding of the important ingredients or components that go into individual player and team success. Our book is limited in scope to the psychological aspects of coaching and does not place any emphasis on offense, defense, techniques, skills, tactics, strategy, drills, or topical subjects of a similar vein. Numerous concrete examples relating to specific sports are given throughout for illustrative purposes only and are included to clarify a particular psychological concept or theory as it pertains to coaching or to the behavior of an athlete or coach.

Effective Coaching: A Psychological Approach is divided into four major sections and twelve chapters. Also note that in this book where the masculine pronoun is used, the feminine term also is equally applicable, since a coach or athlete can be of either sex. Thus we have avoided the use of he/she, him and her, and other awkward constructions.

Part One—The Psychological and Societal Phenomena of Athletics and Coaching consists of three chapters. The opening chapter is an overview that discusses coaching as a science and an art. Here we also introduce sport psychology and the application of sport psychology to athletic coaching.

EFFECTIVE COACHING

A PSYCHOLOGICAL APPROACH

About the authors

Donald E. Fuoss held collegiate and scholastic coaching positions in the East, South and Midwest before coming to California State University, Sacramento. In 1975, he relinquished his position as Director of Intercollegiate Athletics, and presently he is a Professor of Physical Education. He received his Ed.D. in the organization and administration of physical education and athletics from Columbia University in 1952.

Dr. Fuoss has lectured at approximately 75 sports clinics throughout the United States and Canada, and is author of more than 75 articles and 7 other books including *Effective Football Coaching: Game-Winning Techniques for Preventing Mistakes and Errors (1981).* He was a member of the 1967 Rose Bowl Champion Coaching Staff.

Robert J. Troppmann is Chairman of the Physical Education Department, Redwood High School, Larkspur, California, and Head Football Coach at the College of Marin, Kentfield, California. He received his M.A. in physical education from San Francisco State University in 1949.

He has written numerous articles and four books including *Winning Drills for Offensive and Defensive Linemen* and *The New Revised Master Defense Guide* (1981). He received the 1971 National High School Coaches Association Distinguished Service Award.

Fuoss and Troppmann are co-authors of *Creative Management Techniques in Interscholastic Athletics,* and presently are preparing other texts for publication.

An integral aspect of coaching—the societal role expectations of a coach—is discussed in Chapter 2. Superiors, subordinates, peers, players, parents, the media, and fans all have expectations of a coach, and every individual has his or her own expectations. Resolving role conflict at times results in stress, personal strain, and indecision. A coach should be fully cognizant of the nature of coaching and either accept it or choose another profession.

The concluding chapter in the introductory section discusses unique features indigenous to coaching. In one sense, coaching is a most rewarding and satisfying experience. In another sense, coaching is at times frustrating, soul-searching, gut-wrenching, sometimes literally killing, and not infrequently a thankless experience. Emotional tension is a factor that should be seriously considered before one enters coaching. Not all individuals thrive and are productive when working under tension and in stressful situations, such as those of the coach's domain. Obviously a coach's behavior affects a player's behavior.

Part Two—The Philosophical and Management Dimensions of Coaching consists of two chapters. Despite the fact that it is virtually impossible to separate the components of one's personal philosophy of life, one's professional philosophy, and one's coaching theory or philosophy since they are so closely interrelated, each having a direct bearing on the other, an attempt is made to do so in Chapter 4 only for the purpose of discussion. This is followed with a discussion in Chapter 5 on management, decision making, and other skills and processes necessary for effective coaching. For the coach-manager to be effective, he or she not only needs to be familiar with the various functions, concepts, and techniques of management, but she or he will need to be knowledgeable of the advantages and disadvantages of a particular concept or technique. A coach must be able to predict what will result both favorably and unfavorably from the application of management principles. This dimension of coaching is frequently minimized or overlooked.

Part Three—The Psychological Dimensions of Coaching: Understanding Human Behavior consists of five chapters dealing with psychological concepts, theories, and principles that are applicable to sport and athletic coaching. Sport psychology encompasses many interrelationships among the coach, the athlete, and the sport, and the effective use of these relationships results in more effective coaching. There is much more to coaching than only the application of technical, tactical, and strategical "know-how."

The act of communication symbolizes the need an individual has to maintain contact with his or her environment and, for this reason, it can be seen as supplying one of psychology's central themes. Seldom, however, is this theme discussed in detail in coaching textbooks. In coaching, no single behavior is more important than the process of communication. The purpose of Chapter 6 is not only to familiarize the reader with the process of communication and to examine what causes distortions, interferences, and weak communication, but to suggest ways to communicate more effectively. In turn this should lead to greater coaching effectiveness.

It is important for the individual who is a coach to understand the developmental and maturational processes of a human being in order to coach effectively; these are discussed in Chapter 7. Understanding the physiological differences in athletes is paramount if a coach is to succeed in his or her chosen profession. This phase of coaching must receive major consideration in training the athlete for competition. Training must be geared to the individual characteristics and maturational factors, regardless of sex.

Personality, motivation, and learning are all closely interrelated, and each is discussed in separate chapters. Coaches are interested in the study of personality since it may offer some hope of interpreting the mystery of what motivates behavior, especially when behavior is different from what a coach expects or from what the coach would have done. Chapter 8 offers a system of categorizing a wide range of behaviors but, more importantly for the coach, we offer a study of personality—the possible key to predicting human behavior.

There is no single way to approach the subject of motivation. Certainly there is no dearth of psychological literature available on motivation, and the concepts and theories explained in Chapter 9 on the psychology of motivation should aid the reader. However one should learn this if nothing else—one learns a great deal about a person by recognizing his or her needs and then aiding the individual in fulfilling those needs. This can be a success formula in any human pursuit.

The concluding chapter in this largest section of our book deals with the psychology of learning. While a coach may possess a well-rounded philosophy and a sound coaching theory, he or she will not enjoy coaching success unless ideas and "know-how" can be conveyed to others. The methods or means he or she uses to convey ideas and concepts are important, as is *how* he or she teaches or coaches, which is the "art" of coaching. It is through the learning process, which includes communication, that the coach's goals for his program and his sport are transmitted to others. Coaches are teachers; coaching is teaching; and teaching is the management or guidance of learning. The learning process, the learner (athlete), and the conditions for learning are all discussed in Chapter 10.

The concluding section consists of two chapters. Part Four—The Social Psychological Dimensions of Coaching: Social Influence deals with theories and styles of leadership behavior and the psychology of group behavior.

Typically every coach is expected to provide leadership and to be able to motivate his or her players and assistant coaches. Since leadership is a phenomenon that concerns two or more individuals in a particular relationship, Chapter 11 is concerned with how coaching leadership styles influence individual and group behavior in athletics and sports. Leadership styles refer to the qualities of the relationship and the followers in a situation.

The concluding chapter in the book deals with the psychology of group behavior. Within every formal structure there exists a social system of the members of the informal or emergent organization. In sports, team or group members—whether they be players or coaches—interact and relate to one another in performing their assigned duties designated by the formal authority structure. They establish relationships within their own groups in order to satisfy affinity and achievement needs. Thus the emergent organization converts the formal organization structure into a living, functioning, goal-directed group. These group characteristics are identified and discussed in Chapter 12.

From a personal standpoint of the dozen books we have authored and co-authored collectively to date, the writing of this one was the most difficult, the most time-consuming, and at times the most frustrating. Upon its completion we now feel it is also the most rewarding in a psychic sense. We hope this book will aid the reader—coach, athlete, or student—at least in some small measure to better understand sport science's last frontier.

DONALD E. FUOSS
ROBERT J. TROPPMANN

ACKNOWLEDGMENTS

Many people made this publication possible. We thank everyone who helped in the preparation of this book. Certainly the production of any book is never a single effort, and this one is not an exception. The interpretations and applications, however, are our responsibility.

We are grateful to the authors and their publishers who granted us permission to quote from their publications. Without their cooperation this book would never have been written.

Appreciation is also extended to those undergraduate and graduate students in the Physical Education Department, California State University, Sacramento, who researched individual independent study projects on different topical subjects in this book, and to former and present teaching assistants and office aides who located many library sources for our writing. Also, a public expression of appreciation is extended to a colleague, Dr. Frank Jones, who teaches undergraduate and graduate courses at CSUS in sport psychology, for making available to us numerous sources of information from his professional library, and with whom we engaged in dialogue frequently to discuss psychological concepts and their application to athletics.

Most especially we must thank Wayne Anderson, our editor. He deserves our thanks for many reasons, especially for his encouragement and patience. We also wish to thank our manuscript editor, Joan Knizeski, for her thoroughness and professionalism—it was a pleasure working with her. And the senior production supervisor, Jan Lavin, deserves our warm gratitude for care and diligence in getting this book out.

Finally, without the assistance, encouragement, and unfailing support of our wives, Frances Fuoss and Marilyn Troppmann, this book would not have become a reality.

A grateful "thank you," while inadequate, to all who assisted in the preparation of this book in any manner, is expressed with our sincere personal gratitude.

DONALD E. FUOSS
ROBERT J. TROPPMANN

CONTENTS

THE PSYCHOLOGICAL AND SOCIETAL PHENOMENA OF ATHLETICS AND COACHING

CHAPTER 1

An Overview: Psychology, Sport Psychology, And Athletic Coaching

How do the theories and principles of psychology apply to athletics? How can one know and learn more about psychology without having a sport psychologist work with the coach and athlete? Does sport psychology deal only with the problem athletes, or should a coach be concerned with the normal developmental aspects of athletes, too? What information, knowledge, and expertise is necessary to be a "good" or successful coach? What is the most effective type of coaching leadership? Are there specific personality traits or dispositional characteristics one must possess to be successful? What are effective teaching–coaching principles? How does a coach communicate and motivate effectively? Is coaching an art or a science? Is there a systematized body of knowledge based on scientific principles that a coach can turn to in order to obtain valid and reliable coaching know-how?

WHAT IS COACHING "KNOW-HOW"?

The inexperienced or novice coach is not the only person seeking answers to these questions. The experienced or veteran coach, even if highly successful, continues to seek answers to these and similar questions. The quest for knowledge or the search for a "better way" is never ending for the sincerely dedicated, truly professional individual who is engaged in coaching athletics.

An eminently successful veteran high school coach commented, "I usually judge another person's coaching know-how not necessarily by what he says, but more often by the questions he asks. I have noticed over the years I have been in coaching that frequently the losers have all the answers, and the winners ask all the questions.''

No coach ever need be embarrassed because he or she does now know the answers, nor should one be ashamed or hesitant to ask questions in an effort to secure meaningful answers. A coach would be remiss if he did not attempt to seek answers. Our objective throughout this textbook is to provide information with which one can resolve answers to the above questions, and others, concerning numerous psychological aspects of coaching today's athletes.

Coaching ''know-how'' has at least three interrelated components: knowledge, competencies or skills, and attitudes or philosophies.

Knowledge

Athletic coaching is an applied social science that involves an extra dimension—the interaction with people and the knowledge of how to influence them. There is a body of knowledge—the concepts, principles, and functions of administration or management—that is a prerequisite for coaching success. Coaching knowledge can be acquired in numerous ways: as a former participant in athletics, as a ''student'' of the game, as a coach, through formal and informal schooling and training, through personal development effort, and by on-the-job experience as an assistant or head coach.

The Science of Coaching. Is athletic coaching a science? A *science* is a systematized body of knowledge; a system or method based or purporting to be based on scientific principles. A science is based on information that has been empirically verified through the scientific method, which involves identification of conditions or facts through observation and verification of principles through experimentation. For example, the science of psychology is empirical, which means it is based on controlled experiments or objective and precise observations. When certain facts and principles are interrelated into broader conclusions, they constitute the theory of a particular science or body of knowledge. Verified principles of a science are useful for a practitioner or for one applying the science, because it makes it possible to forecast or predict the outcome of specific actions.

While many people think that coaching a sport or activity is only X*s* and O*s*, game tactics, and strategies, coaching is actually an eclectic discipline since it relies on other more narrow knowledge-oriented disciplines for its basic scientific foundation. Coaching is also dependent on other more specialized disciplines for much of its theoretical thrust. Since coaching deals mainly with individuals and groups, doctrines and methods from psychology, sociology, anthropology, and other disciplines contribute to the field of athletic coaching.

A Body of Knowledge. Despite the fact that athletic coaching is considered an applied science, it does have a body of knowledge that may be studied. A sport or a technique may be studied or learned like systematized facts, so that, in a broad sense, coaching would fall under the definition of a science, although it would not be in the same realm as the science of psychology. Athletic coaching as a science is still one of the least developed of all sciences. The encouraging point is that its body of knowledge continues to expand steadily. Prior to the mid-1960s, there was a paucity of materials and information available on the psychological dimensions of coaching.

Relevant to offensive and defensive systems of play, tactics and strategies, drills, and analyses of the mechanics and techniques of individual and team skills of a number of sports and activities, particularly football and basketball, there continues to be a proliferation of materials and information. Although this is important, it contributes only to a technical knowledge of sports.

Obviously there is more to coaching athletics than the mere dissemination of sport technology. Spectators, coaches, and others at times fail to understand that coaching deals primarily with people. Despite the fact that for thousands of years human beings have inhabited the earth, our knowledge of human behavior is still in its formative stages. Also, coaching lacks a generally accepted body of knowledge that can encompass all major variables and aspects of coaching. Without such a body of knowledge, athletic coaching remains primarily an art. Experience continues to be the best teacher, although, at times, trial-and-error methods of gaining experience prove to be grossly ineffective and inefficient. Yet it is only through experience that a coach comes to feel completely comfortable in applying different techniques, concepts, and theories.

COMPETENCIES OR SKILLS

While a *science* is something that is learned (''to know''), an *art* is something that is practiced (''to do''). Therefore, while athletic coaching knowledge and theory comprise a science, coaching practice or application, like the disciplines of medicine, engineering, and education, is an art. To be effective, a coach must develop competencies or skills of at least four types: technical skills, conceptual skills, managerial or administrative skills, and interpersonal or human skills.

Technical Skills

Briefly, technical skills relate specifically to one's major field of coaching interest. Just as individuals acquire technical know-how relevant to being electrical engineers, accountants, English teachers, real estate brokers, or criminal lawyers, others acquire technical know-how pertaining to being gymnastic, wrestling, golf, football, swimming, and track coaches, or coaches of other sport activities. Coaches can become highly specialized in their particular area of interest. For example, there are linebacker, defensive secondary, receiver, quarterback, offensive and defensive line, and other coaching specialists in football; pitching and base running coaches in baseball; field, relay, and sprint coaches in track and field; swimming and diving coaches; and other types of coaching specialists. A coach's professional specialization, formal education, experience, and background will form a strong foundation for developing this ability, along with the coach's continued interest and personal motivation. Although there is nothing inherently wrong with becoming highly specialized in coaching a single phase of a particular sport, one would not be wise to do so to the exclusion of gaining knowledge, competencies, and expertise in conceptual, managerial, and interpersonal skills.

Conceptual Skills

There are "followers" and there are "leaders." The followers wait for others to devise the plans and to determine operative know-how. Thus successful leaders are innovative and creative, and possess analytical decision-making and problem-solving skills. One who can conceptualize can see the "big picture" and has the ability to draw together the fragmented parts. When attempting to resolve a problem, not infrequently an individual who lacks conceptual skills will erroneously treat the symptoms as the problem because of an inability to see the "big picture."

Conceptual skills are an important part of one's philosophy. They are especially important for a head coach who has subordinates, since it is imperative that a head coach perform certain managerial or supervisory functions if his or her coaching is to be effective and efficient. *Effective* coaching is doing the "right things" to achieve desired results and to reach predetermined objectives or goals; *efficient* coaching is doing "things right" in the prudent allocation and utilization of resources including manpower, which would involve players, coaches, supportive staff personnel, and others.

Administrative or Management Skills

While coaches are first and foremost teachers, the higher the level of competition and the larger the coaching staff, the more head coaches become administrators and the less they are involved in actual teaching–coaching. Effective and efficient utilization of time alone dictates the role change of a head coach under such conditions. Since practice sessions and field/floor coaching are the "fun" part of a coaches's job, administrative and supervisory aspects of coaching are often disliked. Administrative details frequently are avoided and minimized by coaches, especially at lower levels of athletic competition. Many coaches simply do not envision themselves in such a role and fail to develop skills in the management functions of planning, organizing, directing, staffing, and controlling. The successful coach is a strong organizer and planner and an adroit decision maker. These and other abilities, in turn, are grounded in more basic cognitive skills, such as interpersonal skills.

Interpersonal or Human Skills

For leadership positions, probably the most critical skills are those that are interpersonal in nature. To be effective a coach must learn to assist others in self-motivation. ✓ ③ Furthermore conciliatory skills of persuasion and the ability to influence others become paramount for effective leadership and necessary to accomplish individual and team objectives and goals. It is only by attaining the latter that the organization can achieve a high degree of success. Acquiring human relations skills, or a behavioral approach emphasizing the human aspects of coaching, is equally as important as acquiring technical skills.

It is most important that a coach understand the people with whom he or she works and is associated. A head coach should strive to learn each individual's personal needs in addition to one's professional goals where staff members are involved. Human relations deal with psychological aspects, perceptions, learning processes, emotions, personalities, and attitudes. Any success a coach attains will depend on how successfully and satisfactorily the coach deals with athletes, coaches, students, parents, staff personnel, superiors, friends, boosters, critics, community members, and others. In exerting social influence, a coach has various roles and expectations. *Roles*

The Art of Coaching

The application of a body of knowledge that constitutes a science is called an art. An ✳ *art* is the skill in performance acquired by experience, study, or observation; it is the systematic application of knowledge or skills in effecting a desired result. For example, the skill of the physician involves an understanding of the knowledge comprising medicine, and the application of this body of knowledge is through the art of treating patients.

Similarly, the skill of the coach involves understanding the body of knowledge that comprises athletic coaching in general and the sport the individual in particular coaches. The application of the principles and concepts is through teaching, leading, directing, and coordinating the players and assistants and their activities— which is an art. *How* a coach teaches in terms of interpersonal skills or human relations is equally as important as *what* a coach teaches. This facet of coaching is interrelated with *attitudes,* which is the third component of coaching "know-how".

Coaching: A Science and an Art

Thus coaching is both a science and an art. Athletic coaching may be considered a science in that a body of knowledge exists that relates to coaching practices. It is not a pure science, but it is an applied science.

Coaching is mostly an art in that one's coaching skills are usually developed through actual on-the-job experience and application. Coaching is difficult because each sport or activity seems to differ in that certain types of individuals appear to participate in certain types of sports. Then, too, each coaching situation is different.

Coaching is also highly individualized. A style that works well for one coach in a particular situation may not produce the desired results for another coach in a similar situation, or even for the same coach in a different situation. There is *no* one best way to coach. Every coach must discover, therefore, what works and what does not work. A coach cannot become effective merely by adopting the practices or the coaching style of someone else. Each coach must develop a natural style and follow practices that are consistent with one's own personality and philosophy.

No one can read a book on athletic coaching or learn a body of knowledge that comprises "coaching" and from this alone be an effective coach. A coach's skills are developed and sharpened through practice. Knowing the science of coaching will certainly speed up the learning of the art and will greatly assist the coach in making effective decisions. However, knowledge is not the only prerequisite for being an effective coach. The controlled environment of the knowledge-oriented physical sciences must be contrasted with the dynamic environment of the art-oriented social sciences, in which testing knowledge through practice in a variety of situations is an inevitable feature of expanding the discipline. Throughout our presentation our intent is to include pertinent information that presents coaching as both an applied science and an art.

ATTITUDES OR PHILOSOPHIES

A third interrelated component of coaching know-how involves attitudes or philosophies. Attitudes derive basically from value systems and beliefs related to oneself, work, and relationships with people. The ways in which we acquire knowledge and skills are, in part, a function of our attitudes. Attitudes will also determine the application of knowledge and techniques. In addition, attitudes are important in determining coaching competencies and success. They tell us what kinds of needs are dominant in a certain individual at a certain period of time.

Since our intent is to place parameters around the meaning of sport, we limit our discussion specifically to athletics and the application of sport psychology to athletic coaching. In order to do this, however, we must define and briefly interpret the terminology applicable to coaching psychology.

WHAT IS SPORT?

Sport in its variety of forms has permeated the human culture since recorded history. In many societies sport has held a prominent position as a social institution, which continues to be the situation in the United States. We concur with Billing (1975) that a taxonomy of sport form is needed because there has been a rapid growth of sport, and because the term *sport* has a variety of meanings covering a broad spectrum of events and activities. However, for the purpose of our discussion neither Billing's nor any other system of classification need be included here. We need only distinguish between sport and other activities.

Sport or Athletics

Although the definition of *sport* may not include the word "athletics," a definition of athletics typically includes sport, exercises or games, and the practice or principle of athletic activities. Therefore, throughout this book the terms *sport* and *athletics* are used interchangeably and synonymously, mindful of the distinction that *sport* is broader in scope that *athletics*. Also, while sport is a major concern in contemporary American life, the principle sporting and recreational activities of the American public are not our concern in this book. Our focus will be on organized individual and team games, sports, and athletics that are usually under the direction of a coach. Loy (1968) supports our contention that sport, which includes athletics, is an institutionalized game involving physical prowess, strategy, and chance, in combination. To be an institutionalized game, there must be published rules defining the manner of play and a declaration of winners. Physical prowess, while playing a dominant role in the outcome of the contest, is not limited to strength and endurance, but includes all of the highly complex and coordinated bodily movements indigenous to specific activities. Also, it must allow for the application of strategy by the competitors, and there must be some element of chance involved in the conduct of the activity.

Some sport sociologists and psychologists, physical educators, and others make a distinction between sport and athletics on the basis of the primary objective of each. The objective of sport reputedly is merely "to have fun," while that of athletics is "to win." For our purposes this issue is moot, because we do not feel these objectives are incompatible in athletic coaching and participation.

Coach and Coaching. A coach is a person who instructs or trains performers in the fundamentals and various techniques of a sport. In certain sports activities, such as gymnastics and figure skating, a coach usually works closely with an individual performer in perfecting various maneuvers and in creating practically flawless performance of a routine. In team sports a coach usually teaches fundamentals and techniques, conducts practices, develops plays, and tries to win the game or contest by directing offensive and defensive tactics and by making substitutions. A coach in a team sport may be a player who directs team play, a nonplayer who has to perform all the various duties of a coach alone, or a member of a large coaching staff who generally concentrates on a particular specialized aspect of play, such as pitching in baseball or dash events in track.

WHAT IS PSYCHOLOGY?

Psychology is derived from the Greek words *psyche,* which means "mind" or "soul," and "logos," which means "study." For many years the commonly accepted definition of the word *psychology* meant the "study of the mind or soul," and the subject was considered as part of philosophy. Toward the end of the nineteenth century psychology began to dissociate itself from philosophy and began to be recognized as a separate science.

The most commonly accepted present-day definition of psychology is "the study of behavior." While this definition is simplified, it does not offer a completely insightful answer to the query "What is psychology?" since the study of psychology is very broad in scope. Its subject matter covers all behaviors that are observable (overt) which human beings exhibit and all those hidden (covert) processes such as emotions, thoughts, and motives that go on inside human beings. The study of behavior covers a wide range of events—from the activity of one-celled microscopic organisms, through animal and human actions, to the categorization and prediction of national habits and the interaction of nations. On another plane, it ranges from a study of brain cell activity to a study of total body fatigue. On still another plane, it ranges from the chemistry involved in memorization to the complexity of attitudes and value systems. Obviously, a number of these aspects are outside our scope of discussion. In studying the various aspects of the subject, one should bear in mind that the two fundamental aims of psychology are to understand and to predict behavior. Thus one can readily see the value of psychology to the coaching profession.

Subfields of Psychology

Different psychologists specialize in different subfields of the discipline, which may be categorized as follows; experimental psychology; clinical, counseling, school, and community psychology; developmental and educational psychology; personality and social psychology; and personnel, organizational, engineering, and consumer psychology. Only the first four broad categories are most applicable to coaching.

Experimental Psychology. This area generally involves research, usually within the context of a laboratory, that is conducted on the most fundamental psychological processes, such as perception, learning, memory, motivation, and emotions. However, psychologists in several different subfields conduct experiments, not just experimental psychologists.

Clinical, Counseling, School, and Community Psychology. Historically, these subfields of psychology were all concerned with helping people deal with psychological problems. Today, however, there are applied psychologists who are concerned with normal development, not just problems. Usually, clinical psychologists diagnose psychological difficulties and provide therapy for those who need it. Counseling psychologists provide occupational and career counseling, marriage counseling, and rehabilitation counseling, as well as other types of counseling. School psychologists work with children who may be having "problems" in school, consult with teachers and parents, and help to design special school programs for gifted and educationally handicapped children. Community psychologists specialize in preventing and treating psychological problems at the community level, which would include youth groups. All of these specialties are primarily concerned with the practice of psychology rather than research, although many psychologists in these fields also engage in research.

Developmental and Educational Psychology. Developmental psychologists are concerned with the development of human capacities and behavior, from conception and birth, through old age, to death. Educational psychologists are involved with the design of educational settings and techniques as well as with the training of teachers. In developmental and educational psychology, research and practice are often closely intertwined.

Personality and Social Psychology. Psychologists in these related fields are concerned with the nature and dynamics of human personality and with the ways in which people's behavior is affected by other people and by the social environment.

Applied Psychology

While the services and research of many of these psychologists could benefit coaches and athletes, the applied psychologists are the most useful for their developmental insights on athletes as well as their research into problem-solving behavior. Applied psychology is the utilization of theories and principles developed through psychology for practical ends. The science of psychology is quite different from what people who have never seriously studied psychology usually believe it to be. The scope of the subject of psychology is much greater than is generally perceived, and many of its findings are vastly different from what people, including many coaches and athletes, have generally taken for granted about human nature. Therefore, psychology is applicable to coaching; however, at present many coaches and others remain unconvinced of the contributions of sport psychology to the field of athletics.

WHAT IS SPORT PSYCHOLOGY?

The opening paragraph of this chapter listed more than half-a-dozen questions that illustrate several areas of concern dealing with sport psychology. Tutko (1970) pointed out that frequently the essential clinical areas that influence performance are overlooked by coaches. Sport psychology attempts to apply psychological facts and principles of learning, performance, and associated human behavior to the whole field of sports. A coach should be concerned with the psychological, emotional, and social benefits, not only the physical ones, that an athlete is likely to be exposed to from participating in athletics. Cratty (1973) maintained that sport psychology research can and does affect, aid, and influence the decisions of coaches, since the study of sport psychology has the common interest of learning more about the athlete and sport. As Singer (1972) pointed out, sport psychology has led to the recognition of a science of human behavior which has partially replaced earlier theories that were based on common sense, instinct, tradition, popular beliefs, and half-truths. More recently, Landers (1979) concurred that the boundaries of sport psychology are not easily established. He stated:

> In its broadest sense, sport psychology can be defined as the scientific study of behavior in a sport or sport-related context. It is an attempt to understand the ''how and why'' underlying sport behavior. As this definition implies, the central focus is on sports for males and females of all ages and levels of competition. This includes field studies ranging from unstructured noncompetitive sport-related forms such as jogging, cycling, weight training, to high-level competitive athletics. Sport psychology also includes laboratory studies employing motor tasks which simulate in abstract form relevant features of the sport situation. In addition, sport psychology includes a clinical dimension, where qualified clinicians diagnose and treat the psychological problems of athletes. . . .

Coaches from the days of Knute Rockne to the contemporary coach have been, rightly or wrongly, applying their own common sense brand of psychology to their coaching without really concerning themselves with any research that might be available. Coaches always try to get their athletes ''up'' for the game or contest and have developed their own way of attempting to motivate athletes. Mentally and physically preparing atheletes for the contest has always been an important goal of the coaching profession that has existed down through the decades. It was not until the era of the ''counter culture'' and sports revolution that the term sport psychologist became prominent in the coaching profession.

Earliest Venture into Psychology in Sports

Perhaps one of the earliest ventures into psychology in sports, in a professional and systematic way, was initiated by Philip K. Wrigley, president of the Chicago Cubs baseball team. Wrigley decided to have a comprehensive, scholarly study made of the team to determine what went into the makeup of a championship baseball team. (At the time of the study the Cubs had won the pennant in 1929, 1932, 1935, and 1938.)

Suinn (1976) pointed out,

> Wrigley sought to combine psychological tests, such as reflex and sight anticipation and baseball aptitude tests, such as running, hitting, throwing. He expected to develop a profile of a champion against which young prospects could be measured.
>
> Wrigley hired the then head of the department of psychology at the University of Illinois to carry out the research. The one flaw was the reaction of the ball players. In those days, they were made nervous by anybody who could read and write; to work with a psychologist suggested to their peer group that they were a little flakey and therefore subject to much locker room ridicule. So they guffawed and cursed and made fun of everything the psychologist tried to do. ''We were too far ahead of our times,'' Wrigley said.[1]

Do Not Wait Until Game Time. Suinn's (1976) discussion of this topic is also helpful, so we will quote him at length:

> On a less systematic basis, the value of ''psychology'' as they understood it, that is, superficially, has long been appreciated by people in sports. Football coaches and others were famous for using locker room pep talks to get their players up for a game. However, there is more to it than a locker room speech on the day of the game.
>
> ''If you don't get your players ready on Monday through Friday,'' said Ara Parseghian, formerly the coach at Notre Dame, ''a locker room speech on Saturday afternoon isn't going to help you.''
>
> He meant psychologically ready as well as physically ready. Coach Parseghian did not, for example, schedule the team's heaviest physical drills for Friday but for Wednesday afternoon. His idea was to bring the players to an awareness of their physical peak in mid-week, then to let them taper off physically while they built up psychologically. Parseghian felt the physical tapering off, combined with the intense psychological build up on that campus, created an anxiousness for action that would be satisfied on Saturday afternoon. ''They're all ready to go physically but you hold them off, like thoroughbreds in the starting gate. You hold them off, and off, and off, until boom! They've got their chance to go.''

The Use of Psychology to Affect Performance

Furlong's (1976) thoughts on psychology and its relationship to sports are also insightful:

[1]Suinn, Richard M. ''Body Thinking: Psychology for Olympic Champs.'' *Psychology Today,* Vol. 5, July 1976, p. 39. Reprinted by permission of *Psychology Today* Magazine. Copyright © 1976. Ziff Davis Publishing Co.

The efforts of individuals in sport to use psychology to affect their own performance, although in a primitive way, have been more the result of personal inspiration than organized thought. They work out ways to psych themselves up or to psych their opponents out. The former involves building up one's own concentration of an opponent. An example of this would be Jimmy Connors, who sometimes bounces a tennis ball an inordinate number of times, perhaps 18–20, before serving. His opponents sometimes claim this is just a device to psych them out, to get them to thinking angrily about his bouncing of the ball instead of his serving the ball.[2]

Problem Athletes

One of the first books dealing with various types of problems, *Problem Athletes and How to Handle Them* (1966), was co-authored by sport psychologists Bruce Ogilvie and Thomas Tutko, founders of the Institute for Study of Athletic Motivation, San Jose State University. Based on their experience as psychologists and consultants for more than two dozen professional teams in basketball, football, ice hockey, and golf, and their work with many high school and college teams, Dr. Ogilvie and Dr. Tutko's book was designed so that a specialized interest in psychological principles and studies could ultimately provide a more factual and scientific basis for handling the individual athlete. Since their pioneer work, increasing numbers of other interested scholars have undertaken research on the psychological nature of athletics.

Research Clinics and Athletic Institutes

The International Society for Sport Psychology (ISSP), founded in 1965, and The North American Society for the Psychology of Sport and Physical Activity (NASPSPA), founded in 1967, whose membership is open to all professionals interested in sport psychology, both support and promote scientific research in sport psychology and their proceedings are published.

A number of public and private institutions, organizations, and foundations have established laboratories to conduct scientific research on subjects who engage in physical activities. Athletes are tested under stress conditions that are similar to those experienced when one participates in athletics. As one specific illustration, Dorothy V. Harris, a specialist in sport psychology and physiology, founded the national research conference, Women and Sport, in 1972, and became Director (in 1974) of the Center for Women and Sport, which is a part of the Sports Research Institute at the Pennsylvania State University. The national research conference in 1972 was the first to look at the female athlete from physiological, psychological, sociological, and biomechanical perspectives. The institute that Dr. Harris founded

---

[2]Furlong, William Barry. "Psychology on the Playing Fields." *Psychology Today*, Vol. 5, July 1976, pp. 40–41. Reprinted by permission of *Psychology Today* Magazine. Copyright © 1976. Ziff Davis Publishing Co.

was the first and only research organization in the United States at that time devoted entirely to the scientific study of the woman athlete. Before Dr. Harris' work there was a dearth of research and material available on the subject of women in sports because women were stereotyped, there was little societal interest, and there was no equal opportunity for girls and women to participate in athletics. There are now research sources available on the female athlete which dispel many of the myths and untruths that have been perpetuated up to now. Such information is of special interest and value to men who are coaching female athletes.

THE APPLICATION OF SPORT PSYCHOLOGY TO ATHLETIC COACHING

Considering the popularity of sport, its length of existence, and its impact on society, until recently relatively little meaningful research had been completed relevant to predicting athletic performance. Consequently, the application of sport psychology to coaching is still in its formative years.

Research in sport psychology, in order to improve athletic performance, has been used for many years in other countries. In the Unitded States we are basically just beginning to aid the coach in making valid and reliable decisions concerning athletic performance. Yet much of the research may be labeled theoretical or simply a study for its own sake, as compared to practical or applied research applicable for utilization by coaches. Undoubtedly a number of individuals, including many coaches, look at much theoretical research as practically useless and not directly applicable to their purposes.

Science and the Future of Sports

Perhaps the above viewpoint was best summed up by an editorial that appeared in *Scholastic Coach* (1978), by Herman L. Masin, editor, who wrote,

> Having always believed that the greatest advances in sport will come from the laboratories of our sports scientists, we've been dismayed by the inability of our researchers to communicate with the outside world.
>
> Our scientists seem to be writing their papers for one another rather than for the people who need them most, the working coach and physical educator.
>
> How frustrating it is to keep coming across all sorts of intriguing research, only to find it unsuitable for general consumption, thanks to all the abstruse formulae and scientific jargon. . . .
>
> Year after year we keep lamenting about this to the sports researchers, and they always agree with us . . . and continue to keep filling the pages of the scientific journals with the recondite reportage.

Masin (1978) concluded his remarks by including an editorial entitled "Science and the Future of Sports" (1977) by Dr. David L. Costill, former president of the Americam College of Sports Medicine, who according to Masin, " . . . echoes everything we've been saying about sports scientists. . . ."

Educate the Coach and Athlete. Dr. Costill made several noteworthy points that have merit for both coach and athlete:

- Begin to relate research findings to the athlete's specific problems. Too much useful information remains buried in the minds and publications of the researcher. If a sound rapport is to be established, efforts must be made by the researcher to educate the coach, athlete, and general public.
- Make an honest effort to interpret the results of the research in terms that the athlete can understand, since the sport scientist quite readily uses the time and energies of the athlete. The failure to communicate is a common source of irritation to coach and athlete.
- Provide answers to practical questions. Too often the scientist is accused of using the athlete to make a few entertaining observations, but then neglects to provide satisfactory, understandable feedback to the athlete and coach.[3]

Dr. Costill concluded his editorial by stating, "Those who attack the applied problems in sports must be responsible for closing the gap in communication with sports practictioners."

In the same vein, two well-known sport psychologists, UCLA's Bryant Cratty and Illinois' Rainer Martens, wrote of the disparity between the sport psychologist's research and the sport practictioner's acceptance and application. Dr. Cratty (1973) supports our contention that, because of abstract theorizing or statements concerned with the obvious which are often caged in psychological jargon, undoubtedly many coaches question how textbooks and other materials on the psychology of physical activity can aid them in their coaching. Dr. Martens (1979) discussed the dissatisfaction with the existing scientific paradigm of social psychology and its adoption in sport psychology. Martens focused on the inadequacies of laboratory experimental research, and as a partial solution suggested that sport psychologists trade their smocks for "jocks," turning their efforts to multivariate, long-term field research.

A Panel of Sport Psychologists. William Straub, Ithaca College (1977) moderating an AAHPER panel, "The Role of the Sport Psychologist for Excellence in Athletic Performance," stated, "I think it is safe to say that the sport psychologist is not sought out to the extent that we would like. I have heard it said that most professional teams and some intercollegiate teams will have a sport psychologist on

---

[3]Masin, Herman L. "Here Below." *Scholastic Coach,* Vol. 47, No. 8, March 1978, pp. 16–17. Quoting David L. Costill, "Science and the Future of Sports." *The Physician and Sportsmedicine,* Vol. 5, No. 6, June 1977. Reprinted by permission.

their staff in the near future.'' According to Dr. Straub, we are at the forefront of some significant developments in the area of sport psychology. The role of the sport psychologist at present is a diverse one, but Straub believes that in the next few years this role will become clarified. Helping teams to win is important, but also fostering the humanistic aspect of sport is a point stressed by Straub. Finally, Straub mentions the need for better instruments for testing and predicting athletic performance (Straub, 1977).

The consensus of the AAHPER panel members (Singer, Tutko, Williams, and McCullagh) indicated that they were all committed to improving the athletic situation in which there are many participants. Even though there is much talk about the way in which a sport psychologist can work with the elite—the outstanding athlete—there seems to be much concern about the other 99 percent of the participants in athletic programs of all kinds.

It was further suggested by the AAHPER panel members that there is much to be done on all levels to make the athletic program more effective. It was also agreed that it was important to translate academic jargon into a language the coach and the athlete could understand.

Research Contributions and Limitations. While some professional and intercollegiate athletic teams have used the services of the sport psychologist to test individual athletes for future performance or potential, the question utmost in the minds of most athletic coaches is, ''How can the sport psychologist help our team?'' For the present, the coach must realize that it is difficult to prescribe rules and principles of behavior that will necessarily hold true in the more arousing environment of an athletic event. Many of the areas currently being investigated by sport psychologists, physical educators, and others, even under controlled testing conditions, cannot provide answers with clear-cut predictions of future performance.

Speaking as a panel member at the AAHPER Seattle Convention (1977), Daniel Landers stated, ''It is important for the athlete and coach to know that incorrect predictions are unavoidable. They have been particularly unavoidable where personality traits have been used to predict successful athletic performance. Often the same test will yield entirely different profiles. We have very few studies that have been conducted in a field study. Most studies are conducted in the laboratory and until this situation changes, it is going to be very difficult to extend our body of knowledge to the kind of things that the coach and the athlete want to know.''

Coaching Today's Athlete

Just as the problems, forces, and issues which surround and shape athletics today are different from those of 5, 10, or 20 years ago, so is today's athlete different. Numerous studies have been made that show conclusively that over the past 40 years boys and girls in the United States have generally grown larger physically than their parents; they also have better developed motor skills. Frequently, if they participate in sports, they are better athletes than their elders were as youths. Also, today's athlete is more knowledgeable, more intelligent, and much more inquisitive than the athlete of previous generations.

Sports and athletics are no longer the relatively simple "rah-rah" activities that many older people remember; nor is today's coach the omnipotent authority he once was. Many long-believed and highly cherished ideals relevant to the value of athletic participation, as well as the ultimate authority of the coach, have been questioned, tested, and in numerous instances refuted by some of today's athletes. Many coaches are uncertain how to deal with today's problems in coaching. Some coaches do not attempt to resolve some of the "touchy" problems. Other coaches handle them badly. The psychology of athletics is probably the sole remaining untapped and relatively untouched area in sports.

The uncertainty of the value of sport psychology to the coach probably arises because most coaches lack knowledge of the scope of the subject. In all probability typical coaches believe sport psychology deals only with "problem athletes"; they are not familiar with the potential of sport psychology as an aid in doing their work more effectively.

Sports, the athletes, and the coaches themselves have all become more complex. Presently, there are more participants engaged in more sports than at any other time in this country's history. Coaching was once considered strictly the coach's domain, in that a *coach* coached "his boys," but now many other professionals, such as medical doctors, psychologists, physiologists, kinesiologists, sociologists, physical educators, and others, have become interested in testing and researching athletics and athletes. Much more information is now available to a coach than at any time previously, and such research could benefit both coach and athlete.

Summary

While coaches should be interested in how sport psychologists can help them and their athletes, a more important question is how can a coach know and learn more about psychology without the availability of a sport psychologist?

Our objective is to present psychological concepts, theories, and principles that are applicable to sport and athletic coaching. While on occasion an individual athlete may be able to apply principles of psychology to his or her training regimen, in most instances the coach must tie it all together and integrate the athlete's viewpoint into the cohesive team structure in order to optimize the individual's talents and skills. Therefore, a coach is professionally compelled to continue to acquire knowledge. Sport psychology encompasses many interrelationships—those among the coach, the athlete, and the sport—and the effective use of this information results in effective coaching. There is much more to coaching than the application of technical, tactical, and strategical "know-how."

REFERENCES

Billing, John E. "A Taxonomy of Sport Forms." Proceedings *NCPEAM*. Phoenix, Ariz. January 2-9, 1975, pp. 34-39.

Cratty, Bryant J. *Psychology in Contemporary Sport: Guidelines for Coaches and Athletes.* Englewood Cliffs, N.J. Prentice-Hall, 1973.

Furlong, Willima Barry. "Psychology on the Playing Fields." *Psychology Today.* Vol. 5, July, 1976, pp. 40-41.

Landers, Daniel. "The Role of the Sport Psychologist for Excellence in Athletic Performance." Panel. Seattle, Wa. AAHPER Convention, 1977.

Landers, Daniel M. "Sport Psychology Today." *Journal of Sport Psychology.* Vol. 1, No. 1, 1979, pp. 2-3.

Loy, John. "The Nature of Sport: A Definitional Effort." *Quest X.* May 1968, pp. 1-15.

Martens, Rainer. "About Smocks and Jocks." *Journal of Sport Psychology.* Vol. 1, No. 2, 1979, pp. 94-99.

Masin, Herman L. "Here Below." *Scholastic Coach.* Vol. 47, No. 8. March 1978, pp. 16-17, quoting David L. Costill. "Science and the Future of Sports." *The Physician and Sportsmedicine.* Vol. 5, No. 6, June 1977.

Ogilvie, Bruce C., and Tutko, Thomas A. *Problem Athletes and How to Handle Them.* London. Pelham Books, 1966.

Singer, R. N. *Coaching, Athletics, and Psychology.* New York. McGraw-Hill, 1972, p. 2.

Straub, William. "The Role of the Sport Psychologist for Excellence in Athletic Performance." Panel. Seattle, Wa. AAHPER Convention, 1977.

Suinn, Richard M. "Body Thinking: Psychology for Olympic Champs." *Psychology Today.* Vol. 5, July 1976, p. 39.

Tutko, Thomas A. "Some Clinical Aspects of Sport Psychology." *Quest XIII.* January 1970, pp. 12-17.

SELECTED READINGS

Billing, John E. "A Taxonomy of Sport Forms." Phoenix, Arizona. Proceedings NCPEAM. January 2-9, 1975, pp. 34-39.

Cratty, Bryant J. *Social Psychology in Athletics.* Englewood Cliffs, N.J. Prentice-Hall, 1981.

Lilliefors, Jim. "Thomas Tutko: An Interview With a Leading Sports Psychologist." *Runners World.* July 1977, pp. 43-45.

Lindgren, Henry Clay. *An Introduction to Social Psychology* (2nd ed.). New York, N.Y. John Wiley & Sons, 1973. (See in particular Chapter 1.)

Martens, Rainer. *Social Psychology and Physical Activity.* New York, N.Y. Harper & Row, 1975.

McNeil, Elton B., and Rubin, Zick. *The Psychology of Being Human* (2nd ed.) New York, N.Y. Harper & Row, 1977, pp. 5-28.

McPherson, Barry D. "Past, Present, and Future Perspectives for Research in Sport Sociology." *International Review of Sport Sociology.* Vol. 10, 1975, pp. 55-69.

Neal, Patsy. *Coaching Methods for Women.* Menlo Park, Calif. Addison-Wesley, 1969.

Ogilvie, Bruce C. "Walking the Perilous Path of the Team Psychologist." *The Physician and Sportsmedicine*. Vol. 5, No. 4. April 1977, pp. 63–68.

Rushall, Brent S. "Applied Psychology in Sports." In *The Status of Psychomotor Learning and Sport Psychology Research*. Brent S. Rushall (ed.). Dartmouth, Nova Scotia. Sport Science Associates, 1975, pp. 7.1–7.32.

CHAPTER 2

Societal Role
Expectations of a
Coach

In most sports the individual who directs the team from the sidelines or bench, determines the game tactics and strategy, and makes substitutions, is generally called "Coach." In baseball this individual is called "Manager." In other sports the individual the public would normally identify as a coach or manager may be known as the field leader, or the court leader, or the ice leader, or simply as "The Man." Regardless of the title that is affixed, the individual in the role position of head coach is responsible for how the team performs and is accountable to many "publics." These "publics" have numerous expectations of the team and of the individual in the role position. Inexperienced coaches in particular are frequently unaware of the set of expectations which society places upon them.

There may be incongruity between the role set of expectations perceived by others for the coach and those perceived by the coach. The result is role conflict and role strain. Role expectations of a coach are an integral aspect of the psychology of coaching.

ROLES AND SOCIAL SYSTEM

Psychologists Kagan and Havemann (1976) defined *role* as "The kind of behavior that society expects from a person in a given position." Here the discussion is limited to the coach. Role relates to a position, not to an individual. It relates here to the position of "coach," not to the expectations regarding the person who happens

21

to be the coach. The prescriptions for the specific coach's behavior result from the position of coach, not from his or her personality or individual characteristics. Personality influences how the individual will fulfill this role, but the basic role pattern derives from the position.

Generally society's perceptions and expectations of the coach or teacher, like the lawyer, minister, physician, and others in the professions, are different from those individuals who engage in other kinds of work. Despite the fact that those individuals in the professions are most likely to be involved in multiple roles outside of their chosen profession, generally each is known and referred to first and foremost in terms of his or her profession. This, too, applies to the individual in the coaching profession.

Role Set: Anticipatory and Obligatory

A *role* set is composed of the different orientations that are expected of an individual who occupies a particular position. These different orientations result from the varying expectations of individuals who interact with the person functioning in the position. Role expectations are *anticipatory* in that there is a regularity to the expected behavior of the role partners, that is, the individual and the group, and *obligatory* in that one is obligated to fulfill our (society's) expectations. For a coach, whether he be a head or an assistant, there are expectations by his or her superiors, associates, peers, subordinates, and others. Also, each individual has his or her own personal expectations and aspirations relevant to the coaching position. Therefore, one can readily deduce that the expectations are actually a set or composite of all expectations, and role set is determined by the social system. Many coaches do not fully comprehend the relationship between their position and the social system's expectations. Most prefer not to be accountable to the numerous "publics."

Multiple Roles

The terms role or role set and multiple roles are often confused and used erroneously. While role relates to a position, multiple roles actually relate to many *different* positions that a person holds in *different* groups or organizations.

Frequently, it has been stated that a coach plays such various roles as disciplinarian, guidance counselor, salesperson, diplomat, psychologist, leader, teacher, strategist, among others. These many roles are all within the single role set of the position of coach since he or she is *expected* to be a leader, discipline the players, be diplomatic, be a strategist, be a tactician, and to fulfill other expectations. It is all part of a coach's job.

While a coach may be expected to play many roles, none is more important than that of teacher. For example, Scott (1951), Moore (1970), Sabock (1973), Gallon (1974), Bucher (1975), all former coaches and members of college and university faculties, have referred to coaching as teaching. In consensus, "a good coach is a good teacher." Clary (1976) discussed the "winning philosophies" of eight National Football League coaches, each of whom referred to the fact that "coaching is teaching." Cope (1977) and Zimmerman (1980), both writers for *Sports Illustrated,* and Bisher (1980), for *The Sporting News,* and others, all have done feature articles on Chuck Noll, the Pittsburgh Steeler's head football coach, who is often quoted as saying, "I'm a teacher." Frequently Noll adds, "Players win, coaches teach them. I teach."

Since the most common synonym used to identify a coach is "teacher," frequently that person is referred to as a "teacher–coach" or "coach–teacher," especially at the scholastic and collegiate levels. While the obvious is that coaching is teaching, the inference is that coaches are teachers first. It is the same implied inference that is attached to the term student–athlete, in that the athlete should be a student first. While these terms and precepts have been and are a fundamental part of the philosophy of many in the coaching profession, there are those who disdain both terms and their inferences, feeling that the sole purpose of both coach and athlete is to win at any cost. When such philosophy prevails, under the aegis of the educational umbrella, role conflict and role strain occur.

For example, a coach in multiple roles may be one who is a husband (or wife), parent, Republican, Lutheran, Rotarian, musician, and a member of various coaching organizations. Each of these positions or roles involves a set of expectations that obviously will differ. Therefore, every person faces multiple sets of expectations, that relate to one's behavior, depending on the different groups or organizations in which one is a member. However, at any particular moment, a person never fills all of his or her possible role categories. Some remain or become latent, while others are active. For example, a succession of roles emerge throughout the day for the typical coach. Many relate to the individual's work and position (role set) as a coach, and others relate to positions the coach holds in different groups or organizations (multiple roles). The expected and appropriate behavior for each, in turn, may be completely unexpected and inappropriate for the next. We are concerned only with multiple roles where they contribute to role conflict and role strain, the latter having deleterious effects on one's coaching effectiveness.

Role Conflict and Role Strain

The term *role conflict* refers to that situation in which a person confronts competing or conflicting expectations. *Role strain* is a broader term that includes not only role conflict but other situations in which the person has difficulty meeting role expectations.

Role conflict occurs when administrators or management have definite expectations that are different from those of the coaching staff. Role conflict may also occur when "outside" groups who have no official connection with the team or institution identify with the team, athletes, coaches, or sport solely because of their interest, and they too have definite expectations of the head coach directing a particular team. The coach may prefer not to be accountable to ''outside'' expectations; yet it is an aspect of coaching, frequently unpleasant, that is impossible to ignore.

Role strain is a problem caused by the fact that a person cannot always know what role others expect one to play, especially when one occupies several different positions in society at the same time or moves from position to position. Basically, there are three types of role conflict.

Person-Role Conflict. Every coach formulates certain basic philosophies and has specific needs, values, and abilities that he or she may bring to the position. Not infrequently, these may be inconsistent with the expectations others have for the coach. There may be objections to the coach's leadership style, manner of attempting to motivate others, coaching methods, tactics, and overall strategies. Those individuals in superior (''power'') positions may try to force the coach to change his expectations. Plans of action may be suggested, inferred, or directed to the coach in a manner the coach considers to be unethical, illegal, unprofessional, untenable, unacceptable. A coach's moral code or strong personal beliefs may not permit him to engage in and accept proposed plans of action.

Person-role conflict may come about as a result of what is referred to as *role overload,* a situation in which the expectations of others may exceed what the coach can produce or accomplish. Role overload may arise because the coach does not have adequate knowledge or the ability to do what is expected in his or her position; a sufficient amount of time may not be available to accomplish expectations; or resources for accomplishing goals and expectations may not be available.

An illustration would be a college coach being informed by his president that the sports schedule is being upgraded; the team is going to compete in a tougher conference; no additional scholarships are available to match those of the schools against whom the coach and team will be competing; there will be no special admissions or reserved slots for athletes, and established high academic standards will be maintained; an already undermanned coaching staff will not be increased; and the coach is expected to turn around a losing program within three years or he will be dismissed!

Intrarole Conflict. Such conflict occurs as the result of people in the role set having differing expectations regarding the position. In many head coaching positions, the head coach may or may not have the ''clout'' that the coach and possibly the subordinates envision and that the coach's title may erroneously infer. The individual in such a position undoubtedly is in the middle—between superiors and subordinates—which may lead to intrarole conflict. Many illustrations could be cited, but three will suffice.

A professional athlete negotiating with the general manager over a significant salary increase, expects the head coach to support his or her request, especially if the athlete has performed well. Management expects their head coach to help hold the line on salary increases. The coach may agree in principle to the salary increase because he or she feels the athlete has contributed significantly to the team's (and coach's personal) success, but management's view is contrary. The head coach experiences intrarole conflict since each has different expectations of his position.

In another illustration, an assistant coach at the scholastic level makes an obvious critical tactical error that results in the loss of a championship game. The head coach feels that it is his prerogative, since the sports program is his responsibility, to dismiss the assistant coach. The superintendent and principal maintain that none of their head coaches can exercise such autonomy and ultimate authority. The assistant coach maintains he is also a mathematics teacher and he does not expect to be dismissed from his teaching–coaching position solely because of the coaching error. The administration feels the head coach's viewpoint is unrealistic in expecting to exercise such autonomous authority merely because of his position as head coach, despite his accountability for the success of the sports program.

An athlete is arrested for creating an off-campus disorder. His coach wants to discipline the athlete, but not dismiss him from the squad. The administration has a contrary point of view. The coach maintains, because of his position, it is his responsibility to discipline the athlete as he deems appropriate. The administration feels differently and expects the coach to dismiss the athlete from the squad. The athlete expects the head coach to handle the disciplining of the players, but he does not expect to be dismissed.

In all three illustrations the head coach is in the middle—between superiors and subordinates—with contrary expectations regarding the coach's position, which causes intrarole and/or person-role conflict.

Intrarole conflict also occurs when the source of expectations is different. Elaborating slightly on different aspects of the above disciplinary case will illustrate this point. Initially, the principal informed the coach that *all* disciplinary problems in which the coach's athletes are involved outside of the classroom would fall within the coach's domain, and the principal expected the head coach to handle them. Later, the principal criticized the coach for being too strict on some occasions and too lax on others in disciplining his squad members. The coach feels he is consistent in his behavior, and his athletes do not feel their coach is unfair in handling disciplinary problems of the squad.

On another occasion, despite the principal's previous instructions to the coach about the handling of disciplinary problems, the principal informed the coach that he or she should bring all·of the team's disciplinary cases to the administration first. The principal informed the coach he would then decide which problems the coach would handle and which the principal would handle personally. The principal's behavior expectations are inconsistent, and the coach experiences intrarole and/or person-role conflict.

Interrole Conflict. The demands of the multiple role expectations may lead to interrole conflict. A coach's spouse and family may expect him or her to participate in church, social, and possibly fraternal or civic activities during the sports season, despite the fact that the coach may feel that the myriad expectations of the coaching position do not permit him or her to engage in any activities other than that of coaching. A coach undoubtedly will engage in some activities outside of coaching, possibly acquiescing to the pressures of others, because of the need satisfaction which is associated with the activities of each group. However, the coach may also attempt to resolve the role conflict in some other manner.

Resolving role conflict is a daily part of individual behavior. How one handles various types of conflict depends in the final analysis on the individual. Not all conflict can be resolved without a certain amount of stress, personal strain, and indecision. A coach should be fully cognizant of the nature of coaching and either accept it or reject it. Another course of action may entail choosing another profession, occupation, or career if the coach cannot live with the roles, rules, expectations, and pressures of coaching. The various types of conflict can be partly resolved by prudently managing time, establishing goals, setting priorities, "managing" the environment, and by the coach formulating meaningful and realistic philosophies, including the development of a sound person philosophy.

Incongruent Expectations and Role Conflict. While this chapter focuses on the expectations and role conflicts of the head coach, a person in this position should also be keenly aware of the position in which assistant coaches, athletes, and others are placed when demands are made on them that are at variance with the significant expectations of other individuals and other roles. Motivation and leadership are vitally important factors in helping others to accomplish goals and objectives and to realize their potential.

COMPOSITE ROLE SET EXPECTATIONS OF A HEAD COACH

If a head coach does not have any assistants, his position and role are similar to that of a first line supervisor in industry; he has superiors above him to whom he is accountable, and his line position is superior to the workers (players) under his jurisdiction.

Where a head coach has assistants, his position and role are like that of a middle manager; he has superiors over him and his subordinates (assistants) are accountable to him. In actuality, in both analogies a head coach is accountable to his athletes, as well as the assistant coaches, despite the formal organizational structure that places assistants and athletes in "subordinate" positions. The application of a head coach's personal philosophy and leadership style will be the determining factors in the coach's interpersonal relationships with assistants, associates, and athletes, not the formal organizational structure that places the head coach in a superior line position over assistants and players.

Expectations by Superiors: Administration and Management

Where there is a formal organizational structure, such as in the private and public sectors of business and government, the role of the individual who holds a subordinate position is more than partially determined by those in the superior line positions, who are above the subordinates. Following the concept presented previously that a head coach is like a first line supervisor or a middle manger, the role is defined by the coach's superiors or *management*. Generally a coach either is given a specific job description or is informed in some manner of his duties, responsibilities, and what is expected of him. Therefore, this partially defines the coach's role, that is, what management expects of the individual in the position of a head or an assistant coach.

Professional Coaching. In professional sports a head coach may also be the general manager, although in most instances he has a general manager in an executive position over him. In such circumstances the head coach is likely to have other executives and owners in superior line positions above him, too. It is not unusual for management, and possibly stockholders in such situations, to set very high expectations for the professional coach. The coach may acquiesce to others' high expectations, although they may be unreasonable and unrealistic. Not infrequently role strain or role conflict occurs. The job turnover of professional coaches in virtually all sports is very high.

Collegiate and Scholastic Coaching. At other levels of competition, a head coach will also have administrators or "higher-ups" to whom he or she is accountable and who set expectations for the coaches. It may be a principal and a superintendent at the scholastic level; a dean, a vice-president, or a president at the college or university level.

Administrators directly above an athletic coach in the administrative hierarchy at both levels of competition are likely to be department heads or athletic directors. Also, at both levels, there probably will be an athletic board and possibly a faculty representative of athletics to whom coaches *may* be accountable. Not infrequently board of education members at the scholastic level and trustee members at the collegiate level have expectations of the coaches and partially define the expected role of the coach.

Contrary to public opinion, seldom does a head coach have the complete autonomy and authority to conduct and administer the athletic program or sport, for which he is totally responsible and fully accountable, as he perceives it should be done. While this causes role conflict and role strain, the administration of present-day athletics in America is hierarchically structured in this manner. The expectations of how the coach should do his job, and how the coach's hierarchical superiors perceive he should do his job, frequently are incompatible.

Expectations of Athletes

Many studies and surveys have been conducted to determine the expectations that athletes have of coaches. Not surprisingly Snyder (1972a, 1972b, 1975) found through his research that the coach serves as a role model, advisor, and socializing agent for his players. LeGrand (1973), in "What Athletes Look for In Their Coaches," reported that athletes expect coaches to know their sport (subject), to know their players and to be able to relate to them in a variety of situations, and to possess the expertise and know-how of effective teaching–coaching methods to bring both subject matter and the players "together."

Eva Balaza (1974) conducted a clinical investigation of the psychological and social variables associated with the personalities of 25 female athletes who competed in the 1972 Olympics, and one interview question was, "What role did the coach play and how was he perceived by his athletes?"[1] Dr. Balaza reported that she had anticipated good relationships and warm feelings would be expressed by those interviewed, but she did not expect them to express so much emotional involvement and enthusiasm, devotion, and gratitude toward their coaches, such as, "He was a good friend, a father and a teacher all put together." While Balaza commented on the reference to the father figure, she noted the affection and respect each girl had for her own father, which the psychologist perceived resulted in a good relationship with the male coach. Balaza also queried the athletes about how they might feel had their coach been female. Despite the fact that all of the female athletes, except two, had male coaches, most of the athletes expressed the same positive feeling might hold true in relating to a female coach. Several athletes expressed the viewpoint that if a girl and her mother got along well, then it was possible that a female athlete would present a mother figure to the athlete and there would be a good coach–athlete relationship.

After analyzing the tapes of the Olympic competitors, Balaza perceived there was a uniqueness about the athlete–coach relationships that went far beyond skill training. The girls' remarks bespoke of humanistic coach–athlete interactions, where the coach helped the athlete optimize her potentiality. Dr. Balaza concluded, "These are the words (on the tapes) that describe an 'educator' in the purest sense of the word. . . ."

Athletes not only expect skills in know-how, in terms of knowledge and teaching–coaching methodology, but an athlete expects his or her coach to display competencies in interpersonal or human skills in the coach–athlete relationship. Their expectations are neither unrealistic nor unreasonable. Any professional person would likely include these as part of his or her own personal expectations, too.

Expectations by the Parents of the Participating Athletes. Up through the scholastic level of competition, and to some extent at the collegiate level, if a player

---

[1]Balaza, Eva K. "The Female Athlete and Her Coach." *Scholastic Coach,* Vol. 44, No. 3, November 1974, pp. 72–77. Reprinted by permission.

has not yet reached adulthood, the coach of a sport is also accountable to the parents of players, particularly where the physical and mental well-being of their son or daughter is concerned. A coach's position carries a surrogate parent role, and as such this role includes certain expectations by most parents who have sons or daughters participating in athletics under a coach's tutelage.

Most parents probably evaluate the athletic performance of their children objectively and realistically. At times, it is emotionally painful for parents to acknowledge truthfully the fact that their son or daughter should not be in the starting lineup or is not a skilled performer, but most parents can accept this reality. However, no parent expects his or her child not to be given adequate opportunities to display their capabilities and athletic skills. Parents do expect coaches to develop the athletic potential of their children who participate. They certainly do not expect a coach to make discriminatory decisions to exclude their son or daughter from athletic participation. Frequently heard is the allegation that a coach has the team "picked" before the season. The implication is that regardless of what a player does the coach is not going to rate objectively all players solely on the basis of performance. While it is difficult to comprehend why a coach would not evaluate objectively in order to select the best performers who can make the optimum contribution to overall team performance, this charge is made frequently about some coaches. Parents also do not expect a coach to play their son or daughter while he or she is injured, nor do they expect a coach to physically or psychologically abuse or misuse their child.

Expectations of Peers, Assistants, and Others

As a result of interpersonal relationships, peers and subordinates have definite expectations of one in the formal organization structure who is in a leadership position of motivating and who performs necessary management functions. These expectations are strongly influenced by the social setting of the group. Not all head coaches readily acknowledge this, but in the real world they are accountable to their players as well as their assistant coaches and peers.

Expectations of Media and Fans. Although a coach may prefer not to acknowledge it, in a sense a coach is accountable to the media, writers, and sportscasters, and to the spectators and fans. Citizens in many communities tend to identify with and support successful athletic teams, as do student bodies on high school and college campuses.

Athletic teams at each level of competition have their own followers with their own special brand of loyalty, support, dedication, and display of emotions toward "our team" whether it is a Little League baseball team in Pennsylvania, a gymnastics team in Connecticut, a Pop Warner football team in North Carolina, a girl's basketball team in Iowa, the Big Red machine in Cincinnati, the Cowboys in Dallas, the Lakers in Los Angeles, the Razorbacks in Arkansas, or any team of the Fighting Irish anywhere. As supporters their goal, individually and collectively, is for their team to go undefeated, to win a conference, league, and division championship, to go to a bowl, to win a national championship or gain national recognition, and to be declared *Number 1*! When these expectations are not met, frequently the performance of the coach and/or the team is criticized by the media, fans, boosters, and such ambivalence is seldom understood and never appreciated by coaches and athletes who are attempting to do their best. In some situations these expectations are virtually insatiable and create many pressures for coaches and athletes.

Expectations of the Individual Coach

In addition to the expectations of others, every individual has his or her own expectations. These may be as realistic or as unrealistic as the expectations others have of the individual coach. Each coach has certain values, attitudes, and knowledge that he or she brings to the position which can influence the individual's interpretation of how one is supposed to act.

Expectations are powerful factors in motivation. Motivation is a function of the goals of the individual, whether that person expects his behavior, based on opportunities available to him, to be important in achieving these goals, or whether he will be rewarded accordingly if he undertakes or accomplishes those tasks or goals. Since the expectations of others will influence what a coach does, two additional expectations also influence a coach's behavior: the expectations the coach has of whether he will be successful in handling the tasks or alternatives open to him, and the expectations that the coach has if he does not engage in these tasks, providing it will result in the ultimate outcomes desired.

Self-concept. The psychology of motivation is discussed in another chapter. Only the importance of self-concept—which has a direct bearing on one's motivation—is included here. One's self-concept is the set of expectations one has as to how one should behave in a given situation. Each person has a concept or picture of "self" that one uses as a central point of reference for one's thoughts, emotions, and behavior. Depending on varying degrees of accuracy and the different levels of awareness of self-concept, one may or may not be all that one professes to be to oneself and to others. Regardless of such accuracy or awareness, the self-concept one has becomes the focal point in his or her behavior and motivation.

Distortions of Self-concept. There are varying degrees of distortion in one's self-concept for a number of reasons. For example, one may feel one has numerous competencies and proficiencies as a coach, or as an athlete one may feel he or she is strong, skillful, talented, graceful, athletically inclined, but due to one's own perceptions of self, and for other reasons, one's self-picture may be greatly distorted.

A second distortion is the result of how other people see us and of their expectations of us. The so-called "looking-glass self" is how we react to other people's reaction to us, and sometimes the results are similar to looking into a funhouse mirror while wearing badly fitted glasses. One's perception of self tends to fit rather well into cultural or social definitions of the particular roles one fills in society, and the concept of self is the basis of our relationship with other people. The self-concept is also a mechanism one utilizes to bind oneself to society, and to anything else to which one can relate.

It is significant to point out that an individual's self-concept, although relatively enduring and consistent, can change. Significant changes in self-concept generally take a period of time. One's self-image can be positive, healthy, and growth-oriented, or it can be wretched and miserable. Obviously, there are human beings, including coaches and athletes, in both categories.

The Reality of Failure. The reality of failing to fulfill the composite role set of expectations of a coach, especially in professional athletics and not infrequently for collegiate and scholastic coaches of "revenue-producing" sports, leads to job insecurity, role strain, and role conflict. Unique aspects indigenous to the coaching profession that can have a debilitating effect on the self-image of a coach are discussed in the next chapter.

The Profession's Expectations

Every profession has anticipatory and obligatory expectations of its membership. The teaching–coaching profession is not an exception. When one enters the field of coaching, that individual assumes an obligation to conduct himself or herself in accordance with the profession's high ideals and standards, which are usually delineated in its code of ethics, and to uphold these standards.

Competencies of a "Good" Coach. A profession also expects its members to acquire competencies and skills in all job or career-related areas. When one acquires these competencies or skills, he or she is usually identified as a *good* lawyer, a *good* physician, a *good* teacher, a *good* coach, whichever is the appropriate profession. So that one may have some idea of whether or not he or she possesses the essential qualities of a *good* coach, here is a list that presents four broad areas of skills or qualities:

- *Technical sports knowledge.* Do you have a thorough and comprehensive technical knowledge of all aspects of the sport which you coach—offense, defense, strategy, tactics, techniques, skills, fundamentals, and rules—and do you study the game *all ways* and *always*?
- *Characteristics and needs of participants.* Do you understand the characteristics and needs of the participants at the level at which you are coaching—mentally, emotionally, physically, and socially—or are they merely "X*s*" and "O*s*" and bodies?
- *Teaching skills.* Are you skilled in the art of teaching? How well do your players comprehend and execute successfully what you teach them? You

may possess vast technical knowledge and know-how of your sport, but can you teach effectively?
* *Desirable personality and character traits.* Do you have the "X" ingredient—energy, enthusiasm, stability, dedication, honesty, integrity, courage, loyalty, sense of humor, and other highly desirable personality and character traits that "rub off" on the participants and others, that are "caught" more often than "taught," and that produce pride and morale which are necessary ingredients to be winners?

Summary

The role expectations of a coach form an integral aspect of coaching. Every person faces multiple sets of expectations that relate to one's behavior, depending on the different groups or organizations in which one is a member. This would include family, church, community, and other personal activities.

Role expectations relating to coaching are many: expectations of the administration; expectations of the athletes; expectations of the parents; expectations of peers and assistants; expectations of the media and fans; and, in addition to the expectations of others, every individual has his or her own expectations, a self-concept.

Resolving role conflict is a daily part of individual behavior. How one handles various types of conflict depends in the final analysis on the individual. Not all conflict can be resolved without a certain amount of stress, personal strain, and indecision. A coach should be fully cognizant of the nature of coaching and either accept it or choose another profession.

The coaching profession expects its members to acquire competencies and skills in all career-related areas. When one acquires these competencies or skills, he or she is usually identified as a *good* coach. For the sake of self-examination, one can look at four basic areas that describe a good coach: technical knowledge, characteristics and needs of participants, teaching skills, and desirable personality and character traits.

REFERENCES

Balaza, Eva K. "The Female Athlete and Her Coach." *Scholastic Coach.* Vol. 44, No. 3, November 1974, pp. 72–77.

Bisher, Furman. "Noll Flamboyant as Blue Serge Suit," *The Sporting News.* Vol. 190, No. 2, September 6, 1980, p. 15.

Bucher, Charles A. *Administration of Health and Physical Education Programs Including Athletics* (6th ed.). St. Louis, C. V. Mosby Company, 1975, p. 224.

Clary, Jack. *The Game Makers.* Chicago, Ill. Follett Publishing Company, 1976, p. 10.

Cope, Myron. "Better Than Working for a Living." *Sports Illustrated.* Vol. 47, No. 11, September 12, 1977, pp. 37–38, 41–42.

Gallon, Arthur J. *Coaching Ideas and Ideals.* Boston. Houghton-Mifflin, 1974.

Kagan, Jerome, and Havemann, Ernest. *Psychology: An Introduction* (3rd ed.). New York. Harcourt Brace Jovanovich, 1976, p. 563.

LeGrand, Louis E. "What the Athletes Look for in Their Coaches." *Scholastic Coach.* Vol. 43, No. 3, November 1973, pp. 92, 94.

Moore, J. W. *The Psychology of Athletic Coaching*. Minneapolis, Minn. Burgess Publishing Company, 1970, p. 1.

Sabock, Ralph J. *The Coach*. Philadelphia. W. B. Saunders Company, 1973, pp. 6–23.

Scott, Harry A. *Competitive Sports in Schools and Colleges*. New York. Harper, 1951, pp. 263–264.

Snyder, E. E. "A Study of Selected Aspects of the Coach's Influence on High School Athletes." *The Physical Educator*. Vol. 29, 1972a.

Snyder, E. E. "High School Athletes and Their Coaches: Educational Plans and Advice." *The Sociology of Education*. Vol. 45, 1972b, pp. 313–325.

Snyder, E. E. "Variations in Team Status and the Coach's Influence." *The Physical Educator*. October 1975, pp. 124–126.

Zimmerman, Paul. "Part 1. Man Not Myth," and "Part 2. The Teacher." *Sports Illustrated*. Vol. 53, No. 4, July 21, 1980, pp. 58–73, and Vol. 53, No. 5, July 28, 1980, pp. 28–35.

SELECTED READINGS

Fordham, Sheldon, and Leaf, Carol Ann. *Physical Education and Sports: An Introduction to Alternative Careers*. New York. John Wiley & Sons, 1978, p. 153.

Landers, D. M. (ed.). *Psychology of Sport and Motor Behavior II*. Penn State. HPER Series, No. 10, 1975, pp. 65–180. (Proceedings from the North American Society for Psychology of Sport and Physical Activity.)

Marshall, Joe. "Let's Face the Music." *Sports Illustrated*. Vol. 48, No. 5, January 30, 1978, pp. 18–19.

Looney, Douglas S. "There Are A Lot of People Who Think I'm a Phony and Now They Think They Have the Proof." *Sports Illustrated*. Vol. 52, No. 12, March 17, 1980, pp. 34–45.

Martens, Rainer. *Social Psychology and Physical Activity*. New York. Harper & Row, 1975.

Neal, Patsy. *Sport and Identity*. Philadelphia. Dorrance Co., 1972.

Sage, George H. "The Coach as Management: Organizational Leadership in American Sport." *Quest*. January 1973, pp. 34–40.

Walsh, Joe. "The Coach: A Teacher in Conflict." *Journal of Physical Education*. May–June 1973, pp. 107–108.

Zimmerman, Paul. "Part 1. Man Not Myth," and "Part 2. The Teacher." *Sports Illustrated*. Vol. 53, No. 4, July 21, 1980, pp. 58–73, and Vol. 53, No. 5, July 28, 1980, pp. 28–35.

CHAPTER 3

Unique Features Indigenous to Coaching

If a survey were conducted of coaches asking how they got into coaching as a career, the results would reveal that some made the determination early in their life to pursue coaching, others sort of "backed" into the job in that they had intended initially to do something else, and others although already in coaching were still uncertain of whether they actually wanted to continue it as a life's work. Few people have an in-depth knowledge of the nature of coaching before they gain experience in the field. There are some coaches who are uncertain whether they are working in a trade or a profession, and many do not know the difference between the two. Almost without exception none think of coaching as a terminal career, other than those who enter it with the intent of coaching only for a limited period of time and then moving on to pursue a different field of endeavor. No one can know in advance the pressures and stress or the pitfalls of coaching until they experience them personally, since only insight and knowledge can be gained on the job. Since most undergraduate coaching courses and the current literature in the field deal with methods, techniques, and systems and may only deal in a cursory manner with a limited number of the unique features indigenous to coaching, the result is a serious void in the preparation of coaches. Our intent is to discuss coaching from an inside perspective, not from how the general public typically perceives the nature of the work. A number of different features of coaching are unique and unlike those found in other careers and professions, and should be of interest to the individual considering coaching as a career or the novice coach in the profession. In turn, these features or characteristics of coaching have a direct bearing on the philosophy, motivation, and behavioral patterns of a coach.

COACHING: EMOTIONAL AMBIVALENCE

Athletic coaching poses a perfect example of the twin horns of a dilemma. On one hand, coaching is one of the most rewarding and satisfying experiences known to an individual. The self-actualizing coach is likely to find coaching as fulfilling and satisfying as the surgeon who performs a successful operation, or as the lawyer who wins a judgment for his client. It is working with young people, watching them grow and mature, and their being better individuals as a result of having "played for you" that makes coaching so rewarding. From a personal standpoint, coaching is satisfying, rewarding, fulfilling, and self-actualizing for the coach.

On the other hand, at times athletic coaching is frustrating, soul searching, gut wrenching, sometimes literally killing, and, not infrequently, a thankless experience. Because athletics are competitive, coaching is stressful and demanding. Over a period of time this can have a devastating effect on a coach's physical and mental health. Generally someone wins and someone loses. At times merely winning is not enough. While no player ever intentionally makes critical errors that lose games, such errors do occur. Unfortunately, and frequently unjustly, the blame is attributed to the coach. Few critics ever realize that only a single team can be Number One in their league, conference, division, or nationally. No individual or team consistently goes undefeated every year.

Clary (1976) made a candid observation, with which we concur, that due to the high visibility of coaches and the popularity of certain sports, coaches literally have "no place to hide" and it is folly to assume that people will fail to notice it when their team loses. Also, because of the inherent nature of athletics and coaching, seldom is it possible to satisfy many people, much less trying to satisfy all of them. Rarely can one in coaching even satisfy himself or herself, because once one wins there is usually the strong compulsion that one must win every time thereafter. If the compulsion is not self-imposed, it is likely to be imposed by others' expectations of the coach and team.

John Wooden retired at the termination of the 1975 intercollegiate basketball season, after having directed his UCLA Bruins to an unprecedented tenth NCAA national basketball championship in his concluding game as a coach. Wooden reputedly informed his players, "I'm bowing out. I don't want to. I have to" (as reported by Moses, 1975). On another occasion Wooden was quoted by the *Los Angeles Times,* "They think when you win a lot that it's easy. The fact is, the more you win the harder it is to keep on doing it."

The Emotional Drain and the Possibility of "Burning Out"

Psychologist Christina Maslach (1977) of the University of California at Berkeley referred to a number of people in high-stress, heavy human contact occupations who may become "burned-out emotionally." While athletic coaches were not identified per se in Dr. Maslach's study, many coaches take on all of the categorized symptoms she described of individuals who work in high-stress occupations. Obviously there are degrees of emotional burn-out ranging from temporary to severe and from short to long duration but, as Professor Maslach pointed out, sometimes the only cure is a complete change of occupation or work. Over a period of years we have observed that some individuals either do not have the emotional temperament or, after a period of time, coaching becomes too much of a strain on them mentally and physically; so they leave the profession.

Fordham and Leaf (1978) support our premise that emotional tension is a factor that should be seriously considered before one enters coaching. Since a team or a coach's product appears before a discriminating audience on a regularly scheduled basis, the way they perform is a direct reflection on the coach and his or her ability to teach. The concern over winning and losing adds to the emotional stress every coach experiences. The stress occurs in direct proportion to the ambition of the coach, the popularity of the sport involved, and the interest of the community toward that sport.

A number of professions precipitate psycho-physiological stress, and coaching is one of them. Although outward behavior is often a sign of stress, some coaches will experience stress without demonstrating it overtly.

High Emotions at Games. In "Tranquilizers, Towel Chewing, Tantrums: All Are Part of Coach Stress" (*The Physician and Sportsmedicine*, 1976), the author identified a former highly successful collegiate basketball coach who quit because of the physical and emotional pressures of coaching. The article reported that the stress on the coach resulted in several serious illnesses after which he opted to terminate his basketball coaching career in order to extend his life.

Allsen, Olsen, and Fisher (1974) have shown that during a football game the coach's heart rate increased enough to suggest that there was stress on the cardiovascular system. Gazes and associates (1969) found that apparently healthy football and basketball coaches have symptomless tachycardia during their games. The responses to the stress of their games were heart rates averaging 63 beats per minute above their resting rates. McCafferty and associates (1978) conducted a series of investigations to try to determine if the stress on "minor" sports coaches was similar to that on coaches of "major" sports. They concluded that there is considerable stress on a coach's heart during competition and that any sport—major, minor, individual, or team—imposes stress on the coach. The coach's perception of the game and the meaning of the outcome are sources of the coach's stress, not the competitive requirements of the game itself.

In recent years the media has reported that several well-known collegiate coaches have suffered heart attacks, two of whom underwent open heart surgery, and yet they returned to the rigors of major college coaching. There have been other coaches at other levels of competition who have been incapacitated too, as a result of the pressures and stress of coaching. Some have returned to coaching; others have not. It would not be an unfair assumption to state that probably most coaches possess many "Type A" characteristics. Research confirms that the "achievement-oriented, competitive behavior" of Type A people is a significant risk factor in heart disease (Brody, 1980). Reputedly Type A Americans are produced by what some psychologists have dubbed "the Little League syndrome," the belief that everyone has to be Number ONE!

Coaching Becomes an Obsession

Masin (1975) editorialized on "the biggest upset of the year," Ara Parseghian's resignation as the head football coach at Notre Dame. Masin queried how a coach in the prime of his professional life, well-known, highly respected, literally on top of the world, could quit? Masin maintained the answer was relatively simple for those who are aware of the rigors and demands of the man-killing job of big-time coaching; namely, the stress of coaching was undermining Parseghian's health, and as Masin commented, "It is a sad price to pay for the pursuit of excellence."

In mid-December 1974, when 50-year-old Ara Parseghian announced his resignation from Notre Dame University and from coaching football, an *Associated Press* release covering the story quoted the highly successful coach as follows: "I just felt I should get away from coaching for at least one year. I just need time to rejuvenate myself physically and emotionally.... After 25 years as a head coach, I find myself physically and mentally drained. This is certainly not an impulsive move.... My health and the welfare of my family was more important than anything else."

In Masin's (1975) editorial wherein he described coach Parseghian as the "biggest of winners," he candidly stated, "you can imagine what the losers go through...."

Many people wonder why one would subject himself to the demands, pressures, and stresses of coaching, especially "big time" major college coaching. Masin (1975) supports our own personal experiences and observations:

> Maybe it's because they're possessed. Coaching isn't a job to them. It's a calling. Much of their tension is self-induced. They work around the clock for months at a time. They neglect their families. They have little or no time for relaxing pursuits. No matter where they are or what they're doing, some part of their mind is going click-click with the Xs and Os.

They are goaded by one thought, winning. Nothing is more galvanically stimulating than coaching a game, pitting every nerve and brain cell against the other guy. And nothing is more ecstatically thrilling than walking off the field a winner.

That, more than the money, is why every coach gives so much of himself. To many of them, coaching is the only time they come completely alive.

The word for this is obsession. It accounts for the incredible excellence of our teams and athletes. It also sometimes accounts for authoritarianism, venality, and breakdowns. . . .[1]

The Pressures of Coaching Can be Fierce

From our experiences and observations in coaching, we have known of head coaches who were "all nerves." They could not sleep the night before a game or eat anything the day of a game. They had to rely on sedatives to calm themselves prior to a game or after a contest. Dr. Keith P. Henschen (1973) in "Post-Competition Tension . . . How Are You Handling It?" stated, "Research indicates that most athletes experience one of three emotional states after a contest, regardless of its outcome: (1) depression, (2) euphoria, or (3) aggression, intrapunitive or interpunitive." It is obvious that some coaches experience the same emotional state and display the same behaviors as their athletes, only for the coach the intensity is likely to be greater and of a longer duration.

"Last Season at USF: Gaillard Resigns, Blames Pressure to 'Win Them All'" was Michelson's (1977) sports headline caption announcing the resignation of the University of San Francisco's highly successful basketball coach, who the year before had been selected by his peers as Coach-of-the-Year after a 29-2 season's record. Michelson quoted coach Bob Gaillard as follows: "You used to be able to win 20 games in a season and be considered a success. But that's all changed. Last Spring, at the NCAA tournament finals in Atlanta, I talked to John Wooden for about an hour one night. He kept saying that it was almost necessary to go undefeated every year to keep people satisfied, that if you didn't maintain that kind of excellence you were in trouble."

To the rational person it is difficult to comprehend how a coach can torment himself mentally and physically by going through the emotional "wringer" game after game during the sports season, especially when the individual maintains he "likes to coach." While there are pressures and stress in many different types of work, it appears due to the nature of the job that pressures and stress are greater in coaching than in many other types of work. The prospective and novice coaches cannot comprehend coaching pressures and stress since they have not been subjected to them previously. The experienced coach, while not liking what the pres-

---

[1]Masin, Herman L. "Here Below." *Scholastic Coach,* Vol. 44, No. 6, February 1975, pp. 12–13. Reprinted by permission.

sures and stress do to his physical and mental well-being, accept them as "part of the job." Not all individuals thrive and are productive when working under tension and in stressful situations such as coaching.

Irrational Behavior. Masin (1974) cited a friend whom he identified only as being a "mature, intelligent, though volatile guy" who had quit basketball coaching after an outstanding career and had just concluded his first season as a spectator. Masin quoted his friend as saying,

> I cringed every time I saw a coach jump up and go ape, or watched him drop to his knees and scream at somebody, or run up and down the sidelines coaching or complaining at the top of his lungs.
>
> So many coaches go completely out of control and lose every semblance of dignity, manliness, and restraint. They become maniacs. It shakes me up because I know that I was no better. I shrivel inside everytime I think of what a spectacle I used to make of myself. . . .[2]

While it may be difficult for some coaches to exercise personal constraint, others purposely are visibly demonstrative because they perceive their role expectations as calling for a display of volatile behavior. It is utilized as an attention-getting technique by some coaches with their intent being to "shake up" their players, the officials, and/or the spectators in an effort to "make something happen." Some spectators, athletes, and other coaches may consider such behavior as nonprofessional. It frequently serves as an acceptable role model behavior for the inexperienced coach and, as a result, many young coaches emulate and perpetuate this type of behavior which makes coaching more stressful. Regardless of the reason, whether it is lack of personal constraint or it is utilized as a psychological ploy, such displays of hyperemotionalism tend to make a mockery of the coaching profession.

EVERYONE IS AN "EXPERT"

As Clary (1976) pointed out, most everyone is an "expert" coach, and many are prone to share their unsolicited opinions with whomever they feel should have the benefit of their expertise. These same individuals who share their viewpoints freely on coaching, not infrequently with the coach if they have access to his or her attention, would seldom attempt to tell lawyers, physicians, or the clergy how to conduct their professional business. Nor would these same individuals, who may not be expert craftsmen either, think of giving instructions to jewelers, brick masons, mechanics, or carpenters on how they should perform their work skills. Yet a coach is not accorded this courtesy and does not enjoy the same degree of respect as other

[2]Masin, Herman L. "Here Below." *Scholastic Coach,* Vol. 43, No. 6, February 1974, pp. 12–13. Reprinted by permission.

professionals and craftsmen. This unique aspect of coaching exerts much pressure on a coach, something the prospective or novice coach cannot fully visualize or comprehend. The experienced coach may never fully comprehend the behaviors of others relevant to this facet of coaching, but he or she learns to live with this uniqueness indigenous to the profession. To survive and maintain emotional stability, a coach must learn how to live with critics, being cognizant of the fact that it is an impossibility to satisfy completely very many of the ''experts.''

THE WORK IS ENDLESS

A recognized coaching cliché is, ''Coaching is like threading beads on a string with no knot, there is no end to the job!'' While an experienced coach readily concurs there is actually no end to one's work in coaching, the prospective or inexperienced coach will have difficulty perceiving anything beyond the seasonal work in his or her sport. Modern-day coaching has become year-round in most sports.

Another coaching cliché is, ''Winners are workers,'' but unfortunately not all ''Workers are winners.'' Hard workers in coaching generally are winners, but there are many factors, other than merely being a hard worker, that determine coaching success.

A *Sports Illustrated* article (1973), ''A Hundred Percent is Not Enough'' by George Allen and Joe Marshall, sheds some light on a hard-working coach. ''Try 110% instead,'' said George Allen, then the Washington Redskin coach, citing why he believed in the work ethic. ''The world belongs to those who aim for 110%, who believe the future is now, who think there is no off-season and who don't take long lunch hours.''

It has been the co-authors' experience over a number of years, knowing and being associated with professional, college, and high school coaches, that many coaches, particularly those in football and basketball, adhere to the ''long day-short night'' work ethic. Coaching for many does become more than a job; it becomes an obsession.

Win!

In the final analysis, both working and winning are expected of a coach, although a coach's major effort should be work to win. Not all coaches want to work hard enough to win. They *wish* to win but it is only a wish, and they do not want to make the personal sacrifices in terms of time and energy to do what is necessary to achieve that goal. Don Coryell, coach of the San Diego Chargers, was quoted by Dave Distel (1979) as saying,

> You can want to win, and you can *really* want to win. You have to want to win enough to practice hard Christmas eve and then come in and practice hard Christmas day. You have to want to work five months with only one day a week off. . . . Everyone's trying to

win, and there is no question that some coaches work harder than others, but that's not the only important thing. Why can some guys sell houses and others can't?

Bob Oates (1979) pointed out that, "Hard work and long hours made Dick Vermeil a winner with the Philadelphia Eagles. The fact is Vermeil's passion for work, and for inflicting it on others (his team practices three hours a day), has already made him a legend in the East.

"Each week, working day and night, Vermeil sleeps three nights in his office, assuming that he gets to bed at all. . . . ''

At times winning is not enough, and the pressures and stress of trying to win and being afraid of losing are almost always present. Losing coaches almost always are fired, but winning coaches get fired, too.

Those who have succeeded (identified frequently as "winners"), as well as those who have failed (losing coaches, who should not necessarily be labeled "losers"), represent the young and old, the inexperienced and experienced, the hard and soft, the good-natured and foul-tempered, the proud and profane, the articulate and inarticulate, and the dedicated and casual. Most are intense and dedicated, some more than others, but dedication alone is not sufficient to produce winning teams. Coaching is much more difficult than the lay person perceives, and there is no clear-cut way to succeed at it. One cannot copy another who is a winning coach, for there seems to be some subtle, secret chemistry of personality that enables a person to lead successfully and to motivate others, and no one really knows what this is.

Duffy Daugherty (1975), former Michigan State football coach, believes that a coach must be himself. If a coach is a quiet person by nature, he should coach that way; if he is a "holler" guy, outgoing, extroverted, he should coach that way. Within the confines of one's personality, the coach should be himself and should not try to be someone or something he is not.

One cannot coach without enthusiasm. When the time comes that a coach does not obtain satisfaction from coaching, it is time to reevaluate one's personal and professional goals. It may be time to seek a different line of work. For many coaches that "time" seldom coincides with their retirement age.

The coach should recognize that the game is not the ultimate, but is of small importance in comparison to the total life we live. However, the game must be important to the coach, and it is a game that is meant to be played to be won. Regrettably, because of societal expectations and pressures, many coaches leave the profession because in time they perceive that coaching is no longer fun, and for them it ceases to be a game. Many perceive that every contest is a life-and-death struggle that must be won if they are to survive in coaching.

EVALUATION IS BASED ON THE PERFORMANCE OF OTHERS

While a coach expects to be evaluated formally by management, administrators, and others in superior line positions, and informally by peers, assistant coaches, players, and the public, not all coaches readily recognize that they are actually judged or evaluated on the basis of the performance of others. Therefore, the personal and professional well-being and financial security of the coach frequently are in the hands of others, so to speak. A coach certainly does not have the same degree of control over his professional fate and career that other professionals have over their own individual destinies. The nature of athletic coaching is different from that of other professions in that the coach is judged rightly or wrongly, but almost solely, on the performance of his or her athletes, the final score, and the coach's record. Inevitably, the first question asked of athletes and coaches is, "Did you win?" or "Why did you lose?" If an individual or team has an overall winning record with the exception of a single loss, the first question generally asked is, "Which team (or performer) beat you?" or "What was the score?"

Society does not impose the same standards on other professionals, asking physicians, lawyers, teachers, and the clergy to post their annual and cumulative won-lost records. For those professions, the "wins" are always made known, but the "losses" are seldom made public. When a loss occurs, the blame may be attributed to the patient or the client or the student or to the nonbeliever. Not so for the coach when a loss occurs. On the profession of coaching, Dick Vermeil was quoted by Oates (1978) in the *Sporting News* as saying, "An artist can hang his work on the wall and people will come in and see it any hour any day. A salesman has his records to show. But in this profession you are judged by what happens in two and one-half hours (once a week). The results of all you've done, or tried to do, are out there every Sunday for others to evaluate."

Invalid Evaluative Criteria

Measurable factors, such as lack of player personnel in terms of quality and quantity, frequently are discounted or overlooked by many people not directly involved in coaching the team or the participants. Negative personal traits and characteristics that players may possess such as immaturity, instability, lack of courage, lack of desire, and lack of dedication to excel may not be taken into consideration by individuals not connected with coaching the sport. The same "experts" would not expect a talented jockey (coach) to win an important racing event without a good horse (personnel) and a good trainer (management), but these same individuals expect a coach to win without good player personnel. Much of a coach's success depends on the player personnel available to the coach and the ultimate win-loss record of the team or individual performers under the coach's jurisdiction.

Masin (1975) cited several well-known professional basketball coaches who won when they had good personnel and lost when their good players were injured, traded, or retired. Masin editorialized, "Every coach knows the game and how to teach it. The secret of winning is personnel. If you have it, you win. If you don't, you lose. . . . That's the way the ball and the reputation bounces, and it's totally unfair to the coaches who bounce with it."

LITTLE SECURITY IN PREVIOUS WINNING RECORD

A time-tested cliché, "Coaches are hired to be fired," is a recognized truism by most experienced coaches at every level of competition. Novice coaches generally recognize the validity and reality of this truism within a short period of time after entering the profession. There is no valid way to substantiate the cliché, but several unofficial sources bear out the reality of the fact that there is a high turnover of professional and collegiate coaches annually. *Sports Illustrated*'s Marshall (1978) pointed out that, since 1975, 24 head football coaches, excluding four interim coaches, had been hired by the National Football League's 28 teams within that three-year period. Shortly after the article's publication (January 30, 1978), two coaches who had been on a "hold" basis were replaced and, before one-third of the regular 1978 NFL season had been completed, three additional head coaches had been replaced, and several others were on a "hold" status during the season.

The Sporting News (September 18, 1979) listed 25 major college head football coaching changes in effect prior to the 1979 season. Smith (1977) in *Chronicle of Higher Education*, "The Old Coach-in Motion Play," cited the fact that more than 200 football and basketball college coaches changed positions prior to the 1977 season. It would be erroneous to infer all coaches were fired. Some coaches retired from the rigors of coaching of their own volition, while others moved out because they were terminated. Some of those remained connected with athletics in a different capacity, others did not. Some moved laterally to other head coaching positions, while some head coaches moved downward from head to assistant coaching positions. Still others moved upward in terms of having been elevated to head coaching positions.

There are approximately 1600 collegiate institutions, of all sizes, not all of whom compete in intercollegiate football and/or basketball. Obviously there are considerably greater numbers of scholastic teams, although there is no practical way of determining the number of coaches who are replaced each year.

Norm Sloan, former head basketball coach at North Carolina State University, was quoted in the *NCAA News* (1977) as saying, "People are getting tenure and security in every profession except coaching. Coaching is the only profession in which you have to prove yourself as much in the 30th year as in the first year."

Indiana University's effervescent and likable head football coach Lee Corso authored an article entitled "J. S. Game—Win or Gone" (1977), in which J. S. stands for "Job Saver." Coach Corso's caption is highly appropriate and tends to refute the popular myth, "It's not whether you win or lose, but how you play the game." Candidly and realistically in many coaching situations, it is win or gone! There is little security in a coach's previous winning record.

THE EFFECT ON THE COACH'S FAMILY

While physicians, lawyers, and others are likely to be away from their families to a limited extent due to the demands of their profession, coaches, depending on the level of competition, are likely to be away from their families frequently due to the nature of their work. The result of a survey conducted by Sabock and Jones (1978) dealing with the attitudes of male high school coaches' wives revealed that the three biggest problems or concerns the wives had relevant to the husbands' coaching were the excessive job demands in terms of time away from wives, children, and families; the health and well-being of the husband–coach because of job pressures resulting in tension, anxiety, ulcers, and possible heart attacks; and irregular home schedule, meals, trips, and transportation problems.

The Sabock-Jones survey of coaches' wives also revealed that the husband–coaches missed many of the activities in which their children were involved because of the amount of time spent away from home as the result of the demands of coaching. The wives were forced to handle the disciplining of the children by themselves on most occasions. The most frequent complaint from the wives' viewpont was the amount of time the husband–coach spent away from home.

When the Wife is the Coach

It is interesting to note the responses of the husbands who were queried when the wife was the coach. While the number of responses Sabock and Jones (1978) secured from wives who were coaches were small, since the number of married women who are high school coaches in Pennsylvania still is relatively few and many male coaches still coach high school girls' teams, the one consistent negative thread concerned the demands on the wife's time. As Sabock and Jones pointed out, "Men who are married to coaches are faced with coming home to an empty house during the season, possibly getting dinner ready, helping clean the house and spending each evening with an exhausted wife."

The results are most interesting, and understandably coaching has a definite effect on the coach's family. The prospective and novice coach may have a tendency not to consider such factors. The experienced coach is likely to minimize or overlook the effect coaching has on his or her spouse and family, most likely feeling "it is part of the job," possibly to the detriment of the spouse and family.

A TERMINAL MEANS OF LIVELIHOOD

Seldom does one retire from coaching in the same sense that one normally retires from another profession, trade, or business at the mandatory age of 65 or 70, especially at the collegiate and professional levels of competition. When one retires from coaching, forced or voluntarily, one usually has not yet reached the mandatory age, and frequently the coach must continue to make a livelihood in some manner other than athletic coaching. Age becomes a discriminatory factor in the hiring of coaches, since coaching is considered a young person's game.

Fred Jacoby (1978), Commissioner, Mid-American Conference, conducted a survey of Big Ten Conference football coaches that revealed that, of the 84 assistant coaches, 11 or slightly more than 13 percent were 20 to 29 years of age; 45 or almost 54 percent were 30 to 39 years of age; 22, slightly above 26 percent, were 40 to 49 years of age; four were 50 to 59; and only two assistants were 60 to 69 years of age. Approximately 93 percent of the total number of assistant coaches at that time were not yet 50 years of age. Of the ten head football coaches at the time, seven of them were in the 40 to 49 age category, one was 50 years of age, and another was 37 years of age. Of the head coaches, 90 percent were not older than 50 years of age at the time of the survey.

As Fuoss (1979) pointed out, age does become a discriminatory factor despite present laws to the contrary. There are certain unofficial recognized "time plateaus" and expectations for coaches in terms of age. Generally, if a football coach has not been named to a head coaching position at a small or major college by 40 years of age, his chances of securing such a position diminish with each succeeding year. It may be that, even with former head coaching experience, no candidate beyond 45 years of age will be considered. It depends on whether one is moving up from high school to collegiate coaching or whether one is changing positions as an assistant, going from one major staff to another.

Active Coaching Career

A young person entering the coaching profession seldom if ever takes into consideration the fact *that 15 to 20 years is likely to be his or her maximal period of time in the profession.* Obviously this is an insufficient period of time to coincide with the individual's mandatory retirement age. Rare is the individual who enters the coaching profession and who thinks of his or her career in these terms. The individual with little or no experience has no frame of reference, and so it is not unusual to look at one's career in terms of the immediate present or the near future. Then, too, after a period of time even an experienced coach may be labeled "too old," although the coach may be in mid-life. Prior to the 1979 season, a coaching acquaintance with 27 years experience in the profession, the last 16 as an assistant coach with a professional football team, found his coaching career terminated at 52 years of age when there was a change of head coaches and two members of the staff were not retained by the new head coach. Unable to secure a coaching position prior to the 1979 season, our ex-coach acquaintance started training as a life insurance salesman, bitter that he did not get any severance pay when he was terminated, and that he had been unsuccessful in securing a coaching position at *any* level of competition despite 27 years experience in collegiate and professional football coaching.

Jacoby (1978), in "Where is Your Next Job," concluded: "There are only so many chapters in each person's book of life. . . . However, nothing is forever. You must prepare for the day you will not be in coaching. It is wise and prudent to give serious thought and plan for your next job change so that you will have a viable future with available options.''

Fordham and Leaf (1978) support our contention that the active coach, particularly for those in head coaching positions, averages about 15 years, and a majority of coaches quit coaching long before they retire from the teaching profession. While this situation can only occur where the coach has already gained tenure as a teacher, this avenue is not open to one who has been hired strictly on the coaching track. Not infrequently problems arise for the coach who returns to full-time teaching. One problem may be that the ex-coach has to re-tool skills and acquire additional knowledge in order to teach in a subject discipline if he or she has not been teaching classes as well as coaching. Classroom teaching is much different from on-the-field coaching, and the ex-coach is no longer in the spotlight that he or she may have enjoyed for a number of years. There are a number of other aspects of full-time classroom teaching that may confront the ex-coach, especially if the removal from coaching was not of his or her own volition. If the transition is not smooth, there may be problems not only for the coach but also for the administration who will encounter difficulties trying to fire a tenured faculty member. Frequently ex-coaches become bitter because of having been forced out of coaching and back into teaching. If they fail to give less than 100 percent as teachers, this causes problems with other classroom teachers.

A current problem in the scholastic ranks is one of coaches leaving the field because of the lack of funds for equipment and transportation or a lack of administrative support for the athletic program in general. This type of coach, who possibly has 15 to 20 years left until retirement, returns to the classroom, leaving the coaching jobs to someone else. Declining enrollment and lack of funds prohibit school administrators from hiring new teacher–coaches in some districts. Thus the coaching positions are being filled by paraprofessional or ''walk-on'' coaches who come in after school hours to coach the different teams. Although this situation may not be the norm, a vast majority of coaches still face the fact that when they retire from coaching it will not coincide with their mandatory retirement age since the typical coaching career is 15 to 20 years.

FREQUENT COACHING CHANGES

Depending on one's personal goals, motivation, and professional aspirations, a coach is likely to have several coaching positions in his or her career. There is no one set pattern, but typically one moves from a high school position to the college ranks, and some then go into the professional coaching ranks. One usually starts as an assistant, then moves to a head coaching position. But one does not always move up in coaching. Some move laterally, others move downward, and still others move out of the field after a period of time. It is likely, however, if one remains in the field of coaching for a number of years, the individual will have opportunities to move to other positions.

Depending on the individual's aspirations and opportunities, it appears that over the course of a coaching career the typical coach is likely to hold approximately six different positions as an assistant and/or head coach, but still not reach the mandatory retirement age while in coaching. At the other end of the spectrum is the coach who holds a single coaching position for his entire career and retires from it because of mandatory age requirements.

Termination from a position is always an ego-shattering and traumatic experience for the coach and his family. Job change, either forced or of one's own volition, can be a highly emotional experience. An assistant coach, for example, may be very competent, but usually his career depends on the head coach's success. The head coach may be fired or change positions by choice, which may cause a termination of the assistant's position or force the assistant into a job change, too. The assistant coach and his family may or may not wish to change positions at that particular time. Where children of school age are involved, this presents a number of problems and stress within the family. Moving and relocation expenses, especially as the result of a sudden termination or job change, may bring on a financial crisis for the coach and family with limited financial means.

Author Jim Benagh (1976) discussing ''big time'' athletics tried to present in a humorous vein the situation that many college football coaches who are sudden jobseekers frequently find themselves in about the time of the annual American Football Coaches Convention each year in January. While it is amusing to refer to the ''All Time All-Lobby Team'' of coaches who parade the lobby of the convention site in order to secure coaching positions, it can be a traumatic crisis for a coach who has been terminated and is unsuccessful in securing a new position.

Fuoss (1979), in ''Blueprinting Your Coaching Career,'' *Summer Manual,* American Football Coaches Association, acknowledged this plight of coaches, but suggested ways one could give his career and life direction and how one could keep open his job opportunity wedge over an extended period of time. Fuoss also included the need to assess and mold one's career and life in the event one left the field of coaching before the mandatory retirement age.

IF YOU ARE INTERESTED IN MAKING MONEY

The remainder of the above heading should read ''then coaching is the wrong career to pursue.'' No attempt will be made here to categorize coaching salaries because too many factors are involved in determining what an individual will be paid for coaching duties.

Salary depends on the level of competition, the head or assistant coaching position, the responsibilities, the sport, and frequently whatever the salary negotiations will tolerate. Much depends on how badly the employer wants to hire the individual coach, the maximal salary that the employer can offer within established guidelines, and what salary can be legitimately justified to those accountable for funding. The other party to the salary negotiations is the candidate–coach, and it frequently comes down to how badly he or she wants the coaching position and what the individual will accept as a salary. Whatever the amount, considering all of the previously discussed factors, one earns one's salary in coaching!

For the most part coaching salaries are comparable to those of teaching, especially at the scholastic and collegiate levels, and must adhere to specified salary guides for all faculty members. On the scholastic level a coach receives a teacher's salary plus a stipend called an extra-service contract, which is usually not adequate compensation for the hours put in and the amount of work that has to be accomplished.

There are well-known "name" coaches at large collegiate institutions, especially in football and basketball, who considerably supplement their regular coaching salary through clinic speaking engagements, their own television shows, publications, and endorsements. However, these coaches are the exceptions and are relatively few in number, as is the motivated high-school teacher and the university professor, similarly the exception, who successfully supplements his or her teaching salary to an appreciable extent by research, consultation, and publishing.

Financial compensation for professional coaches, notably in football and basketball, is considerably more than collegiate coaching for the most part. In many instances assistant coaches in the professional ranks, especially in football and basketball, receive greater financial remuneration for their coaching than do many head coaches of those sports at the collegiate level. Very few of these coaches, professional or collegiate, receive income comparable to that of the top lawyers or physicians. If the amount of time involved in coaching were taken into consideration on an hourly basis, few individuals in professions other than coaching would work so long for such minimal compensation. Sabock and Jones (1978) reported that, while they did not solicit responses from high school coaches' wives in their survey relevant to salary, the consensus of the unsolicited responses was that coaching was not worth the time their husbands spent on it when one looked at the amount of money the coaches received. This might lend some support to the notion that people do not stay in coaching for the money or, conversely, if a person is interested in making money, coaching is the wrong career to pursue.

It is the general consensus of most people who are familiar with the coaching profession and knowledgeable of the typical financial compensation that most coaches receive that, if a coach were to spend the same amount of time in some other occupation that he spends in coaching, he would be making a lot more money. Like the ministry and teaching, coaching is frequently referred to as a labor of love. Many individuals in these professions feel the psychic rewards are far greater than the monetary ones, and this is why they are ministers, teachers, and coaches. While all three professions have some features that are similar, no other profession has as many unique features as those that are indigenous to coaching, and these have a direct bearing on a coach's philosophy, work, and the relationship he or she maintains with assistants, players, and others.

Summary

Few people have an in-depth knowledge of the nature of coaching before they gain experience in the field. In a sense, coaching is one of the most rewarding and satisfying experiences known to an individual. And yet at times athletic coaching is frustrating, soul searching, gut wrenching, sometimes literally killing, and, not infrequently, a thankless experience. Emotional tension is a factor that should be seriously considered before one enters coaching, since not all individuals thrive and are productive when working under tension and in stressful situations such as the coach's domain.

One cannot coach without enthusiasm. The coach should recognize that the game is not the ultimate, but is of small importance in comparison to the total life we live. However, the game must be important to the coach, and it is a game that is meant to be won.

People do not remain in coaching for the money or, put another way, if a person is interested in making money, coaching is the wrong career to pursue. Like the ministry and teaching, coaching is frequently referred to as a labor of love. Many individuals in these professions feel the psychic rewards are far greater than the monetary ones, and this is why they chose to be ministers, teachers, and coaches. While all three professions have some features that are similar, coaching has many unique features, and these have a direct bearing on a coach's philosophy, work and the relationship he or she maintains with assistants, players, and others.

REFERENCES

Allen, George, and Marshall, Joe. "A Hundred Percent Is Not Enough." *Sports Illustrated.* Vol. 39, No. 2, July 9, 1973, pp. 74–76, 80, 83, 84, 86.

Allsen, P., Olsen, D., and Fisher, A. "The Effects of Stress Situations in Football Games on the Heart Rates of Football Coaches." Read before the annual meeting of AAHPER. April 1, 1974.

Associated Press. "Irish Coach Parseghian Quits—Will Rest For at Least One Year." December 4, 1974.

Benagh, Jim. *Making It To #1: How College Football and Basketball Teams Get There.* New York. Dodd, Mead and Company, 1976, pp. 137, 139.

Brody, Jane E. *New York Times News Service.* "Study Links The Rat Race To Heart Attack: Here's a 'Type A' Checklist." Reported in *The Sacramento Bee.* September 21, 1980, p. A19.

Clary, Jack. *The Game Makers.* Chicago, Ill. Follett Publishing Company, 1976, p. 10.

Corso, Lee. "J. S. Game-Win or Gone." *Summer Manual.* Americal Football Coaches Association, 1977, pp. 84–86.

Daugherty, Duffy. "Some Thoughts on Coaching." *San Francisco Coach of the Year Football Clinic Notes.* Edited by Bob Troppmann, 1975, pp. 66–68.

Distel, Dave. "Chargers' Coryell—San Diego Coach Specializes in Intensity and Turn-arounds." *Los Angeles Times*. December 28, 1979, Part III.

Fordham, Sheldon I., and Leaf, Carol Ann. *Physical Education and Sports: An Introduction to Alternative Careers*. New York. John Wiley & Sons, 1978, p. 153.

Fuoss, Donald E. "Blueprinting Your Coaching Career." *Summer Manual*. American Football Coaches Association, 1979, p. 66.

Gazes, P. C. Sovell, B. F., and Dellastatious, M. W. "Continuous Radioelectrocardiographic Monitoring of Football and Basketball Coaches During Games." *American Heart Journal*. Vol. 78, 1969, pp. 509–512.

Henschen, Keith P. "Post-Competition Tension. . . How Are You Handling It?" *Scholastic Coach*. Vol. 43, no. 4. December 1973, p. 52.

Jacoby, Fred. "Where is Your Next Job?" *Summer Manual*. American Football Coaches Association, 1978, pp. 73–75.

Kolbenschlag, Mike. "Tranquilizers, Towel Chewing, Tantrums: All Part of Coach Stress." *The Physician and Sportsmedicine,* Vol. 4, no. 1, January 1976, pp. 97, 99, 101.

Marshall, Joe, "Let's Start the Music." *Sports Illustrated*. Vol. 48, No. 5, January 30, 1978, pp. 18–19.

Masin, Herman L. "Here Below." *Scholastic Coach*. Vol. 43, No. 8, 1974, p. 10.

Masin, Herman L. "Here Below." *Scholastic Coach*. Vol. 44, No. 6, February 1975, pp. 12–13.

Maslach, Christina. "Burnout: A High Price for Caring." *The National Observer*. July 11, 1977, p. 14.

McCafferty, William B., Gliner, Jeffery A., and Horvath, Steven J., "The Stress of Coaching." *The Physican and Sportsmedicine*. February 1978, pp. 67–71.

Michelson, Herb. "Last Season at USF Gaillard Resigns, Blames Pressure To 'Win Them All'." *The Sacramento Bee*. September 9, 1977, p. D-4.

Oates, Bob. "Honored Coaches Can Expect Ax." *The Sporting News*. April 8, 1978, p. 70.

Oates, Bob. "Eagles' Vermeil—Hard Work and Long Hours Made Him Winner in Philly." *Los Angeles Times*. December 28, 1979, Part III.

Sabock, Ralph J. and Jones, David. "The Coaching Profession: Its Effect on the Coach's Family." *Athletic Journal*. Vol. 58, No. 9, May 1978, pp. 42, 44, 45, 62.

Sloan, Norman. "Opinions Out Loud." *NCAA News*. Vol. 14, No. 7, July 15, 1977, p. 2. (Quoted from the *Dallas Times Herald*.)

Smith, Steve. "The Old Coach in Motion Play." *Chronicle of Higher Education*. July 18, 1977, pp. 9–10.

Sporting News. September 18, 1979.

Wooden, John. *Sports Illustrated*. As reported by Moses, S. "Pursued By a Very Long Shadow," Vol. 43, No. 43, November 17, 1975, pp. 32–34.

SELECTED READINGS

Associated Press. "McClendon: Educators Must Regain Control." *The Sacremento Union*. January 8, 1980, p. D-3.

Axthelm, Pete. "Quiet Man." *Newsweek*. Vol. 85, April 14, 1975, pp. 93–94.

Costill, David. "Science and the Future of Sports." *The Physician and Sportsmedicine*. Vol. 5, No. 6, June 1977.

Dower, Herb (Ed.). "Coaches Under Glass." *Santa Rosa Press Democrat*. Santa Rosa, Calif. February 19–24, 1978 (five-part article).

Fuoss, Donald E. "Blueprinting Your Coaching Career." *Summer Manual*. American Football Coaches Association, 1979, pp. 63–70.

Governali, Paul. "The Physical Educator as Coach." *Quest* VII. December 1966, pp. 30–33.

Johnson, Warren R. "Emotional Upset and Psychosomatic Problems in Coaching." *The Athletic Journal*. February 1957, pp. 44–46.

Komarovsky, M. "Some Problems in Role Analysis." *American Sociological Review*. Vol. 28, 1973, pp. 649–662.

McKinney, Wayne C. "What is a Good Coach?" *Scholastic Coach*. March 1970, p. 86.

Petrelli, John A. "So You Want to be a Coach?" *Scholastic Coach*. Vol. 44, No. 3, November 1974, pp. 6–8.

Starnes, Richard. "Boosters: A Winning Coach's Best Ally, a Loser's Greatest Foe." *Chronicle of Higher Education*. November 12, 1973, p. 7.

Starnes, Richard. "Tennessee, With $3-Million Sports Budget, Keyed to Winning." *Chronicle of Higher Education*. October 9, 1973, p. 3.

Suinn, Richard M. *Psychology in Sports—Methods and Applications*. Minneapolis, Minn. Burgess, 1980.

Underwood, John. "Special Report—Students Athletes: The Sham, the Shame." *Sports Illustrated*. Vol. 52, No. 21, May 19, 1980, pp. 36–44, 47–48, 53–54, 57, 60, 62, 65–66, 71–72.

Will, Geroge F. "The George Will Column: 'Type A' Person Strives To Develop 'Type B' Characteristics." *Washington Post*. As reported in *The Sacramento Bee*. October 2, 1980, p. B11.

Two

THE PHILOSOPHICAL AND MANAGEMENT DIMENSIONS OF COACHING

4

A Dynamic Philosophy for Coaching Effectiveness

How an individual views relationships, things, events, and the values affixed to them, is that individual's philosophy. A coach's overall philosophy is made up of interrelated components of one's personal philosophy of life; the philosophy one has toward one's position and work as a coach; and the strategical, tactical, and operational philosophy of the sport one coaches. These are the cornerstones of the foundation on which each coach builds his or her life, work, program, and sport. Since it is impossible for an individual not to perceptualize, have beliefs and attitudes, and to affix values, everyone has some sort of a philosophical base that motivates their overt and covert behavior.

The truism, "Philosophy is the pursuit of wisdom, and wisdom continues to pursue philosophy," rings true. The continuing development of these components for a coach is an evolving, dynamic process to the degree that he or she continues to seek wisdom throughout life. The philosopher Epictetus stated, "The beginning of philosophy is to know the condition of one's own mind." While the application of this statement seems simplistic, for many individuals it is not. Many people are uncertain in their beliefs and values, and the result is that they vacillate from one course of action or opinion to another. For an individual in a leadership position, such as a coach, the results can be chaos, confusion, and possibly total disorder. For the coach the end results are likely to be an unsuccessful program, a losing sport, ineffective coaching, and a dissatisfied person. The coach's constituents are likely to be dissatisfied, too.

THE DEVELOPMENT OF A PHILOSOPHY

Each component of one's life is not a separate entity because each has a direct bearing on the others. Obviously, since coaching may be succinctly described as a "people's" business, a coach's personal perceptions of human relationships are critical in dealing with players, subordinates, associates, and others connected directly with his or her work and the position as coach.

As an aspiring or an inexperienced coach may ask, "How and where do I get a coaching philosophy?"—as if it were something relatively simple that could be gleaned from a book or obtained from attending a clinic or a coaching seminar. In reality a person acquires an overall philosophy as the result of varied experiences throughout one's entire life. Coaching philosophy may be acquired as a result of experiences one has had as a former player and coach. A coach's philosophy is influenced by what one reads, sees, hears, and experiences. For example, Steadman (1980) quoted Pittsburgh's Super Bowl coach Chuck Noll as follows: "I learned early as a coach that there's more than one way to do a thing. I've been influenced, one way or another, by everyone I have come in contact with, the coaches I worked for and those working for me. I learn from my players, too. It happens all the time." A coach may be influenced by the strategy, tactics, or the personal demeanor of other coaches and participants in numerous sports at all levels of athletic competition. These experiences will influence an individual in formulating, broadening, and revising a personal philosophy that will dictate everything he or she does as a human being and as a coach, because the individual will affix to these experiences his or her own set of values, beliefs, concepts, and attitudes. In so doing, one formulates one's philosophy.

While one's personal philosophy begins to be formulated early in life, a coaching philosophy would usually not begin to develop until the individual started to think of a career or to take a definite interest in coaching. It is important for prospective coaches to begin formulating a sound philosophy of coaching during their undergraduate years. Each person should take advantage of the opportunity to broaden his knowledge by testing his or her ideas on others in order to receive the benefit of their wisdom. In turn, this aids in clarifying one's thinking and in adopting other sound ideas.

Why Develop a Philosophy?

Philosophy is concerned with answering fundamental questions. Specifically, for the coach seeking answers to *what, why,* and *how,* a philosophy will provide guidelines for determining the needs, as well as the pathways for meeting these needs. Since coaches are challenged and questioned by many people in today's society, it is essential that a coach knows *what* he believes and *why* he believes it. Despite the democratic decision-making process advocated by some critics of athletics that athletes should make all of their own and the team's decisions, in the final analysis coaches must decide what is best for their players, team, themselves, a. the sport they coach. This is not to infer that coaching staffs should fail to secur input from their squad members. It is important for a head coach to orient and indoctrinate staff and players as to the head coach's beliefs pertaining to the sport in which they are all involved. The coach's philosophy provides his or her staff and players with a sense of direction. They, in turn, through the sport and program, generally reflect the head coach's philosophy. Not all coaches make known the detailed specifics of their philosophy, so that their staff members, players, and others may be uncertain of their head coach's beliefs and wishes pertaining to such matters as training rules, practice sessions, style of play, discipline, personal appearance, codes of conduct, and so forth. Some coaches may not think through various aspects of their philosophy. For example, one young head coach decided it would be more democratic for each of his assistants to handle the disciplinary problems of the players each coached, including imposing their own sanctions, without first establishing mutually agreed on team member behavior codes with specified sanctions to be imposed uniformly. The results were player rebellion, low morale, and a losing season. In reality each coach was applying his own perceived philosophy, since neither the staff nor players had been oriented as to the head coach's philosophy.

"Wait-See" and "Do Right" Philosophies. A different type of error is the coach who does not want to expend the time to orient or indoctrinate others as to his philosophy, utilizing either a "wait-see" philosophy or a blanket "do right" philosophy to cover all situations that may arise and cause problems, after which the head coach's philosophy is made known relevant to the particular situation. In the "wait-see" philosophy if action is taken, it is always *after* the fact. Or action may be taken on one occasion but not another so that inconsistency occurs in similar circumstances, and this causes additional problems.

In the blanket "do right" philosophy, the players may be merely informed by the head coach that they are always expected to "do right" or corrective sanctions will be imposed by the coaching staff. This, too, is *after* the fact, and unless the policy is spelled out initially, so that the players know the details of the head coach's philosophy, conflicting individual value judgments are inevitable. What an athlete or group of players may perceive as "right" for them and the team may differ from the coach's point of view.

Both the "wait-see" and "do right" philosophical points of view are analogous to the "fire fighter" philosophy, which waits until a fire occurs before attempting to take precautionary measures. If a coach has a clearly delineated philosophy and policy, it is like the "fire preventer" who does all he can initially to prevent fires from occurring.

In athletics the team is the unit in which instruction of the individual most commonly takes place, and it is essential that a coach's philosophy be clearly defined, first to the coach, and then to the assistants and players. In some sports, team coordination involving specific plays, patterns, and unit assignments is more important than in others. In all sports where individuals compete for a school, the team concept exists and concern for others on the team and team goals are present. The basic premise of athletic competition is to achieve through personal, individual successes; this may then culminate in the ultimate achievement of winning a contest, game, race, or match. The individual athlete thus can have both a personal success and a success as part of a winning team.

In competitive situations involving teams, the democratic process in its purest sense would not be successful. Contributions by individuals to the decision-making process are important and valuable, but ultimately one person must collate, evaluate, and take long-range or on-the-spot action and consider the individual and the team. This person is the coach, and the role is to a great degree authoritarian. The reponsibility cannot be delegated to others. Because the coach is devoted not only to improving the athlete but also to self-improvement, the margin of error is always present. The coach will learn from such errors and future athletes will benefit from this experience.

Changing Philosophical Beliefs and Values

The erroneous inference should not be drawn that once an individual acquires basic beliefs they are always held steadfast throughout life. Fundamental beliefs generally are formulated early in life and depend on the inculcations of one's value system, such as the individual's personal and social ideals or standards that may be used to evaluate and regulate one's own and others' behavior. These involve judgments of what is proper, good, right, true, desirable, acceptable, or their counterparts, and how one perceives different situations. Due to social and technological changes in our culture and the mores of society, the beliefs and attitudes of people are likely to change to some degree. What an individual believed to be right and true at one time may not be the situation later in one's life. One's basic beliefs, although well-established, may be modified, revised, or even abandoned at a later date as one matures and acquires additional knowledge and wisdom. One must formulate his or her own beliefs or philosophy. They cannot be borrowed *in toto* from others. A coach should reflect his own thoughts as his true self and allow his human qualities to show; an individual cannot be something he or she is not. Regardless of the number of years a person is in the coaching profession, certain basic concepts and beliefs are likely to remain fairly steadfast as the tenets of a coach's philosophy, whereas coaching theory or philosophy is just as likely to change. Change is not necessarily good or bad, but inevitable. Regardless, a coach should constantly reevaluate his or her beliefs about life, coaching, and coaching theory. Frequently such a reevaluation is based on learning experiences encountered in life generally, and in the coaching profession specifically.

If a head coach is to provide the necessary leadership for effective coaching in order to achieve the desired goals, it is imperative to develop a sound overall philosophy in the three areas mentioned—in one's personal philosophy, in one's view of one's position, and in one's sports philosophy. All three are interrelated, and these will determine not only the way a coach conducts the program, but also the degree of success that person ultimately achieves individually and collectively as the leader and head coach of the sport.

DEVELOPING A PERSONAL PHILOSOPHY OF LIFE

Much of the base foundation of how a coach views coaching will be intertwined considerably with how that individual views life and relationships with others. Dr. Roy Menniger, fourth president of the world renown Menninger Foundation and author of "Responsibility to Self" (1972), pointed out the necessity of a personal mental checkup in which each individual examines his own motivation and goals in life. A careful self-scrutiny and self-appraisal will aid the individual in exercising some control over his own destiny.

Typical of the self-examination queries, or Menninger's "keys," would be seeking soul-searching answers and meaningful dialogue with oneself similar to the following:[1]

- What are my goals in life?
- Toward what objectives am I aiming, and how realistic are they?
- How well do they incorporate what is *really* important to me?
- How well do they actually express my values?
- Are they real or only for show?
- Are my goals solely materialistic?
- To what purposes have I dedicated my efforts and life?
- What are my personal priorities in life?
- Does how I utilize the vital resources of time and energy truly reflect my priorities?
- Is there an imbalance in the use of my time and energy in that my own needs come first? Last?
- Do I accept the concept of balanced responsibility which implies a willingness of responsibility for my own attitudes, feelings, failures, and prejudices instead of projecting and displacing my feelings and attitudes onto others or forces external to myself?
- Do I possess the courage to face myself honestly and fairly?
- Can I accept disappointments and losses?

[1]Menninger, Roy W., M.D. "Responsibility to Self." *Menninger Perspective*, Vol. 3, No. 4, June/July 1972. Adapted with permission from *Menninger Perspective*. Copyright © 1972 by the Menninger Foundation.

- What is the consistency and quality of my personal relationships with others?
- Are my human relationships important? Superficial, meager, unrewarding?
- Of my relationships, is there a quality of involvement wherein there is a mutual willingness to share, to listen, to give?
- From whom do I receive emotional support, and to whom do I give emotional support?
- Do I possess the capacity to care, to love, and do I really invest myself in others, becoming involved, listening to them, and caring about them?
- How truly do I possess love of self in terms of pride, self-esteem, a person of value, an individual of worth?
- Is my love of self mature and realistic, and can I extend my love to help others in a respectful and genuinely caring manner?

Many psychologists, physicians, and others have postulated than an individual's relationships to others mirror that person's relationship to self. Dr. Menninger (1972) concurred, maintaining that how well a person deals with others will depend on success in managing oneself in relation to the provocative and difficult questions posed above. Answers to a number of these questions are not simplistic and in some instances, depending on the individual coach seeking to establish a philosophy of life, they are not all answerable. One's philosophy is not formulated quickly, but is built cumulatively throughout one's life. Forthright answers to multipurpose questions pertaining to one's motivations and goals in life need to be examined repeatedly.

In developing one's personal philosophy, it is important for a coach to establish a strong self-image. One should make every effort to recognize one's strengths, weaknesses, motives, desires, and drives, and learn to live with them. As a result, a coach will be better able to handle success and failure, trials and tribulations, frustrations and anxieties, as he or she strives to meet personal and professional goals and aspirations.

Principles, Attitudes, and Values

In the development of a philosophy and in the application of philosophical beliefs, whether they be personal, professional or coaching theory, one will seldom be unsound if he or she builds on and operates from a strong base of fundamental principles. A *principle* is an ethical code of standards and a basic quality determining intrinsic nature or characteristic behavior. A principle is a statement formulated as a guide to action. Principles are not designed to be irrevocable laws, but rules of conduct that help us cope with life's situations.

An *attitude* refers to a set of beliefs about a given object or situation. A *value* represents an end-state or goal. A value goes beyond the specific things and conditions to a long-range concern with standards of conduct and the ends to be served.

Examples of values are honesty, integrity, loyalty, fair play, sportsmanship, all of which for generations have been recognized as concomitant values of athletic participation. Obviously, these have not always been realized, since much depends on the individual athlete's own value system and attitudes, and those of the teacher-coach also.

Concisely, attitudes are perceptual sets of responses to persons, things, and events. Attitudes go with us in our encounters and are perceptual sets that affect our responses. Both attitudes and values are motivational-perceptual states that define what an individual expects and desires, and they therefore affect behavior. They both are acquired from contact with others. Many social psychologists and sociologists maintain that virtually everything studied in social psychology somehow involves attitudes and values. In the broadest sense, they are psychological representations of the influence of society and culture on the individual. For example, tastes, preferences, manners, and morals reveal this particular influence. But attitudes and values also retain the flavor of particular individual experiences, mainly from past social interaction.

Prioritizing Values. Most every individual has some general idea of the priorities that are most important in his or her life. But probably few people take time to carefully prioritize their values in relation to their importance. The following checklist of selected items of individual value may enable a coach to conduct an introspective examination by prioritizing them, from the most important to the least important.

self	compassion	trust	individuality
family	success	honesty	equality
fellow man	power	loyalty	tolerance
community	respect	competition	conformity

It may not be too difficult for a coach to measure the value of two similar or opposite items, such as prioritizing self or family, or comparing success to failure, or honesty to dishonesty. It is more difficult to prioritize a dozen or more items. The checklist is a relatively simple exercise dealing with self-appraisal of one's values. The real merit in prioritizing values comes in their application when an athlete and/or coach is confronted with apparent incongruous choices, such as sportsmanship–unsportsmanship, honesty–dishonesty, and so on, that surface in athletic competition and coaching.

Perceived Attitudes Toward People

While a coach deals with things and events, more importantly a coach interacts with people. A large measure of one's success in any endeavor is the relationship with others, and this is especially true in a "people's business" such as coaching. Consequently, how a coach perceives other people and his or her relationship with them is most important. Much of this depends on one's personal philosophy, which in turn is interrelated with one's personal and professional goals and motives.

"I-Me" or the "We-Our" Philosophy. While most coaches stress the importance of team unity, loyalty, and self-suppressed player individuality in order to produce a winning team in which all will share the success, not all coaches practice what they preach. There are coaches who use their players, assistants, and others for their own selfish purposes. They are more concerned about "I-me-my-mine," *my* record, *my* image, and *my* career, and not too overly concerned about the well-being of those to whom a head coach is expected to provide leadership and motivation. Assistants and players may be perceived merely as "stepping stones" or rungs in the head coach's career ladder to be stepped on or over as the coach tries to climb upward in the coaching ranks. Such an individual seldom understands the cardinal principle that in helping others to achieve success he or she generally will achieve success, too.

The opposite of the "I-me" philosophy is the "we-our" philosophy. When this philosophy is evident within any team, whether it be assistants or squad members, feelings of trust, respect, esprit de corps, camaraderie, loyalty, pride, and good morale prevail. The results are cooperation, cohesiveness, and effectiveness in the accomplishment of team goals. Consequently, the individuals involved satisfy their needs and achieve success also. If the reader will analyze carefully the demeanor of individuals on any winning team, whether it be in business, athletics, or any other field of endeavor, the "we-our" philosophy will be evident.

Invited to speak to a group of businessmen in Arizona about applying his coaching principles to their types of business, Penn State's Joe Paterno said, "it's easy to be pretty good, but it takes another dimension to be the best. You've got to forget about 'I' and 'me' and think about 'we' and 'us.' Sometimes that's not easy to get across when you're dealing with strong-minded, aggressive kids. To get it across, a coach has really got to believe in it. A coach has got to be unselfish and make sacrifices himself. He can't get through to his kids if he's got his eye on a job somewhere down the road" (Foust, 1977).

"Xs," "Os," "Studs," "Animals," or Human Beings? Some coaches consider players only in terms of height, weight, body type, speed, athletic skills, "Xs" and "Os," and not as human beings. Some may refer to their players as "studs," "animals," "jocks," or in other uncomplimentary terms. The terms probably are not meant to be derogatory, but they certainly are not laudatory terms to describe some mother's son or a father's daughter when speaking of their ability as an athlete. When such terms are utilized the athlete is identified as though he were a nonentity, with the emphasis on the physical skills, not on any other sterling qualities that a person may possess. It probably makes little difference to the coach who perceives athletes in such a light, that each player is a human being with individualistic emotional, social, and physical needs, which he or she is seeking to fulfill by participating in athletics.

The Principle of Individual Differences. Perhaps the single most important principle in a coaching philosophy is the respect for individual differences. Coaches will readily acknowledge individual physical differences and skills, but often neglect the personality structure of an individual.

A coach may emphatically state, "I treat all of my players alike," with the inference being that the coach does not show favoritism or have double standards. Neither is advocated, but the issue is whether or not individual differences are recognized by the coach. In reality it is not possible for any coach to interact and treat all squad members in an identical manner all of the time. Human frailty and the coach's personality deters this from occurring. Every person possesses motives, desires, drives of various intensity, and these are reflected in the coach's behavior. Each coach exhibits degrees of affection and rejection in liking and disliking some people. In this sense a coach does display degrees of favoritism in that typically he or she likes and lauds players who hustle, put forth much effort, and strive to excel, disliking and usually berating those who do not display the desirable qualities of the more highly motivated teammates. At a later point in time if the players' motivation and behavior patterns are reversed, then the likes/dislikes change, and the coach would be better able to support his boast of treating all of his athletes the same. Actually, the coach is recognizing individual differences.

Perhaps the recognition and application of the principle of individual differences may be best illustrated by a statement by John Wooden, one of collegiate basketball's most successful coaches, who was quoted as informing his players, "There may seem to be double standards at times as I most certainly will not treat you all alike in every respect. However, I will attempt to give each individual the treatment he earns and deserves according to my judgment, in keeping with what I consider in the best interest of the team. You must accept this in the proper manner for you to be a positive and contributing member."[2] We concur with Wooden's sage comments.

Develop Successful People. A person in the coaching profession needs to comprehend that a coach's essential task is to influence others toward successfully achieving their desired predetermined goals. A head coach's most important task is to help players and assistant coaches optimize their potential in satisfying their perceived needs so that they are successful in achieving their desired goals. Only motivated, successful, self-actualizing individuals accomplish important results. Through a coach's careful guidance, direction, and influence, team goals become

[2]According to Coach Wooden, ex-UCLA basketball coach, in a note to one of the co-authors, July 11, 1980, "The quote appeared in a letter I wrote to my returning basketball players at UCLA in the early '70s. . . ."

important parts of each athlete's personal goals, so that an athlete is motivated to try to achieve both individual and team goals. In the accomplishment of individual goals, the athlete also achieves team goals, and vice versa.

Most coaches probably never have the opportunity to work with highly motivated, gifted, "uncommon" athletes. The prospects they coach typically might be identified as "common" or average in terms of their skills and innate ability. However, the coach's job is to develop these prospects into "uncommon" successful people through his or her understanding of human behavior, personality, and motivation, and by utilizing an effective leadership style. Average people who are highly motivated can and do become "uncommon," self-actualizing achievers who become champions and winners, whether they be athletes, coaches, astronauts, or pioneers in other fields of endeavor who achieve success. A coach's job, like that of a teacher, is to help the common person optimize his or her innate abilities to become an "uncommon" successful person.

DEVELOPING A RATIONAL AND PROFESSIONAL PHILOSOPHY APPLICABLE TO COACHING

One's personal philosophy will have a definite bearing on a coaching philosophy—how one regards the sport one coaches, the problems connected with the sport, and the importance placed on these problems. The coach will be motivated to act on these problems in accordance with his or her attitude or point of view toward them. Some of these problems will receive most of the coach's interest, attention, time, and effort, while others will receive little thought and attention because of the low priority the coach places on them. It could be stated that a coach's philosophy is really his attitude about how he perceives the problems of coaching.

Coaching: The Position and the Work

How a coach handles and resolves the problems connected with the sport depends on how that particular coach views his or her position as a coach and the coach's perceptions or attitudes toward the nature of coaching. Therefore, it is well for a coach or a prospective coach to search carefully for candid and meaningful answers to the following questions:

- Why do I (want to) coach?
- What do I (expect to) get out of coaching?
- What are my personal and professional goals?

Just as a player fulfills some of his needs through participation in athletics, many of the coach's needs will be fulfilled through his work of directing or coaching athletes. Just as there are people in other professions and other lines of work for the wrong reasons, there are also people in coaching for the wrong reasons. It is suggested that prospective, novice, and inexperienced coaches would do well to examine the following partial checklist of selected items thinking in terms of motivation of what one wants or expects to receive from his position as a coach and from coaching. The items should be prioritized from most important to least important in order to conduct an introspective examination of one's needs, personal and professional.

pay/financial gain	peer recognition	achievement through risk
status	social benefits	opportunity for
power/authority	new experience	advancement
respect	job stability	self-actualization

The priority and importance that each coach attaches to the items in the checklist will be reflected in his relations with people, events, and things, and in the goals that he sets for himself, the assistants, and the team, personally and professionally. Depending on the situations the coach encounters, it is very likely that as he or she gains experience in coaching not only will the prioritized dimensions be rearranged, but they will also receive greater or lesser emphasis in terms of importance. Experience shows that as many coaches reach mid-life and mid-career they choose to leave the field of coaching because their needs have changed and coaching no longer fulfills their personal and career needs.

The Coach's Philosophical Views. A candid introspection of personal and professional goals—why one wants to coach and what he or she expects to acquire from coaching, plus the individual's prioritized list of needs—will reveal much about the coach's personality, motivation, and philosophy. While there are different names or terms used to identify various kinds and types of coaches, Sabock (1973) and others categorize them similarly as idealists, rolling stones, climbers, ambitious coaches, and hangers-on.

Idealists, purists, or "straight arrows" are those coaches who have deep-seated convictions about the inherent values of athletics. They usually maintain high standards of ethical conduct for themselves, their players, and for the purist rules of the game. Winning by chicanery or unfairly is foreign to their beliefs and prostitutes the integrity of the game. While they may be fierce competitors, winning is merely a by-product that occurs as the result of every individual on the squad doing his best for the good of the team. Much emphasis is placed on sportsmanship, team cohesiveness, winning only by strict adherence to the rules, and the true spirit of the competitive process. Purists enjoy coaching and are more concerned with inculcating the positive value of sports than devising ways to bend the rules to win. Nor do the idealists believe in "using" their players and others for their own personal gain. They are more concerned about their players deriving the maximal benefits from competitive athletics than they are in furthering their own ambitions at the expense of their players. Also, their philosophy is likely to be that, if they work hard and do a good job coaching, win or lose, their efforts will be recognized and they will be rewarded for "playing by the book." Many do not actively seek other positions once they locate a situation that is compatible to their high ideals, since they tend to remain and become actively involved in the community where they reside. While there are numerous individuals with high ideals in the field of coaching, coaches in the profession who are purists are no longer as significant in total numbers as in past decades. Since societal expectations create a mania for winning, many times, virtually at any cost, the purists believe these realities in present-day athletics taint and make a mockery of the high standards that should be taught through participation in sports. The idealists and others maintain that the coaches who engage in questionable practices are unethical and detrimental to the coaching profession.

Perhaps the poet Sir Henry Newbolt summed up the purists' philosophy of athletic competition best when he penned the lines:

> To set the cause above renown,
> To love the game beyond the prize,
> To honor, while you strike him down,
> The foe that comes with fearless eyes. . . .

"*Rolling stones,*" "travelers," "nomads," "movers," "jumpers," and "leapers" usually change jobs frequently. Usually they are opportunists to the extent that they are always looking for a better coaching situation. They may be motivated to change because of financial and professional advancement and/or for the opportunity to coach at a higher level of competition. The opportunity to coach in a better situation will likely be the most predominant factor because they may end up receiving less financial compensation for their coaching at a higher level of competition, depending on the situational variables. A coach's career plan may be only to remain a year or two in a series of coaching positions, moving on every time an opportunity is available, theorizing it is better to acquire diverse experience in a number of situations than to remain in one situation indefinitely. However, incompatibility and displaying a meandering career philosophy may also send the wandering coach on his way. If the coach does not get involved with the school and community, other than through his coaching activities, this is likely to be perceived as the desire not to put down roots. Loyalty is a two-way street. The coach's superiors may feel that, since the coach displays no loyalty about staying and likely will jump at the first job offer, why should they display loyalty by retaining him? While numerous jumpers and rolling stones frequently do move on with their superior's blessings, others are asked to move because they do not "fit in."

"*Climbers*" are those whose goal is to reach the top in coaching. The manner or method in which they choose to "climb" is the critical factor. If their methods are ethical, they are to be commended; if unethical, they are a discredit to the profession. Regrettably, when someone refers to a "climber," typically the inference is that the individual will utilize *any* means, including *using* others to reach his goal. Not infrequently the "climber" is also a wanderer moving from job to job, because the unethical climber's modus operandi is unacceptable to ethical coaches and administrators.

Ambitious coaches may be "climbers," "travelers," and idealists, too, when their motives and conduct are not unethical. They are goal-oriented and opportunists, ready to move when the situation presents itself rather than waiting for a situation to fit their timetable. However, most do not climb over others or misuse and manipulate people to accomplish their goals.

"Hangers-on" are those coaches who have been in coaching for a number of years but, after a period of time, despite the fact that they no longer find the work satisfying, continue going through the motions. Such an uncomplimentary appraisal certainly does not apply to all long-time coaches, because many continue to contribute to the profession and find coaching rewarding and satisfying. Our inference is to two specific types of hangers-on. One is the coach who would like to relinquish his coaching duties, but is compelled to continue coaching since there are no other career alternatives available to him. Another is the type who should leave the field of coaching, and may even desire to do so because of the physical and psychological demands of the job, but hangs on only because the title provides him with ego satisfaction. Psychologically he is fearful of leaving coaching because he will miss "playing the role" the title implies. In fairness to the latter type, in all probability he has been so involved over the years that he does not know what it would be like not to coach. He is aware of the fact, however, that if he gives up coaching he will probably be unable to return to it again. The hanger-on coach many times is like the fighter past his prime who continues to go through the motions of fighting despite the fact that he has lost his "heart" and motivation.

Situational Factors in Coaching. When entering the profession, the novice seldom thinks about the situation or climate of the first coaching position. The beginning coach generally has little or no frame of reference with which to make a comparison with the first coaching assignment. Even if the individual has been exposed to a quality, winning athletic program through participation as an athlete, in all probability the novice coach has not had a real opportunity to gain an in-depth knowledge of the inner workings of the successful program other than through casual observations.

In a short period of time, after being on the "inside," the coach realizes there is much more to building a successful athletic program and winning than merely having technical, tactical, and strategical knowledge of the sport. A reliable philosophy and a favorable environment contributes greatly to coaching success.

It is likely in a person's coaching career, as the individual gains experience, there will be opportunities to teach and coach in situations or environments more conducive to the personal goals of the individual involved. As each coach's philosophy varies relevant to the goals and destination he or she is seeking in coaching, there are numerous factors surrounding opportunities in the profession that one should consider. A cursory list of the factors one would want to consider relevant to a coaching situation are as follows:

- Type, location, and philosophy of the institution
- Attitude of the administration and the faculty toward athletics
- Sports tradition at the institution
- Financial support for the sport and athletic program
- Type of community, enthusiasm, and support for the sport and athletic program
- Player personnel available
- Number of assistant coaches
- Realistic opportunities to build a successful program and produce winners
- Coaching duties
- Other duties the coach is expected to perform
- Chances for advancement, including salary increments
- Fringe and other benefits

A salient point frequently overlooked by coaches with limited or no experience is that not all situations are conducive to building a successful, winning athletic program. Often a candidate for a coaching position will evaluate only the tangible physical factors, which may range on a continuum from excellent to deplorable or nonexistent, and fail to ascertain exactly what the philosophy of the institution is and the attitude of the administration and faculty toward athletics. There is considerable evidence to support the allegation that many administrators, faculty members, and others synonymously associate winning athletic programs with the well-publicized ills in present-day athletics. Consequently, at many institutions some sports are merely tolerated rather than fully accepted by the faculty and the administration, vigilant in their "watch dog" role. They fear the sport or program may get too big, win too much, and the "athletic tail will end up wagging the academic dog!" While there is no denying that an overemphasis on a sports program may include setting aside or ignoring rules and engaging in much of what is "wrong" in athletics, winning per se is not "wrong" unless rules are circumvented solely to produce wins. If the sports program is conducted within the rules, regulations, and spirit of the competitive process and consistent winning is the result, this should be identified and lauded as excellent teaching–coaching and effective learning, not as an overemphasis on athletics.

Evaluation of Situational Factors: S-W-O-T-S. One method of comparing coaching positions or of evaluating factors is to utilize a SWOTS model: Strengths, Weaknesses, Opportunities, Threats, Suggestions, as illustrated in Figure 4-1. For the individual who is entering his or her initial position in the field of coaching, it is likely the novice coach will not have another position with which to make a comparison (Coaching Situation ''B''). One would do well to utilize the SWOTS model in order to determine its situational strengths, weaknesses, opportunities, and threats. The suggestions (conclusions) might be *not* to accept the position if the negative factors greatly outweigh the positive attributes of the position. The beginning coach is likely to understand that he will not be offered every position he goes after but, without any experience in the job market, he might fail to realize that he should *not* accept every position he is offered. In numerous situations the chances of succeeding as a winning coach simply are not evident.

In the event one is considering another position, SWOTS may be used to compare the two coaching situations (Figure 4-1). Regardless of the circumstances,

	Coaching situation "A"	Coaching situation "B"
Strengths—		
Weaknesses—		
Opportunities—		
Threats—		
Suggestions—		

Figure 4-1. S.W.O.T.S. analysis for evaluating coaching positions.

all factors should be categorically listed, analyzed, and evaluated. Eventually an objective decision can be reached by the candidate which may be included under "Suggestions." The individual could list suggestions for improving the program or bargaining points for further discussion and consideration of the new position. Or the conclusions might be not to accept the new position offer, but to list suggestions on how to improve his or her current coaching situation and program. Despite SWOTS or any other technique used to aid an individual in making a decision, a coach still sometimes may regret having turned down a position and later may wish he had accepted it; or after accepting a position he may later regret having accepted it. All of the situational variables and facts are never available at the time the position is offered for a coach to be absolutely certain he is making the *right* decision.

The "As Is" and "Could Be/Should Be" Situation. When one moves to a new coaching position, one must recognize the "as is" situation and work toward a goal-oriented, results-getting "could be" or "should be" situation in order to build a successful, winning program. Many times a new coach is impatient. Rather than work to improve a poor "as is" coaching situation, he dissipates time and energy lamenting about how deplorable his rundown situation is. If one were to analyze and evaluate all of the head coaching positions in collegiate football and basketball, one would find a limited number of super-coaching positions in comparison to other positions. The objective here is not to exalt the super-coaching positions and to demean all others, but to point out that most of the present-day athletic powerhouses at one time were merely "also rans" or poor "as is" situations until a coach took command and turned the program around. At the time the coach might have been either an assistant who moved into a head position or a head coach who had not yet established his reputation as a dynasty builder of winning athletic teams. Specifically, Alabama, Ohio State, Michigan, USC, UCLA, Marquette, Penn State and others in the past at a point in time all had losing or mediocre football and/or basketball programs until new coaches changed "as is" situations into "could be" or "should be" goal-oriented winning situations.

It is important that an in-coming coach try to envision realistically the potential of a new situation and work to optimize the position potential to his expectations. This entails goal setting with time expectations for achieving the desired results, although they may or may not materialize on schedule.

Goal Setting: S-C-R-A-M

The starting point for all achievement is desire and a definiteness of purpose. To become a successful, winning coach, one must have a strong burning desire *to be* and *to do*. It cannot be a hope or a wish or a vague groping to be successful, but it must be a strong desire to be a success. It must be a definite realistic goal. Practically all decision making entails the option of trade-offs. Therefore, a coach must decide what he is willing to give up in order to attain personal success. It is not sufficient merely to say, "I want to be a winning coach." One must establish goals of when and how. One must create a definite plan for carrying out his desire to be a successful coach. Then the coach must put his plan into action. An outstanding characteristic of high achievers is their goal orientation. Although goal setting typically comes easy to a self-motivated person, anyone can learn to set reasonable goals and work toward them. It takes motivation and know-how to proceed, and the determination to achieve success. One might want to use the SCRAM format for setting realistic goals. Goals should be *S*pecific, *C*hallenging, *R*ealistic, *A*ttainable, and *M*easurable.

In goal setting there are several important points that should be remembered:

1. Make your goals objective and set specific deadlines; avoid such subjective terms as more, enough, less, and a lot; state specifically how much of what, by when, and starting when; target dates for completion/accomplishment are imperative.
2. Put your goals in writing. Psychologically one will feel obligated if the goals are written, and it is beneficial to sign off in a contractual sense.
3. Review your goals often. Review strengthens one's drive toward achievement and helps to reconcentrate one's efforts in the proper direction.

While goals may be difficult, if they are realistic and attainable, one is more likely to be motivated to produce a better performance than would be possible with easy goals or a general goal of merely "to do one's best." If a person creates a goal and then meets it within a specific time period, this person has achieved a first success pattern. In determining needs, the only reason people set goals is because their "needs" demand to be satisfied.

Objectives Become Goals. Prior to goal setting, a coach might do well to study management by objectives (MBO) research in order to practice coaching by objectives (CBO). Advocates who have practiced MBO successfully herald it as a key to improving group motivation, performance, communication, and job attitude (Steers and Spencer, 1978). A coach is encouraged to study MBO philosophy and the process of achievement motivation before setting goals for himself, assistants, or team members. For a coach merely to post a "list" of goals for the team, for example, and let it go at that, some anxiety will be created but for the most part the job will not get done.

When you choose a goal, you must consider the time and the place where you are trying to achieve that goal. When asking yourself what it is you want to do, also ask yourself, "Is this the right time for me to aim for this particular goal? Am I in the right place to achieve these goals?" Once you recognize the trend, act! While the time to act may be "now," many fail to act immediately. If you wait, conditions may change and you may be unable to attain your goal(s).

Many "experts" have suggested that it is highly desirable to put everything down on paper that an individual wants. However, it is well to remember that on paper these "wants" are nothing more than dreams. An individual may wish to select the items that are a part of his or her immediate wants and needs and decide how he or she is going to secure them. Once this is accomplished, a coach can start to program his or her objectives into goals. Some of the individual wants could be short term, while others may be intermediate or long term.

The time span should be realistic in terms of the individual's skills, ability, and expertise. Goal setting helps to push the individual's ability so that he or she will learn new skills as a result. With new-found skills, goals in the future will be of a shorter time span because the individual first learns to discipline himself or herself in relation to time. Start with goals that are small so that the individual can experience achievement.

Persistence in Attaining Goals. Persistence is a state of mind; therefore, it can be cultivated into a highly desirable habit. Like other states of the mind, persistence is based on definite causes, among them are the following:

1. Definiteness of purpose. Knowing what one wants is the first and perhaps the most important step toward the development of persistence.
2. Desire. It is comparatively easy to acquire and to maintain persistence in pursuing the object of intense desire.
3. Self-reliance. Belief in one's ability to carry out a plan encourages one to follow the plan through with persistence.
4. Definiteness of plans. Organized plans, even though they may not be completely formulated, encourage persistence.
5. Accurate knowledge. Knowing that one's plans are sound and are based on experience of observation is very important. Guessing instead of knowing destroys persistence.
6. Cooperation. Sympathy, understanding, and harmonious cooperation with others tend to develop persistence.
7. Will power. The habit of concentrating one's thoughts on the building of plans for the attainment of a definite purpose leads to persistence.
8. Habit. Persistence is the direct result of habit. The mind absorbs and becomes a part of the daily experiences on which it feeds.

Career Goals: Self-Analysis. Let us look briefly at formulating career goals by examining a series of questions where the individual, from the prospective or novice to the experienced coach, can do a self-analysis by carefully thinking through and then *recording* his or her responses to the following questions:

1. Where are you now? What is your present status/position?
2. Where are you going? What is your immediate career goal or objective? How/when do you expect to accomplish your immediate career goal?

3. What are your assets/strengths? What have you to offer?
4. How are you overcoming your liabilities/weaknesses? What are you pre-
    pared to do to improve the quality of what you offer?
5. What do you want to be or do with your life? What is your ultimate career
    goal?
6. When do you expect to get there? How/when do you intend to reach your
    career goal?

Figure 4-2 illustrates an individualized profile form that may be used as a
follow-up to the self-analysis questions used for goal-setting purposes in order to
''blueprint'' one's coaching career.

Although a further discussion of career goals, as well as that of matching up
personal competencies with job skill requirements, is outside the scope of this book,
one must ''blueprint'' and monitor one's coaching career carefully, having a specific plan in terms of goals and the time it takes to reach career plateaus successfully
(Fuoss, 1979).

Team Goals: Coaches and Athletes. Before the season starts, it is advisable for
coaches and players to formulate individual and team goals and objectives, as well
as the means of accomplishing these desired ends. It is important that each person
know what is expected of coach and athlete, and what they may expect from each
other. All efforts and energies of the coaching staff and athletes must be channeled
in the same direction if the objectives and goals are to be successfully achieved. An
outstanding example is winning the National Championship, an ultimate individual
and team goal set by Paul ''Bear'' Bryant, his coaches, and the University of
Alabama football squad members every year. Bryant-coached teams have achieved
this singular individual and team goal more often than any other institution competing in major college football. Coach Bryant not only sets individual goals for
himself, but encourages his assistant coaches and players to set individual goals,
too.

In all probability all of the goals sought by squad members and the coaching
staff, if they are to be achieved, will be accomplished through a joint effort via the
sport's program or activity. It is for this reason that it is tremendously important that
players and coaches know the common goals they are seeking. Many do not! As a
result all may be individual members of a group or team physically, but lack group
or team cohesiveness and unity because all are not psychologically aware of each
member in the group.

Once a goal has been set, the next step is to provide ''triggers'' in order to
remind the individual(s) of the commitment. ''Triggers''—visible on the calendar,
lockers, and bulletin boards—are constant reminders of the goal that is being
sought. For example, if coaches and players all have an individual and team goal of
going undefeated, winning their conference, sectional, and regional championship,
and winning a national championship, the ''trigger'' card would list and publicize

Projected date for final completion of specific plan: Indicate definite, attainable, and realistic date _____

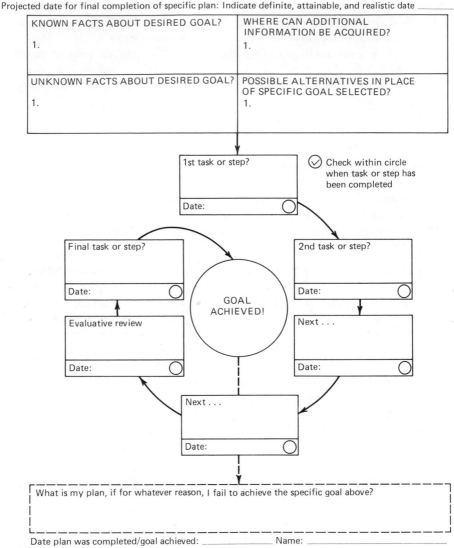

Figure 4-2. An individualized goal-setting plan. (Remember an individual's goals develop from one's perceptions of one's needs.)

the short-range and intermediate goals of winning each of the scheduled contests in order to accomplish the ultimate goal of winning the national championship. A "trigger" is reduced by one every time a plateau is reached, still encouraging players to strive to reach the ultimate goal. Each time an individual or team reaches a plateau, each will experience personal and group accomplishment. In recent years there have been instances where teams have not won all of their games, but have been declared national champions in their sport because their record has been better than other teams striving for the same ultimate goal. Therefore, if a short-term or intermediate goal is not successfully achieved, the entire plan is not abandoned as it may still be possible to achieve the ultimate goal despite temporary setbacks along the way.

The Competitive Process: Purpose and Desired Results

A coach's philosophy should evidence his attitudes toward his professional duties in an attempt to assist the athletes developing high ideals of physical, mental, spiritual, and social well-being. In addition to these values, the coach must be concerned with developing motor and cognitive skills, and the coach's philosophy should include providing experiences that will help the athlete develop moral and ethical character, proper health habits, personality, and the respect for the rights of others and human dignity.

A coach's philosophy should reflect an example of sound character, intellectual judgment, and true sportsmanship; it should foster the democratic principles of society; and it should also show confidence in the ability of athletes to think for themselves and to respect the individual worth of each person whom he or she comes in contact with. A coach should provide experiences that will enable each athlete to overcome fear and to handle his or her own body skillfully for one's own safety as well as the safety of others. The coach should give guidance to the athletes so that they may give self-direction to their lives and become good citizens.

Principal Benefits To Be Derived. Every scholastic and collegiate athletic endeavor should make a contribution to the overall education of the participants, in order to assure the beneficial aspects of athletics. As part of a coach's philosophy, the sport one directs and coaches should offer the following benefits to the participants:

- The desire to strive whole-heartedly toward excellence
- The realization that anything of real value will not be achieved without hard work
- Development of a healthy attitude toward competition
- Development of a spirit of cooperation
- Practical experience in making decisions
- Development of a desire for wholesome, rewarding, and aesthetically pleasing physical activity

A coach must be aware that the overall purposes of any endeavor related to education are to recognize the capability of the individual and then provide an opportunity for this person to develop to his optimum. The coach must provide experiences in these activities that are primarily physical, so that the maximum contribution can be realized while developing an athlete's greatest potential.

Code of Ethics. Coaches must be mindful of the history and evolution of the coaching profession if they are to serve effectively in the educational development of young people who are participating in athletic programs.

Historically, the scholastic and collegiate athletic programs belong to the students who participate, from which it is expected they will derive laudable benefits. The burden of proof rests largely with the coaching profession. Justification for including it in the scholastic and collegiate programs rests on the dual premise that it provides both physical benefits and character values for those who participate.

However, it has become increasingly clear during recent years in particular that, because of the tremendous increase in the number of players, teams, and coaches, there is need for reviewing and perhaps updating an operating code of principles and ethics.

In dealing with goal setting and objective achievement, it is important that the people who are working with the student–athlete clarify and distinguish ethical and approved professional practices from those that are detrimental and harmful. By *ethics* we mean the basic principle of right action. Ethics stress the proper functions of the coaching profession in relation to the institution, athlete, and community and imply a standard of character in which the public has trust and confidence. The ultimate success of any code of ethics rests primarily with the coaches.

Winning and Losing. Over the normal course of events at most levels of competition, winning and losing occurs in cycles. Although there are a few teams that win consistently, and there are those that lose just as consistently, most teams experience both up and down years. This is especially true at levels of competition where active, aggressive recruiting is either nonexistant or is greatly restricted for whatever the reasons, and the coach has to rely on the "call-out" and "walk-on" prospects to build a team. The coach's competitive nature and personality may be such that he has great difficulty accepting the "as is" situation, especially if he has coached previously in a situation where he recruited and had a winning record. Much nonproductive energy will be dissipated by the coach, leading to greater frustration if the coach does not recognize it is impossible to control all factors in every situation and if he is fearful of losing. His personality may be such that he simply cannot acknowledge losing and will not accept it. Such a philosophy results in much psychological stress, especially if, in addition, the coach becomes angry because he must compete against teams made up of recruited athletes.

Regardless of the circumstances, games and contests will be won that were expected to have been lost and there will be those that were lost that should have been won. If one remains in coaching for any period of time, he or she most certainly will experience the up-down cycles, be the donor-recipient of "giveaways," and be forced to adopt a pragmatic philosophy pertaining to winning and losing. Sometimes coaches are not well-grounded in their fundamental beliefs concerning the avowed purpose and desired results of athletic competition, failing to fully comprehend why individuals compete in athletics. Coaches do not handle victory and defeat well. While the code and spirit of competitive athletics postulate being modest in victory and gracious in defeat, outward manifestations of behavior by coaches and their players do not always exhibit a desirable, socially accepted demeanor. Some coaches are unbearably boastful in victory and intolerable "sore losers" in defeat. Frequently their players display the same undesirable behavioral characteristics because a coach's philosophy and behavior usually are reflected through his or her squad members since the coach is the role model. There are some coaches whose disposition and personality are such that it probably would be better if they were not in the coaching profession. The same observation may be made of some people in other professions and trades, too.

Humiliating Your Opponent. On some occasions a coach is likely to find himself in the position where his team completely dominates and outclasses the team that it is competing against. While it would be dishonest to ask his players to perform less than their very best, generally a coach can keep from running up the score and humiliating the opposition by removing his regulars and permitting the substitutes to play, and by restricting play selection in some sports. It is difficult to know exactly when to "call off the hounds," since a coach and his players are always definitely interested in attaining the highest rating possible by the media. However, there is some question of the value of "steam rollering" an opponent, running up a huge score, and humiliating the players, coaches, institution, and supporters of the hapless team. Some members of the coaching "fraternity" are not adverse to running up the score if the opportunity presents itself later on to oppose a coach who has shown evidence in the past of having poured it on hapless opponents. It is for this reason that, if a coach wins "big" during an up cycle, it is likely his team will lose "big" during a down cycle, as this, too, has a tendency to even out the longer one remains in the profession. While the situation may be such that a coach can do little about losing badly especially in a down cycle, a coach can certainly control to a large measure whether his team wins by a reasonably respectable or a lopsided score. The media is responsible for some of this stress, as well as a coach's ego, since team rankings are involved and frequently teams have to run up scores and defeat opponents badly to be ranked high in the polls.

Emphasize Winning, But Not At Any Cost. Frequently the charge is made of sports at all levels of competition that there is too much emphasis on winning. It should be borne in mind that from time immemorial the object of athletic competition has been to win, despite an attempt in some quarters in recent years to try to refocus the emphasis on "everyone wins" or "no one loses." Since we are a competitive society, this focus does not seem to be pragmatic. The emphasis would be more realistic if it were placed on adhering to the rules and the spirit of the game.

It is when the rules are bent or broken in pursuing the goal of winning that an element foreign to the basic idea of sports is introduced. One must also make a distinction between professional and amateur sports. In professional sports the pressures of winning are paramount since this involves money, jobs, and livelihood, and these transcend the world of fun and games.

There is absolutely nothing inherently wrong in teaching athletes to play to win or to excel and be the best one can be, providing this can be accomplished within the spirit and the rules of the game. The desire to win, however, does not excuse the coach from violating the rules, using unethical means to gain an advantage, or abusing athletes to win at all costs.

Perhaps John Brodie (1974), former Stanford great and all-pro quarterback, stated it best when he said,

> You play to win. There's no doubt about that. But if winning is your first and only aim, you stand a good chance of losing. You have the greatest chance of winning when your first commitment is to a total and enthusiastic involvement in the game itself. Enthusiasm is what matters most. If I was enthusiastic about the game, enjoying it, and doing my absolute best, then I had the best chance of winning it. But then I could also handle losing, because I had done my best. If you can't handle losing, you'll never be a big winner. It's never easy to lose. But if I knew I had performed at the top of my ability, with total involvement, that would take care of the winning or losing. . . .
>
> The goal, it seems to me, is to be as good as you can be. If this makes you number one, fine. If not, you haven't lost anything, and you have gained a lot. . . .[3]

Life is an endless cycle of large and small wins and losses, and woe betide the individual, coach or athlete, who cannot handle the highs and lows of everyday living. This is a lesson that is offered to be learned by participating in athletics.

Handling Success and Failure. A well-known axiom, "Success requires no explanation, and failure permits no alibis," certainly is true in athletics where the scoreboard is used as the barometer that indicates wins and losses. Unfortunately, the scoreboard is also frequently used by society as the sole criterion of success or failure of a coach, team, or sport. By determining success and failure by using the final scores of only several games, or even the won-loss record of a coach and team for a single season, one does not accurately depict coaching failure or success. It usually takes several years for a coach to turn a losing program around, produce a winner, and be labeled a success. Several classic examples from professional football are illustrative. Few people remember that the long-time, highly successful Dallas Cowboy's coach, Tom Landry, with many wins including two Super Bowl victories, had losing seasons for the first five years and a record of 7-7 his sixth

---

[3]Brodie, John, and Houston, James D. *Open Field*. Boston: Houghton Mifflin Co., 1974. Copyright © 1974 by John Brodie and James D. Houston. Reprinted by permission.

year. While the Pittsburgh Steelers under Chuck Noll have won an unprecedented four Super Bowl championship games within a six-year period, few people recall that Coach Noll's record in his first year with the Steelers was 1 and 13. Noll and Landry have each won more than 100 games in their professional football coaching careers. Conversely, there have been coaches at other levels of competition who have won "big" initially in their first or second year, at times having undefeated teams, never to produce winning teams again.

When one enters coaching, he or she must adopt a philosophy barometer as to how to measure coaching success, because some coaches cannot stand the pressure and humiliation of being labeled a loser or failure. It has been stated many times that often the difference between success and failure is such a thin line that one person achieves success because of perseverance and staying power, whereas another person foregoes the opportunity because he fails to persevere, quits, and is dubbed a failure. Usually the person who fails to prepare properly is the loser and a failure, too. The winner or successful person does all that he can to prepare for winning. High achievers psychologically always expect to win and, because of their perceptions of only winning, they are successful performers, whether they are coaches or athletes. Others do not expect to win, only to compete, but eventually and ultimately to lose.

One should realize that all successful coaches first did a certain amount of dreaming, hoping, wishing, desiring, and planning before they reached their goal. They were not indifferent, lazy, lacking in ambition or desire. Most all who succeed have had poor starts and setbacks before they finally "arrived." No one is ever defeated until defeat has been accepted as a reality. Those who wish to excel must go beyond the average. It is very easy to be ordinary, but it takes much determination and hard work to excel. One should not rely solely on "luck." In place of the word "luck," which by itself has little value in achieving success, it would be well to substitute the word *opportunity*. Opportunity plus preparedness equals success. It is a rare case when an individual achieves success through a fluke, such as relying on sheer "luck" to guarantee achieving success.

Dealing with Coaching Pitfalls Philosophically and Psychologically

Since coaching is acknowledged to be a high-risk, high-profile type of work, a coach should analyze carefully the pitfalls and unique features indigenous to the job, then develop some operable strategies for handling them. The sooner a coach can make these determinations and establish perimeters around his job and the nature of his work, the easier it is for him. Otherwise a coach is likely to worry unnecessarily about the pitfalls, especially that of being unjustly fired. A coach may vacillate and be uncertain of his beliefs, especially if he feels he is forced at some point to compromise himself but really does not wish to do so. Every coach would do well to establish his career "game plan" first and then get on with the job of coaching.

The most rational approach is to recognize the pitfalls and psychological pressures as part of coaching, live with them, try to do an outstanding job, play by the rules, but work for change to improve your situation, and in turn hope to lessen the pressures and minimize the pitfalls. This may be dubbed the "straight arrow" philosophical strategy.

The "win at any cost" strategy implies doing anything to win. The prevailing logic is, "If I don't win I'm going to be fired anyway, so I might as well 'cheat' if I have to in order to win." There is also the inference that everyone else "cheats." While the "straight arrow" alternative may not get you fired even if you have a losing record, the coach who gets caught cheating most likely will be fired even if he wins. Also, that individual's future in the coaching profession is limited.

A third strategy is to leave coaching pressures and pitfalls behind and pursue a more realistic and enjoyable means of making a livelihood and fulfilling your needs. After a period of time, a coach may decide that he would be happier doing some other type of work.

A coach should be truthful with himself and recognize he may not have the temperament or personality, competencies or expertise, to be a coach. He may not want to continue in coaching, or he may be a happier person not being a head coach. Often it comes as a surprise to an individual to learn that he or she really does *not* like coaching, or that it is different from what the individual thought coaching would be like. There are those in coaching, as in other professions, who fail to recognize that they are not "cut out" to do the type of work they are doing. Not every person who initially wanted to be a lawyer, physician, scientist, or astronaut ended up being in that profession. Some tried and in time recognized the fact that they really did not want to do with their lives what they thought initially they wanted to do. The same is true of coaches. Merely wanting to be a coach at an early stage of one's life is not a valid reason by itself for continuing to pursue a career in coaching if the work does not continue to be fulfilling and satisfying, or if one is overwhelmed with the pitfalls that prevail. Not all coaches who make a career change do so because they have been fired. Many make career changes of their own volition for reasons involving their own personal motivations.

DEVELOPING SOUND COACHING THEORY OR PHILOSOPHY

A third component of developing coaching philosophy deals with strategical, tactical, and operational planning, concepts and theories pertaining to the specific sport one coaches. Strategy and tactics, as applicable to coaching, are terms that are used interchangeably, and frequently erroneously. There is no great harm in utilizing these terms interchangeably, except one may be referring to strategy when more correctly one actually means tactics. Strategy is more commonly used than tactics, since strategy includes the application of tactics.

Strategy and Tactics

From a military standpoint, strategy is the science or art of military command as applied to overall planning and conduct of combat operations. In general, *strategy* is a plan, method, or series of maneuvers for obtaining a specific goal or result.

Tactics are the techniques or science of securing strategic objectives, especially the art of deploying and directing one's forces against the opposition. It is also a variety or instance of the use of strategy, and it is the art of devising or employing plans to secure a goal. It is a mode of gaining an advantage or success.

Specifically, strategy in athletics refers to the art and science of conducting that particular sport's campaign in which a coach directs and maneuvers his or her players within the rules as they play against their opponents. It involves both long-range objectives and immediate tactics. It refers to offensive and defensive choices made by the coach and players, in addition to numerous other facets of the game that might eventually affect its outcome. These are planned for in advance and then undertaken during the contest in order to gain an advantage over the opposition.

A coach is a strategist as he prepares in advance for upcoming games by drilling and practicing his players in specific offensive and defensive stratagems. A coach becomes a tactician during the contest when he makes decisions as to when to employ his predetermined strategy. Strategy, then, may be thought of as game generalship since tactics refer to short-range moves or skills that make long-range strategy possible during the actual contest. Situational contingencies—such as when to utilize a play action pass in football, or when to bunt or hit away in baseball to advance a runner, or when to adhere to "freeze" play late in a basketball game when ahead—would all be tactical moves. Generally these are referred to by the media, spectators, and by some coaches as coaching strategy. A coach's devised game plan is often referred to as the overall strategy for a particular contest, although it is more likely a series of tactical moves that will be utilized when specific situations arise during the contest. Game strategy does not merely happen. It must be planned for and then practiced if it is to be successfully used during a contest to gain an advantage over the opposition.

Generalship and Gamesmanship

While the terms strategy and tactics may be used interchangeably without loss of meaning, not so with the terms generalship and gamesmanship. While both may be thought of in terms of tactician and strategist, generalship implies a positive connotation and gamesmanship has a negative connotation. Both may be part of a coach's philosophy, whereas other coaches may refuse to employ gamesmanship tactics. A number of people, including some coaches, do not know the difference between generalship and gamesmanship.

Coaching *generalship* may be thought of as knowing what to do and then having your players do it since it is synonymous with "leadership." *Gamesmanship* is the art of winning games by doubtful expedients without actually violating the rules. The "sucker shift" and the "volleyball spike" are examples of two tactics that were used by some coaches in the past to gain an unfair advantage over opponets, until these measures were prohibited by the football rules committee. An athlete instructed to feint an injury to stop the clock when his or her team has no times out remaining, and a coach who instructs his pitcher to "brush back" a batter in order to disrupt the batter's confidence and rhythm are examples of controversial tactics that are in the "gray" area of gamesmanship. Both are violations of the rules, but intent would be difficult to prove. Unfortunately, many people correlate gamesmanship with a vision of a master strategist–tactician who cleverly out-coaches another, or with the concept of "oneupmanship" where a coach goes "one up" in gaining an advantage over another. Usually the coach gains this advantage because of his perceived wisdom, experience, cleverness, and expertise, but seldom is what the coach does perceived as being unethical or illegal. Many believe gamesmanship denotes clever exploitation of bending permissible rules. However, no coach is likely to build an enviable record strictly by utilizing gamesmanship. A coach may win several games because of some tactic he used which was innovative and unexpected but, after opposing coaching staffs see the tactic several times, it becomes familiar and its use predictable. Perhaps contrary to public opinion, most coaches do not want to win by questionable or unethical tactics. But this actually depends on a coach's personal, professional, and coaching philosophy.

Philosophy and Coaching Theory Influence Strategy and Tactics

As one prepares for competition, and during the course of the competitive event, whether it be individual or team, strategical planning and tactical maneuvering depend on one's philosophy of how he or she perceives the event or game can be won: (1) success-oriented selection or (2) failure-avoidance selection.

Success-Oriented Philosophy and Selection. The theory of success-oriented philosophy and selection is that the individual, coach or athlete, concentrates on success, not on failure, which may be offensive or defensive in nature. His chief rationale is that by concentrating on offensive tactics or outscoring, outhitting (baseball), pinning his opponent the quickest (wrestling), outrunning (track) his opponent, he will win. While individually or as a team he may "jump" on his opponent quickly in order to exploit tactical errors, he does not wait explicitly for his opponent to make errors and mistakes. Conversely, while his play may result in some tactical errors, his theory is to continue to attack offensively as he is success oriented in his strategical planning and selection of tactics. He concentrates on achieving success offensively, rather than on waiting for his opponent to fail.

Failure-Avoidance Philosophy and Selection. The theory of failure-avoidance selection is two-pronged: (1) an individual competitor or team plays conservatively, not taking unnecessary risks in any strategical planning or tactical selections; and (2) as a result an individual or team is in a better position to exploit the opposition when he or they make a mistake. Conversely, if he or his team makes an error, it is not of great magnitude. While the ultimate goal also is to win, emphasis is more on defensive and conservative tactics, permitting the opposition to defeat itself through its own errors.

There are coaches who have achieved outstanding winning records adhering to one coaching philosophy or the other. However, if a coach has athletes who are bigger, quicker, and faster, and he has a greater number of them than his opponent, he will probably win adhering to either philosophy and tactical selection. Since all contingency variables are situational, it is unlikely year in and year out that a coach will continue to garner the superior personnel. There is a tendency for this variable to occur in cycles, especially at the scholastic level of competition. Therefore, it is likely many coaches combine elements, where possible, of both philosophies so that to adhere to parts of both would not be totally incongruent in one's coaching theory.

Depending on whether the coach's philosophy is founded on success-oriented or failure-avoidance selection will determine his priorities of the components of the overall game and the style of play he teaches.

Prioritize

Regardless of the sport, it is impossible to spend an equal amount of time practicing every segment of the overall sport. For example, if one is offensive-minded and is attempting to teach numerous offensive patterns and variations, it is very likely the coach will not have sufficient time to practice all of the offensive patterns alone, much less the remaining different components of the *overall* game. Should a coach try to do so, and it requires a disciplined head coach not to become enraptured with offensive plays, other segments of the overall game will be sorely neglected. The teaching-coaching methods and techniques, practice organization and practice sessions, and game strategy and tactics will depend on the individual coach's philosophy or coaching theory. This in turn will depend on the priority; in football, as an illustration, he gives priority initially in his thinking and planning to offense, defense, and the kicking game. He may prioritize them in that order, or he may prioritize the components as defense, kicking game, offense. Every coach must attempt to establish at least in his own mind the priorities he is going to place on each component of the sport he coaches.

For example, if the coach places offense as his first priority, the emphasis is on *possession* of the football. His basic coaching philosophy is that he wants possession in an attempt to get more points on the scoreboard than his opponent. In formulating his philosophy, kicking is the least important, and his team will only punt the football when forced to do so. It is likely he will almost never punt the ball on other than fourth down since he does not want to relinquish an opportunity to score by sacrificing the football to the opposition on an early down.

The coach who believes in winning games with a strong defense believes in *field position* football. His theory is that if the defense is strong enough his team will keep the opposition from advancing too far and eventually the opposition must kick the football to his team. He looks at the kicking game as an offensive weapon, since he ties it in strongly with defense, and he expects to gain field position with the exchange of the football when his team punts. He is likely more prone to kick on an early down, especially if backed up near his own goal line, since he feels the opposition may load up attempting to block the punt if his team waits until fourth down to kick.

Style of Play

In addition to a sound coaching philosophy on possession versus position, which lends itself to football for the purpose of illustrating our point, a coach of any sport must keep abreast of changes, especially in a team sport concept, where modification and variations of offensive and defensive play are constantly changing. This is not to imply that a coach should change merely because of a popular trend or what is "fashionable" at the time. However, the coach should be knowledgeable of what is going on in his or her sport and adapt to new trends if it is feasible.

In basketball there are at least two different theories of play. One is the pattern style and the other is the free-lance type of game, and the coach will have to decide philosophically which style of play to use. Yet no two coaches have exactly the same idea about the way the game should be played, and the coach will have to develop his own philosophy or coaching theory. A well thought out philosophy represents the springboard for the detailed development of an offensive and defensive scheme, embracing the coach's own ideas and theories.

A Hodge-Podge System. Many coaches are guilty of changing to a new offense or defense in their coaching theory merely because it is popular at the time, or of attempting to "combine" theories and come up with a "hodge-podge" or smorgasbord type of offense or defense, with the feeling that this will solve their problems. Changing offensive and defensive styles from week to week or year to year is bound to produce a great deal of confusion, especially in the minds of the players who must be "sold" on the coach's basic philosophy relative to offensive and defensive schemes. The coach should also realize the fact that he and his staff may have very limited knowledge of what they are adopting and trying to accomplish with a new offense or a new defense.

Many coaches derive their style of play from their own experience as players. Familiarity with certain techniques and respect for a former coach and his or her ideas relative to the game deeply influence the novice coach. Many coaches make the mistake of installing the complete offensive or defensive theory that they learned during their competitive days with no new thoughts added. This produces a poor reproduction of the original. A head coach would be wise to use the basic theory he has learned and practiced as a player, or an assistant coach, but he should apply his own mental initiative to the squad's demands and limitations.

Summary

While one is likely to enter the coaching profession as a young person already possessing a personal, dynamic philosophy of life, an individual acquires most of his or her professional philosophy of coaching athletics and coaching theory through one's interests and experiences in the field of coaching. Acquiring philosophy is a long-time process over much of one's life. As an individual continues to pursue wisdom, his philosophy is built in layerlike fashion on a foundation of values acquired early in one's life. Despite the fact that it is virtually impossible to separate these components since they are all closely interrelated and each has a direct bearing on the other, we have attempted to do so in this chapter only for the purpose of discussion.

REFERENCES

Brodie, John, and Houston, James D. *Open Field*. Boston. Houghton Mifflin Company, 1974.

Foust, Tom. "Paterno Says Rules Are Too Complicated." *The Arizona Daily Star*. April 12, 1977.

Fuoss, Donald E. "Blueprinting Your Coaching Career." *Summer Manual*. American Football Coaches Association, 1979, pp. 63–70.

Menninger, Roy W. "Responsibility to Self." *Menninger Perspective*. Vol. 3, No. 4, June/July 1972.

Sabock, Ralph J. *The Coach*. Philadelphia. W. B. Saunders Company, 1973, pp. 32, 83–84, 142.

Steadman, John. "Noll's Strong Character Shows in Steelers." *The Sporting News*. January 26, 1980, p. 21.

Steers, Richard M., and Spencer, Daniel G. "Achievement Needs in MBO Setting." *Personnel Journal*. January 1978, p. 26.

SELECTED READING

Biemiller, Lawrence. "The Continuing Scandal of College Athletics; Business's 'Dangerous' Presence on Campuses." *The Chronicle of Higher Education*. Vol. XXI, No. 6, September 29, 1980, p. 23. From a cover story of *Newsweek*. "The Shame of College Sports." September 22, 1980.

Fisher, Craig. "We're Number One." *The Physical Educator*. Vol. 28, No. 4, December 1971, pp. 183–186.

Garloch, Larry. "The Philosophy of a Beginning Coach." *Coach and Athlete*. Vol. 42, No. 2, October 1979, pp. 6, 20.

Moore, J. W. *The Psychology of Athletic Coaching*. Minneapolis, Minn. Burgess Publishing Co., 1970.

Phillips, B. J. (Reported by Peter Ainslie/Tuscaloosa.) Cover story "Football's Supercoach: Paul 'Bear' Bryant." *Time*. Vol. 116, No. 13, September 29, 1980, pp. 3, 70–74, 76–77.

Tutko, Thomas A., and Richards, Jack W. *Psychology of Coaching*. Boston. Allyn and Bacon, 1971.

Underwood, John, *The Death of An American Game: The Crisis in Football*. Boston. Little, Brown and Company, 1979.

5

Management, Decision Making, and Other Functions, Skills, and Processes for Effective Coaching

There is a similarity between successful people in middle and executive management positions in industry, business, and government, and head coaches of athletic teams who are in organizational structures over subordinate personnel. All must be able to perform, to a high degree, specific management functions and skills in planning, organizing, staffing, directing, and controlling, and must be adroit decision makers. While each has his or her own particular technical or operational skills as the result of specialized training and education, to be highly successful each must possess management skills, too. A universally accepted operational definition of *management* is "the accomplishment of predetermined goals and objectives through the efforts of others," which applies to every individual in a management position of a hierarchial organization structure regardless of one's technical or operation skills, including the coach–manager.

MANAGEMENT–COACHING: THROUGH THE EFFORTS OF OTHERS

Where one must rely on the accomplishment of goals and objectives through the efforts of other people, as in coaching, if success is to be achieved, a head coach is required to give guidance, direction, control, recognition, leadership, and motivation to other people's efforts to accomplish specific tasks. Success in any venture, including coaching, does not occur as the result of "luck," but comes about through careful planning, hard work, and wise decision making. The effectiveness of any organization, program, or activity, including the coaching of a team and its performance, depends on how well they are managed. By working together in planned, organized, directed, and coordinated efforts, head and assistant coaches and players are able to accomplish individual, team, and programmatic goals and objectives that each could not attain otherwise.

Merely being in a management position, regardless of whether it is in business, industry, government, or coaching, does not guarantee that the manager will be effective and efficient. An oft-repeated quote is, "There are three types of people: those that make things happen, those that watch what is happening, and those who do not know what has happened." A paraphrased version of the above is, there are three types of managers: "Those who know, those who don't know, and those who don't know they don't know!" Successful managers, regardless of the sector in which they work, through the management process not only plan for what is going to happen, but they make things happen. They know what is happening and why, as they monitor their plan throughout. The end result for the manager–coach is efficient and effective coaching, a successful program, and a winning team.

COACHING: MANAGEMENT AND TECHNICAL FUNCTIONS AND SKILLS

A successful, winning program is the result of organized effort with a "prime mover" head coach in the leadership position performing two sets of skills: those of planning, organizing, staffing, directing and controlling, plus technical or operational skills that relate to the tasks performed as part of the coaching work flow. While coaches will readily recognize the latter functions and skills since these relate specifically to the teaching–coaching of a particular sport or a specialized phase of it, frequently head coaches fail to recognize that they also perform the functions and skills of a discipline and body of knowledge identified as *management*. The purpose of this chapter is to make the reader more aware of management and decision-making processes so that he or she will be able to coach more effectively.

THE ROLE OF MANAGEMENT

Generally, the role of management is to plan, organize, integrate, and interrelate organizational activities and resources for the purpose of achieving common objectives. Specifically, the responsibility of a coach–manager is to direct his or her sports organization or program so that it is effective in goal accomplishment. Coaches select, slot, and integrate the human elements and resources available to them so that the resultant coordinated activity will optimize performance. Typically, resources are identified as people, materials, machines, money, and methods, including technologies. When unmanaged and uncoordinated, the result is confusion and "drift." Managed resources and coordinated effort have a synergistic effect, where the simultaneous actions of the separate elements become greater than the sum of the effects taken independently.

The Management Process

Rather than considering management as a group of people, as it is frequently done when identifying superior-subordinate relationships, the discipline of management has focused on the activities managers engage in. Accordingly, management is process and as such it is dynamic and changing.

Management deals with human organizations in that a manager coordinates the activities of subordinates so that organizational or program goals may be achieved. As such the manager directs and coordinates the activities of people in a superior-subordinate A/B relationship. In coaching, A is the head coach or superior and the Bs are the assistants and players or subordinates.

A coach–manager is concerned with effectively and efficiently achieving organization or program objectives and goals. Succinctly, *effectiveness* is "doing the right things" and *efficiency* is "doing things right." Effectiveness means making the right choices in terms of desired results or goals. It involves decision making that is related to establishing goals, selecting proper alternatives, and evaluating situations so that decisions are made that enhance the program or sport.

The meaning of management efficiency is broader in scope than is suggested by "doing things right." *Efficiency* is the proper utilization of all resources, including people, methods, money, material, and machinery, in the achievement of established goals or the implementation of decisions. Candidly, the proper utilization of resources applied in the management process means economical output in terms of the most quantity and best quality at the least cost in the shortest period of time. It involves achieving goals with the least waste and greatest economy of resources. It is as applicable to coaching as it is to government, business, or industry. Economic resources in industry and business, however, take on a different importance than those in coaching and government, since both the goals being sought and the resources available are different. Any manager who squanders resources through mismanagement is considered inefficient and is not fulfilling his or her responsibilities. The mismanagement of people is a common error. The economic law of efficiency, "Be efficient or die," is as applicable to present-day coach–managers as to managers in private and public sectors.

A pragmatic premise underlying management, which is frequently the sole criterion for the coach–manager and others, is that leaders are ultimately evaluated on how effectively the organization or program they direct is achieving its objectives. Managers are selected to direct, coordinate, and control (monitor) the organization or program in order to achieve its objectives (goals). Organization or program goals are established by individuals as a result of group processes that modify what each will do individually.

FUNCTIONS OF MANAGEMENT PROCESS

Management has been dissected into subfields based on the discipline's functions of planning, organizing, staffing, directing, and controlling. Different writers may use slightly different terms. Leading may be used in place of directing, but the five that have been identified continue to have wide acceptance as the basic elements of the management process.

A decision is made about a plan; it has implications for organizing; leadership is necessary to implement or actuate the plan through joint human endeavor; and the resulting performance must be controlled or monitored throughout. In each instance a manager has to make decisions pertaining to *what* is to be done; *when, where,* and *how* it is to be done; *who* is to do it; and behind each of these decisions is *why*.

Despite the fact that one may be performing operational or technical functions, if one also engages in any of the five management functions, that individual is recognized as performing the functions of a manager. Obviously this would be applicable to coaching, although few coaches view management functions and skills as an integral part of a head coach's work. Too often, head coaches and other managers devote too much time to performing their technical skills, whereas the time could be better utilized in reaching their goals and objectives if they devoted more to the managerial dimensions of their position. Field and court coaching are fun and typically most coaches derive much satisfaction from participating in the technical work flow of coaching. On the other hand, the management functions of coaching require much conceptualization, decision making, and coordination. When this does not occur or receives only cursory attention by a head coach, the collective group effort is uncoordinated, inefficient, and ineffective. Too often skill in management functions is either played down or overlooked when compared to technical skills. Yet every successful coach possesses and exercises management skills, although it may be evident only to those individuals directly involved with the program.

Linking Processes of Management

The management process involves more than a person in a superior-line position over subordinates performing the five basic functions of the discipline. Coach–managers must also be skilled decision makers and have unusual communication abilities in order to be successful. The coach–manager is one who, through the linking processes of communication and decision making, performs the basic management functions of his or her group or program in order to achieve its goals and objectives. If successfully performed, the results are coordination of the program's activities and external adaptation. Communication and decision making are also referred to as intervening management processes because they connect and interrelate the previously mentioned management functions. However, these two processes are not solely associated with the management process and are applicable to the operational or technical aspects of coaching, too. When an individual plans, organizes, staffs, directs, and controls group activities, he or she is engaged in functions that are exclusive to the management process. An individual can plan and organize his or her own work, but, since it does not involve a group, or an A/B relationship, it is not considered management.

Communication and decision making are referred to as the linking processes of management because a manager can perform management functions such as planning and organizing only by making decisions and communicating these decisions to others. Communication and decision making are ubiquitous processes that relate to essentially everything that a coach–manager does. For these reasons, communication and decision making are extremely essential to the success of a coach–manager and receive consideration along with the primary functions in all comprehensive treatises on the management process.

Integrative Conditions Resulting from Managerial Action

Coordination and adaptation are two other management-related processes that are difficult to conceptualize. They are separately identified, but in a literal sense they are conditions that result from actions taken relating to the basic management functions. Effective planning will contribute to coordination as well as effective organizing. If a coach–manager fails to schedule meaningful work for his assistants and players, coordination will break down. Many writers consider coordination to be the epitome of the management process and hence the essence of management. Certainly one major objective of performing management functions is to achieve internal coordination of all elements.

The difficulty in evaluating coordination and adaptation from a management standpoint is that there are no processes or concepts that exclusively "coordinate" or "adapt." Coordination and adaptation are achieved only through the management functions of planning, organizing, staffing, directing, or controlling. No specific body of knowledge or set of management techniques relates exclusively to coordination or adaptation, since both conditions result from the manner in which the five primary management functions are performed. In order to be successful as a coach–manager, one must have an awareness of one's players and assistants as well as a broad understanding of interrelated elements, relationships, and situational variables and contingencies, so all can be coordinated. Coaches cannot be static in their thoughts and actions since they are responsible for shaping and modifying their program and sport so that it is successful in adapting to the changing conditions in the environment. Darwin's law, "Adapt to survive," is applicable to all managers including the coach–manager.

As illustrated in Figure 5-1, after securing pertinent information relevant to the "as is" situational variables and contingencies, a coach–manager engages in communication and decision making, which are frequently identified as linking or intervening processes and not as functions of management since they are applicable to all human endeavors. Thus the coach must also perform the primary management functions in order to achieve the desired conditions through coordination and adaptation, to attain the sports or program's collective objectives—these are the goals, desires, or targets that have been identified after careful consideration by management (the head coach), with input from the coaching staff and squad members. Feedback from each of these boxes, as illustrated in Figure 5-1, returns to the

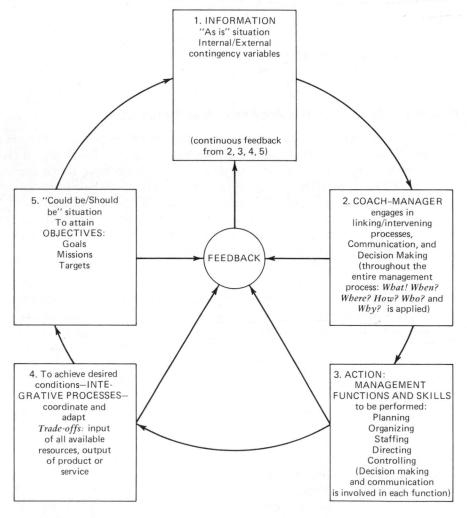

Figure 5-1. The management (flow) process—a circular, continuous, dynamic, and ongoing process.

to "catch up," the time factor alone will not permit him to do so during the actual sports season. Someone likened a coach's job to that of stringing beads on a thread with no knot; there is no end to the job! Therefore, a coach's overall plan must be well formulated prior to the season, so that his plan can become operative at the beginning of the sports season. Long-range planning must precede the sports season and continue throughout and after the regular season for effective coaching to take place.

For effective coaching to occur during the sports season, there must be year-round planning leading up to the in-season, the extent and detail depending on each particular coaching situation. Also, the overall details of the plan must be activated by individuals being made responsible and accountable for carrying out delegated specifics of the plan; this is a control or the monitoring function of the head coach. It all commences with a plan which then must be organized in detail. In its simplest form, planning involves establishing objectives and organizing all efforts to attain them.

In the development of a plan, three types of decisions (Figure 5-2), are necessary: (1) strategical, (2) tactical, and (3) operational; and all are fused together to attain the objectives and goals that have been identified. *Strategical* planning is long range, usually determining how available resources (player personnel skills, coaching expertise, and so on) will be used to achieve objectives. *Tactical* planning is concerned with implementing the strategic plan. In industry tactical planning typically has a 3 to 5 year time span. In coaching tactical planning is more immediate instead of intermediate, such as devising a specific game plan for an upcoming opponent. *Operational* planning is the *who* and *how* in a detailed timetable.

In most sports programs for effective coaching to take place during the time or season that the sport is actually in progress, there are three additional seasons where planning and organizing must occur: the *post*season, the *out of* season, and the *pre*season. Using scholastic and collegiate sports as the basis for discussion and as illustrations, three seasons coincide with the academic school year, namely, August–September of one year to the following May–June of the next year, and the out-of-season period for virtually all scholastic and collegiate sports is during the summer vacation months.

At the conclusion of the regular sports season or the *in*-season, the *post*season plan should become operative, eventually moving into the *out-of*-season plan. At some point in year-round planning, the out-of-season plan terminates and, for the traditional fall sports, the preseason plan becomes operative. The latter leads into a general plan for the in-season, with the specific details and the logistics for making the plan function being worked out and organized by the coaching staff weekly and daily, such as practice and game plans. There are always meaningful, purposeful, and relevant tasks, chores, activities, and specific "things to do" if the overall coaching is to become effective. Therefore, the year-round plan is actually the plans of all four seasons tied and fused together to form the sport and the program's plan.

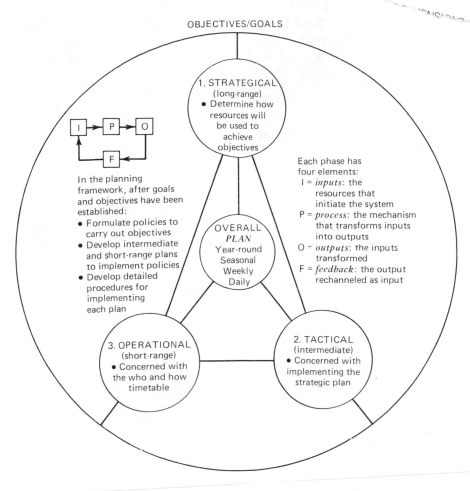

OBJECTIVES/GOALS

1. STRATEGICAL
(long-range)
• Determine how
resources will
be used to
achieve
objectives

In the planning
framework, after goals
and objectives have been
established:
• Formulate policies to
carry out objectives
• Develop intermediate
and short-range plans
to implement policies
• Develop detailed
procedures for
implementing
each plan

OVERALL
PLAN
Year-round
Seasonal
Weekly
Daily

Each phase has
four elements:
I = *inputs*: the
resources that
initiate the system
P = *process*: the mechanism
that transforms inputs
into outputs
O = *outputs*: the inputs
transformed
F = *feedback*: the output
rechanneled as input

3. OPERATIONAL
(short-range)
• Concerned with
the who and how
timetable

2. TACTICAL
(intermediate)
• Concerned with
implementing the
strategic plan

Figure 5-2. The development of a plan involves making three types of decisions: strategical, tactical, and operational.

Plan Ahead By Seasons. While tactical and operational decisions are being made for the current season at that particular time of the year, strategical decisions for upcoming seasons in the future are also being made so that the overall plan for the sport and the program are always ongoing. For example, while the actual playing season of the sport is in progress and the major emphasis is to devote time and attention to the tactical and operational decisions relevant to the opposition and to winning games, some attention is also given to strategical decisions for the post-season, out of season (summer), and possibly even the preseason. The point is that for coaching to be effective, one cannot wait until that particular season arrives to start the initial planning. There is a general strategical plan for each of the seasons, which is refined into tactical and operational plans once that particular season arrives. Yet, there is always planning ahead for the upcoming season as part of the overall plan for the sport and program.

There is always an on-going list of planned ''things'' to be done by seasons. They should not be merely time-fillers and busy work that many coaches seem to get involved in because of the profession's ''expected-to-work-long-hours syndrome,'' but selected tasks, ''things,'' that are relevant and fused together into the overall plan for a more effective coaching schedule. Initially the ''things'' should be merely listed, and then prioritized in rank order. It is virtually impossible to list and prioritize at the same time.

Prioritize. While it is suggested that a coach and his staff enumerate all of the ''things to do,'' it is impossible and impractical to give the same degree of attention to every item; it is also unnecessary to do so. Therefore, all activities or ''things'' need to be prioritized in rank order from most to least important for each of the four seasons, and monitored carefully, or a coach is likely to discover later on that he and his staff have spent little or a disproportionate amount of time on some activities to the detriment or exclusion of others that were more important and that should have received more attention.

Figure 5-3a, the Priority Planning Triangle (solid bold lines), illustrates that all items listed ''to be done'' should then be divided into three major categories: (1)

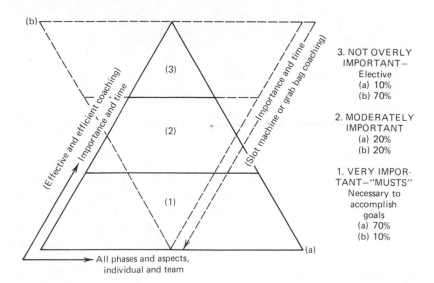

Figure 5-3. (a) The priority planning triangle (solid lines), and (b) the inverted priority triangle (broken lines).

Very Important—"Musts," (2) *Moderately Important,* and (3) *Not Overly Important.* Therefore these tasks and "things to do" are not only listed by seasons, but they are prioritized within each of these three major categories in rank order of importance. Whether it is the overall master plan or the daily practice plan, five types of decisions must be made for effective coaching:

- *What* needs to be done?
- *When* will it be done?
- *Where* will it be done?
- *How* will it be done?
- *Who* will do it?

Why? is germane to all of the five types of decisions.

The broken lines in Figure 5-3*b* illustrate the Inverted Priority Triangle, both in terms of "things to do" and in reference to a timetable, where a head coach and staff do *not* clearly identify, prioritize, and monitor the program or sports activities and tasks. When this happens, the head coach is not creating and managing a favorable environment conducive to success.

The Seasonal Plan

Limiting the discussion to the actual sports season and specifically to the *very important "musts"* category, it may be necessary to reorder the priority of "musts" because of numerous variables or situational factors that influence and affect the successful completion of tasks. For example, certain key players and the team may not "come along" and develop at the rate of speed that was first estimated and anticipated when the list was initially devised. The teaching and acquisition of motor skills and the individual and team playing techniques are not only sequential, but the time allotted to teaching and mastering specific skills is speculative and variable and depends on many factors. The *very important "musts"* list may have to be restructured, which in turn will have a direct bearing on the other two categories, since everything is done within a time frame.

The Priority Time-Pie. While the priority planning triangle illustrated in Figure 5-3*a* is divided into thirds as a system of classifying three broad levels of categories, this is for diagrammatic purposes only since each coaching situation is different and must be tailor-fitted individually. While there are basic *musts* to be accomplished every year in every sport, a "down cycle" in playing personnel, a new coaching staff, upgrading the schedule, new opponents, or other contingency factors of a similar nature would mean that in order to produce a representative (and one would hope) winning team, the list of *musts* would be greater in number and by necessity would receive more time and a higher priority over those items in the other two categories.

Some of the items in the *must* category will be handled quickly while others may take more time than initially planned. Therefore, within the constraints of time and finances, some of the musts may not get done in preparation for an opponent. A coach and a team may get by without having accomplished some of these musts, but during the course of a particular contest a coach may realize his error of omission. In preparation for his next opponent it is likely that he will go back and spend more time on the musts which he failed to accomplish previously. As a result, the *moderately important* and *not overly important* or *elective* categories would receive proportionally less importance, priority, and time.

In strategical, tactical, and operational planning, a coaching staff should list all of the "things" they would like to accomplish in the preparation during the season for an upcoming opponent. Theoretically and logically all of the *must* tasks should be accomplished before moving to the prioritized list of *moderately important* activities; if time permits, finally the staff can begin the last category of *elective* "things." Once again, however, if the "things" are not monitored carefully, a coaching staff will discover that they are not accomplishing their specific desired objectives and goals. The time devoted or allocated to the accomplishment of the designated activities, items, and "things" must be closely monitored because there is only a specific total amount of time available daily, weekly, seasonally, and yearly to work for the accomplishment of the sports program.

An Illustration. Eventually most every coach is faced with preparing his or her team for a contest after sustaining an unexpected loss, especially if defeated badly. A coach has three alternatives: (1) change nothing and continue with the overall plan, retaining the same priorities in the three categories as before; (2) abandon the plan and place more emphasis on additional offensive plays, defensive alignments, and new tactics, which would be away from the *musts* and would place more emphasis on the electives (it is always "fun" to add new "wrinkles" and gadgets); or (3) place even more emphasis on the basic *musts* and eliminate everything that is not overly important in getting ready for the next contest.

The preservice student and the novice coach are likely to select the second alternative above, while the experienced coach is likely to select the third or first alternative, in that order of preference. A head coach may feel that his team is progressing slowly and that despite the loss they were defeated by a superior team; thus he decides to stick with his original plan. More than likely, however, the experienced coach is apt to give even greater priority to the *very important musts*, recognizing that it is the fundamental execution of basic skills and techniques, and not plays, that wins contests. It is likely he would want his players to perform fewer offensive plays and defensive alignments with greater perfection than to add more to what they are already executing poorly. If this were his rationale, he would select the third alternative.

If a coach does not prioritize the *musts* and the *moderately important* activities, he will dissipate most of his time and effort on the *elective* things to do. For example, he may spend more time on practicing plays and putting in new "wrinkles,'' or in doing other ''fun'' things, than he does in teaching–coaching his players the basic fundamentals of his sport. Under such circumstances the priority triangle becomes inverted (Figure 5-3b) as the least important phases of the game receive the most attention and the most important ones receive the least. Such lack of planning usually leads to ''slot machine'' or ''grab bag'' coaching.

Slot Machine or Grab Bag Coaching. There is a style of coaching characterized by frequent and at times massive changes, which is analogous to the individual who keeps pulling the handle on the slot machine or reaching into the magic bag of chances, with the idea of trying to find the winning combination. Usually this coaching theory or philosophy is not well-founded or sound if the individual perceives that winning is the result of gimmicks, gadgets, and fooling the opposition. Just as one may hit the jackpot or blindly choose the prize from the grab bag occasionally, whether it be in gambling or coaching, the odds are prohibitive of continuing to win or select the ''right'' combination over a period of time. More frequently it is the inexperienced coach who turns to slot machine coaching simply because he has not yet learned that one cannot build a solid winning program on chance or grab bag methods. However, it is not always the inexperienced coach, since there are occasions when seasoned coaches, who should know better, revert to slot machine coaching, perhaps because they panic and try desperately to win.

Plan and Prepare Well. Most every experienced coach questions himself about his practice plans and teaching methods, especially if he is not a highly consistent winner. A winning coach is likely to feel he has found ''the best way'' and is not as likely to revise his practice regimen to any appreciable extent unless it can be proven to him there is still a better way that will make him a more consistent winner! Typical questions a coach is likely to ask are:

- Am I covering all of the essentials?
- How often should I cover certain phases of the game?
- How much time and attention should I devote to certain areas?
- Am I overlooking any phase or aspect that I should be including?
- Am I spending too much (or not enough) time covering certain areas?
- What have (and haven't) I covered?
- Too much (or not enough) scrimmaging?
- Will the team be ready to play by game time?

Probably very few coaches feel totally confident they have covered everything in preparation for an upcoming opponent. However, if they have a seasonal master plan of what they must and should teach–coach, and if they have maintained records of what they have taught and the amount of time devoted to teaching–coaching, they go into competition feeling reasonably well-assured that they can adjust to the unexpected should it occur, and they are confident of victory because they have prepared well.

Management of Time Skills

There are skills that must be developed in a specific time frame if one is to coach and manage effectively. Time is a paradox. While it is true that no coach ever seems to have sufficient time, in reality all coaches have the same amount of time. Everyone has all the time there is, since there simply is not any more time available! Each of us has 24 hours in every day, 168 hours in every week. We cannot borrow time from yesterday to use today, nor can we store up time today to use tomorrow. Each one of us has time to utilize as we wish, and it is up to each coach individually to make the most of each 24-hour period. This statement is so simplistic that many coaches and others fail to comprehend it. As some anonymous philosopher once stated,

> Yesterday is a canceled check.
> Tomorrow is a promissory note.
> Today is ready cash. Use it.

The problem is not how much time one has, but how one spends the time that is available. As Ben Franklin stated, "It is what you do with time, not time itself, that is worth money." Therefore, if because of situational contingencies a coach only has one hour per day practice time, as compared to another coaching situation where a coach has two-and-a-half hours per day available for practice, the first coach must perform his or her coaching and management skills both on and off the practice field more efficiently in order to compete with the latter coach. The extra hour-and-one-half the first coach does not have available for practice time on the field must be spent in developing and honing the basic plan, in organizing, staffing, and directing the plan, prior to implementing and practicing it on the field, and then in controlling or monitoring the plan during practice. Many times successful coaches cite the fact that they seldom "out-coach" their opposition, but frequently they will speak with pride of "out-working" them. The latter does not necessarily mean longer hours on the job, but almost always means performing coaching and management functions and skills better than the opposing coach. People do not necessarily fail in coaching or any other profession because they lack skills. Many times they are unsuccessful because they do not prioritize the "must do's" (Figure 5-3) or properly organize their time in seeing that the "musts" are effectively performed and accomplished. Time is a rigid barrier *all* coaches encounter.

CONTROL AS A MANAGEMENT FUNCTION

There is no one best way to plan or control. All planning and control systems must be adapted to the situation. It is the failure to perform a control function that causes many problems and is responsible for most failure, second only to no plan or a poor plan initially. While this may sound like an indictment to some coaches, and may be difficult to comprehend by serious-minded coaches, there are individuals in coaching as well as in the business world who sort of "wing" their plans. Since they do not have a definite formulated overall plan, their controls are indefinite, too. Most coaches probably have some sort of a plan, although their control function might be little more than cursory or practically nonexistant.

Controlling is the measuring of performance to ensure that results are consistent with the plan. The types and varieties of control systems tend to duplicate the types and varieties of plans. In the business world the following are the typical types of control: goals and strategy, organization structure, social, financial, budgets, production, quality, and audits, a number of which may also be used in coaching to obtain desired feedback. It is the failure to obtain and utilize systematic feedback in teaching, learning, and coaching that causes many problems and frequently is responsible for the lack of coaching success.

While the scoreboard or where an individual or team "places" are definite instruments of measurement, game competition is the ultimate, and feedback is only partially obtained after the contest. Individually or as a team, each would perform more consistently, and one would hope more successfully, if valid and reliable feedback were secured prior to game competition rather than after it. Briefly, the methods of measurement vary, depending on the type of control, and include qualitative findings and quantitative data, judgments, observation, interaction, reports, and so on, which are acquired on a systematic basis. When operations and results are consistent, no controls involving corrective action are required. However, when exceptions exist, either the plan must be changed or modified. Without effective planning and control, the program or organization is in "drift" condition.

Control as an Operative Function in the Management Process. In a broad sense, _control_ can be considered as any restraint, curb, or regulation on behavior or organizational processes, although in the business world it is even more restrictive since it relates to the systematic measurement and revision of behavior or processes. Sociologists and psychologists view control in terms of the processes that influence and affect behavior, whereas in the business world control relates more to regulating operations and resource allocations within an organization. Since resources include people, money, materials, machines, and methods, both concepts of control as expressed are applicable to coaching if effectiveness and efficiency are to be achieved. Control guides behavior and organizational activity into useful channels, helps ensure that resources are efficiently utilized, and keeps the sport or program functioning in a coordinated fashion. Its purpose is the measuring of performance to ensure that results are consistent with the plan.

Broadly stated, activities are carried out through a sequence of planning, execution, and control. Planning involves the establishing of strategy and objectives and then the determining of the activity sequence and resources necessary to attain them. Planning provides a sense of direction to a program, as well as to individual subunits, and is an important integrating force, serving as a prerequisite for the effective handling of other management functions. Because of the interdependence of this entire cycle, planning, execution, and control are considered as one continuous dynamic, ongoing process. The feedback mechanism of control should be constantly modifying and adjusting plans, so that any artificial separation between the planning and control of the process is misleading. However, there is always the possibility of mistakes in judgment where one does not impose control measures. The coach may not think it important to do so, such as his failure to follow up on monitoring assigned tasks and responsibilities assigned to assistant coaches. Or he may secure data and information which indicates that the plan is off-target or off-schedule, and yet he may fail to implement corrective measures, or he may impose the wrong corrective measures. No effort will be made to analyze either of the latter two problems, other than to point out that production and quality controls in coaching, although different in content from the traditional ones in industry, are as applicable to coaching as they are to the business world. Social control content, applicable to industry and to coaching too, includes roles, expectations, group norms, customs, values, leadership styles, and so on.

Assigning Responsibilities and the Need for Follow-up Monitoring

Frequently coaches diagram offensive plays and defensive alignments and devise strategies and tactics, but fail to take into consideration that their symbolic X*s* and O*s* represent people who must carry out those offensive and defensive assignments in order to achieve success. The same principle applies to the "things" that are to be done. A head coach can devise a detailed list of "things" he would like to see done by his assistant coaches, but many situational factors may prohibit the realization of all of the head coach's expectations.

While a head coach must be pragmatically realistic, for every "thing" to be done, each task must be assigned to someone to do. Not only are numbers of subordinates important, but the experience of each subordinate or assistant coach is important, too. Theoretically, if a head coach feels there are 100 important "things" that can be delegated to subordinates and he has two assistants, each has 50 to accomplish; with four assistants, each has 25 tasks to accomplish. However, because of individual differences in experience or expertise, it is very likely one or two staff members will have more tasks to perform than others. Also, some tasks are more complicated, time-consuming, and of greater importance than others. These are situational factors that a head coach must take into consideration; he or she will also have to take care not to overburden some coaches with so many tasks that it is impossible for them to succeed at any.

Not infrequently the time factor is overlooked; the failure of the head coach to follow up and monitor the assigned activities or tasks to make certain they have been done or to determine the exact status of the assigned tasks is also a major problem. While a head coach may delegate a number of tasks or "things" to be done, some cannot be delegated to subordinates since the expectations of the position demand that the head coach do specific tasks. However, those tasks and activities that can, should be delegated and then monitored. The control function of the management process is imposed to make certain the plan is being activated and not merely being discussed verbally. Planning, activation, and control should be an interrelated, continuous process.

DECISION MAKING AND OTHER MANAGEMENT SKILLS FOR COACHES

Since all management activity involves decision making, many people consider decision making to be synonymous with management. Of the five management functions, however, decision making is more closely associated with planning than any of the others, because initially there must be a *plan*—whether it is to try to resolve a particular problem, to develop seasonal-weekly-daily practice schedules, or to conceptualize an entire year-round program before that plan can be organized, directed, staffed, and controlled. Obviously each management function involves decision making (Figure 5-1).

Some decisions are made intuitively by coach–managers, and many are made as the result of one's judgment based on one's experience or frame of reference in coaching. A third method in making decisions involves an analytical problem-solving approach. This technique is especially important and necessary where more serious or far-reaching consequences are likely to occur as a result of one's ultimate decision. All managers, including coaches, should be familiar with the problem-solving approach for reaching decisions, because one's limited experience and expertise does not always permit one to make wise decisions intuitively or judgmentally. The latter two types of decisions will be discussed only briefly; the suggested steps for making decisions by an analytical process will be listed and discussed in greater detail.

CRITERIA FOR MAKING DECISIONS

Regardless of the method, all choices are influenced by the desire to achieve certain ends or goals. Therefore, in reality all decisions are *future* oriented and should be predictive in nature. This is to rationalize, "If I do this (as the result of my decision), then this should occur." One makes a decision to move from one state of affairs to new conditions or the desired state of affairs, such as from the "as is" situation to the "could-should be" coaching situation. The basis or criterion for this decision may be simply a "hunch" (intuitive), or it may be made based on the criterion of experience (judgmental), or it may be through careful analysis of available alternatives and then a decision of which is the most pragmatic. When the latter occurs, decision making is not treated as a discrete event, but as a process, since a coach–manager must engage in considering alternatives and evaluating information relative to these alternatives before making his or her choice. Decision making is not only the result of decisions made previously by a head coach and others, but problem-solving decision making is a process. For the most part our discussion refers to the formulation of a coaching plan (Figure 5-2), as applied to the management process (Figure 5-1). It is readily acknowledged that the decision-making process in problem solving is time consuming, which few coaches feel they can afford. However, despite this apparent disadvantage, to devise a sound plan the entire coaching staff must invest the time.

Intuitive decisions are made when an individual has no knowledge of the factors underlying a problem or is unfamiliar with workable solutions. Sometimes the coach has merely a ''hunch'' or a ''feel'' for what action should be taken. This ready insight into solutions cannot be completely dispelled in explaining the limited success of certain coaches in some situations, but since it represents little more than guessing, it is hardly acceptable as a basis for directing a year-round athletic program or seasonal activity.

Decisions based on judgment are actually the type that consume most of the typical coach's time. A coach's knowledge and experience gained through tenure in a particular coaching situation helps him or her to be accurate in making decisions regarding routine matters. Through experience one learns to rely on ''rules of thumb'' that guide one's decisions in coaching matters. Through this common sense approach a coach often makes dozens of decisions where there is no need to investigate the circumstances thoroughly because he or she is familiar enough with the activities to predict the outcome.

Problem-Solving Skills

Employing the problem-solving approach in decision making requires different kinds of skills than those one employs when one makes intuitive and judgmental decisions. It involves the development of problem-solving skills with which one learns to sense and recognize *what* causes problems and *why* they occur; one learns approaches and plans for getting things done, as well as how to set up acceptable goals and objectives. These functions and skills may be identified as analysis and ideation. *Analysis skills* involve both examining and determining what needs to be accomplished; and *ideation skills* refer to the abilities to develop ways to use analysis to make the program, sport, and the coaching staff more effective.

Both analysis and ideation skills require what psychologists lable *cognitive skills,* which are mental processes or skills that require the ability to think clearly. Solving problems, conceptualizing, determining goals and objectives, analyzing, and interpreting are examples of cognitive skills that a coach would utilize. Frequently it is the acquisition of cognitive skills that separates successful head coaches from unsuccessful ones, head coaches from assistant coaches.

The Decision-Making Process in Problem Solving. A decision is *not* simply a choice to proceed with a course of action. It is an ongoing goal-oriented process involving the development of alternatives, the collection and analysis of data, and the whole sequence of events that occurs, starting with the proper identification of the problem, until that point at which the problem is effectively resolved. Frequently the identification of the problem is not as simplistic as it may appear, as a common error is to deal erroneously with the symptoms instead of the problem. Also, the number of steps in problem solving are arbitrary, and some information is collected in every phase of the process. In addition, in many situations all steps may not be necessary because situational variables are different and seldom remain static; thus, the resolution of the problem may become more difficult or simpler. Some problems may be unresolvable, and others may literally resolve themselves over a period of time. However, it is the overall methodology of problem solving that deserves recognition, and it is convenient for analytical purposes to segregate the method into phases or steps. The following steps in problem solving are suggested:

1. Identify and define the problem or barrier.
   - What is wrong or what needs to be done?
   - Is it one big problem or a collection of minor situations?
   - Is it a clear problem or a camouflage for a different problem?

2. Analyze the problem.
   - Separate it into parts.
   - Determine nature, functions, and interrelations of its parts.

3. Collect data to solve the problem.
   - Seek all data that refers to the problem.

4. Analyze the data.
   - Reaffirm if the correct problem was identified and defined.
   - State the data and its bearing on the problem.

5. Arrive at solutions.
   - Identify constraints relating to a decision or solution.
   - Define the most conspicuous solution and its rationale.
   - Cite an alternative solution(s) and its rationale.

6. Test solutions and obtain feedback.
   - Determine if the decision is achieving the results desired.
   - Measure results, which are considered a part of the control function of management.
   - Be prepared to make alternative solutions when necessary.

This problem-solving process assumes an ideal situation in which human rationality is maximized in making decisions. However, rarely does decision making

proceed in the logical sequence presented. A coach–manager frequently not only lacks resources such as money, manpower (people), and methods of obtaining complete data to be this thorough, but if under pressure especially during the sports season he or she may lack the significant element of time. The simplified process of correctly identifying problems, developing alternatives, and then making the "best" decision or choice at that particular time is a vital framework for objective and effective decision making. However, it is recognized that usually it is impossible for any coach–manager to know all of the facts because of the constraints of time alone in most decision-making situations. Therefore, one cannot possibly have all of the necessary and accurate factual information, know all of the possible alternatives available, and be able to anticipate all results since this is not consistent with the world of reality. Yet one must make decisions, cognizant of the fact that information is limited and may be inaccurate, realizing also that uncertainty is a normal variable in all decision-making processes. Despite these limitations, several conclusions are evident regarding the decision-making process.

Conclusions Pertaining to the Process. First, decisions seldom stand alone as separate entities; they tend to be interrelated and sequential. Every decision is based on a previous decision (Figure 5-1). One decision typically leads to the need for other decisions. The decision process typically involves the selection of certain means to achieve particular ends. Usually these ends are intermediate steps to broader ends, relating to the goals of the individual, the sport, and/or the program. All major decisions also typically involve numerous minor implementing decisions relating to the functions of management.

Second, after analyzing advantages and disadvantages, it should be recognized that all decisions eventually involve trade-offs. Of the alternatives selected, each will typically have some features that are superior in some respects to those of other alternatives. At times the advantages of one alternative are only gained through sacrificing the benefits of others. As a result the coach–manager's decision frequently is an exercise in evaluating trade-offs where choices may involve some form of compromise. One's philosophy and subjectivity will determine the extent or degree of compromise, if any, if values or beliefs are involved in resolving the problem or issue in the decision-making process. One cannot overlook the primary human forces that are dominant in the situation being faced. Therefore, two sets of factors are involved in decision making: rational decision processes and methods of analysis, such as have been described, and the pressures that come to bear on the coach–decision maker resulting from the particular individual or individuals he identifies or is involved with in an influential relationship. A coach not only wants to make what he or she perceives is a "right" decision, but a coach is anxious to have a decision accepted and carried out by his or her subordinates, and approved by the coach's superiors as well. Those individuals who see themselves as losing through the decision will probably resist the proposed action, and those who perceive themselves as gaining will apply pressure to have the decision consummated.

In few coaching situations does a coach have a completely free hand to make decisions unilaterally on *all* matters involving his athletes, just as few other supervisors or managers involved in organizational or programmatic processes have sole autonomy and ultimate authority in decision making. All managers, including coaches, are always subject to opposing forces and constraints that limit their authority and influence, including those from within their own group on whom occasionally they may rely for a power base if decisions rendered do not gain acceptance by other individuals in the group.

Despite these limitations, decision making is an act of choice where an individual decides to pursue a course of action selected from a number of different alternatives. Decision making is the intervening or linking process of management (Figure 5-1). It is the action by which the functions of planning, organizing, directing, staffing, and controlling are carried out. Obviously the process is not utilized when decisions are made on the basis of intuition by hunches or guessing. And, as previously mentioned, routine decisions are made on the basis of judgment, where repeated experience dictates what action will normally be successful. However, problem solving is an analytical process using a method like that used in scientific inquiry, involving a much more complex analytical process than decisions based on judgment alone. Also, the climate of the program or situation relating to the decision is an important factor in the decision process. One of the foundations of success, and also one of the most difficult to build, is the ability to make wise and prudent decisions. Among the major causes of failure, being indecisive is probably at the top of the list because it is difficult on occasion to make a decision and it is easy to procrastinate. As the leader, a head coach's responsibility is to face problems and to make decisions wisely.

Knowledge-Based Skills

The second group of functions and skills involves specific knowledge or techniques, relevant to planning and organizing the specifics of the program the coach is directing. How a coach directs and organizes staff and players, develops practice schedules and game plans, evaluates performance and makes routine decisions, depends on one's knowledge-based skills. How a coach applies his or her knowledge-based skills depends on the individual's decision-making process.

Human Relations Skills

The third set of functions and skills relates to communication, motivation, and development of effective relations with superiors, subordinates, players, and others; these are often identified as skills in public relations. Human relations skills would also include a coach's leadership style and his or her effectiveness in shaping and managing the contemporary environment or climate of the program, activity, or sport. An individual in coaching has many opportunities to create a favorable climate via public and human relations with superiors and administrators, assistant coaches and supportive staff, players, alumni, students (at the collegiate and scholastic levels), spectators, game/contest officials, and others.

Affective Development Skills

The fourth group of coaching–management activities is much more difficult to define. By *affective* skill, we mean a coach's influence on the attitudes, emotions, and values of subordinates, players, and others. This group of skills involves those personal characteristics that truly distinguish effective leaders. Such characteristics include being willing to accept and seek increasing responsibility and to make unpopular decisions, showing concern for both personal achievement and the needs of others, expending energy to achieve, and being aware of one's personal limitations as well as strengths. This fourth set of characteristics overlaps all of the other categories.

All four sets of functions and skills are necessary and are often used simultaneously. The categories relate specifically to skills utilized in the performance of management functions, all of which an individual must exercise in the position and role of head coach. The better a coach performs these functions and skills, the more likely the individual will be able to create and manage a favorable climate for coaching success.

Summary

In the contingency or situational approach to coaching and management, for the coach–manager to be effective he or she not only needs to be familiar with the various functions, concepts, and techniques of management, but one needs to be knowledgeable of the advantages and disadvantages that occur when he or she utilizes a particular concept or technique. One must be able to predict what will result both favorably and unfavorably from the application of management principles. A coach–manager needs to be able to analyze the situation he or she is confronted with in order to determine which concepts or techniques will be the most effective. After analyzing the trade-offs involved when one uses particular concepts or techniques, a coach–manager is better able to match up the proper ones with the needs of specific situations, which should result in successful management.

SELECTED READINGS

Bisbee, Charles. "Challenge Yourself to Success." *Nations Business*. November 1969.

Certo, Samuel C. *Principles of Modern Management: Functions and Systems*. Dubuque, Iowa. Wm. C. Brown Company, Publishers, 1980, pp. 47–227.

Fuoss, Donald E., and Troppmann, Robert J. *Creative Management Techniques in Interscholastic Athletics*. New York. John Wiley & Sons, 1977.

Grieve, Andrews. "The Coach's Handbook." *Scholastic Coach*. Vol. 32, March 1969, pp. 58–61.

Glueck, William F. *Management*. Hinsdale, Illinois. The Dryden Press, 1980, pp. 198–331.

Ivancevich, J. M., Donnelly, Jr., J. H., and Gibson, J. L. *Managing for Performance*. Dallas, Texas. Business Publications, 1980, pp. 49–120.

Lakein, Alan. *How to Get Control of Your Time and Your Life*. New York. Peter H. Wyden, Publisher, 1973.

Love, Sydney F. *Mastery and Management of Time*. Englewood Cliffs, N.J. Prentice-Hall, 1978.

Mackenzie, R. Alec. *The Time Trap*. New York. McGraw-Hill Company, 1975.

Massengale, John D. (Ed.) *The Principles and Problems of Coaching*. Springfield, Ill. Charles C Thomas, 1975. "Organization Begins with the Coach," Dale Hanks, Chapter 40, pp. 309–314.

Reynolds, H., and Tramel, M. E. *Executive Time Management: Getting 12 Hours' Work Out of an 8-Hour Day*. Englewood Cliffs, N.J. Prentice-Hall, 1979.

Sage, George H. "The Coach as Management: Organizational Leadership in American Sport." *Quest*. January 1973, pp. 35–40.

Stram, Hank. "Great management is the foundation of a great team." *The Sacramento Union*. January 17, 1979, p. C-5.

Three

THE PSYCHOLOGICAL DIMENSIONS OF COACHING: UNDERSTANDING HUMAN BEHAVIOR

6

The Psychology of Communication and Coaching Effectiveness

The act of communication symbolizes the need of the individual to maintain contact with his or her environment, and for this reason alone it can be seen as supplying one of psychology's central themes. Humans interact with each other through the communication process, although understanding and being understood frequently does not occur. Yet in coaching, no single behavior is more important than the process of communication. Communication has much to do with the structure, activity, and effectiveness of an organization and group, whether it be in government, business, industry, or coaching an athletic team.

Early studies treated communication merely as a tool, but now communication is recognized as a universal linking process applicable to most all human endeavor. There is a growing recognition of the dynamic role of communication within the life of a group or organization, not solely because it is utilized everywhere, but because weak communication is one of the most common barriers relating to program, group, and individual effectiveness. The purpose of this chapter is not only to familiarize the coach and the coach to be with the process of communication and to examine what causes distortions, interferences, and weak communication, but to suggest ways to communicate more effectively. In turn, this should lead to greater coaching effectiveness.

CRITICAL PROBLEM: INEFFECTIVE COMMUNICATION

There is considerable evidence to indicate that communication breakdown frequently is a critical problem in almost every aspect of human endeavor where two or more people are involved. In the field of management, as an illustration, not only does the prestigious *Harvard Business Review* consistently deal with the topic, but practically every issue of other management magazines contains one or more articles on communication (Lorey, 1976). The consensus appears to be that more than 80 percent of the managers have identified ''communication'' in response to the question, ''What causes you trouble in your job?'' While this illustration relates specifically to managers in business, it could well apply to all other trades and professions including coaching–teaching since a frequent lament is lack of communication. However, as both Tutko (1974) and Lyon (1973) pointed out, despite the necessity of improving communication between coach and athlete, the current available literature offers little concrete information or practical suggestions on how this can be done. Our intent is to resolve this problem.

A "Communication Gap"

Sometimes when there are communication barriers or a lack of communication or a breakdown in communication, someone refers to this as a ''communication gap.'' The most simplistic diagram illustrating the communication process would be a straight line, the shortest distance between two points. However, a more realistic diagram of communication would be a wavy line, or a series of circles, a tangent or a trajectory, that may or may not eventually reach its intended objective. The very nature of the organizational structure of coaching, designed as it is to facilitate interaction and move management, coaches, and team toward goal accomplishment, provides barriers to effective communication. Communication is downward, upward, lateral, and diagonal.

A different kind of ''communication gap'' occurs when someone is not involved in direct communication or is receiving information secondhand. In professional sports in particular, this dilemma seems to occur frequently. The owner of a professional team may choose to deal directly with his coach, but without the general manager being fully knowledgeable of the specific contents of the discussion, so that a communication gap then exists between the general manager and the coach. With agents representing many professional athletes, depending on the scalar chain of management and the head coach's span of authority and control, an agent and the owner or general manager may communicate without player and/or coach being fully knowledgeable of the specifics; thus a ''communication gap'' occurs between the player and coach, both of whom have not directly communicated with the agent and owner or general manager. More often, however, the ''communication gap'' is the direct result of their failing to interact with each other.

Coach and Athlete: "We Can't Communicate." Frequently coaches will say of an athlete, ''I can't talk to him''; ''He simply doesn't understand what I'm saying''; ''He's a loner who doesn't communicate with anyone''; ''I've told him a hundred times, but. . .''; or other similar statements with negative connotations.

On the other hand, athletes may say of a coach, ''He doesn't talk to me''; ''He never tells me anything''; ''I don't understand him''; ''He never explains what he means''; ''He's always hollering and shouting, but. . .''; or other similar statements with negative connotations.

These statements are not too dissimilar, and all indicate a breakdown in the communication process, although there are other dimensions of coaching involved since communication is only the linking process. All dimensions of coaching are interrelated because it is virtually impossible to be effective in such areas as leadership, motivation, learning, teaching–coaching methods and performance, practice organization, game tactics and strategy, when the universal linking process of communication is ineffective.

In ''Talk? It's Really an Issue in Sports,'' *Los Angeles Times*' sports columnist Bob Oates (1978) quoted a former National Basketball Association coach as saying, ''Five years ago management fired a coach because he didn't have charisma or couldn't relate to his team. Today the word is 'communicate.' They fired me because they said I wasn't communicating.'' Regardless of the specifics in this particular situation, coaches are frequently accused of not communicating with some of their athletes, and in turn coaches often indicate there are communication breakdowns between them and some of their athletes.

Communication Breakdown. Dealing with communication breakdown is not a simple matter. Usually it is symptomatic of more basic difficulties within the organization, squad, team, group of players, and coaching staff or between individuals. Individuals restrict or distort communication because of distrust, fear, conflict, bias, or other such factors. Improved communication can be achieved only by eliminating or reducing these human frailties and perceptions. The deficiency of the information can be overcome by improving the system, and by the head coach performing the required managerial functions and skills that are ingredients for coaching success.

Some communication breakdown is directly attributable to a lack of skills, such as listening and speaking, but most occur because of the failure to understand people's behavioral patterns and the relationships between the source and the receiver, whether it be the talker and the listener, the writer and the reader, or the performer and the audience, and the complex nature of the communication process itself. While this can be illustrated by simple diagrams, in reality barriers frequently make effective communication extremely difficult to achieve.

WHAT IS COMMUNICATION?

Since one frequently hears or reads about the communication process, both *communication* and *process* need to be defined for purposes of clarity and understanding. *Communication* is the imparting or interchange of thoughts, opinions, or information by speech, writing, or signs; it is the transmission and the exchange of information conveying meaning between two or more people. A *process* is a systematic series of actions directed to some end; it is a continuous action, operation, or series of changes taking place in a definite manner. It is a continuous, ongoing event, developing changes or dynamic interrelationships.

Communication Is Behavior. Human behavior is typically social behavior, characterized by people interacting with others. This interaction is communication and is the outward manifestation of perceptions, attitudes, feelings, needs, drives, interests, emotions, and values. Through an individual's actions, these behavioral characteristics are communicated to others. Furthermore, the same external factors that affect behavior, such as peers, group norms, and the expectations of others, also affect how and what we will communicate. Since communication is behavior, evaluating the effectiveness of communication and the means of improving it are dependent on the behavioral concepts that are discussed throughout this book.

In addition to communication being behavior, it is also listening and understanding. It is not necessarily talking, unless both the sender and the receiver understand each other. Effective communication requires that both communicators be on the same current or wavelength. When they are not, it is analogous to plugging an a-c iron into a d-c electrical outlet; a fuse is blown!

Communication Terms Defined

Before analyzing and discussing the communication process, let us define some common terms that will be utilized throughout, mindful of the fact that sender and receiver, both communicators, are both human organisms who exist in similar states. Therefore, an analysis of behavior from a communication standpoint applies equally to communication sources and receivers.

Here are some dictionary terms, modified and synthesized for our discussion of the communication process and the context it has in this book.

Send (verb) To put into some state or condition. To dispatch by means of communication. To convey or cause to be conveyed or transmitted by an agent.

Sender–encoder (noun) One who transmits a verbal and/or nonverbal messages. (Example: coach, athlete, teacher, spectator.)

Receiver (noun) One who receives something; a recipient. Also called the *decoder*. A person who receives incoming signals and converts them to perceptible forms. The receiver–decoder of the message sent by the sender–encoder. (Example: athlete, coach, student, audience.)

Message (noun) The basic theme or significance of something. Something sent. A communication in writing, in speech, or by signals (code). A messenger's (sender–communicator's) errand or function sent by verbal or nonverbal means. (Example: information about tactics or strategy transmitted by language or signs, such as "pass," "kick," "bunt," "take one" (strike), "hit-and-run" (or "run-and-hit"), and so on.)

Channel (noun) A means of passage. A means of communication or expression. A way or course of thought or action. (Example: visual, auditory.)

Encode (verb) To put or convert a message into a code. To transfer from one system of communication into another. (Example: a coach's selection of terminology to describe systems, techniques, tactics, strategy, methodology, etc., based on his or her intent and the comprehension level of the athlete or the one for whom the message is intended.)

Decode (verb) To convert a message from code into plain text or ordinary language. (Example: athlete interpreting or understanding coach's message according to coach's specific use and the athlete's comprehension of vocabulary, terminology, etc.)

Feedback (noun) The return (by the receiver–decoder) of a portion of the output (message) of any process or system to the input (sender–encoder). The partial reversion of the effects of a process to its source or to a preceding stage. (Example: verbal or noverbal, such as "Yes," "No," "I don't (do) understand," nodding head affirmatively, shaking head negatively, quizzical facial expression, applause, restlessness, and so forth.)

Interfere (verb) To hinder, impede, meddle. To inhibit clear reception of broadcast (by sender and receiver) signals. Something that causes or produces confusion. (Example: *internal* interference is usually found in encoding/decoding, such as the coach uses vocabulary (terminology) that the athletes do not understand, or young athletes, never having been exposed to the sport before do not know what to expect or do not see the intricacies of the game. *External* interference is usually found in the channel, such as noise or distractions while the coach is trying to teach/demonstrate/explain techniques, methods, tactics, etc.)

Perception (noun). The act or result of perceiving (awareness, discernment, insight). Perception involves the way a person views or "sees" reality, assigning meaning to reality based on one's frame of reference and on other factors, which are discussed in detail throughout this book. (Example: perception is the *"I"* behind the eye that sees!)

TYPES OF COMMUNICATION

There are various types or kinds of communication: intrapersonal, interpersonal, group, one-to-group, and nonverbal communication. There are various dimensions of nonverbal communication that directly affect all communication.

Intrapersonal and Interpersonal Communication

Intrapersonal communication is the communication we have with ourselves in that we listen to what we say; we read what we write; we think; we are both the sender and the receiver. The dynamics of the intrapersonal communication cycle are complex and involve diverse processes and components. However, in coaching one is more concerned with one-to-one and coach-to-group communication.

In interpersonal communication there must be a minimum of two parties involved for communication to take place, and the exchange must be meaningful. The sender intends to affect the response of a particular person or group of persons. The message or communication content may be received by the person for whom it was intended, or by persons for whom it was not intended, or both. Depending on the communication situation, the message that is received may be distorted, so that the sender's intention of affecting a response in the interpreter does not materialize to the sender's expectations.

The elements and structure of a language do not themselves have meaning. They are only symbols, sets of symbols, cues that cause us to bring our own meanings into play, to think about them, and to rearrange them. Communication does not consist of the transmission of meanings. Meanings are not transmittable, and meanings are not in the message; they are in the message-users.

Serious communication breakdowns can be attributed to the false assumption that there is meaning in the message. A common perpetuated misnomer is that words have meaning, but do not mean the same to all people. It would be more accurate to state that words do not mean at all; only people mean, and people do not mean the same by all words. Meanings are personal since they are learned, and they differ from person to person. One learns words and acquires meanings from them by perceiving a word as related to objects or to other words, for which one already has affixed meanings. Interpersonal communication is only effective when the receiver interprets the sender's message the way the sender intended it.

Group and One-to-Group Communication

Group communication is actually interpersonal communication. A group, such as members of a coaching staff or a squad, is a number of persons who communicate with one another over a span of time, and who are few enough in number so that each individual is able to communicate with all other members of the group face to face and not secondhand. Communication patterns within a typical group usually reflect that certain individuals talk with every other member, while certain other people avoid talking with each other.

The one-to-one or public-speaking situations of one-to-group are an important part of a coach's job and are an equally important part of the communication process, too. A coach may be in the role of a public speaker to inform, to instruct, to convince, to persuade, to inspire, to entertain. While the ingredients of the communication process are the same in one-to-one and one-to-group situations, it is easier for the coach (speaker) to revert to one-to-one with his athletes even in a one-to-group situation, than it is to do this when he is public speaking. Smaller or more intimate groups, such as athletic teams or squads, are likely to be more receptive to the speaker and more influenced by the coach, for reasons mentioned previously, than the audience in public-speaking situations.

Nonverbal Communication

Any means the individual utilizes to convey ideas, feelings, information, thoughts, or attitudes to others involves communication. Much of the communication that affects people is never verbalized. Facial expressions like smiling or frowning, gestures such as an upraised open palm, or a clenched fist, a pat on the back, a slap on the buttocks, a handshake, or any observable behavior can transmit a nonverbal message. People are often not only unaware of the effects of nonverbal messages, but many are also unaware of nonverbal messages they transmit or receive. The lack of awareness of nonverbal communication elements can result in ineffective communication. Yet the most meaningful expressions of motivation for some people are communicated on the nonverbal level.

Body Language. *Kinesis* is from Greek and means *motion* or *to move*. *Kinesics* is the study of body movement and the visual aspects of behavior. Our objective here is not to include numerous illustrations of kinesics or body language that depict when an individual is "open" or "closed," since there are a number of books available on the subject (Fast, 1970, 1977; Henley, 1977). Despite the popularity of such books, some psychologists and others feel that the study of body language has not been sufficiently extensive to determine direct relationships between specific body movements and meaning. We wish merely to point out that body language can support and supplement verbal communication; it can also be used to hide attitudes and feelings and to contradict verbal statements. Perception is in the "eye of the beholder," and it is impossible for another person to interpret how the beholder perceives body movements. Therefore, it is easy to misinterpret body language. Judgments about the meaning of body movements must be made carefully since no single body movement can be considered an absolute indication of an individual's feelings, attitudes, or emotions. Yet it is inevitable that one will interpret a person's body movements, giving much credence to the clichés: "Actions speak louder than words," and "Judge a person not by what he says, but by what he does."

Spatial Relations. *Spatial* means relating to, occupying, or of the nature of space. *Proxemics* is the study of how individuals structure and use space. Spatial relations or proxemics affect communication because individuals learn and use what is considered the appropriate distance to maintain in communication situations.

In observing humans interact, one learns that this "appropriate" distance varies. The appropriate distance for communicating with a coach, a teacher, a physician, or many other individuals is probably *not* the same as the distance used in communicating with friends and peers. Psychologists and sociologists have revealed that individuals usually maintain a greater distance from people that have a status higher than theirs, and from those whom they dislike. Conversely, most people will move closer in communicating with individuals whom they like.

Spatial relations relevant to the size and location of one's office and its furnishings (object language) also affect communication. In many coaching situations where lack of space is not a prohibitive factor, most head football and head basketball coaches are assigned private offices. Head coaches of other sports may not be accorded this distinction, but a private office assignment conveys a nonverbal message of importance.

For example, a prospective coach or novice coach is not likely to be aware of the fact that administrative policy may specify that *only* head football and head basketball coaches be assigned single-office space twice the size of other head coaches and assistant coaches. The policy may specify further that two assistants are to be assigned per single office. Management and administration obviously are aware of spatial relations when making these determinations.

The location of a head coach's office, or a department head's office, or that of an athletic director, and the manner in which the office is furnished, can convey the nonverbal message of importance, status, and position. Policy may dictate the size, type, and even make of office furniture assigned to coaches. An assistant coach's office is likely to have different furniture than a head coach's office; and this is likely to be the distinction between head coaches of "major" sports and those who coach "minor" sports. Looney (1980) pointed out a number of the above points wherein he cited the head coach of a major sport at a name institution where $50,000 had been expended to have the coach's office redone, despite the fact that at the time his team was winless and the institution's sports program reputedly was going "bust." Our point is that both the amount and type of space, where the office is located, as well as how it is furnished, does communicate nonverbally. Spatial relations are significant aspects of any communication situation.

Object Language. An *artifact* (or *artefact*) is usually a simple object, such as a tool or ornament, showing human workmanship or human modification. Object language or artifacts refer to the communication that results from the display of material things. The way an individual utilizes artifacts communicates a message about the user. We are not judging a coach's use of artifacts in decorating his office. We are merely stating that numerous mementos, photos, citations, honors, trophies, awards, and similar artifacts may serve as a psychological barrier in the communication process. In a given situation these numerous objects, as well as a coach's nonverbal and verbal communication, could adversely affect the communication process between coach and athlete. Also individuals convey object language by their selection of clothes, eyeglasses, jewelry, hairstyle, and other personal items or apparel.

Use of Voice. *Para* from Greek, means *akin to;* beside; along side of; beyond. Thus *paralanguage* is concerned with how something is said, rather than *what* is said. Paralanguage deals with voice qualities (tone, rhythm, resonance, tempo); vocal irregularities (er, huh?, humm!, silent pauses); and vocal qualifiers of intensity (loud/soft), rate (fast/slow), and pitch (high/low). It is the combination of these elements that results in each individual having unique speech patterns. Also, it is because of the individual speaker's vocal qualifiers of intensity, rate, and pitch that frequently the intended receiver and/or others "hear between the words" of the spoken message.

Use of Time. *Chron,* or *chrono,* is from Greek and means *time. Chronemics* means the use of time. In our American society many individuals are "time conscious" in a "hurry-hurry" life style. An individual's attitude toward time is communicated by the way the individual deals with it. Most head coaches are very "time conscious." An assistant coach arriving late for a staff meeting may communicate a lackadaisical or an indifferent attitude toward work and the sport he or she is involved with. Also, it may communicate lack of respect for colleagues, disrespect for the head coach, and inconsideration on the part of the errant assistant who has infringed on the other staff members' prudent use of time. Subordinates are usually never expected to arrive late for an appointment or a scheduled meeting with a superior, such as at a conference or staff meeting. In the business world and in most every other known endeavor that involves a superior-subordinate relationship, the unwritten rule is, "Don't keep the 'boss' waiting!"

Conversely, if the "boss" keeps the subordinate(s) waiting by reporting late for scheduled appointments or staff meetings, the unwritten code is, "Rank has its privileges." While the subordinate(s) may feel differently, the nonverbal communication when a superior is late is that he or she simply could not get away from another important function or meeting or he or she would have been on time for the present appointment. When a head coach is late for a staff meeting, assistants may or may not proceed on their own, depending on the situation and the circumstances.

When an assistant is late for a meeting with other assistants, but the head coach is not involved, this is usually acceptable by the other peers as long as the errant assistant is not always "running late." If the latter occurs, then colleagues might interpret such behavior as lack of respect or simply inconsiderate behavior.

Interestingly, spatial relations comes into play at staff meetings, too. Going on the assumption that designated seating is *not* assigned by the "boss," other than that every subordinate "knows" never to sit in the chief executive's power seat at the head of the group, there may be a "jockeying for position" by subordinates sitting in the conference room to gain close proximity to where the "head" person sits to conduct the meeting. Where one is seated at a meeting or conference conveys nonverbal communication and indicates one's influence and power.

In some coaching situations it is extremely difficult to have regularly scheduled meetings involving the entire staff because of the myriad duties and responsibilities other than coaching that conflict. Being late for scheduled practice sessions, however, is an entirely different matter since this "time," when properly scheduled and blocked out in advance, is usually "honored" and is seldom violated at any level of competition. Coaches and players are usually properly routinized so as not to commit infractions by reporting late for practice sessions.

Many head coaches consider anything short of a dire emergency (and not too many emergencies are tolerated!) as inexcusable. If a head coach is tardy, usually practice sessions commence on time if the sessions are well-planned and properly organized. If an assistant coach is tardy, usually adjustments are made quickly and practice commences on time.

Sanctions are usually imposed on players who are late for practice. For the player or assistant coach who is continually late to practice, in many situations this results in the dismissal of the individual from the team or staff.

Most organizations, which would include the management of an athletic team, develop definite standards to be observed in the use of time. The standards may vary as the result of the individual's position, status, and worth to the organization, and as a result of the nature and circumstances of the situation. But the failure to adhere to written or "unwritten" standards of behavior relevant to the use of time communicates nonverbal messages that can reduce the individual's chances for success—whether the person is a head coach, an assistant coach, or an athlete.

Communication Behavior Is Broad in Scope. People can communicate on many levels, for many reasons, with many people, and in many ways. To coach effectively one is likely to utilize spoken, written, pictorial, gestural, group, mass, action, sensory, symbolic, auditory, and other types of communication to convey ideas, to demonstrate techniques and skills, and to teach plays, systems, tactics, and strategy, in individual, group, and team practice sessions, and during athletic contests. These examples in no way are all-inclusive, but merely illustrate some of the communication patterns in coaching.

COMMUNICATION AND COACHING

Effective communication requires much more than merely knowing techniques or mastering skills. From a coach's standpoint, communication is broad and integrative because it encompasses essentially everything that occurs in the field of coaching. The head coach is the focal person in that he or she is the administrator or chief executive of the sport that he or she coaches. The staff and players look to the head coach for leadership, motivation, and all organizational and management aspects of the program. Therefore, effective communication is an integral part of the coach's professional life as well as personal life and it contributes optimally to any measure of success the coach attains. Where group processes are involved, effective communication skills are very important. Trust, confidence, respect, cooperation among people are also tremendously important.

Without effective communication, including the intangibles mentioned, it is difficult for effective joint action or understanding to take place. Since a head coach's function is to optimize the effectiveness of group activity that includes coaching staff subordinates as well as players, communication becomes one of the vital aspects of a coach's work.

Time Spent Communicating and Leadership/Motivation

Numerous studies have revealed that approximately 70 to 80 percent of a manager's time in business, industry, and government is spent in some form of communication. Depending on a coach's position, sport, number of assistants and squad members, and the level of competition, it is likely that many coaches spend as much time communicating as do other middle managers. While no known research is available to support this statement, it would not be an inaccurate presumption to state that most coaches probably spend at least half of the hours of every day engaged in various types of communication.

Leadership and motivation are mentioned together frequently because a leader is expected to motivate; each is discussed later in detail in separate chapters. In fact, many management studies of communication have been conducted in conjunction with leadership and motivation. Gaining the support of others, whether in the field of management or coaching, is highly dependent on communication skills. Whether staff or players, communication serves as a vehicle. And a trait that tends to be common among leaders is the ability to communicate. The leader–coach sets the stage by communication. If one's leadership style is open, straightforward, information-seeking, and encourages feedback, this will strongly influence the organization to take on these characteristics. Leadership and communication are both forms of behavior As outlets of behavior, they will be characterized by the same traits that are dominant in an individual's personality.

THE COMMUNICATION PROCESS

A communication situation involves the production of a *message* by someone, a *sender–source* or one sometimes referred to as the communicator, and the receipt of that message by someone, a *receiver–interpreter,* sometimes also referred to as a communicator.

One- and Two-Way Communication

In simplistic terms the three basic elements in the communication process are the sender (S) who transmits a message (M) through a channel to the receiver (R) who interprets the message, as is illustrated in Figure 6-1*a*. At times this one-way process is illustrated by a straight line S-M-R, or S-M-C-R; S-M-R infers that a channel must be utilized to transmit the message, and S-M-C-R includes the channel (C) in the formula. However, this straight-line oversimplication or half-cycle, one-way process is incomplete since there is no feedback from the receiver to the sender. Effective communication is normally a two-way process, as illustrated in Figures 6-1*b* and 6-2, because the receiver's feedback must reach the sender to finish the communication process, to let the sender know that the original message was interpreted and the receiver has reactions. In the feedback cycle the process is reversed; thus the receiver becomes the sender, and vice versa, so that both are referred to as the communicator.

Encoding-Decoding Processes

Figure 6-2 illustrates the two-way circular communication process in which the source–sender communicator encodes the original message into the actual message being sent, which the receiver–interpreter communicator decodes. When the receiver sends feedback, he or she has now become the sender, and the original communicator becomes the receiver. Therefore, the encoding and decoding processes exist within *both* communicators.

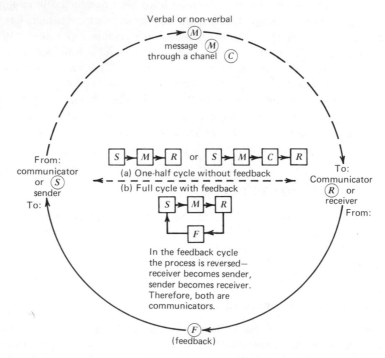

Figure 6-1. (*a*) One-to-one linear communication *without* feedback, and (*b*) effective communications: a two-way circular process.

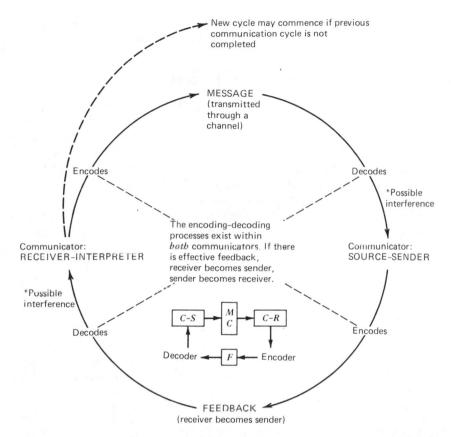

Figure 6-2. Since encoding and decoding processes exist within *both* communicators, interferences frequently lead to a "communication gap."

Most models of the communication process are "idealized" in that they assert what communication "should be" and "would be" if all variables are operating simultaneously. The primary value of an idealized model is as an illustration of the dynamics of the communication process, while permitting a discussion and a visual examination of the relationships among variables in the process. However, ineffective communication is prevalent, usually as the result of internal and/or external interferences, which can cause a breakdown in the ongoing process. As illustrated in Figure 6-2, possible interference can occur in the first half of the cycle, so that the interpreter does not even receive the actual message from the source as the sender intended; or possible interference can occur in the feedback phase of the communication cycle. Also, as is illustrated in Figure 6-2, if the original message is not complete, a new cycle may commence. Specific reasons why ineffective communication occurs will be discussed shortly, although it will be better understood if we first look more closely at the components of the communication process.

Components of the Communication Process

While the source and receiver are discussed separately for analytical purposes, and it appears in illustrated models as if there is a beginning and an end of communication, source to receiver, this is not the case since both are communicators, encoding and decoding throughout the circular communication process (Figure 6-2). A necessary condition for human communication is an interdependent relationship between source and receiver. Each affects the other. Source and receiver are dyadic concepts, each requires the other for effective communication.

When two people interact, they put themselves into each other's shoes, try to perceive the world as the other person perceives it, try to predict how the other will respond. The goal of interaction is the merger of self and other, a complete ability to anticipate, predict, and behave in accordance with the joint needs of self and other. Interaction may be defined as the ideal of communication—the goal of human communication. All communication is not interactional since much of our social behavior involves attempts to find substitutes for interaction.

We can communicate without interacting to an appreciable extent. However, to the extent that we are in an interactional situation, our effectiveness, our ability to affect and be affected by others, increases. As interaction develops, expectations become perfectly interdependent. The concepts of source and receiver as separate entities become meaningless, and the concept of the process becomes more clear.

THE SOURCE–SENDER COMMUNICATOR

For effective communication, four factors must be taken into consideration within the source, the encoder of the original message. They are one's communication skills, attitudes, knowledge level, and position within one's sociocultural system.

Communication Skills

There are five verbal communication skills. Writing and speaking are encoding skills; reading and listening are decoding skills. The fifth is critical to both encoding and decoding: *thought* is involved in purpose itself. Obviously there are other encoding skills such as diagramming (drawing) and gesturing (hand signals), which a coach utilizes, but what is said about writing and speaking can also pertain to the other encoding skills as well.

As source–encoder, a person's level of communications skill affects one's ability to analyze one's own purposes and intentions as well as one's ability to encode messages that express what one intends. Examples would be a coach's use of vocabulary, symbols, and gestures to express his thoughts, meaning, and intent; how a coach arranges words so his intended meaning is clear; how he pronounces words; and how he encodes messages that have a good chance of being decoded accurately.

An Illustration. The observations of a junior high school teacher–coach working with inexperienced students on the flying rings in a physical education class will illustrate a number of points from a negative standpoint where the communicator's intent and meaning were not clearly expressed through his message to a gymnast. The instructor's encoded message was not decoded and received by the youngster as intended by the encoder.

The instructor was standing in a position at the side of the mats, perpendicular to the "flying" path of a seventh grader, so that he could properly observe, "spot," and instruct the student. The inexperienced student's in-flight path was forward, approaching the instructor's lateral position. As the young boy's feet touched the mat, he was running in order to pump and pick up more speed to get a higher arc on the flying rings. As the student ran through and was abreast of the instructor, in a low voice, the instructor said, "OK, you can come down now." To the instructor this meant, "Stop pumping your feet on the forward run through and start dragging your feet on the mat as you descend, until you stop and dismount from the rings." The inexperienced seventh grader decoded the instructor's message differently. He let go of the rings at a height of more than 12 to 15 feet above the gymnasium floor! The young student sustained a double compound fracture of the arm and was fortunate not to have suffered more serious injuries. This true story illustrates a lack of communication skills by both the source and the receiver.

Attitudes

The source's (and receiver's) attitudes are a second factor. The attitudes of a communication source affect the ways the person communicates. Unfortunately, the word "attitude" is not easy to define, although a simplistic explanation may be that one's attitude is one's disposition or manner with regard to a person or thing. While social scientists have considerable difficulty in determining what they mean by "attitude," nonetheless, a person's attitudes are important factors, whether one is encoding or decoding in the communication process.

The attitude or self-image one has *toward* or *of oneself*, whether favorable or unfavorable, is most important. The whole complex of variables that go together to comprise the individual's personality is related to the concept of self-attitude in communication.

The attitude the sender has *toward the receiver*, the other person in the communication process, is equally important. We like some people; we may not like others; or we may even dislike them. Once again, one's *attitude* may be favorable or unfavorable toward the other person.

Whether one's attitude is favorable or unfavorable *toward his subject matter* is revealed by the writer–speaker–source, and also by the reader–listener–receiver. Some topics we prefer communicating about because they are enjoyable and bring satisfaction; other topics we would rather not discuss. We may be compelled on occasion to engage in less enjoyable topics, although we may not feel favorably toward communicating about such subject matters or the consequences of our actions. In many acts of communication we are constrained to express a point of view that will give rise to conflict. Such statements are not always easy to make. It is a well-known fact that negative feelings are less readily expressed in face-to-face communication than are positive feelings. Also, it is recognized that many people commonly bias their public remarks in a positive direction in comparison to their private and personal evaluations, which may be very different.

Illustrations. One's attitude toward oneself, and others, is likely to be expressed favorably when your athletes give near-perfect performances, such as establishing a new swimming or track record, scoring the winning point or match in tennis or basketball, scoring on a perfectly executed punt return in football or a squeeze play in baseball, having an undefeated season, and being selected "Coach-of-the-Year" in the sport you coach. Attitudes are likely to be expressed unfavorably when your team loses a game that it was expected to win, when you must reprimand an athlete for breaking training rules, when you must respond to an irate parent of a student–athlete, when your quarterback throws an interception that results in a touchdown for the opposition, when your pitcher walks in the winning run in baseball, when a double fault gives your opposition the point-game-match in tennis. A person's attitude is an important factor in the communication process.

Knowledge Level

It is obvious that the quantity and quality of knowledge a source has about his subject will affect his message. One cannot communicate what one does not know, or communicate with optimal effectiveness content material that one does not understand.

Illustrations. If a football coach who has played the pro set in college and possibly in the professional ranks decides to teach the veer offense in his first high school coaching assignment, his knowledge of the subject probably will be suspect. The same would be true of the basketball coach who attempts to teach the fastbreak offense, but lacks players with the height to get the ball off the defensive board and lacks the guards who must possess quickness.

Conversely, a coach can have too much technical knowledge of a subject if the squad members are unable to comprehend fully what the coach is trying to teach. A simple illustration would be a coach who attempts to teach multiple defensive and offensive patterns without first determining whether the athletes comprehend the fundamental skills of the sport. One's knowledge of communication affects one's communication behavior whether one is the source or the receiver.

Sociocultural System

No source or receiver communicates as a free agent; one is always influenced by the position one holds in a sociocultural system. Limiting our discussion to the source, although the information is equally applicable to the receiver, it is important to know the cultural context in which the coach or athlete communicates, the cultural beliefs and values that are dominant for those involved, the forms of behavior deemed acceptable or unacceptable, in short, the operating philosophy. To use the current jargon, all these have a bearing on "where the coach or athlete is coming from" when he or she communicates.

People in different social classes communicate differently, just as people from different cultural backgrounds communicate differently. Social and cultural systems partly determine the word choices that people make, the purposes they have for communicating, the meanings they attach to certain words, their choice of receivers, the channels they use for this or that kind of message, all of which are influenced by a source's position in a sociocultural system.

Illustrations. Whether a coach is experienced or inexperienced, whether he is young in years or an older coach, whether he has a winning record or a losing one, whether he is a head coach or an assistant coach, the type of sport and the level of competition engaged in, whether the coach is respected, admired, and liked or not respected and disliked—all these factors relate to the sociocultural system and to a coach's (sender's) communication effectiveness.

Los Angeles Dodger captain and second baseman, Davey Lopes, maintains the prerequisite for effective communication is an in-depth knowledge of the persons one means to communicate with. Oates (1978) quoted Lopes as saying, "It's difficult to reach anyone unless you know his personality. You have to know what upsets him, you have to know his moods. Then you'll know why he does certain things. I think this is the whole key to being a successful baseball manager. There's a whole lot of talk about communication, but players today are from so many ethnic backgrounds that if you don't know who they are, you can't talk to them."

Although the next logical step in the communication-process model after the source–encoder is the message and the channel of communication, since there are similarities in the presentation and context of material between the source and the receiver, the receiver will be discussed next.

THE RECEIVER—INTERPRETER COMMUNICATOR

Much of what we have discussed about the source–encoder is also applicable to the receiver–decoder of the original message. The individuals at both ends of the communication process are quite similar; and when one engages in intrapersonal communication, the source and the receiver are the same person. He who is a source one moment has been a receiver. The messages one produces are determined by the messages one has received, since forces impose on one prior to the moment of encoding. The same is so for the receiver, as this person, too, can be looked on as a source. During a given communication situation, one often behaves as both a source and a receiver. Certainly, a person will perform source behaviors in the future, which will be affected more or less by the messages sent to the individual as a receiver.

Communication Skills

To communicate effectively, the receiver is the most important link in the communication process. When we write or speak, it is the reader or listener who is our focal point. This concern with the receiver is a guiding principle for any communication process. When the encoder makes any decisions with respect to the communication, he or she must always keep the decoder in mind. If the receiver does not have the ability to listen, to read, to think, this person will be unable to receive and decode messages that the source–encoder has transmitted.

An Illustration. The instructor/gymnast in the anecdote above illustrates all of these points—namely, to communicate effectively the receiver is the most important link in the process. While a typical reaction may be, "Anyone with common sense would know not to let go of the rings in mid-air," or "The young student should have known what the instructor meant," the fact of the matter is that from what actually occurred the gymnast (receiver) did not have the ability to listen, to think, to receive, and to decode the source's (coach's) message as the sender intended. Others may say that the youngster decoded the sender's message just as it was transmitted, although the feedback the instructor received was certainly not what he had intended.

Other Communication Factors

The other communication factors—attitudes, knowledge level, and sociocultural system—are the same for the receiver as for the source. What has been presented and discussed for the source is also applicable for the receiver.

When the source (coach) chooses a code for his message, he must choose one that is known to the receiver (athlete). When the source selects content in order to convey his purpose and intent, he selects content that will be meaningful to his receiver. When he treats the message in a specific way, part of his treatment is determined by his analysis of the receiver's communication (decoding) skills, attitude, knowledge, and place in a sociocultural context. Clearly, the source "targets" a message to a particular receiver.

Interdependence and Relationships

Both communicators can be analyzed in terms of their communication skills, attitudes, knowledge levels, cultural contexts, and their place in multiple social systems. What may not be apparent is the interdependence of the source and receiver in such an analysis. Many of the key determinants of communication involve the relationships between source and receiver characteristics. A great portion of communication theory must be *dyadic* in nature; that is, it must emphasize relationships and deemphasize one-person characteristics. Our discussion and analysis must be phrased in terms of the relationships between communication components, rather than in terms of the values of a particular component for a given person. This is not to say that individual characteristics are not important, they are, but usually in the context of their relationship to other factors with which they operate conjunctively.

THE MESSAGE

The message is the actual product of the source–encoder. When a person speaks, one's speech is the message; when one writes, the writing is one's message. When one gestures, the movements of one's head, body, extremities, the expression on one's face, are the message. When one diagrams (offensive and defensive patterns), the graphic illustrations are one's message.

Message Factors

At least three factors need to be taken into account in the message: the message code, its content, and the treatment. Each factor has elements, and these elements have different structures. When one learns to distinguish and to name objects, one isolates units and labels them as object *elements*. Then, when one puts these units together in some way, he or she places them in a structure. While it is debatable which is more important in communication, having good ideas or elements, or having good organization or structure, you cannot have one without the other or neither can exist. Also, there is no fixed unit to which one can refer at all times as an element, and no fixed sequencing of units to which one can refer at all times as a structure. What we look on as elements and structure will depend on our purpose and our level of analysis. Let us look at the three elements of interest—message code, content, and treatment—each of which includes elements and structure.

Message Code

A code is a system of signals for communication; a system of words or other symbols arbitrarily used to represent words. Languages are codes. The English language is a code: it contains elements (sounds, letters, words) that are arranged in certain meaningful orders. Anything is a code (music, dancing, painting) that has a group of elements (a vocabulary) and a set of procedures for combining these elements meaningfully (a syntax). *Dactylology* is the art of communicating ideas by using finger gestures, as in a manual alphabet used by the deaf. American sign language, known as Amesian, is a code. Different ''wig-wag'' (hand signal) systems are used extensively by players, coaches, and officials in present-day athletics.

In producing or receiving messages, we require the use of a code. It produces a message, we encode it; we choose symbols and arrange them in a systematic way. Whenever we encode a message, we must decide which code, what elements of the code we will select. In receiving a message, we decode it. We try to translate this code into our own words in a way that is meaningful to us.

Illustrations. Most everyone is familiar with the more common signals used by game officials: in baseball signals for balls and strikes, safe or out; touchdown, safety, personal foul, illegal motion in football; charging, blocking, and a technical foul in basketball.

We are also familiar with coaches using hand signals in baseball to indicate tactics and strategy, such as pitch out, walk, pick-off, take a pitch, bunt, hit away, hit-and-run, or a catcher's hand signals indicating the type of pitch. Also, in football and other sports a hand signal system is frequently utilized to encode the content, treatment, and transmission of messages.

Message Content

Briefly, *content* may be defined as the material in the message that is selected by the source (coach) to express his or her purpose. It includes the assertions, judgments, and information which one presents. Without going into further communication semantics, it is enough to state that content, like code, has both elements and structure, but for our purpose no further discussion is necessary as our example will illustrate these points.

An Illustration. By utilizing a series of hand signals from the sidelines, a coach can communicate and transmit offensive plays, including the offensive formation and the starting count, such as: ''I'' right (formation), 38 pass (play action pass off a running play fake), ''on three.'' In using this type of system, the quarterback need *not* determine when to use his repertoire of offensive plays, since the decision is made by the coach in the scouting booth or on the sidelines. All the quarterback need do is ''read'' the hand signals from the sidelines and match up each series with a specific play he has been taught for that game. In this situation the signals are codes because they are structured in ways meaningful only to a specific team's quarterback and several coaches. The method of structuring the message and the treatment and channeling of the message content will be illustrated next.

Message Treatment

The *treatment* of a message may be defined as the decisions the communication source (coach) makes in selecting both codes and content. In the normal course of events where the source encodes his or her message by speaking or writing, as compared to utilizing sign language (wig-wag system), the personality and other individual characteristics of the source determine the treatment he or she will give to the message. In other words, each of us has a particular style of speaking and writing: specific encoding patterns. Each person arranges message elements in certain ways and not in others. One's communication skills, attitudes, knowledge, culture, and position in social systems dictate certain choices on the part of the sender, as well as on the part of the receiver. Since we have already discussed these, let us look at an illustration where code, content, treatment, and the channel of communicating the message are combined.

An Illustration. By a series of hand and foot signals a coach on the sidelines in football can indicate to a designated defensive player various alignments, stunts, and pass coverages, such as "52, Blitz, Red." The defender (receiver) in turn conveys the information to his teammates. By the positioning of his feet or by touching various parts of his lower extremities, a coach can indicate the desired defensive alignment, which might include two dozen or more stunts for the down linemen; by touching his body above the waist, dividing his torso in thirds, he can signal various movements to linebackers and/or safeties, when they are involved in the coordinated defensive stunts; and by hand and fist signals indicating motion away from or toward his body, up or down, and in other ways, the sideline signal flasher can encode messages that signify pass coverages, each of which correlates with specific defensive alignments and stunts.

The neck, ears, face, head, and other parts of the coach's anatomy may be touched to wig-wag a coded message from the sidelines. It is not unusual for the coach on the sidelines who is flashing signals to have a repertoire of 50 different ones per week. At the major college and professional levels of competition the signals change every week, and the encoded messages and signals are taught only to several defensive players, one of whom reads the signal flashed to him in the defensive huddle. He encodes the message in the huddle, informing his teammates of the defensive alignment, stunts, and coverage.

To acknowledge (feedback) to the flasher that he has received the sideline signals, the defensive signal caller may touch his chin quickly with his fingers as he stands in the defensive huddle. If he does not read or understand the signal, he may indicate such by tugging his face mask quickly. The sideline signal flasher will then give him his signals again.

THE CHANNEL

A *channel* may be defined as a means of access; a course into which something may be directed; a route through which anything passes or progresses. While the word is used to mean many different things, in communication theory it is applicable to modes of encoding and decoding messages. We are referring to the five senses: sight, hearing, touch, smell and taste.

In communicating we must decide which channels we will use. What kinds of messages should be transmitted orally, such as on the practice field, in meetings, during the competition or contest? Which kinds should be transmitted visually, such as through written or typed instructions? What kinds of messages should be transmitted to athletes visually but nonverbally, through pictures or by symbols rather than words, such as offensive and defensive playbooks (without written/typed instructions or materials)? What kinds of messages should be transmitted physically, through demonstrations and touch, by having the athletes perform certain fundamentals, skills, and techniques? A source (coach) cannot discuss or make decisions about the selection of channels independently of his decision on the content of the message. The content, the code, the treatment of the message, are related to one's choice of channels. At the same time, knowledge of our receivers is related to choice of channels: can the receiver (athlete) decode better by seeing, by hearing, by touching? In the illustration where offensive and defensive signals were flashed from the sidelines, the coach's message could have been transmitted to the huddle via a substituting player each time. Finally, the source (coach) himself is related to the channels he selects. Is he a better communicator when he speaks, when he writes, when he demonstrates (or has someone demonstrate)? Is the situation such that, for whatever reasons, to utilize a particular channel and not others is more advantageous?

Utilize More Than One Channel

Experience shows that to coach effectively and for learning to take place, more than one channel will have to be utilized. A receiver is more likely to decode a message accurately if the receiver can see it and hear it at the same time. It is a well-established fact that an athlete (receiver) cannot retain as much oral information as he can visual information, other things being equal. When motor skills are being taught, oral and visual information is of little value unless the athlete can practice the skill or technique that has been explained to him or the athlete has seen demonstrated. Athletics has the primary purpose of teaching gross motor skills rather than verbal skills. Perceptual development, information feedback, and communication play important roles in the development of these physical skills.

FEEDBACK

The term *feedback* implies a point of view. One individual makes a response, performs an act. This response is perceived by a second individual and is responded to. He reacts to the original message. There must be some *response* by the receiver to the sender's message which tells the source how his or her message was received. This is known as *feedback,* which is the partial reversion of the effects of a process to its source or to a preceding stage. Effective communication takes place when the receiver interprets the sender's message the way the sender intended.

When there is intrapersonal communication, when one communicates with oneself, the messages one encodes are fed back into one's system by one's own decoder, and this is known as feedback. In interpersonal communication, if the source decodes the message that he encodes, if this message is put back into his system, this is known as feedback.

Feedback Is the Weather Vane

It has been said, "Feedback is the weather vane of a relationship!" By listening to the receiver's words and voice and by watching his or her movements, the sender can tell how effectively he or she communicated (got the message across). The receiver usually tells the sender in some way how accurately he or she received the message. This reaction of the receiver, verbal or nonverbal, is feedback. Once the sender gets the feedback, he or she can decide what the next message should contain.

Action-Reaction Interdependence

Communication often involves an action-reaction interdependence. Feedback provides the source with information concerning his success in accomplishing his objective. In doing this, it exerts control over future messages which the source encodes. One consequence of a communication response is that it serves as feedback to both the source and receiver. The action of the source affects the reaction of the receiver; the reaction of the receiver affects the subsequent reaction of the source. The source or the receiver can make use of the reactions of the other.

Reactions allow the source or receiver to check himself, to determine how well he is doing in accomplishing his purpose. Feedback also affects subsequent behavior, if the source and receiver are sensitive to it.

Communication sources and receivers are interdependent on themselves for their existence and for their feedback. They continually exert influence over themselves and others by the kinds of responses that they make to the messages they produce and receive. Clearly, person-to-person communication permits maximum feedback; all available communication channels can operate. The source has also an opportunity to change his message on the spot as the result of the feedback he or she gets.

An Illustration. An athlete indicates he or she does not understand, and if the sender (coach) is sensitive to feedback, the coach will repeat the instructions. If the coach reacts subjectively and emotionally and indicates that the athlete is stupid, lazy, or goofing off, the receiver (athlete) will react much differently to negative feedback than if the coach repeats his instructions.

If the receiver (athlete) reinforces the sender (coach) that he is a good teacher-coach, the coach may become a better teacher-coach. Any athlete or coach can testify that he or she gives a better performance when his or her audience reacts favorably, when they make responses that the coach and/or athlete can use as positive feedback.

Action-reaction relationships are significant in analyzing communications. Feedback is an important instrument of affect. The reactions of the receiver are useful to the source in analyzing his effectiveness. They also affect his subsequent behavior because they serve as consequences of his prior responses. If the feedback is rewarding, he perseveres. If it is not rewarding, he changes his message to increase the chances of being successful.

Frequently we overlook the importance of feedback. We fail to realize the extent to which we can affect the receiver's behavior and, in turn, how the sender's behavior is affected.

COACH AND ATHLETE: TECHNIQUES FOR IMPROVING COMMUNICATION

Effective communication depends on more than a knowledge of concepts, models, and the process of communication. These are not too difficult to comprehend, but the effective implementation of techniques is difficult and, most often, time-consuming. The chances for effective communication are greatly enhanced if the environment is conducive and receptive for effective communication to occur. Where there is mutual trust, respect, confidence, and cooperation between coach and athlete and members of the coaching staff, communication is usually open and effective. Before the most effective communication technique can be selected, however, it is necessary to develop a sensitivity to people, which actually depends on one's philosophy toward others and on a coach's particular leadership style. This style is dependent in turn on the coach's philosophy, a power-oriented versus achievement-oriented approach. In the former approach, a coach attempts to motivate through fear, threats, and possibly intimidation, which greatly inhibits open and effective communication, as compared to utilizing positive motivational appeal in an achievement-oriented approach.

Face-to-face communication is extremely difficult for some people. Some make it more difficult than it need be because of poor communication habits. Both sender and receiver must concentrate if as much meaning as possible is to pass between them. Each must be alert to every clue given by the other as to what he or she is trying to communicate. As we have already stated, there are numerous factors that affect the process of communication. It is customary to concentrate almost solely on words, but words are conveyors of meaning. The receivers of our words are the only ones who can attach to them the meanings they have learned in their past. Consequently, we may learn poor communication habits that result in diluted or distorted communications. Our purpose here is to discuss a half-dozen bad habits that have been gleaned from various sources. If the reader has any of these poor communication habits, he may or may not be aware of them. These bad habits can be reduced and eventually eliminated by those individuals who would like to communicate more effectively.

Verbal Crowding

When the receiver hears the beginning of what one says, assumes he knows what the other has in mind, and commences his response before the other has completed his thought, this is known as verbal crowding. It is also bad manners. By the receiver forming a hasty assumption, the latter shuts off the speaker (verbal crowding) from expressing what the speaker has in mind. Behaviorally it demonstrates an attitude, namely, lack of interest and respect for the other persons's ideas.

Impatient Listening

There are numerous books, articles, courses, and seminars on the "Psychology of Listening" and "How to be a Good Listener." If one continually interrupts another, seizes every opportunity to be the speaker, does not like to be a listener, stops listening, and turns on his own stream of words at first opportunity, he is a rude impatient listener. He or she would be an excellent candidate for one of the above-mentioned seminars or courses.

Stumping

There are various reasons for "taking the stump." It may be that one merely feels his own importance and wants to express his personal ideas, with little regard for others. Or one may have limited knowledge or not be conversant on a number of different topics; so a person "stumps" regardless of the relevancy of the topic, introducing his favorite subject or interest of the moment to cover his own inadequacies. For whatever reason, when "stumping" occurs, effective communication is minimal or it is not a two-way, complete process.

Grasshoppering

For the individual who tries to converse in meaningful dialogue, when the other party "grasshoppers" this is very annoying. It destroys continuity when meaningful conversation is occurring, and an individual interjects, "That reminds me . . . ," and off he goes on another subject. This is "grasshoppering." For some people this is compulsive, and frequently the content of "That reminds me" is trivial, gossipy, folksy, or of a "story-telling" nature.

By-Passing

Not the same as "grasshoppering," but like it in that "by-passing" moves the conversation away from its original subject. In "grasshoppering" the intent is obvious; in "by-passing" both parties discover they are *not* talking about the *same* subject, though they thought they were. When they discover they are not operating on the same wavelength, so to speak, they quickly return to points germane to the topic under discussion. By-passing can be reduced, but never completely eliminated.

Wandering-Off

Due more to lack of concentration, lack of interest, or indifference rather than to senility or mental incapability, one sometimes mentally leaves the situation. It is most obvious when one is speaking and does not complete the train of thought he or she was pursuing, such as when one is telling a joke and never delivers the punch line. The individual merely stops speaking and wanders off mentally. He does not necessarily shift to another topic, but does not complete the topic he or she started.

Another form of "wandering-off," not quite as obvious to others in a group if they are intent on carrying the conversation, is the individual who simply does not get involved in the conversation. For all practical purposes the individual is present physically, but mentally absent from the conversation. Mind-wandering would be very obvious if two people were attempting to converse, but one party did not become involved in the conversation.

Techniques for Improving Communication

In addition to eliminating the bad habits mentioned, the following techniques or methods are suggested as ways of improving communication:

- Reduce "social distance" and status awareness. ✓
- Utilize multiple channels of communication where possible. ✓
- When and where possible, eliminate interferences which disrupt or distort. ✓

- Interpersonal or one-to-one communication, face-to-face, is superior to other types in many situations.
- Utilize direct communication whenever possible. ✓
- The source or sender must accept the responsibility for the effectiveness of the communication.
- When possible, and where applicable, provide the receiver with complete details of the subject being discussed, such as who, what, when, where, why, and how.
- Simple direct language is most effective.
- Try to show the receiver the benefits in the communication.
- Learn to listen and to concentrate on what the other person is saying, and do not "listen between the words."
- Obtain feedback since it is necessary for understanding.
- Be cognizant of the effect of "body language."

If one will implement these suggestions when communicating with others, providing one is sensitive to others and their needs and the environment or climate is conducive to open communication, the potential rewards of more effective communication are unlimited.

Summary

The act of communication symbolizes the need for the individual to maintain contact with his or her environment, and for this reason alone it can be seen as supplying one of psychology's central themes. Humans interact with each other through the communication process, although understanding and being understood frequently does not occur. Yet, in coaching, no single behavior is more important than the process of communication. Communication has much to do with the structure, activity, and effectiveness of an organization and group, whether it be in government, business, industry, or athletics.

The purpose of this chapter is not only to familiarize the reader with the process of communication and to examine what causes distortions, interferences, and weak communication, but to suggest ways to communicate more effectively. In turn, this should lead to greater coaching effectiveness.

There is considerable evidence to indicate that communication breakdown frequently is a critical problem in almost every aspect of human endeavor where two or more people are involved. Sometimes when there are communication barriers or lack of communication or a breakdown in communication, someone refers to this as a "communication gap."

Effective communication depends on more than a knowledge of concepts, models, and the process of communication. These are not too difficult to comprehend, but the effective implementation of techniques is difficult and, most often, time-consiming. The chances for effective communication are greatly enhanced if the environment is conducive to effective communication. Where there is mutual trust, respect, confidence, and cooperation between coach and athlete and members of the coaching staff, communication is usually open and effective. Before the most effective communication technique can be selected, however, it is necessary to develop a sensitivity to people, which actually depends on one's philosophy toward others and on a coach's particular leadership style.

REFERENCES

Fast, Julius. *Body Language*. Philadelphia. M. Evans with J. B. Lippincott Co., 1970.

Fast, Julius. *The Body Language of Sex, Power and Aggression*. Philadelphia. M. Evans with J. B. Lippincott Co., 1977.

Henley, Nancy M. *Body Politics: Power, Sex and Non-Verbal Communication*. Englewood Cliffs, N.J. Prentice-Hall, 1977.

Looney, Douglas S. "There Ain't No More Gold in Them Thar Hills." *Sports Illustrated*. Vol. 53, No. 15, October 6, 1980, pp. 30, 35–37.

Lorey, Will. "Mutual Trust is the Key to Open Communications." *Administrative Management*. September 1977, p. 70.

Lyon, Leland P. "Psychology of Sport: Coach–Athlete Communication." *Scholastic Coach*. Vol. 43, No. 3, November 1973, pp. 72–74.

Oates, Bob. "Talk? It's Really an Issue in Sports." Quoted in *The Sacramento Bee*. April 23, 1978, p. C-1.

Tutko, Thomas. "Psychology of Sport: More of Coach–Athlete Communication." *Scholastic Coach*. Vol. 43, No. 6, February 1974, pp. 72–74.

SELECTED READINGS

Baker, Larry L. *Listening Behavior*. Englewood Cliffs, New Jersey. Prentice-Hall, 1971.

Batchelor, James, and Goethals, George. "Spatial Arrangements in Freely Formed Groups." *Sociometry*. Vol. 35, 1972, pp. 270–279.

Becvar, Raphael J. *Skills for Effective Communication: A Guide to Building Relationships*. New York. John Wiley & Sons, 1974.

Bullowa, Margaret. *Before Speech, The Beginning of Interpersonal Communication*. New York. Cambridge University Press, 1979.

Goeller, Carl. *Writing to Communicate*. New York. Mentor Executive Library, 1974.

Koehler, J. W., Anatol, K. W., and Applbaum, R. L. *Organizational Communication Behavioral Perspectives*. New York. Holt, Rinehart and Winston, 1976.

Lane, Margaret. "Are You *Really* Listening?" *Reader's Digest*. Vol. 117, No. 703, November 1980, pp. 183–184, 186, 188.

Lockhart, Aileene. "Communicating With the Learner." *Quest*. Vol. VI, May 1966, pp. 57–67.

Molloy, John T. *Dress For Success*. New York. Warner Books, Inc., 1975.

Myers, G. E., and Meyers, M. T. *The Dynamics of Human Communication*. New York. McGraw-Hill, 1973.

Patton, B. R., and Giffin, Kim. *Interpersonal Communication: Basic Text and Readings*. New York. Harper & Row, 1974.

Wagner, Hugh, and Pease, Kenneth. "The Verbal Communication of Inconsistency Between Attitudes Held and Attitudes Expressed." *Journal of Personality*. Vol. 44, March 1976, p. 1.

Wells, Theodora. *Keeping Your Cool Under Fire: Communicating Non-Defensively*. New York. McGraw-Hill, 1979.

Wilkinson, Charles. *Speaking Of: Communication*. Glenview, Ill. Scott, Foresman, 1975.

7

Developmental Psychology and Coaching Effectiveness

More than 300 years ago the poet John Milton wrote, "The childhood show the man, As morning show the day," and psychology has shown that he was, at least in part, right. Kagan and Havemann (1976) pointed out that studies of the same children from infancy to adulthood show that some of the behavior and personality traits of the adult can indeed be traced to events and influences in childhood, particularly those occurring during the first 10 years. Developmental psychology is concerned with the development of human capacities and behavior from conception through old age. This chapter provides an overview of contemporary developmental psychology and its application to coaching.

WHAT IS DEVELOPMENTAL PSYCHOLOGY?

Ausubel and Sullivan (1970) described *development* as changes that occur as a function of time. In their view, development "pre-supposes that some degree of lawful continuity prevails between successive stages of an ongoing growth process and that the priorities of prior phases contribute to the form and substance of subsequent phases. . . ."

Their definition is based on the view that development occurs partly as a result of genetically controlled structural changes occurring within the individual. On the other hand, developmental psychologists Ausubel and Sullivan recognize the role of environmental factors in determining change. The recognition of the interactive

contributions of *both* hereditary and environmental factors in determining development is the hallmark of the interactive stance that characterizes much of modern
developmental psychology. The concepts of nature (heredity) and nurture (environment) will be discussed in detail in the two chapters that follow.

Early developmental psychology focused on the biological foundation of behavior and on physical growth, and initially the field was known as *genetic* psychology. The term was abandoned for the more general term *developmental* psychology, however, since the former gave the erroneous implication that genetic
psychology was concerned only with the investigation of innate determinants of
behavior. Emphasis on time rather than on genetic constitution permitted developmental psychologists to assume that development could be a product of learning as
well as maturation. Currently the field of developmental psychology is in a state of
contention regarding how much emphasis to place on organismic and environmental
variables as determinants of development as is reflected in Kagan and Havemann's
(1976) definition of developmental psychology: "The study of the processes by
which the newborn baby acquires his patterns of overt behavior, thinking, and
problem solving and the motives, emotions, conflicts, and ways of coping with the
conflict that will go to make up his adult personality."[1]

It is important for the individual who is a coach to understand the developmental and maturational processes of a human being in order to coach effectively. It is
not unusual for most coaches to get caught up with the mystique of coaching, the
tactics and strategies of the game, and literally forget about the fact that the participants who are human beings execute the skills, techniques, tactics, and strategies of
the game. Therefore, it is important for a coach to teach and coach his or her sport
cognizant of the norms of the age group under the coach's tutelage, yet allowing for
individual differences. In addition to nature and nurture, norms and individual
differences are basic concepts in developmental psychology.

THE CONCEPT OF INDIVIDUAL DIFFERENCES

One of the most reliable conclusions that can be made regarding people is that they
display individual differences in their behavior. Just as no two sets of fingerprints
are the same, no two people have the same interests, aptitudes, ambitions, or
physical features, despite the fact that people frequently try to stereotype individuals
by body types, personalities, or other means. It is an established fact, although not
always recognized, that if a group of individuals are subjected to the same practice
conditions, influenced by the personality of the same coach, and are motivated
under the same kinds of conditions, their final performances will *not* be the same
but will differ widely.

Most developmental psychologists place strong emphasis on the individuality

---

[1]Kagan, Jerome, and Havemann, Ernest. *Psychology: An Introduction* (3rd ed.). New York: Harcourt Brace Jovanovich, 1976, pp. 451–554, 558. Reprinted by permission.

of the person, which is reflected in the concept of individual differences. Such a concept holds that individuals invariably differ from one another in the extent and manner of their growth, and developmental progress tends not to be uniform in all areas within the individual. For example, physical growth may progress at a different rate than intellectual growth.

Respect for Individual Differences Is Effective Coaching

One of the most important concepts in a coaching philosophy is the respect for individual differences. Many coaches do not fully comprehend how important and how meaningful it is to recognize truly an individual's differences. Typically most coaches will recognize and make exceptions for individual differences in the skills and techniques of their athletes, but a number of the same coaches may *not* recognize or tolerate individual differences in personality. Athletes have different backgrounds, arousal levels, and aspirations, and each reacts differently to stress and pressure. Recognizing these individual differences is an important aspect of coaching. Since coaching is "people-oriented" in that a coach deals with human beings and not "things," it is necessary to comprehend the basic nature of human behavior. Even though understanding people is central to being an effective coach, this is not an easy task, because scientific knowledge of human behavior is still very limited. Basic questions as to whether abilities and personality characteristics are inherited or developed through experience are still subject to speculation.

Many forces shape human behavior, with the result that it is difficult to isolate specific factors and determine their precise influence. Accordingly, behavioral analysis must take into consideration a wide variety of interacting variables.

Norms

Although developmental psychologists have emphasized the uniqueness of the individual, they have also been heavily committed to the discovery of general principles of development that apply to all individuals. As a result normative statements about the characteristics of particular age groups have been constructed which provide broad guidelines for coaches and others. For example, knowledge of developmental age norms related to physical and mental skills have made it possible to design instructional programs with physical and learning activities appropriate for specific age groups.

HAVIGHURST: THE DEVELOPMENTAL TASKS OF LIFE

For the past 30 years Robert J. Havighurst, Professor of Education and Human Development and a member of the Committee on Human Development at the University of Chicago, has influenced the basic concept of developmental psychology. Dr. Havighurst's *Developmental Tasks and Education,* first published in 1948 in pamphlet form, elaborated on and republished in 1952, went through 17 printings and has been translated into more than a half-dozen languages, and was recently revised and republished again in 1972. It continues to be a "classic" and one of the most widely quoted sources in the entire field of developmental psychology. Our references are to Professor Havighurst's 1972, 3rd edition.

Definition: Developmental Task

"Living is learning, and growing is learning," according to Havighurst, and one learns to walk, talk, throw a ball, and do numerous other learning tasks throughout one's life. The human being learns his way through life. Living in a modern society is a long series of tasks to learn, where learning well brings satisfaction and reward, while learning poorly brings unhappiness and social disapproval. Havighurst (1972) stated, *"A developmental task is a task which arises at or about a certain period in the life of the individual, successful achievement of which leads to his happiness and to success with later tasks, while failure leads to unhappiness in the individual, disapproval by the society and difficulty with later tasks."*

Havighurst summarized and discussed six age periods, with six to ten developmental tasks described for each period. The number of developmental tasks is somewhat arbitrary, since it depends both on the bio-social realities out of which the tasks arise and on the refinement of analysis made by Dr. Havighurst. Some of the tasks are broadly defined and could be broken down into smaller tasks. The inclusion of Havighurst's six age categories and the developmental tasks for each age period will not be listed, nor will the nature of the tasks, their biological, psychological, and cultural basis, and the educational implications be included in our discussion since this is a book-length subject in itself.

We suggest that the reader pursue this source of information further in order to comprehend more fully Havighurst's developmental tasks of life as it does have special significance and meaning for the individual who is coaching. Briefly, Havighurst's developmental task concept is a "middle ground" between two opposed theories of education: the theory of freedom, which asserts that the child will develop best if left as free as possible; and the theory of constraint which proposes that the child must learn to become a worthy, responsible adult through restraints imposed by his society. A developmental task is midway between the individual's need and a societal demand. It assumes an active learner interacting with an active social environment. Accordingly, it is a useful concept for those who would relate human development and behavior to the problems and processes of education, including coaching.

DEVELOPMENTAL TASKS IN RELATION TO COACHING

In Havighurst's paradigm of developmental tasks, most scholastic and collegiate coaches would not be overly concerned with the age extremes in the continuum, since the individual is too young in the first (birth to 6 years) and too advanced in years in the last (middle age, about 30 to 60 years) to participate in organized athletic competition, for the most part. We are cognizant of "as is" situations, however, where there are 5, 6, and 7 year old children, early childhood in Dr. Havighurst's paradigm, participating in *organized* athletic competition. *Time* (June 26, 1978) reported "six and seven-year-old girls growing up with soccer on Long Island," and *UPI* (July 5, 1978) reported, "5 Year Old Boy Sets Marathon World Record." The latter, a story from Junction City, Kansas, reported that "Bucky Cox, of Lawrence, Kan. ran the 26 mile, 385 yard course through central Kansas in 5:25.9, breaking the previous unofficial record by more than 30 minutes." It was the youngster's first marathon, and in it he set a world's record for his age group."

At the upper end of the continuum there is "masters" competition for individuals 50 years of age and older. These are individual concerns, however, and numerous factors are involved when one participates in athletic competition at a very early or an advanced stage of life.

If a child is not developmentally prepared, or an adult has aged to the point where his or her capabilities have diminished, an intensified, prolonged, training regimen under competent coaching will *not* achieve effective results. There is also the possibility that psychic damage to young athletes could be more harmful than the physical abuses they are subjected to. Psychiatrist Dr. S. Harvard Kaufman (1980) of the University of Washington decried the psychological stress to which many athletes are subjected, beginning with Little League baseball and culminating with professional athletics. Dr. Kaufman stated, "In many ways the psychic damages to athletes were more harmful than the physical abuse to which they subject themselves," referring to "exaggerated salaries paid . . . [to] young people as a result of competition in the slave market. No longer are contestants taught to think but only taught to carry out orders as pawns on a large chessboard, whether you call it a gridiron, a floor, an arena, or anything else." Dr. Kaufman continued, "Physicians are taking a greater part today in recognizing and correcting the causes of and treating physical injuries." But he notes little time has been spent on the psychic elements of sport.

Indeed, the psychological trauma exerted on youngsters by some coaches and some parents may be of more concern than the Little League elbow injury, for example.

The Individual Must Be Developmentally Prepared

When an infant is born, that child develops according to stages common to all healthy children. From primarily reflexive or physical behaviors, to perceptual-motor, cognitive, and conceptual activities, a child advances in a manner dictated by genetic factors, but influenced strongly by environmental influences. While children are naturally limited by the neurological and maturational stages of their development, this does not preclude the possibility that they can and do perform in many endeavors far exceeding typical expectations.

There is little doubt that the early years of an individual's life are formative ones. Chronological or motivational ages in the early years of a child's life cannot be precisely pinpointed with any degree of validity and reliability for the learning of athletic skills. Research supports the contention that most children are not able to perform activities requiring good coordination of the whole body before the age of 7 or 8 years, and introducing them too early to such activities only results in unskillful performance or failure. This does not preclude the teacher–coach who can simplify and modify sport skills for the appropriate age of the child so that he or she can perform skillfully and achieve success.

LEARNING AND MATURATION

An individual in the coaching profession must be aware of how maturation and learning occur. Throughout, it will be helpful to bear in mind that the two sets of processes that jointly account for development are learning and maturation. For better comprehension, these terms need to be defined.

Learning

Since the psychology of learning and performance is discussed in Chapter 10, here the subject is treated minimally. According to McNeil and Rubin (1977), "Learning, refers to relatively enduring changes in behavior that take place as the result of experience. Clearly, learning takes place throughout life, in the home, at school, on the job and in most other places as well."

Kagan and Havemann (1976) defined *learning* as, "The process by which overt behavior and covert behavior become altered or attached to new stimuli."

Therefore, it could be concluded that learning is the modification of behavior through practice, training, or experience.

Maturation

According to psychologists McNeil and Rubin (1977), "Maturation, in contrast, refers to changes that take place without any specific experience or practice. . . . Whereas learning reflects the impact of the environment on behavior, maturation reflects the unflooding of inherited biological patterns that are 'programmed' into the individual."

For example, parents and others may not want a child to crawl and will attempt to "teach" the child to walk at a young age. Typically children begin to crawl when they are about 10 months old, and they begin to walk at about 15 months old. These are time guides that occur typically in many children even if they are not given any special training or reinforcement for these accomplishments. A child cannot be taught to walk until he or she is "ready" (maturation) to do so. At this stage of development the child "learns" to walk because of the biological patterns that are programmed into the child, not because of past experience. Parents and others often get the terms learning and maturation confused. Frequently it is the adult who is reinforced, not the child, when the child performs a task or skill successfully, because of the adult's maturation.

Maturational Trends. There are at least four maturational trends that occur in human development.

> *Cephalocaudal sequence* refers to the progression of the infant's development from head (cephalo) to foot (caudal means tail). The head is most rapid in growth rate, followed by the trunk, and then by the legs. Behavioral development also follows this course.

> *Proximal-distal* sequence refers to the progression of growth from the central parts (proximal means center) of the body, such as the trunk and shoulders, to the extremities (distal, i.e., to the arms and legs, and then to the fingers and toes). In practical terms, a child must crawl before it can walk.

> *Differentiation* refers to the gradual refinement of behavior as growth progresses. The process of differentiation moves from an all-inclusive body reaction to behavior that is narrowly focused toward some goal.

> *Integration* occurs after a baby reaches a certain stage of differentiation, and one begins to notice the many focused responses that are pulled together into larger integrated behavior patterns.

The concepts of differentiation and integration do not relate specifically to physical growth. They are also applicable to the development of intelligence, emotional control, and social maturation over the full range of the life cycle.

While even a brief discussion of maturational trends may not be of interest to some coaches, prospective or experienced, all coaches would benefit from studying and comprehending fully such information regardless of the coaching level of competition. In addition, every coach will benefit immeasurably from studying other sources delineating the physiological, psychological, and sociological characteristics and needs of the individuals of the group he or she coaches. As a result a coach will better understand the behavior patterns and be able to fulfill the needs of the athletes he or she is teaching–coaching.

Havighurst (1972), and others, have categorized the developmental tasks of adolescence from approximately 12 to 18 years of age. One will readily conclude from studying and comparing teenage characteristics of those individuals in grades 9–10 (early to mid-teen years) and those in grades 11–12 (mid-teen to late-teen years) that the differences in characteristics and needs are both obvious and significant. To fulfill their needs, including motivation, and to teach–coach more effectively, a coach must understand the physiological, psychological, and sociological characteristics of athletes at all ages with whom he or she works; the coach must learn to recognize the differences in physical capacities and abilities and provide programs accordingly. The failure to do so generally results in ineffective teaching–coaching.

ATHLETIC COMPETITION AND THE DEVELOPMENTAL GROWTH PATTERN

A basic educational principle is that all programs and activities should fit the individual at each stage of his or her growth level. The intensity and degree of athletic competition to which the participant is exposed should reflect a developmental and sequential pattern. Athletic competition for participants in the early years of their childhood should be of a very low intensity and then gradually be increased through the years as the child becomes older and more mature.

A student's age is the worst possible measure of physical maturity, because of the widely varying adolescent development stages. Yet most high schools traditionally group athletes by age. The result is a high-school athletic injury rate that is very high. Illustrating this point, Gomolak (1975) quoted J. Kenneth Hafner, director of field services for the New York Public High School Athletic Association, as stating: "At 13, boys can vary physically from 90 pounds of baby fat and peach fuzz to 225 pounds of muscle and mustache. To match such opposites in a competitive sport is begging for injury. But by matching the big-youngster-regardless of age, against athletes of similar maturity and skill, injuries are reduced while competition improves."

Understanding the Individual

Despite the fact that much emphasis is placed by most coaches of team sports on group cooperation and cohesiveness, every successful coach recognizes that a team is made up of a group of individuals. At times it may be overlooked or perhaps forgotten that every individual brings to the team or group numerous qualitative and quantitative differences. The physical differences of height, weight, quickness, speed, motor skills, and intelligence are readily recognized and easily measurable. The qualitative differences, such as methods of practice and contest performance, can be evaluated fairly accurately, too. Frequently overlooked, however, is the necessity of assessing aptitudes and special interests of the players who make up the team. Both types of individual differences cause players to vary in their style and degree and intensity of performance, because no two individuals are exactly the same. Successful effective coaching takes into account the individual differences of all players and instills in them the team concept of cooperation, cohesiveness, and unity. This is not an easy task for a coach and is a good indication of his or her skills in the "art" of coaching.

Physiological and Psychological Changes

Although coaches at every level of competition have some common problems with which they must deal, coaches who work with teenagers have additional and different kinds of problems to try to comprehend and resolve since numerous physiological and psychological changes occur in each individual during the adolescent years. To achieve success, the scholastic coach must try to understand, motivate, and show respect and concern for teenagers and their problems, interests, anxieties, worries, and points of view, and be knowledgeable of their physical capabilities and mental characteristics. A teenager, while not a child and not yet an adult, frequently displays childish and immature behavior, but usually wants and expects to be treated as an adult. Many coaches have ambivalent attitudes toward some teenagers because of their wide range of behavior patterns. In regard to sports, while teenagers may want to participate earnestly in athletics, and they may or may not be concerned about winning or losing, depending on the individual, athletics for most are "just a game" and not a "matter of life or death." While they may experience and display frustration, anger, and disappointment in losing or joy, satisfaction, and personal fulfillment in winning, usually it is only for a relatively short period of time, since there are other interests, concerns, and events requiring their attention. Many coaches have difficulty comprehending this point of view since they feel the athlete is not interested or lacks total dedication if he or she does not display the same intensity for winning and achieving success that the coach possesses. For the coach whose job is on the line as the result of losing, his or her perspective is entirely different from the player's, and frequently the result is anger, frustration, hostility, and perhaps even a display of socially unacceptable behavior. Coaches should remember that teenage athletes are unpredictable and that they will undoubtedly display other concerns and interests. Collegiate and professional coaches do not have the same problems as those who coach teenagers, since their players for the most part are in their adult years. However, there are rewards and satisfactions to be derived from coaching scholastic athletics that are not present at the other levels of competition.

FEMALE ATHLETES ARE TRANSFORMING AMERICAN SPORTS

The participation of the emergent female athlete deserves special reference here, not because she is inferior or different, but because much of what once was thought to be factual has been found to be groundless and erroneous in many instances, especially in reference to females participating in sports. It is most important for the male who may be coaching female athletes to understand physiological and psychological differences based on fact rather than on traditional and stereotyped role expectations of the female athlete and her performance. The coach should not perpetuate the half-truths and myths that may surround the female athlete and her participation in sports. Of course, it is equally important that the individual who coaches male or female athletes be selected on the basis of teaching–coaching competencies and skills and not on the basis of their sex.

In a *Time* (June 26, 1978) cover story, "Comes the Revolution," staff sportswriter B. J. Phillips in her outstanding article on women in sports stated, "Joining the game at last, women are transforming American athletics." Phillips supported her contention by citing specific cases of outstanding athletic feats by female athletes as well as other recent research findings. While it is beyond the scope of this text to include compilations of statistics and research supporting the rapid gains and accomplishments of women in athletics, the chief catalyst that has been responsible for the explosive growth of women's sports started with Title IX legislation, which is a section of the Education Amendments Act passed by Congress in 1972 and which became mandatory by law on July 21, 1978. With the opportunity that Title IX legislation provided, there is little doubt that women are transforming athletics.

Research Results Are Positive

While there continues to be much conjecture and speculation about the long-term effects of Title IX, and the reputed inherent dangers of competitive athletics for girls and women participating, there is significant research to support the contention that, in terms of how it affects their behavior, physiology, growth, and development, sports have a positive effect on girls and women. From a purely scientific point of view, however, physicians, psychologists, physiologists, physical educators, and other researchers have not been able to provide all of the answers, and additional research is needed. The proponents and supporters of sports for girls and women are hopeful that the female athlete will derive all the numerous benefits that males have derived from their involvement in sports. It is hoped that the women's and girls' programs will avoid the mistakes and so-called "evils" that have occurred in men's and boys' athletics over the years. There is a feeling by many men and women that if the administrators and coaches of women's and girls' athletics model their program after the men's, they will not benefit from the mistakes that have been made and will fail to exploit the opportunity and capitalize on the potential that athletics holds for them.

The revolution in sports for the female athlete is running full tide, bringing with it a sea of change, not just in activities, but in attitudes as well. "The stigma is nearly erased. Sweating girls are becoming socially acceptable," stated Liz Murphy, coordinator of women's athletics at the University of Georgia (Phillips, 1978).

Let us briefly examine other attitudes pertaining to the female athlete. Not all are positive. Many still have not changed. Some are slowly changing.

Despite the fact that in the last half-dozen years or so the participation of females in sports has escalated at a tremendously rapid rate, and that many physical education activities and lifetime sports are now offered co-educationally, contact sports remain predominately single-sex and separate. Since traditionally athletics have been the domain of the male, the mass populace continues to think of highly competitive athletics in particular as masculine and what the male is supposed to represent in today's society. A major contributor to the literature on the female athlete, Professor Dorothy Harris, Pennsylvania State University, pointed out at the AAHPER Anaheim Convention and later presented in "Research Studies on the Female Athlete" (1975) that "Society continues to applaud the positive psychological and social benefits he (male) gains from participation."[2]

Stereotype Image

In speaking of the psychological demands of competitive athletic experience which are not generally compatible with society's stereotyped image of what the female should be, Dr. Harris continued, "On the other side of the picture, many believe that experience in competitive athletics brings out the undesirable behaviors in the female; indeed it appears to be to her detriment to pursue such involvement. After all, we would not want to make 'men out of little girls' like we make men out of little boys in competitive sports! Therein lies the rub!"

Dan Levin's *Sports Illustrated* (March 17, 1980) article, "There She Is—Miss What?" which dealt with women's bodybuilding, suggested that what the female participants wanted for themselves was not compatible with society's stereotyped image of what the female should be. As Levin pointed out, for some people women engaging in bodybuilding raises complex questions and strikes at deeply held values regarding society's concept of femininity, despite the fact that "femininity" may be difficult to define. The contest judges even had difficulty agreeing on the criteria for judging the female bodybuilders even though all were familiar with the well-accepted standards utilized to judge male bodybuilders. As Levin pointed out, "Women's bodybuilding has arrived—sort of. The girls know what they're doing, but many of the contest judges don't."

Snyder and Kivlin's (1975) study of women athletes, which included aspects of psychological well-being and body image, raised serious doubts about the stereotypes regarding women athletes. They concluded, "even though women athletes have frequently received negative sanctions, their participation in sports has apparently been psychologically satisfying and rewarding. Perhaps the social costs

---

[2]Harris, Dorothy V. "Research Studies of the Female Athlete." *JOHPER*, January 1975, pp. 32–36. Reprinted by permission.

of athletic participation by women today are not as great as previously, and contemporary changes in broadening of sex roles are reflected in the positive finding regarding the women athletes.''

Snyder and Kivlin, like others, also pointed out that further research on women athletes is necessary especially in a period when sex roles are changing.

Androgyny in Athletes

As a spokesperson for the female athlete and women in general, Dr. Harris queries what standard of behavior is being used to determine what is desirable. Traditionally, society has defined feminine and masculine behavior characteristics. In the sports environment, where the behavioral demands are generally the same for those who are participating regardless of sex, perhaps it would be better to look at *human* behavior in an *androgynous* (having both female and male characteristics) sense, rather than as feminine or masculine behavior.

In this text our intent is to present all of our material in this manner, so that it is applicable to the athlete and coach of either sex, and not single out and identify characteristics and behaviors as being specifically masculine or feminine.

Masculinity and femininity, as culturally defined, have been extremely resistant to change; this has been especially true when athletic competition has been concerned. As Harris (1975) pointed out, "The traditional role of the male has allowed him to determine the range of behavior he will condone as being feminine and this does not include those behaviors that appear essential for success in competitive sport. However, 'athlete' has no gender, it is not male or female, it is only a term used to describe human beings in a specific contest." Hammer (1979), "Girls In Sports, Aggressive and Feminine—Can They Be Both?," pointed out that coed sports teams at the junior level may signalize revolution in traditional notions about masculinity and feminity.

While it is apparent that the benefits of involvement in competitive athletics are human benefits and are not sex-linked, and the female athlete stands to gain as much from them as the male athlete, there are others who believe that the failure to develop a satisfactory level of the elusive aspect of masculinity will likely result in social and psychological problems. Fisher (1972) pointed out in his article, "Sports As An Agent of Masculine Orientation," that

> At a time in our society when much attention is being given to Women's Liberation, one should also realize that at the time the young males are undergoing a considerable degree of feminization. It is *imperative* that the masculine concepts of certain sports be retained. The degree of importance of athletic competence is that it helps form the foundation of an adequate assumption of the male role. Something as important as the masculine concept of *certain* sports should not be permitted to go out of existence. Male

children, both present and future, cannot afford to be deprived of yet another factor which influences masculine orientation.[3]

FACTORS TO CONSIDER IN COACHING THE FEMALE ATHLETE

The individual who is a coach must be aware of the research that supports the difference between the male and female athlete in body type, physiological and metabolical factors, and developmental and environmental factors. While there are physiological, psychological, morphological, and metabolical differences, it has been found these differences between men and women are not as diverse as they were once postulated to be. The female athlete is likely to derive the same benefits from sports participation as the male athlete, provided that she too is subjected to a sound rational conditioning and training program and that competition is based on sound judgment.

[handwritten margin note: lit. used to speak of definite differences to coaching]

Do Not Compare Male and Female Performances

Because of biological differences between the male and female, in events involving strength and power most women are incapable of equaling the performance of men. While women can hold their own and excel men in some athletic activities, women's achievements in sports should not be compared to those of the men. In many competitive athletic events, especially if they involve strength and power, women should not be matched to compete against men. In male–female team competition, in order to make the sports experience meaningful, care should be exercised to equalize the teams.

Capabilities of the Female Athlete. Dr. Jack Wilmore, past president of the American College of Sports Medicine, and a long-time investigator of women's physical abilities, has concluded that the physical differences between males and females may be more an artifact of social or cultural restrictions imposed on the female than a result of true biological differences between the sexes. Factually, boys and girls are equally matched in physical abilities up to 10 or 12 years of age. However, through the teens the male becomes considerably stronger and faster while the average female's physical performance declines. The main cause of her decline is simple, Wilmore believes. "Just about the time she starts to menstruate, she learns she must stop climbing trees and start acting like a 'little lady.' As a result, her physical abilities never get a chance to develop" (Katz, 1976).

In one study, Wilmore placed a group of untrained college-age women and men on a 10-week weight-lifting program. He found that the women gained only

---

[3]Fisher, A. Craig. "Sports As An Agent of Masculine Orientation." *The Physical Educator*, Vol. 28, 1972, pp. 96–98. Reprinted by permission.

slightly more leg strength than the men, but they increased their arm and shoulder strength significantly. And while the men's initial upper body strength was about 100 percent greater than the women's, the men's leg strength was only about 25 percent greater. When Wilmore related these values to body weight, the men's leg strength was only about 7 percent greater. Wilmore called this finding "revolutionary." He said, "We've always been told that women are so much weaker than men. Here it turns out that they have almost exactly the same leg strength. This makes sense because women use their legs in everyday life much as men do, walking and climbing stairs, for example, but they don't their upper bodies nearly as much."

Wilmore stated (Katz, 1976),

> Such studies, and others on women's endurance potential and body composition, suggest that biological differences are not the sole reason for the vastly different performance levels of men and women. What we've done in the past is to compare relatively sedentary women with relatively active men, simply because of the different kinds of lives men and women tend to lead. When we look at people who've kept themselves conditioned throughout life, the differences aren't nearly that great.[4]

Dr. Allan J. Ryan, editor-in-chief of *The Physician and Sportsmedicine* (1977), concurs, quoting from a study of 63 female volunteers from high schools who took part in the demanding and vigorous physical exercises for entrance into the military academies. Ryan stated, "Only three failed the exacting military academy physical examination and only two had to drop out during the initial testing. The results of the study indicate that women are capable of undertaking the demanding plebe physical training at the academy, and the investigators concluded that 'women are far better performers than the literature suggest!'" Dr. Ryan concluded, "Those of us who have followed women athletes over the years when they were much less numerous and visible in the United States, but much more in evidence abroad, have always known this."

Fear of Injury

The fear that female athletes are more likely to be injured in sports than males is not supported by evidence. In a survey conducted by the Committee on the Medical Aspects of Sports, of the American Medical Association, the fear of injury to the female athlete was found to be baseless. More and more studies are showing that women were indeed created for vigorous activity. Dr. Christine E. Haycock (1979), associate professor of surgery at the New Jersey Medical School pointed out, "The

---

[4]Katz, Barbara J. "Female Doesn't Mean Inferior." *National Observer,* July 13, 1976, p. 16. Reprinted by permission of the *National Observer*. Copyright © Dow Jones & Company, Inc., 1976. All rights reserved.

reason women athletes sustained more injuries than men in the past was due to poor coaching, improper training and inadequate equipment. Now injuries are decreasing to levels comparable to men's.''

Physiologically female and male athletes react the same to training from a technique standpoint. The differences are basically those of degree and intensity of the training, not in technique. Coaching any athlete, male or female, is probably best done on an individual basis, taking into consideration the ability and potential of each person. We are beginning to realize that a person's apparent masculinity-femininity is far more important than sex in affecting how he or she is perceived regarding athletic competition.

Sports Competition Is Beneficial

From a physiological standpoint, research indicates that sports competition for the female athlete is not detrimental to her health or well-being—nor does it have a harmful effect on the normal functioning of her reproductive system, nor does it cause menstrual problems. To the contrary, it has been found that through participation in athletic activity reproductive processes are enhanced.

Sports Do Not Masculinize Female Participants

Cultural beliefs and social influences, although not as prevalent and restrictive as they were prior to the passage of Title IX, probably have been responsible for much of the negative appraisal of women in sports and many of the half-truths and myths surrounding women's sports. That sports will masculinize women participants is an unfounded myth that still prevails, since the female athlete for the most part does not engage in high-resistance training programs contrary to the previously cited article on women's bodybuilding (Levin, 1980). While there may be some fear that women athletes will be masculinized by developing bulky muscles if they exercise too much, researchers have found that women, unlike men, can substantially increase their strength with almost imperceptible increases in muscle size. Male hormones are primarily responsible for the development of bulging muscles and, while women possess male hormones, research shows that most females have only small amounts in their bodies. Therefore, the hormones that make a male a male and a female a female determine the degree of muscle mass. Physical activity cannot change a person's inherent capacity for muscle development.

Summary

It is important for the individual who is a coach to understand the developmental and maturational processes of a human being in order to coach effectively. Most developmental psychologists place strong emphasis on the individuality of the person, which is reflected in the concept of individual differences. Many forces shape human behavior, with the result that it is difficult to isolate specific factors and determine their precise influence. Understanding the physiological differences in athletes is paramount if a coach is to succeed in his or her chosen profession. This phase of coaching must receive a major consideration in training the athlete for competition. Since *athlete* has no gender, training must be geared to the individual characteristics and maturational factors, regardless of sex.

The benefits and pleasures derived from competitive experiences should be shared by both male and female athletes. It is not important that females equal male records. It is important that they reach their own potential, make and break their own records, and have a significant experience in athletic competition.

REFERENCES

Ausubel, D. P., and Sullivan, E. V. *Theory and Problems of Child Development* (2nd ed.). New York. Grove & Stratton, 1970, p. 3.

Fisher, A. Craig. "Sports as an Agent of Masculine Orientation." *The Physical Educator*. Vol. 28, 1972, pp. 96–98.

Gomolak, Charlotte. "Problems in Matching Young Athletes: Baby Fat, Peach Fuzz, Muscles and Mustache." *The Physician and Sportsmedicine*. Vol. 3, No. 5, May 1975, pp. 96–98.

Hammer, Signe. "Girls In Sports, Aggressive and Feminine—Can They Be Both?" *Parade*. August 5, 1979, p. 7.

Harris, Dorothy V. "Research Studies of the Female Athlete." (Original Source: AAHPER Anaheim Convention.) *JOHPER*. January 1975, pp. 32–36.

Havighurst, Robert J. *Developmental Tasks and Education* (3rd ed.). New York. David McKay Company, 1972, pp. 1–2.

Haycock, Christine E. "Female Myths." *Parade*. September 30, 1979, p. 1.

Kagan, Jerome, and Havemann, Ernest. *Psychology: An Introduction*. New York. Harcourt Brace Jovanovich, 1976, pp. 451–454, 558.

Katz, Barbara J. "Female Doesn't Mean Inferior." *National Observer*. July 31, 1976, p. 16.

Levin, Dan. "There She Is—Miss What?" *Sports Illustrated*. Vol. 52, No. 12, March 17, 1980, pp. 64–68, 70, 72, 75.

McNeil, Elton, and Rubin, Zick. *The Psychology of Being Human*. New York. Harper & Row, 1977, p. 359.

Phillips, B. J. "Comes the Revolution." *Time*. Vol. III, No. 26, June 26, 1978, pp. 54–59.

Ryan, Allan J. "The Capabilities of Women." *The Physician and Sportsmedicine*. Vol. 5, No. 6, June 1977, p. 29. (Study on p. 32.)

Sacramento Bee. "The Slave Market, Sports Psychic Damage Cited." January 13, 1980, p. PC 6. (Quoting Dr. S. Harvard Kaufman.)

Snyder, Eldon E., and Kivlin, Joseph E. "Women Athletes and Aspects of Psychological Well-Being and Body Image." *Research Quarterly*. Vol. 46, No. 2, May 1975, pp. 191–199.

UPI. *Altoona Mirror*. "5 Year Old Boy Sets Marathon World Record." Altoona, PA. July 5, 1978, p. 41.

SUGGESTED READINGS

Ahlgren, A., and Johnson, D. W. "Sex Differences in Cooperative and Competitive At-titudes from the 2nd through the 12th Grades." *Developmental Psychology*, 1979, pp. 15, 45–49.

Atkins, C., Morse, C., and Zweigenhaft, R. "The Stereotype and Recognition of Female Athletes." *The Journal of Psychology*, 1978, pp. 27–31.

Bucher, Charles A. "Athletic Competition and Developmental Growth Patterns." *The Physical Educator*. Vol. 28, No. 1, March 1971, pp. 3–4.

Daniels, Jack. "Physiological Characteristics of Champion Male Athletes." *Research Quarterly*. Vol. 45, No. 4, December 1974, pp. 341–348.

Gander, Mary J. *Feminine and Masculine Role Stereotyping in Physical Education and Competitive Sports*. Produced by the University of Wisconsin Extension, 1974.

Hammer, Signe. "Girls In Sports, Aggressive and Feminine—Can They Be Both?" *Parade*. August 5, 1979, pp. 6–7.

Harris, Dorothy. "Research Studies of the Female Athlete." *JOHPER*. January 1975, pp. 32–36.

Harris, M. B., and Hall, C. "Sex Stereotypes and Rating of Athletes." *Journal of Social Psychology*, 1978, pp. 105, 151–152.

Harrison, Peggy, and Jones, Billie J. "Research and Women in Sports: Closing the Gap." *The Physical Educator*. May 1975, pp. 84–88.

Havighurst, Robert J. *Developmental Tasks and Education* (3rd ed.). New York. David McKay Company, 1972, pp. 1–116.

House, William C. "Actual and Perceived Differences in Male and Female Expectancies and Minimal Goal Levels as a Function of Competition." *Journal of Personality*. Vol. 42, September 1974, pp. 493–499.

Klafs, Carl E., and Lyon, M. Joan. *The Female Athlete: A Coach's Guide to Conditioning and Training* (2nd ed.). St. Louis. C. V. Mosby Company, 1978.

Krone, Chester. "Choosing the Right Sports for Your Child." *Woman's Day*. October 1976, pp. 26–28, 180.

Larner-Romano, Deborah, and Leavy, Jane. "The Sporting Life: Athletics and Fertility—A Medical Controversy." *MS*. Vol. VIII, No. 4, 1979.

Singer, Robert N. *Myths and Truths in Sports Psychology*. New York. Harper & Row, 1975, p. 111.

Wood, P. S. "Female Athletes: They've Come a Long Way, Baby." *Reader's Digest*. Vol. 117, No. 702, October 1980, pp. 126–130. (Condensed from *New York Times Magazine*. May 18, 1980.)

8

The Psychology of Personality: Coach and Athlete

So many approaches to personality have been advanced by psychologists, philosophers, theologians, and social commentators of other disciplines that, even if it were possible, it would be impractical to discuss all of these positions in detail. Our attempt here in a single chapter is briefly to examine a number of the various theories and approaches that psychologists have developed about personality and human behavior.

NO SINGLE UNIVERSALLY ACCEPTED THEORY OF PERSONALITY PREVAILS

The reader should understand that, since wide disagreement prevails over what forces operate to produce the elements of personality, a single theory of personality that explains human behavior to the satisfaction of all simply does *not* exist. Yet of all the areas of psychology that have been researched, no other aspect has received greater attention than that of personality. This truism applies to the field of physical education and athletics, too; much research has also been conducted pertaining to personality development and physical activity.

A survey of the literature, as reported by Cooper (1969), Husman (1969), and others, revealed traditional classifications commonly used to compare *physical activity and personality development*. Here is a partial list of some classifications.

- Recreational and intramurals versus nonrecreational participation
- Indoor versus outdoor activities
- Physical education majors versus nonmajors
- High-ability ranking in a sport versus low-ability ranking
- Individuals in a specific sport versus "normals"
- Individuals in sport A versus individuals in sport B
- High-fitness group versus low-fitness group
- High-motor ability group versus low-motor ability group
- Before contest versus after contest
- Combative sports versus noncombative sports
- Olympic and championship athletes versus lower caliber performers
- Males versus females

To illustrate further the propensity toward the study of personality, Ruffer (1975, 1976) compiled 572 sources in a five-part series in *The Physical Educator,* an original research paper on "Personality Traits of Athletes," that did *not* include any duplication of the same articles in different sources. All of which give the reader some indication that there is not a paucity of research materials on personality as a subject.

EXPECTATIONS FROM THE STUDY OF PERSONALITY

Of all the other topics in psychology, personality has always held the greatest fascination for the nonpsychologist and layperson. The typical coach is not an exception. Coaches are interested in the study of personality since it may offer some hope of interpreting the mystery of what motivates behavior, especially if that "something" is different from what a coach expects. While a coach may overtly try to better understand others, covertly he or she may be trying to better understand "self." If a person can understand himself and what motivates him, he is more likely to better understand the behavior of others.

Personality offers a system of categorizing a wide range of behaviors but, more importantly for the coach, a study of this subject involves the possibility of predicting human behavior. Personality, or at least the understanding of it, appears to be one of the keys to successful and effective coaching. Coaches can utilize their understanding of personality to motivate their athletes, to attempt to predict their successes, to alleviate frustration, to build confidence, and to try to understand others. It is not sufficient for a coach to understand only his own personality or only the personality of his outstanding performers. A coach must have a basic understanding of all individuals on the team. A coach must be aware of the numerous factors that reputedly help make up and develop one's personality. In fact, the consensus is that for one to have a successful team, a knowledge of personality, and those factors affecting personality, is a must.

Antagonistic and Irreconcilable Theories

Unfortunately many people, especially those who are looking for simplistic answers to controversial questions, are disappointed that the study of personality does not provide *the* answer. The topical subject is complicated and there are few "pat" answers since personality, as well as other highly specialized branches of psychology, is fraught with antagonistic and seemingly irreconcilable theories. Basic questions that appear to be more of a philosophical or theological nature, than of a psychological one, remain unanswered or unanswerable; yet on their answers depend other major conclusions. Nature or nurture and determinism or self-determinism suggest two such controversial issues that illustrate different antagonistic and irreconcilable theories in the field of psychology.

Depending on the intent of the individual seeking the answers, not infrequently the less serious person either is content with a superficial treatment of personality or the individual adopts a favored theory as a panacea to the exclusion of all other ideas. Or the individual may become interested solely in some favored segment of the overall field of personality, such as in personality tests. One must be cautious of adopting segments of an overall theory out of context, whether it be personality or any other specialized area in the field of psychology.

WHAT IS PERSONALITY?

Personality is a term used to characterize the *individual* that emerges as the newborn child and who grows, matures, and reacts to the thousands of environmental stimuli that surround him. Personality represents the whole self; it is like a mask in the sense that it is made up of patterns of behavior through which the individual expresses his inner interests. It is the representation of the whole individual resulting from a composite of many factors, such as physical and mental abilities, feelings, interests, attitudes, emotional make-up, and other qualities. Therefore, personality may be considered as the aggregate of all properties or qualities of an individual, both physical and psychological in nature. As such, the definition or concept of personality is much broader than the popular one often accepted by most people, who normally relate "personality" solely to the social skills of an individual. However, even this broader definition has some inadequacies, because personality is not just a composition of certain traits; it is how the individual perceives himself in terms of self-image, as well as how others perceive and are influenced by the individual. Personality, like other human characteristics, represents a unique pattern of traits and conditions that are in constant interaction.

Physical attributes are included as a part of personality because they affect psychological traits. They also influence self-image and the impression one makes on others. For example, the physical features of the attractive or handsome swimmer, or the seven-foot basketball player, male or female, certainly influence how these athletes affect others and how they view themselves.

Numerous Definitions and Theories

Numerous definitions could be cited by such well-known personality psychologists as Allport, Eysenck, Sullivan, Cattell, Hilgard, and so forth, as well as by such sport psychologists as Morgan, Martens, Landers, Singer, Tutko, and Ogilvie, since all have postulated condensed definitions of personality. However, most all psychologists have acknowledged that their definitions are incomplete. More than 40 years ago, Gordon Allport (1937) drew attention to the different meanings of personality by reporting 50 diverse definitions, including his own classic definition that *personality* is the "dynamic organization within the individual of those psychophysical systems that determine his unique adjustments to his environment." Since Allport's definition may well be the most quoted, it will suffice for our purposes here.

However, for the purposes of examining personality research, we should realize that, although there is some basic agreement on what is personality, there are almost as many definitions as there are theories. Personality then takes on flexible meanings. In actuality, we do not know for certain how personality is formed, how it works, what constitutes its components, or what determines the relationship of these components. In a sense, psychology is only concerned with the study of human *behavior;* thus one's personality may be theorized as the total pattern of one's thinking, feeling, and behavior since this pattern demonstrates one's distinctive method of adapting and relating to the environment. Figure 8-1 illustrates a conceptualization of behavior as a two-way process. An individual adjusts to his environment and, in turn, one's personality evolves as a result of this adaptation. One's personality is not static, but is in a constant state of evolution; however, at the same time, one is seeking a steady state in terms of balance with the environment. Most personality psychologists have been content with implicitly assuming that personality serves to guide and determine human behavior.

MAJOR ISSUES IN PERSONALITY STUDY

Before examining and comparing different personality theories, two major issues that are controversial and illustrate the disparities in personality theories need to be acknowledged. They are the nature-nurture debate and the determinism or self-determinism controversy.

Nature Versus Nurture

Is an individual's personality the result of heredity and what one inherits from one's parents, or is personality the result of one's upbringing and environment? There are expert theorists who cite studies supporting their contention that the major determinations of an individual's personality are to be found in a person's constitutional

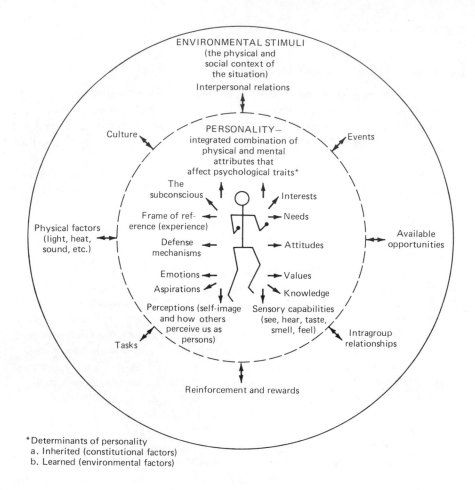

Figure 8-1. Factors affecting behavior: individual personality environmental stimuli.

make-up (nature); and other expert theorists cite studies that support their contention that upbringing (nurture) is the major determinant of an individual's personality.

Despite the research studies and theoretical constructs and their interpretations by the psychologists, the question of *which* has more influence, nature or nurture, is deceptive and probably not answerable when put into an *either-or* format. Probably a better question would be, "How do heredity and environment interact with one another to produce personality?" While the answers may not be completely definitive, we are likely to get better answers than when being forced to make the choice between nature or nurture (see Figure 8-2). However, the recent trend has been to place greater importance on the individual being a product of his environment. Sport psychologist William Morgan (1978) discussed the possibility that "athletes and coaches are victims of their circumstances and not their personalities." Fur-

Question: "How do heredity and environment interact with one another to produce personality?"

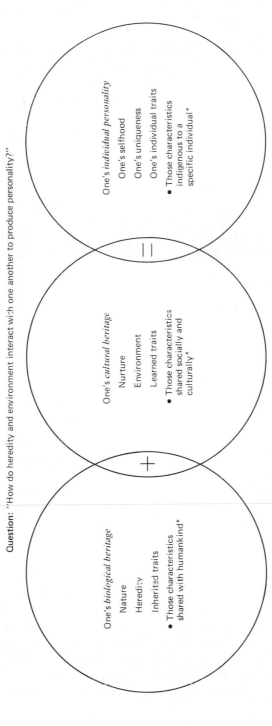

One's biological heritage

Nature

Heredity

Inherited traits

• Those characteristics shared with humankind*

$+$

One's cultural heritage

Nurture

Environment

Learned traits

• Those characteristics shared socially and culturally*

$=$

One's individual personality

One's selfhood

One's uniqueness

One's individual traits

• Those characteristics indigenous to a specific individual*

*The extent, degree or intensity is uncertain, debatable and controversial.

Figure 8-2. The Fused Chain Interaction of one's heredity and environment produces one's personality.

163

thermore, he stated, "their traits have been fixed by heredity and the first few years of life."

Determinism or Self-Determinism

Do forces outside the person control the individual (determinism), or does one have a choice in shaping one's own personality (self-determination)?

Determinists believe in the philosophical doctrine that every event, act, and decision is the inevitable consequence of antecedents, such as physical, psychological, or environmental conditions, which are independent of the human will.

Self-determinists theorize that humans are more than empty organisms at the mercy of the rewards and punishments of their environment, and that a person's inner life is the source of one's decisions and aspirations. Free will, willpower, free choice, "mind over matter," "pulling oneself up by one's own bootstraps," determining one's own fate or course of action without compulsion—these are some of the words a self-determinist would use.

While some psychologists contend it is an either-or issue, Rychlak (1968) and others contend that in a personality theory it is possible to accept and integrate *both* viewpoints without compromise.

THE PSYCHOANALYTIC STRATEGY

Psychoanalysis is a strategy that emphasizes the importance of events within the mind (intrapsychic events). The term *psychoanalysis* has the following three common referents:

- It refers to a theory of personality, particularly personality development from its earliest stages of childhood.
- It is a method of scientific investigation that studies intrapsychic phenomena —*psychoanalyzing* an individual's random thoughts, dreams, mistakes, and other forms of behavior in order to determine their meaning or psychic significance for the person.
- It is the name of the *therapy,* that is, psychoanalytic psychotherapy, in addition to a *process,* which is being used to bring about a personality change.

The focus of psychoanalytic theory is on the intent—the "why?" or the unconsciousness. The implicit belief is that once the "true" intent or the "real" reason can be discovered, the behavior can be modified or changed. It means delving into one's motives, the intrapsychic forces, *not* the social forces, in the assessment of the individual's personality.

Despite inherent liabilities of the psychoanalytic theory, originally advanced by Sigmund Freud, and still being practiced and modified by other Freudians and Neo-Freudians, psychoanalytic theory has dominated the study of personality. Freud's work and writings continue to have a profound influence on psychology today despite his demise at age 83, more than 40 years ago (1939). Also, it should be borne in mind that each of the personality strategies has liabilities.

THE DISPOSITIONAL STRATEGY: ATTRIBUTIVE AND PROPULSIVE APPROACHES

Dispositional psychologists believe that there is a good deal of generality in human characteristics, so that a person who acts in certain ways in one situation will also tend to act in those ways in other situations. The dispositions suggested by various psychologists to account for personality can be divided into two broad classes: *attributive* and *propulsive*. The distinction between these two classes of dispositions is imperfect, although it is valuable for empirical research.

Attributive Approaches—Trait and Type

These approaches to personality specify dimensions that explain a person's behavior because he or she is that way, such as, "He behaves that way because he *is* agressive," or "He is the aggressive type," or "She doesn't communicate with anyone because she *is* shy." Frequently trait and type are used as summary labels to conveniently explain observed differences in behavior.

Credit for setting the rudiments of the first modern biological-type approach to personality belongs to a German psychiatrist, Ernst Kretschmer (1921, translated 1926), who, along with his colleagues, developed a "constitutional inventory" in order to determine types of physiques. Sheldon (1942) followed up on Kretschmer's lead, studying and classifying physiques in order to identify temperamental components or traits. He posited that for each body type there is a related personality pattern. Williams (1967), and many others who have followed, hypothesized that because there are differences in the physical constitution of individuals often these differences cause differences in behavior. It is apparent that this assertion, if viable, has far-reaching consequences for both predicting and understanding individual differences in personality.

Allport's Trait Approach

In 1931 Allport (1966) took a dispositional position that he described as *heuristic realism,* specifically, "the person who confronts us possesses inside his skin generalized action tendencies (or traits) and that it is our job scientifically to discover what they are." Allport's original statement of the characteristics of traits first appeared in 1931 and was judged to be defensible in 1966. Here are Allport's (1966) eight assertions:[1]

1. Traits have more than nominal existence.

2. Traits are more general than habits.

3. Traits are dynamic, or at least determinative, in behavior.

4. Traits may be established empirically.

5. Traits are only relatively independent of other traits.

6. Traits are not synonymous with moral or social judgments.

7. Traits may be viewed either in light of the personality which contains them (i.e., idiographically), or in light of their distribution in the population (i.e., nomothetically).

8. Acts, and even habits, that are inconsistent with a trait are not proof of the nonexistence of the trait.

Allport proposed that an individual's traits may be classified in terms of the degree to which they pervade, or become diffused, throughout his personality. The most pervasive traits are referred to by Allport as *cardinal dispositions,* which dominate the individual's entire existence, and *central dispositions,* which refer to the relatively small number of traits that tend to be highly characteristic of the individual. *Secondary dispositions* are those characteristics of the individual which operate only in limited settings.

Allport also posited that traits may be viewed as *common* traits, that is characteristics that allow for comparison between one person and another, or *individual* traits, that is, the unique characteristics of the individual that do not lend themselves to comparison across persons. Allport was particularly concerned about seeking out the individual's personal key qualities.

Earlier Allport (1961) referred to the concept of "selfhood" as *proprium* (the organization of personality) which the individual used to unite the seven aspects of selfhood; Allport listed these in the order of their probable occurrence in the growing child.[2] *Proprium,* Allport asserted, is an important concept of personality, and one's self-image becomes a major organizing factor in one's life. Furthermore, Allport posited that motivation is found *within* the structure of personality (traits), rather than as an independent force, which is different from Freud's concept of motivation. Since Allport was a prolific writer, his monumental research on personality traits is frequently cited.

[1]Allport, G. W. "Traits Revisited." *American Psychologist,* 1966, pp. 1–21.

[2]Allport, G. W. *Pattern and Growth in Personality.* New York: Holt, Rinehart and Winston, 1961, pp. 228–229, 235–237, 365–366. Copyright © Holt, Rinehart and Winston, 1961. Reprinted by permission.

Cattell's Trait Approach: Factor Analysis

Raymond B. Cattell (1965), a prominent dispositional psychologist, along with many other researchers, believed a common method had to be employed to interrelate the various findings of trait research and to allow the simultaneous examination of many traits. A statistical technique with these properties is available and has come to be called *factor analysis*. Cattell maintained that there is a common structure across personalities that must be determined empirically, in the same way that the elements of the physical universe were discovered.

Eysenck's Type Approach

Like Cattell, H. J. Eysenck (1967), another prominent dispositional psychologist, has attempted to discover the basic components of personality in an empirical and theoretical fashion, relying heavily on factor analysis to accomplish this goal. However, the level at which each psychologist has chosen to look for the basic dimensions of personality is different. Cattell's research has revealed a relatively lengthy list of *source traits*. Eysenck's investigations have focused on discovering a small number of basic *personality types*.

In relating factor theory to sports predictions, Fisher (1976) observed, "Sport predictions derived from trait assessment have not been successful." Typically, personality traits account for less than 10 percent of behavioral variance in any given situation. This means that 90 percent remains unaccounted for. Such findings certainly breed little confidence in any explanation of future behavior based on the level of the personality trait. Nevertheless, a trait assessment of athletes is likely to be as correct as a coach's subjective evaluations.

Propulsive Approaches—Needs

Propulsive explanations of personality emphasize more dynamic, impelling forces as characterizing the individual, forces which drive (or impede) action. Propulsive views are based on the concepts of need and motive. For example, "He is *driven* to achieve or excel," or "She *needs* love and affection"; both statements imply an active force that controls the individual's behavior. The kind and amount of one's needs *propel* the individual to different courses of action, which give rise to different personalities.

Several dispositional approaches to personality that are distinguished by a focus primarily on the identification and measurement of *needs* as a means of understanding, predicting, and controlling human behavior will be cited and discussed briefly.

Sport Personology. The objective of personality psychology (personology) is to obtain reliable information about personality or individual differences in order to understand and to try to predict human behavior. Psychologists, sport psychologists, and others who study *sport personology,* a specialized area of interest within the larger field of personology, are particularly interested in understanding and predicting human behavior within a sports context. Specifically, their concern is to attempt to determine the role that sport/athletics play in one's personality development or in the change of one's personality; these psychologists also wish to determine the influence of personality on sport or athletic performance.

Researchers such as Martens (1975), and others who continue to investigate sport personology, seek answers to the following types of questions in order to understand and predict human behavior:

- Does participation in athletics generally influence the participant's personality?
- Does the individual's degree of success or failure in sports influence the participant's personality?
- Do changes occur in the participant's personality as the result of engaging in specific competitive athletic experiences?
- Are there critical periods in an individual's development in which participation in sports/athletics may play an important role in personality development or change?
- What attributes of certain sports, such as team versus individual, differentially influence the participant's personality development?
- Do individuals with different personalities perfer or choose specific sports and not choose others?
- Do individuals who engage in sport or athletic participation have different personality profiles from those who do not, that is, athletes versus nonathletes?
- Do various personality profiles determine success or failure in certain sports?
- Is it possible to change the personality of the participant to increase the likelihood of success in sports participation?

Martens (1975) suggested that if the answers to the question, "What are the unique characteristics of superior athletes?" can be identified, the coach can either select athletes with these characteristics or implement programs that can modify the athletes' personalities in conformance with the superior athletes' personalities, resulting in greater success.

Martens also suggested that by fostering personality development there is a considerable social value gained; sports may even have a potential therapeutic value. Of course, by improving an athlete's performance there is an obvious practical value. Coaches and athletes alike are always interested in learning ways in which sports performance may be improved. If knowledge about the psychic constitution of the individual, or his personality, can enhance his performance, then this knowledge is of value.

Murray's Approach to Personality. Henry A. Murray (1962) and his associates posited an approach that deals with "directional forces within the subject, forces which seek out or respond to various objects or total situations in the environment." This approach in itself is not new, as others have suggested the theory of impelling passions and drives, based on the dynamics of Freud's theory which was already well known. However, Murray and his associates wanted to identify and catalog the forces, to assess them in individuals, to determine their relationships with one another, and finally to write a comprehensive theory of personality. Murray did not want to use the phrase "psychology of personality," since he felt it was clumsy and repetitious, so he and his colleagues defined their area of interest as "*personology.*" Murray believed that the individual and his environment must be considered together as a person–environment interaction. However, to begin an analysis of this interaction, forces within the individual (needs) and forces from the environment (press) are temporarily separated. Murray defined a *need* as "an organic potentiality or readiness to respond in a certain way under given conditions. . . . It is a noun which stands for the fact that a certain trend is apt to recur." *Press* represents the equally important forces provided by objects, situations, or events in the environment.

McClelland—Achievement (*n* Ach) Motivation. Murray's dispositional approach to personality has stimulated much research, a prime example being the extensive work of Dr. David C. McClelland and his associates on the achievement motive (1953, 1961, 1965), specifically, Murray's *n* Achievement, abbreviated "*n* Ach". While McClelland and Murray shared a common bias concerning the nature of human personality, the basic strategies of attacking similar problems differ. Whereas Murray chose to catalog and study a large number of needs, McClelland chose to focus his attention on a single need—the need to achieve. The Thematic Apperception Test (TAT) was used by Murray to "reveal things that the patient is unwilling to tell or unable to tell because he is unconscious of them." McClelland used the test to "consciously teach people to think and to be achievement oriented."

According to Liebert and Spiegler (1974), "McClelland's program to foster and increase people's need to achieve is based on principles derived from psychoanalytic, phenomenological, and behavioral personality change principles," which is considered one of the liabilities of the dispositional strategy.

THE PHENOMENOLOGICAL STRATEGY

Phenomenological psychology postulates that effective reality is *reality as it is perceived;* that the reality of phenomena is solely a function of the way in which it is observed. Therefore, what is *real* to a person is that which is in one's subjective world, from one's internal frame of reference. Dr. Carl Rogers, a renowned humanistic psychologist and prominent phenomenological theorist, maintains that in order to change personality one must change the perception of oneself and of one's world.

The implication of a phenomenological orientation or strategy of personality is that a person's behavior can only be understood from his own point of view. Basic approaches to the phenomenological strategy for the study of personality are the self-actualizing humanistic approach of Carl Rogers and Abraham Maslow and the psychology of personal constructs formulated by George Kelly. Only the work of Rogers, who developed a complete strategy for studying personality, will be discussed here briefly. The theories of all three of these psychologists focus on the "higher" functions of humans and consider humans as active, reacting beings who change continuously. Phenomenological strategy emphasizes the present, focusing only on the "here and now" events and problems in its humanistic therapy; psychoanalysis, on the other hand, probes the deep unconscious mind for past events that have caused present personality problems. The latter therapy maintains that past events or causes must first be identified in order to resolve present problems.

Rogers' and Maslow's work deals with *self-actualization*—a belief that each person has a tendency to actualize himself in a way that approaches his or her unique potential. Kelly's theory concentrates on the cognitive constructs through which people view their experiences. Kelly posited that people act in those ways which lead to their being able to predict events in their lives most accurately. Obviously, the specifics of either of these approaches varies for each individual. Their theories are termed "*holistic,*" since they view and understand each of a person's specific acts in terms of his entire personality.

Roger's Self-Actualizing Approach

Rogers (1959) postulated that all behavior is governed by the actualizing tendency that involves all movements of a person in the direction of maintenance and enhancement of the "self," which he considers as *one* motivation.[3] Rogers stresses the importance of consistency between how a person views himself and how he would like to be viewed. As part of his theory, Rogers postulated that all persons have a basic need (*positive regard*) to experience attitudes, such as acceptance, respect, and love, from significant individuals in their lives; furthermore, when a person becomes aware that he is satisfying another's need for positive regard, his own need is satisfied. When one perceives his whole self as worthy of positive regard, he experiences unconditional positive self-regard, which means the individual is accepted and respected.

Rogers' (1959) approach to personality, and that of Maslow's (1954, 1970)

---

[3]Rogers, Carl R. "A theory of therapy, personality, and interpersonal relations, as developed in the client-centered framework." In S. Kock (Ed.), *Psychology: A Study of Science,* Vol. 3. New York: McGraw-Hill, 1959, pp. 184, 256. Reprinted by permission.

too, encompasses the fully functioning person. Both psychologists found that people are fully self-actualizing when

- Their behavior is regulated by their organismic valuing process
- They are open to all experiences
- Their self-concept is whole and consistent with their experiences
- They are free from threat and anxiety, and hence have no defenses
- They epitomize psychological health or adjustment

Despite the fact that many people, including numerous coaches, feel more comfortable with phenomenological ("everyday") psychology than with other complicated theoretical constructs dealing with the study of personality, one must be aware of the liabilities of this particular strategy. Phenomenological personality theory does not explain the development of personality and, as its critics maintain, its theory is mostly descriptive rather than explanatory.

THE BEHAVIOR STRATEGY

In contrast to the three other strategies that have been discussed, the behavioral strategy for the study of personality is directly and ultimately concerned with *overt behavior* for its own sake. The unit of personality in the behavioral strategy is *behavior,* and in this strategy personality and behavior are closer to being synonymous terms than in the psychoanalytic, dispositional, and phenomenological strategies. Behavioral approaches hold that personality can be best explained by examining the external influences on a person.

In addition to the focus on behavior, a second unifying principle of the behavioral strategy is the emphasis on learning. The basic assumption made by adherents of behavioral approaches to personality is that behavior develops and is modified primarily, though not exclusively, in accordance with the principles of learning rather than acquired through heredity and determined biologically.

As Liebert and Spiegler (1974) pointed out, behavioral approaches differ with respect to the form of learning that is emphasized.[4]

Behavioral Approaches: Theories of Learning

The behavioral strategy includes the following three approaches:

1. The *classical conditioning* or *respondent* approach focuses on a person learning new responses by coming to associate a set of circumstances

[4]Liebert, Robert M., and Spiegler, Michael D. *Personality Strategies for the Study of Man* (Rev. ed.). Homewood, Ill.: The Dorsey Press, 1974. Copyright © by The Dorsey Press. Reprinted by permission.

which previously did not elicit a particular reaction with another set of circumstances which has already led to that reaction.

2. In the *operant conditioning* or *instrumental learning* approach, behavior is learned as a result of the consequences a person experiences when he or she performs the behavior.

3. The *observational learning* or *imitation* approach considers learning to be a function of a person's observations of the behavior of others and the consequences of these behaviors.

It is significant that, although the distinction among the three paradigms can be useful, especially pedagogically, in real life most behavior is acquired and sustained by a combination of observational, operant, and respondent learning.

Compared with the psychoanalytic, dispositional, and phenomenological personality strategies, relatively few theoretical constructs are employed within the behavioral strategy. For example, behavioral theories do not posit any kind of unifying force or structure for personality, such as is found in psychoanalytic (ego), dispositional (proprium), and phenomenological (self) personality strategies. Behavior strategy has no similar equivalent. Instead, behaviorists view each aspect of personality semi-independently of all other aspects, which is consistent with the view that behavior is determined by external rather than internal forces.

The behavioral strategy has its liabilities too; for example, it reputedly relies too heavily on the concept of learning to the exclusion of other processes that also have an important influence on personality.

Now let us examine some facets of the personality of the coach and of the athlete, and the application of personality research to coaching and athletic performance.

THE COACH'S PERSONALITY

Each coach and athlete reacts differently to almost any given environmental situation. This reaction depends to a large extent on the nature of the individual's personality. Because of the inherent nature of competitive athletics, and because of the personality of the individual who fulfills the role set and societal expectations of the coach, it is imperative to underscore the influence a coach has on others, particularly the athletes under the coach's tutelage. It is tremendously important that a coach know his own personality. One should "know thyself," one's strengths, weaknesses, motives, desires, and drives. Also, a coach should be mindful of the fact that he or she can truly influence and mold the character and personality of youthful participants in particular. These influences can be positive or negative, beneficial or detrimental, but it is very likely they will be lasting throughout the life of the individual who has been influenced by the "coach."

To attempt to know oneself is a complex matter, and it is not always an easy task because it is difficult for one to be truly objective about oneself. It is a common human frailty to overlook one's own shortcomings, and in reality it is difficult to see oneself as others see us. Frequently, one sees oneself as he or she wishes to be perceived by others. Psychological insight can offer increased effectiveness in coaching. However, one's success in coaching is likely to be diminished by a coach's failure to examine rationally and objectively the basis of one's attitudes and other personality attributes. It is obvious that each coach has certain personality characteristics. The coach's personality affects his or her philosophy of coaching, which in turn reflects the type of team a coach produces.

AN ATTEMPT TO CATEGORIZE COACHING PERSONALITIES

Tutko and Richards (1971) illustrated how coaches with particular personalities produce specific player responses, defining five general categories for coaches: the hard-nosed or authoritarian coach, the nice-guy coach, the intense or "drive" coach, the easy-going coach, and the businesslike coach.[5] Neither Tutko and Richards nor the authors of this publication imply these categories are all-inclusive, nor that every coach will fall exclusively into any one category. These five, however, are the most predominant categories.

____ The coach's personality is reflected in his or her type of discipline, leadership style, methods of motivation, practice schedule, organization, game plan and conduct, coaching philosophy, attitudes, and beliefs, and so on. These factors, in turn, are reflected in the behavior of the athletes, including their attitudes, whether or not their coach is liked or disliked, respected or not respected, and whether the players are relaxed, tense, and so forth. Each "type" or category of coach is likely to surround himself with assistants and players similar to himself who possess the characteristics he possesses and the behavior patterns he displays. In turn, if assistants and players want to be a part of his or her "team," they too are apt to display their head coach's behavior patterns. Not all five categories or types display entirely different personality characteristics, since the intense or "driven" coach is likely to possess some of the same attributes as the hard-nosed coach and the businesslike coach. There are advantages and disadvantages, or "trade-offs," in each personality type. Usually, however, the team reflects the personality of their coach.

A Team Reflects the Personality of the Coach

Perhaps this point may be best illustrated by a personal observation related by Rainer Martens, nationally known sport psychologist from the University of Illinois, speaking in Sacramento, California, March 8, 1980, on "Competitiveness and Youth Sports." Dr. Martens told of a situation where a youngster of 9 years of age, Kevin, went out for a Little League baseball team for the first time. In Kevin's first time at bat, he watched a mature 12-year-old opposing pitcher whiz three fast strikes over the plate without Kevin ever having gotten his bat off his shoulder to swing at any of them. As Kevin walked back to the dugout with his bat and helmet, apparently not affected too much by having been declared out on three called strikes, his coach ran down from his third base coaching box and chastised Kevin. The youngster was a total failure, according to his coach, for not even having tried to hit the ball. Kevin continued back to his place on the bench, humbled and crestfallen. From his vantage point Kevin watched his teammates strike out, too. However, he observed that those who had played previously for the coach reacted by slamming down their protective helmet, throwing their bat, kicking the dirt, sulking and pouting after they had gone down swinging. The response from their coach at the third base line was always, "That's all right. You did okay. Stay in there!"

When Kevin came to bat again he watched the first two called strikes. His coach exploded, "At least swing at the ball!" Kevin swung blindly at the next pitch, over his head, and as he walked back to the bench he remembered the behavior of his teammates when they too had struck out. Kevin slammed down his protective helmet, threw his bat, kicked the dirt, started to sulk and pout, and his coach yelled, "That's all right, Kevin, you'll get a hit the next time!"

As Dr. Martens pointed out, Kevin did not learn how to hit or how not to swing at bad pitches, but Kevin learned that when you did not get a hit with that particular coach you had to express certain behavior to illustrate to him that you were a failure. Kevin wanted to be a member of the coach's "team," so he reflected his coach's behavior and personality.

Effective Coaching

It is not possible for a coach to be all things to everyone. Nor is it possible for a coach to be something he or she is not. One cannot emulate or imitate other successful coaches; one must be his own person.

It sometimes happens that each of the different coaching types is able to handle an athlete of a certain personality type. The authoritarian can handle the "con" type athlete; the "nice-guy" coach, the sensitive player; the "intense" coach appears to be best for the unmotivated athlete; the bright and perceptive athlete responds best to the "easy-going" coach; and the "businesslike" coach is most effective with the talented athlete. However, regardless of the personality of the athlete or coach, all coaches can be effective with each player through insight and effort. Every coach should be sensitive to individual differences of his athletes. Team personality very likely will reflect the coach's own personality. The coach's awareness of this will give him an increased insight into the complex art of handling athletes. In turn this can make the coach more effective and successful in his professional life.

A Profile of Successful Coaches

In their pioneer work in the area of sport psychology, Ogilvie and Tutko (1966), probably the most prolific writers on the subject of personality profiles of coaches and athletes, reported on their study of the personalities of 64 coaches representing the four major sports in America: basketball, track, football, and baseball. They found the coaches to be readily distinguishable from the average male on a number of important human characteristics.

Their profile was almost identical to that of the outstanding athletes Ogilvie and Tutko had observed among Olympic swimming champions, professional football players, professional baseball players, outstanding track and field athletes, and professional basketball players. Quoting psychologists Ogilvie and Tutko (1966), the coaches as a group were found to be:[6]

- Highly success-driven men with outstanding need to be on top.
- They were highly orderly, organized men who preferred to plan ahead and be concerned with looking ahead into the future.
- They tended to be outgoing and warm people who enjoyed being with others.
- They had finely developed consciences and were very much in tune with the appropriate values in our culture.
- They seemed unusually well equipped by personality and temperament for handling their emotions when under considerable stress.
- They were, as a group, open, trusting people who were not excessively defensive in their relationships with others.
- They scored very high in leadership qualities when compared with norms based upon men who were selected or elected leaders.
- They were, as a sample, more dominant, take-charge types of persons who would actively seek roles of leadership.
- They were more prone to blame themselves and accept blame when things go wrong than to pass the responsibility over to someone else.
- They exhibited the highest average of psychological endurance of any sample of men we have ever studied. It appears that ''stick-to-it-ness'' is the most prominent feature of the personality of successful coaches.
- They were unusually mature emotionally and would be described on the basis of their tests as persons who would face reality in a direct manner.
- They were free to express their natural aggressive tendencies in a manner appropriate to their role as a coach.

Positive and Negative Personality Traits for Coaches

For one to establish a self-image and better understand ''self,'' Moore (1970) suggested that a coach utilize a self-evaluation test to determine the degree to which

---

[6]Ogilvie, Bruce C., and Tutko, Thomas A. *Problem Athletes and How to Handle Them.* London, England: Pelham Books, 1966, pp. 18–20, 22–23, 88–106. Reprinted by permission of the authors.

he or she possesses traits that are considered to be socially desirable and technically necessary for success in the field of coaching. In his book, *The Psychology of Athletic Coaching,* Moore offered the following positive or highly desirable coaching traits, with a brief explanation of each attribute:[7]

leadership	reliability	optimism
sense of humor	emotional stability	integrity
friendliness	loyalty	understanding
forcefulness	persistence	cooperation
honesty	ambitiousness	self-discipline
industriousness	creativeness	trust

The list is by no means all-inclusive but, as Moore pointed out, it gives a meaningful insight into the behavioral patterns of successful coaches. If one should indulge in self-evaluation using the listed traits as criteria, one could arrive at a score but, without knowing the degree to which the "good" coaches possess the various traits or characteristics, one would have no basis for comparison. However, there would still be some value in a coach performing this exercise because he or she could get an indication and an awareness of his or her own traits. The same exercise could be performed for the negative traits or characteristics.

Moore listed the following negative traits as those that would lessen a coach's chances for success:[7]

sensitivity to criticism	laziness	worry
disloyalty	poor discipline	discourtesy
emotional instability	intemperance	aloofness
overly critical	selfishness	vulgarity

The same type of profile or rating scale could be used to determine attributes or trait characteristics of athletes, such as speed, agility, quickness, toughness, desire, strength, size potential, coordination, aggressiveness, and pride, with affixed ratings to determine the degree of each attribute as follows: (1) poor, (2) below average, (3) average, (4) above average, (5) outstanding. These attributes of the athlete could be more objectively measured than those attributes listed for the coach. However, one must be cautioned about using any testing instrument incorrectly.

THE ATHLETE'S PERSONALITY

If a coach is able to recognize the different personality traits of the members of the team, he or she will be able effectively to use the varied approaches available to

[7]Moore, J. W. *The Psychology of Athletic Coaching.* Minneapolis, Burgess, 1970, pp. 4–8. Reprinted with permission.

him. Communication, motivational techniques, teaching and coaching methods, and other procedures will vary in accordance with the degree to which the individual athletes show different personality traits.

Each athlete is uniquely motivated to compete for whatever reason he chooses. Frequently the reasons are not evident, since they may be covert and not the manifestations which are overtly displayed. Probably few individuals ever compete to their full potential, although performers who are highly successful, the champions in particular, as a group, tend to share certain traits that typify athletic success.

Being Successful Means Maximizing Potential

Depending on the specific situation which involves numerous variable factors, the typical coach is likely to have few, if any, champion performers. Frequently all a coach can do is seek the performer who is the determined competitor, despite the player's lack of other desirable attributes and physical skills, and attempt to develop whatever potential the athlete may possess. When this occurs, not infrequently the highly motivated competitor is successful and is labeled a "winner" mainly because he maximizes his potential, and the individual is motivated not to be a "loser." He envisions himself only as winning, not losing.

Conversely, an athlete may appear to have many of the desirable attributes and seemingly possess much potential to be a successful performer, but lack some inherent ingredient that prohibits him or her from measuring up to the coach's expectations. Not infrequently coaches label the missing ingredient as the lack of "heart," which has different connotations for different coaches.

Individuals at times even fear success. Ogilvie (1968), Winchel and colleagues (1974), Timnick (1978), and others have referred to the motive of avoiding success as the "success-phobia." Timnick, referring specifically to the research of New York University psychologist Katherine Garner and her publication, *The Success-Fearing Personality,* stated, "The whys of this success phobia—first observed by Freud—are tangled in certain events of very early childhood, the experts say—perhaps in the first three years of life, certainly within the first five." Timnick, referring to people in general, stated that "Psychiatrists say it happens all the time. Many men and women unconsciously fear success.... So much so, in fact, that when they near a long sought goal, they may procrastinate, get anxious to the point of panic, have trouble making decisions, become depressed and develop psychosomatic ills." Dr. Garner, addressing members of the American Academy of Psychoanalysis, was quoted by Timnick as saying, "Accumulated studies give strong indications that fear of success is a phenomenon prevalent in a wide variety of people, and it seems to affect men and women equally" (Timnick, 1978).

A common coaching error is to spend too much time and effort working with the individual who appears to have great potential, but who in actuality never produces to the coach's expectations. Unbeknown to the coach, the potentially outstanding performer may have an unconscious fear of achieving success, or may be content to be a squad member for reasons other than those manifested, but is not desirous of competing to try to achieve success.

While most coaches would probably continue to work with the athlete who has potential but does not perform to their expectations, selection should be based on *actual* player *performance,* not on the *potential* of how a player might perform. Not infrequently a prospect who appears to have little potential in terms of height, weight, and speed may be completely overlooked initially, but when given the opportunity the individual produces beyond the coach's expectations. For want of a better word, if "heart" is the ingredient the second athlete possesses but the potential performer does not, the participant with "heart" is the more reliable performer. To be effective, a coach must focus on performance, not potential.

THE STATUS OF PERSONALITY RESEARCH AND ITS APPLICATION IN SPORTS

Not all of personality research is useful, and perhaps much of it may be inaccurate. This statement is not meant to be an indictment, but it is factually established. Brent S. Rushall, then Coordinator of Applied Psychology at Dalhousie University, Halifax, Nova Scotia, summarized the status of personality research and its application in sports (1973) as follows:

> The standard of research has not been good. The mood of those involved in producing high quality work is one of dissatisfaction. The trend of opinion is one of starting anew and looking at other research and theoretical alternatives. Certainly, researchers need to delve into the theories and scientific methods that are concerned with general behavior. The analysis of behavior will provide an empirical basis for the developing of valid measuring instruments.

Dr. Rushall also pointed out that, not only is the application of personality information to sports sadly neglected, but coaches and teachers are uncertain how to utilize the information they do receive. It is not difficult for sport psychologists and others to compile research information on what athletes are like or what they have done, which most coaches already learn for themselves in time, but as Rushall (1973) stated, "The first big stride in the application of personality information to athletics will be the communication of what must be done by the coach when given the information revealed by a particular test."

Dr. Leon E. Smith (1970), then Professor of Physical Education and Director of the Motor Performance Research Laboratory at the University of Iowa, stated, "Research findings relative to the study of personality and physical performance reveal a mosaic of contraditions."

Cooper (1969) concluded from his review of the literature on athletic activity and personality that, "When one looks at the research done in this area, as in many other areas in their empirical infancy, more questions are raised than answered, more directions mapped out than journeys completed."

Dr. A. C. Ostrow, School of Physical Education at West Virginia University stated in his article, "Personality Research and Sport: Methodological Considerations" (1979),

It is probably a conservative estimate to suggest that several hundred research investigations have been conducted purporting to demonstrate a relationship between personality formation and sport participation. Unfortunately quantity and not quality has most often been the trademark of research in this area. These investigations have sometimes been motivated by an interest in establishing the sport experience as important for desirable or "normal" personality development. Often, however, these investigations have been motivated by what appears to be a simplistic solution to a thesis or dissertation requirement.

Psychological Tests

There are several different categories of psychological tests and within each category are hundreds of specific tests. The trained counselor working with scholastic and collegiate students will probably not be familiar with all of the tests. However, the use of tests by trained counselors may prove of some aid to the coach. The coach should understand the following about psychological tests in general:

- Tests are better for measuring present and past behavior than for predicting behavior, although some tests make quite good predictors.
- No psychological test is foolproof, although some are highly sophisticated and would be difficult to "beat."
- While one may learn many "things" about a person through psychological testing, it is not possible to learn "everything" about the individual even if an extensive battery of tests is used.
- Some of the major categories of tests are personality tests, intelligence tests, achievement tests, aptitude or skill tests.

Identification of Personality Tests

Alderman (1974), in his publication *Psychological Behavior in Sport,* observed,

The major research thrust into the personality of athletes has been aimed at the identification of personality traits. These investigations, using mainly group personality tests, have been directed toward determining which traits correlated most highly with outstanding athletic ability in high school, college, national and international competitors.

Though the numerous traits identified in these studies are naturally restricted to the kinds of tests used, a fairly comprehensive picture of the athlete's personality trait structure has begun to appear.[8]

The objective personality questionnaires used to investigate athletic personality include the same instruments that have been used most frequently for the selection of personnel in business or industry. A brief summary of the personality tests and inventories most often used in the past follows:

Edwards Personal Preference Schedule (EPPS). This test was designed to evaluate the relative strength of fifteen of the manifest needs outlined in Murray's system of human needs.

The Minnesota Multiphasic Personality Inventory (MMPE). This inventory contains items or statements which the subject evaluates as being true or false with respect to himself. These items cover various life experiences common to everyone, including somatic experiences, family relations, sociopolitical attitudes, sexual attitudes, moodtone, and beliefs.

The Eysenck Personality Inventory (EPI). This instrument is designed to measure the two pervasive and relatively independent dimensions of *Neuroticism-Stability* and *Extraversion-Introversion* as identified by Eysenck. Neuroticism refers to general emotional instability and the individual's predisposition to neurotic breakdown under stress, whereas extraversion refers to the uninhibited, outgoing, impulsive, and sociable inclinations of a person.

The California Psychological Inventory. This instrument was specifically designed to evaluate the personality dimensions of "normal" people in a variety of situations. The four major categories for 18 different dimensions are: measures of poise; ascendancy and self-assurance; measures of achievement potential and intellectual efficiency; and measures of intellectual and interest modes.

The Cattell 16 PF Questionnaire. The 16 primary factors identified by Cattell are described as being functionally independent and psychologically meaningful dimensions of a person's personality. This inventory has been used broadly in the investigation of physical educators, coaches, and athletes. Cross-cultural comparisons plus data on age-group competitors greatly increase the reliability of the statements that can be made about the personalities of athletes.

The Athletic Motivational Inventory (AMI). It is the contention of Ogilvie and Tutko (1969) that "successful athletes tend to share certain traits that typify athletic

---

[8]Alderman, R. B. *Psychological Behavior in Sport.* Philadelphia: W. B. Saunders, 1974, pp. 127–151. Copyright © 1974 by W. B. Saunders Company. Reprinted by permission of Holt, Rinehart and Winston.

achievement.'' With this in mind, they have, after many years of measuring and evaluating athletes' personalities, designed a personality questionnaire specifically directed toward the evaluation of personality profiles of athletes. This questionnaire, the Athletic Motivational Inventory (AMI), consists of 190 items, with a choice of three responses to each item. The AMI gives a 9-point scale measurement of the individual athlete on each of 11 personality dimensions which are divided into two general areas.

The Use of Personality Tests

Because the coach is in a race against time, he or she often wants to utilize tests—similar to ''taking an aspirin to cure a headache.'' The coach wants something simple and quick, to resolve a problem and to give an immediate answer. Unfortunately for the coach, there is no single test that can do this, nor can a simple test be used in this manner.

As Mudra (1974) pointed out in his article, ''Personality Tests: Panacea or Phantasy?''

> Experts in the field of personality testing claim that it is still in the ''tea-leaf-reading'' stage. It is fairly simple for the psychological counselor to analyze a test and suggest a remedy to the client (coach). But he still leaves the coach to deal with the remedy. The fact that the coach expects the psychologist to know more about the problem than he does can cause the coach to accept almost any remedy suggested by the psychologist.

Alderman (1974) concluded that,

> The personality profiles of athletes based on the measurement of personality ''traits'' do not increase our knowledge of the dynamic tendencies which move people to action. They do not give us a picture of the ''whole'' person, just segments. Also, little attempt is made to show how these traits integrate with each other to cause overt behavior.

While few coaches are professionally trained as psychologists and generally do not have the required specialized expertise necessary to counsel individuals with unusual personality problems, coaches can perform ''everyday psychology'' by showing genuine concern and understanding for the individual as a person. Not infrequently an athlete is viewed by a coach strictly as a statistic, depending on a coach's personal philosophy. Also, ''everyday psychology'' deals with aiding the individual in fulfilling his particular needs. Finally, it is strongly recommended that a coach should try to assist the athlete in getting professional help. Coaches and teachers in scholastic and collegiate institutions often can refer their students and student-athletes to the institution's counseling services. Coaches should utilize these services and professionally trained counselors with specialized expertise whenever possible.

Summary

A single theory of personality that explains human behavior to the satisfaction of all does not exist. Coaches are interested in the study of personality since it may offer some hope of interpreting the mystery of what motivates behavior, especially when an athlete's behavior is different from what a coach expects or from what the coach would have done. Personality theory offers a system of categorizing a wide range of behaviors, but more importantly for the coach, a study of the subject involves the possibility of predicting human behavior. Despite the unresolved age-old argument of whether personality is inherited or learned, the trend has been to place greater importance on the individual being a product of his environment. Much research has been done on athletic activity and personality but, so far, no completely valid and reliable means has been devised to predict with a high degree of accuracy the behavior of athletes.

REFERENCES

Alderman, R. B. *Psychological Behavior in Sport*. Philadelphia. W. B. Saunders, 1974, pp. 127–151.

Allport, G. W. *Personality—A Psychological Interpretation*. New York. Holt & Company, 1937, p. 49.

Allport, G. W. *Pattern and Growth in Personality*. New York. Holt, Rinehart & Winston, 1961, pp. 228–229, 235–237, 365–366.

Allport, G. W. "Traits Revisited." *American Psychologist*, 1966, pp. 1–10, 21.

Cattell, Raymond B. *The Scientific Analysis of Personality*. Baltimore. Penquin Books, 1965, pp. 55–56.

Cooper, Lowell. "Athletics, Activity, and Personality: A Review of the Literature." *Research Quarterly*. Vol. 40, No. 1, March 1969.

Eysenck. H. T. *The Biological Bases of Personality*. Springfield. Ill. Charles C Thomas, 1967.

Fisher, A. Craig. *Psychology of Sport*. Palo Alto, Calif. Mayfield, 1976, pp. 322–323.

Husman, Burris F. "Sport and Personality Dynamics." *Proceedings 72nd National College Physical Education for Men*, 1969, pp. 56–70.

Kretschmer, Ernst. *Physique and Character: An Investigation of the Nature of Constitution and the Theory of Temperament*. W. J. H. Sportt (Trans.). New York. Harcourt, 1926, pp. 9, 21–25, 29, 65.

Liebert, Robert M., and Spiegler, Michael D. *Personality Strategies for the Study of Man* (rev. ed.). Homewood, Ill. The Dorsey Press, 1974, pp. 4, 49, 111, 131, 159, 192, 220–221.

Martens, Rainer, *Social Psychology and Physical Activity*. New York. Harper & Row, 1975, pp. 144–159.

Martens, Rainer. "Competitiveness and Youth Sports." Lecture. American River College, Sacramento, Calif. March 8, 1980.

Maslow, A. H. *Motivation and Personality*. New York. Harper and Brothers, 1954 (2nd ed., Harper & Row, 1970).

McClelland, D. C., Atkinson, J. W., Clark, R. A., and Lowell, E. L. *The Achievement Motive*. New York. Appleton-Century-Crofts. 1953.

McClelland, D. C. *The Achieving Society*. Princeton, N. J. Van Nostrand, 1961.

McClelland, D. C. "Toward a Theory of Motive Acquisition." *American Psychologist*, 1965, pp. 20, 321–333.

Moore, J. W. *The Psychology of Athletic Coaching*. Minneapolis. Burgess, 1970, pp. 4–8.

Morgan, William P. "Sport Personology: The Credulous-Skeptical Argument in Perspective." In William F. Straub (Ed.), *Sport Psychology—An Analysis of Athletic Behavior*. New York. Movement Publications, 1978.

Mudra, Darrell. "Personality Tests: Panacea or Phantasy?" *Scholastic Coach*. Vol. 43, No. 4, May 1974, pp. 20–22, 97.

Murray, H. A. "Uses of the Thematic Apperception Test." *American Journal of Psychiatry*, 1951, pp. 107, 577–581.

Murray, H. A. *Explorations in Personality*. New York. Science Editions, 1962, pp. 61–66, 244.

Ogilvie, Bruce C. "The Unconscious Fear of Success." *Quest X*, May 1968, pp. 35–39.

Ogilvie, Bruce C., and Tutko, Thomas A. *Problem Athletes and How to Handle Them*. London, England. Pelham Books, 1966, pp. 18–20, 22–23, 88–106.

Ogilvie, Bruce, and Tutko, Thomas. AMI. Institute for the Study of Athletic Motivation (ISAM). San Jose, Calif. 1969.

Ostrow, Andrew C. "Personality Research and Sport: Methodological Considerations." *The Physical Educator*. Vol. 31, No. 2, May 1979, pp. 95–96.

Rogers, Carl R. "A Theory of Therapy Personality, and Interpersonal Relations, as Developed in the Client-Centered Framework." In S. Kock (ed.), *Psychology: A Study of Science*. Vol. 3. New York. McGraw-Hill, 1959. pp. 184, 256.

Ruffer, William A. (Ed.). "Personality Traits of Athletes." *The Physical Educator*. Vol. 32, No. 1, May 1975, pp. 105–109. Vol. 33, No. 1, March 1976, pp. 50–55. Vol. 33, No. 4, December 1976, pp. 211–214.

Rushall, Brent S. "The Status of Personality Research and Application in Sports and Physical Education." *Journal of Sportsmedicine and Physical Fitness*. Vol. 13, No. 4, December 1973.

Rychlak, Joseph F. *A Philosophy of Science for Personality Theory*. Boston, Houghton Mifflin, 1968. (See Chapter 8.)

Sheldon, W. H. *The Varieties of Temperament: A Psychology of Constitutional Differences*. New York. Harpers, 1942, pp. 4–6, 14, 290.

Smith, Leon E. "Personality and Performance Research—New Theories and Direction Required." *Quest XIII*, 1970, pp. 74–83.

Timnick, Lois. "Fear of Success." *The Sacramento Bee*. August 13, 1978, p. 3.

Tutko, Thomas A., and Richards, Jack W. *Psychology of Coaching*. Boston. Allyn and Bacon, 1971, pp. 15–39, 41–56.

Williams, R. J. "The Biological Approach to the Study of Personality." In T. Milton (Ed.), *Theories of Psychopathology*. Philadelphia. W. B. Saunders, 1967. pp. 19–31.

Winchel, R., Fenner, D., and Shaver, P. "Impact of Coeducation of 'Fear Success' Imagery Expressed by Male and Female High School Students." *Journal of Educational Psychology*. Vol. 66, No. 5, 1974, pp. 726–730.

SELECTED READINGS

Carron, Albert V. "Personality and Athletics: A Review." In Brent S. Rushall (Ed.), *The Status of Motor Learning and Sport Psychology Research*. Dartmouth, Novia Scotia. Sport Science Associates, 1975, pp. 5.1–5.12.

Hall, Calvin S., and Lindzey, Gardner. *Theories of Personality* (2nd ed.). New York. John Wiley & Sons, 1970.

Jourard, Sidney. *Personal Adjustment*. (2nd ed.). New York. Macmillan, 1963.

Lidz, Theodore. *The Person: His Development Through the Life Cycle*. New York. Basic Books, 1968.

Maslow, Abraham. *Toward a Psychology of Being*. New York. Van Nostrand, 1968.

Maslow, Abraham. *The Farther Reaches of Human Nature*. New York. Viking Press, 1971.

Morgan, W. P. "The Psychomotor Domain: Movement Behaviors." In R. N. Singer (Ed.), *Sport Psychology*. Philadelphia. Lea & Febiger, 1972.

Morgan, W. P. "Selected Psychological Considerations in Sport." *Research Quarterly*. Vol. 45, 1974, pp. 374–390.

Morgan, W. P., and Johnson, R. W. "Personality Characteristics of Successful and Unsuccessful Oarsmen." *International Journal of Sports Psychology*. Vol. 9, 1978.

Suinn, Richard M. *Psychology in Sports Methods and Application*. Minneapolis. Burgess, 1980.

CHAPTER 9

The Psychology of Motivation: Improving Personal Performance

Motivation, perception, learning, and personality are four areas of human behavior that have been studied more than any other by psychologists. While each topic is discussed separately in this book, none is more central to personal performance and success than motivation—whether it is a coach's or an athlete's.

While some members of the coaching profession undoubtedly have benefitted from the voluminous research that has been compiled on motivation, probably most have not. Many sport psychologists maintain, and probably rightfully so, that psychological motivation is the most neglected area of a coach's training. Since few coaches are trained in the field of psychology, it is unfair that a coach should be expected to be an authority on motivation without special training. Since this is seldom the situation, typically a coach can only rely on those experiences that have grown out of trial-and-error or trial-and-success, although he or she may not understand why there were failures or successes.

Most coaches probably take a "commonsense" approach to motivation, namely "a little from here and some from there". This type of "common sense" eclectic approach seems very pragmatic to a coach, since there are numerous definitions and complicated theoretical concepts of motivation. Such complicated motivational theories, as well as other detailed abstract conceptualizations in the field of psychology, are seldom understood by a person not trained in that discipline. The purpose of this chapter is to acquaint the reader with motivational theory and to provide meaningful information that may be utilized as a base on which he or she may build and develop motivational strategy. This chapter builds on the previous one, which discussed the psychology of personality. Motivation is clearly one of the vital aspects of a leadership style and of a coach's effectiveness.

NO SINGLE WAY TO APPROACH THE SUBJECT

Visiting scholar and author George Sage, University of Northern Colorado at Greeley, presented a series of lectures to students and faculty at California State University, Sacramento, on "Sport as a Social Agent" (1977). Speaking on the subject of motivation, Professor Sage began by saying, "The topic of motivation is probably the single most popular topic among coaches when they get together." He quickly added, "There is no single definition of motivation; therefore, there is no single way to approach the subject."

There is an abundance of material authored by coaches on the subject of motivation which tends to support Sage's comment. However, it has been our experience over many years that when coaches get together they tend to be more interested in discussing and securing additional information on systems of offense and defense, drills, tactics and strategies, techniques, and the Xs and Os of the sport, failing to learn more about how to motivate effectively those individuals who are the Xs and Os on paper. Yet in support of Dr. Sage's opening remarks, we concur that motivation is a popular topic among coaches and that most are concerned about learning how to get their athletes to give their best performance. In fact, the most puzzling and complex responsibility of a coach is that of trying to motivate his or her athletes. If coaches were queried, it is likely all would agree that motivation is a vital concern and a major part of their coaching tasks.

We do concur emphatically with Sage that there is no single agreed on definition of motivation and that there is no single way to approach the subject. Personality and learning frequently are intertwined with some motivational theories, and these conceptualizations become quite complicated. Obviously, all of this complicates matters for coaches who are seeking simplistic answers or solutions of how best to motivate their players, assistants, and others.

HEAD COACH: LEADER AND MOTIVATOR

If one follows the job market in coaching and scans job announcements, position descriptions, and evaluative criteria for job performance, probably the two most evident words that are used are *leadership* and *motivation*. They identify salient personal characteristics that employers are seeking in candidates and that all head coaches are expected to possess. Head coaches are expected to provide strong leadership and to motivate assistants, players, and others.

Head coaches are not only held accountable for their own behavior, but their superiors frequently hold them accountable for the behavior of their assistants and players, too. Head coaches also are expected to understand and correct behavior that deviates from the norm or accepted mores of society. To try to understand a person's motivation, one must try to comprehend the "why" of behavior, that is, "the reason or cause of behavior." If a coach is not familiar with motivational theory, he or she is likely to respond to the why, "I simply don't understand that person, or why he (or she) acts that way!" Obviously such a response is not an answer and deals with the symptoms not the solution to a behavioral problem.

The "Why" of Behavior

As Craig, Mehrens, and Clarizio (1975) pointed out,

> Motivation is a very general term for conditions that cause one to begin an activity and pursue it with vigor and persistence. In every day terms motivation refers to the "why" of behavior, just as ability means the "can." When we question one's motivation, we assume he can but ask, "Why does he?" or "Why doesn't he?" . . . Motivation must be considered in any discussion of behavior. . . .

The media has publicized a world-class tennis player who interrupts tournament play to make obscene hand gestures to sport officials, opponents, and spectators; a former vice-president makes the same gross gesture to the media; a former highly successful college football coach vehemently protests an official's decision by tearing up the down markers on the sidelines; a professional basketball player strikes and fractures the jaw of an opposing player; and a professional hockey player performs the same "number" with his hockey stick on his opponent; a football coach does a somersault on the sidelines after the opposing team scores a touchdown; a coach chews a towel and bites his fingernails during a close game; an athlete performs the "spike," "shuffle," and "bop," hanging from the crossbar or the basket (before rule changes) after scoring. The media has also publicized many behavioral acts of unselfishness, courage, humility, and sportsmanship among athletes and coaches.

While sensational and somewhat infamous acts and deeds of individuals gain more attention and notoriety than noteworthy behavior, when an individual performs attention-getting behavior, such as those illustrated, inevitably the first question asked is, "Why?"

General Points of View Relevant to the Scope of Motivation

Both the coach and the psychologist are interested in the "why" of behavior, but they view motivation differently. Generally a coach views motivation in a relatively narrow context; *how to* motivate to improve athletic performance. A psychologist's view is likely to be very broad in scope: namely, *all* behavior is motivated.

From the coach's viewpoint motivation typically is thought of in a limited context of a person (a coach) giving or doing something for someone (an athlete) in order to get that individual "turned on" (motivated or aroused) to do something he or she might not otherwise do. Within the context of athletics, the "something" is to try to get the athlete "turned on" to perform optimally. Many coaches perceive their role responsibility as motivator as analogous to what one does when confronted with a weak battery in an automobile; give it a booster or "hot" shot to recharge the battery!

A popular cliché in coaching is "Every athlete has a 'hot button,' and it is the coach's responsibility to find it and 'turn on' each player!" The simplistic implication is analogous to an individual fumbling around trying to locate a wall switch in a dark room in order to turn on the light. In time the wall switch is located and when the person clicks the "on" switch, the room is illuminated. While the analogy is practical, there will be less fumbling around and more efficient and effective coaching if the coach comprehends how and why the individual is motivated ("turned on"). Since everyone's "hot button" is not the same, not all methods of motivation are effective.

Human behavior, as perceived from the psychologist's point of view, represents a system of complete relationships. The aspect of personality that is associated with enthusiasm in carrying out different activities is called *motivation*. Therefore, nearly all conscious behavior is motivated or caused. Individuals do not act in nondirective, random fashion, but seek rewards and satisfaction for what they do. Behavior is goal directed. The intensity with which people engage in certain activities is a function of the benefits they expect to gain from them.

Therefore, while motivation may be thought of as simply a "desire to do something," which can be as fundamental as getting a drink of water, going to one's job daily as a coach, or reporting for an individual or team sport, motivation also can be as complex as one's mind can imagine. It can be a display of behavior patterns that may be described as unpredictable, erratic, in gross taste, or even socially unacceptable. It could also be the opposite. It can be something done alone or it can be working with others. It can be something requiring a few moments or several years of effort. The individual may or may not know the cause or reason for his or her doing something and for acting in such a manner. However, psychologists maintain that human behavior is not random and is the result of some internal motivation. As observers we can only speculate on what motivates another person, because we do not always understand the reasons for our own actions and our own motivations. However, understanding motivational theory will aid us in our quest to attempt to comprehend the "why" of human behavior.

Motivation and Personality

It is difficult to discuss motivation and personality separately. Freudian psychologists and some other theorists do not attempt to do so. For example, the concepts of self, the need for achievement, the issues of determinism versus self-determinism, and the nature-nurture controversy are several subjects that could be discussed in a single chapter on personality-motivational theory or in separate chapters. There are numerous theories, and there are no simple, uncomplicated, definitive answers to complex psychological functions. The truth of the matter is that not all of the answers have been found to all the queries pertaining to human motivation and personality.

Our intent is not to cite numerous detailed, theoretical constructs which are convenient ways of conceptualizing complex psychological functions, but to offer information that will be meaningful and beneficial to the coach. First, however, a more operative definition of motivation is necessary, other than merely saying that it is "a desire to do something."

WHAT IS MOTIVATION?

Mednick, Higgins, and Kirschenbaum (1975) pointed out that psychologists define motivation in many different ways to express many different viewpoints, and then stated, "The *motivation concept* generally refers to the biological, social, and learned factors that initiate, sustain, and stop goal-directed behavior." As a definition of motivation this is highly acceptable. Another useful definition is that of Kagan and Havemann (1976): "A general term referring to forces regulating behavior that is undertaken because of drives, needs, or desires and is directed toward goals." A simplistic definition of motivation is that which energizes, directs, maintains, and sustains behavior.

Motivation is a response directed toward the reduction of a need. A person has certain needs that create tensions and the individual behaves in specific ways to relieve these tensions. A person has goals that he or she attempts to achieve through behavior. These goals will satisfy certain basic needs or wants of the individual. Motives are the goal-directed "whys" of behavior; needs are its initiating and sustaining forces. Drive is what moves an individual to satisfy his needs, and goals in this context, are anything that will alleviate a need and hence reduce a drive.

For example, a person tries out for an athletic team and attempts to achieve certain goals. These goals will satisfy certain basic needs or wants that a person has, such as a feeling of accomplishment or status. The person makes the team and an intermediate goal is achieved, and the drive temporarily subsides. Intermediate goals refer to subgoals set up for achievement on the path toward the final goal, which is usually remote in time. Intermediate goals help to maintain morale and a long term effort toward the more distant goals, such as to be a regular, move to all-conference, then to all-American, and finally "the best" at a given position.

Salient Points

There are a few salient points relevant to motivation that we should keep in mind:

- Motivation deals with internal conditions that we are unable to observe. We observe outward behavior that results from the internal motives, but we can only infer what leads to the behavior of a person.

- Motivation and behavior are not the same. Motivation is an important factor in determining behavior, but behavior is also influenced by biological factors, social and cultural factors, perception, and similar factors.
- The result of motivation is always activity. A person responds to internal motives by activities directed toward goals that the individual believes will produce satisfaction.
- Human behavior is directed toward attaining goals, and it is assumed that personal needs will be satisfied when the goals are reached. Goals do not control behavior; they influence it and give an individual direction. Goals give a person something visible to work with in attempting to satisfy needs. The attractiveness of the goal is related to the amount of frustration produced by unsatisfied needs.
- As soon as one need is satisfied, another appears. Motivation continues all of the time as an individual is always in a never-ending chain of need fulfillment. However, when a need is satisfied, it does not motivate. There is no longer motivation to direct behavior toward goals related to it. Maslow and other psychologists pointed out that a satisfied need is not a motivator.

Intrinsic and Extrinsic Motivation

As Sage (1977) pointed out, "One way of conceptualizing motivation is to say there are two broad classes of motivation, one is intrinsic, and the other is extrinsic."

Intrinsic. In the field of psychology, *intrinsic* motivation is explained as coming from within or inside the individual. Intrinsic motivators are internal rewards that occur at the time of the performance. As psychologist Edward Deci (1975) observed, "intrinsically motivated behaviors are ones which a person engages in so that he may feel competent and self-determining in relation to his environment."

Illustrations. One is intrinsically motivated if he or she performs an activity for no other reason than for a feeling of confidence and self-determination, a point both Sage (1977) and Martens (1980) made. Intrinsic motivation is an integral part of the learning situation, especially if the individual seeks to learn not for any external reward, but merely for the joy of knowing.

Ladies professional golfer Carol Mann (1978) was quoted as saying, "Each week is different. The money isn't sufficient to motivate you. It's not always so easy to turn your motor on week after week. Pride is the big thing but after 18 years I still get my kicks out there."

Considered by some people to be "the best baseball player in America," California Angles' Rod Carew (1977) was quoted as saying, "I'm happy with what I'm doing. I'm at ease and I've got peace of mind. Money doesn't mean everything to me in life. . . . I'm not on any ego trip to be the highest priced player. Being happy and healthy means more to me. . . ."

In *Intrinsic Motivation* Professor Deci (1975) evaluated the research of psychologists White, Berlyne, Hunt, Piaget, Elkind, Atkinson, McClelland, De-Charms, Heider, and Vroom to establish that intrinsically motivated behaviors do indeed play an important role in human life.

Extrinsic. The principle of extrinsic motivation is that an individual is given an extrinsic reward for performance in the belief that this will keep the person performing. *Extrinsic* motivation is that which comes from the outside, established artificially, and created by rewards. External motivators give no direct satisfaction at the time the act is performed. The rewards are received after the individual performs.

Illustrations. Many coaches, parents, and others put much emphasis on extrinsic motivators. We concur with Martens (1980) that the "message" coming across to most of today's young athletes is to "win that trophy." However, when youngsters in particular engage in organized sports, their involvement and external motivation must be kept in proper perspective. We agree with Martens (1980) when he said, "Awarding young athletes is not intrinsically bad. The key, however, is teaching the child to see the award as a memento of one day's achievement."

Despite what golfer Carol Mann (1978) and baseball star Rod Carew (1977) have been quoted as saying, *Sports Illustrated*'s Special Report, "Money in Sports" (Kennedy and Williamson, 1978), leads one to believe that, for many individuals, money is the only motivator. Psychologists have debated this question for many years. Many professional athletes maintain they do not participate solely for the money, and this may be correct. However, it may be what "money can buy" or "what wealth represents," that satisfies other needs, or merely the fact that they can command and are paid huge salaries. Therefore, whether or not money is a motivator is a qualified "yes" *and* "no" answer.

While coaches are most knowledgeable about extrinsic motivators, they should be concerned about intrinsic motivators, too. Typically the extrinsic factors are usually forgotten, and the intrinsic more lasting.

BROAD CATEGORIES OF MOTIVATIONAL THEORIES

There are numerous theories of motivation, ranging from purely mechanistic behavioral approaches to those that are almost mystical in their view of human activity. However, detailed psychological analyses of motivation will not be discussed.

Murray (1964) proposed that every theory of motivation falls under one or another of four headings, although some theories may fall under more than one heading simultaneously. The four types of motivational theory are cognitive, hedonistic, instinct, and drive.

Cognitive Theory

Cognition is the act or process of knowing. A cognitive theory of motivation is so-called because the cognitive or the thought of the idea is supposed to underlie the observed behavior. For example, if a female thinks she should compete in athletic competition, she proceeds to do so; if she thinks she should not, she does not compete.

One can readily deduce in cognitive theories that the individual acts because of free will. This viewpoint is contrary to the theoretical constructs of psychologists who believe in determinism versus self-determinism, as discussed previously.

Cognitive theories assume that a human being thinks out or plans what he or she is to do. Such theories cannot account for unconscious motivation nor provide a useful means for productive behavior.

Hedonism Theory

Hedonism is the doctrine that pleasure or happiness is the highest good; it is devotion to pleasure. Relevant to motivation, theorists interpret hedonism to mean that a person acts to achieve satisfaction or pleasure and to avoid pain or nonsatisfaction. Hedonism is *not* irreconcilable with cognitive theories of motivation. Feelings of pleasure and pain or satisfaction and nonsatisfaction influence our behavior, which is also influenced by social and cultural factors, perception, and other factors. These feelings are not always consistent within the same person.

Hedonism fails to deal with the problem that pleasure and pain are subjective experiences. Without an objective measurement that can apply to all people, pleasure, satisfaction, pain, and nonsatisfaction cannot form the foundation of a scientific theory of motivation. In spite of the difficulty of working with such a theory, a commonsense and simplistic theory has much appeal, and it is difficult to explain behavior without recourse to hedonism. As a result, virtually every theory of personality or motivation contains some element of hedonism.

Instinct Theory

In our culture instinct theories of motivation are old and popular. To the layperson, instinct offers a simplistic explanation of most all behaviors.

Instinct is understood as an identical behavior pattern found among all humans which is inborn rather than learned. Since early in this century it has been a common practice to label behavior as instinctive, such as referring to the *maternal* instinct or the *social* instinct, or even to explain a variety of behaviors by making such statements as, "She reacted instinctively," "He moved by instinct," "He is instinctively aggressive," and so forth. Over a period of years, the list of instincts became practically all-inclusive, and people became dubious of the whole concept of instinct as applicable to humans. Merely labeling behavior as "instinctive" did not explain behavior and, in a sense, it was no longer subjected to experimental investigation. As a result, most psychologists abandoned instinct theories of motivation. However, instinctive theories have regained some favor in recent years because of the research and writing of several social psychologists, most notably Nobel Laureate Konrad Lorenz, with his studies on various animals and birds (Evans, 1975).

Drive Theory

The majority of today's psychologists are drive theorists of one sort or another; yet, there is some hesitancy about promulgating drives as the *sole* basis for human behavior. Serious philosophical and scientific issues underlying drive theory are the primary reasons why psychologists are reluctant to give it total support.

Succinctly, a *drive* is a physiological condition that moves a person to satisfy his or her needs. A *need* is something required by a person to adjust optimally to his or her environment. The hunger drive, for example, moves the individual to satisfy his need for food. The drive, a physiological condition, causes an organism to become active (hence "motivation"). From these primary physiological drives we can demonstrate the development of secondary or learned drives, from which a theory of motivation, such as A. H. Maslow's hierarchy of motives and needs can be derived.

SPECIFIC MOTIVATIONAL THEORIES

In Chapter 8 several different theories of personality were cited; they are referred to again here briefly as a point of reference in discussing the causes of motivation.

- *Psychoanalytic Strategy* (Freudian psychology). To reduce tension. The source of motivation is psychic energy (intrapsychic events within the mind); its purpose to reduce tension and seek pleasure.
- *Phenomenological Strategy* (Rogerian psychology). To maintain and enhance the self. Rogers described motivation as the result of one unitary motive toward self-actualization.
- *Behavioral Strategy* (Skinnerian psychology). To minimize external stimulation. Motivation is not caused from within, but is external and is caused by the environment (situational). General behaviorists maintain it is necessary to reduce drive.

Content and Process Theories

For purposes of simplification, Fulmer (1977) divided the approach to human motivation as content theories and process theories.

Content Theories. The assumption is that motivation involves something we need to understand about individual behavior; so *content* theories focus on factors within the individual personality and the environment that produce a high level of behavior.

Probably one of the best known and most widely accepted content theorists is A. H. Maslow (1943, 1954, 1970). In his self-actualizing continuum he described individuals as pursuing needs. We will return to discuss Maslow's theory in greater detail later in this chapter.

Process Theories. The assumption that all behavior is learned and results from certain processes that a person has experienced is the basis of *process* theories of motivation. The emphasis of this approach is to structure a person's experiences so that behavior will match predetermined goals. Process theories deal with how behavior is activated, directed, sustained, and stopped.

Probably the best known of the process theorists is B. F. Skinner (1938); he uses what is known as a stimulus-response approach or operant conditioning. In this theory, the individual operates or produces a change in his or her environment in order to receive a reward. Behavior can be motivated by making desired changes in an individual's environment to control through rewarding, or reinforcing, the performance of required tasks.

Individual and Group Motivation

In his article, "Motivation and Performance of Sports Groups," Zander (1975) considered individual and group motivation. In discussing individual performance, he briefly mentioned the supportive approach, the reinforcement approach, and the pride-in-performance approach, none of which are directly concerned with how well a team performs as a unit. These concepts are concerned only with how well each individual performs, or with how hard each individual works to improve his own skill and his rewards. Group motivation, on the other hand, deals with pride and satisfaction in the team. Zander (1975) considered two group-oriented motives: the desire for group success, and the desire to avoid group failure. With success there is a disposition on the part of a participant to experience pride and satisfaction with his group if it successfully accomplishes a challenging task; with failure there is a disposition on the part of a participant to experience embarrassment or dissatisfaction with the group if it fails to accomplish a challenging task.

A knowledge of the psychology of motivation should prove invaluable and beneficial to a coach, who by now must realize that there are numerous theories but not unequivocal answers.

THE MOTIVATION PROCESS

The relationship among needs, goals, and behavior to achieve success is extremely complex. Difficulties can be encountered in different areas in the process of need satisfaction. The intensity of needs change, and goal selection is influenced by numerous social and cultural factors. The following are various models of the motivation process.

Need Satisfaction

The simplest behavioral model of motivation involves the process of a person selecting behaviors he or she believes will lead to the successful attainment of the goal. Figure 9-1 illustrates a motivation process:

1. A person is motivated by an internal need, which creates a state of tension that results in the individual seeking a goal to satisfy the need.

2. Behavior, or the actions of the individual, is directed toward achieving the goals.

3. If Cycle *A:* Success. The actions are successful and the goal is achieved. In homeostasis the need has been partially or fully satisfied, the tension is reduced, and the tendency is to return to a state of less tension or physical and psychological balance.

4. If Cycle *B:* Failure. The goal is not achieved. Thus, the individual may use *constructive* behavior by substituting a different goal which he believes will satisfy his needs, and the process begins a new cycle. Or *defensive behavior* may be elicited in the individual; in this case, the person may try to convince himself (although the process is generally believed to be unconscious) that a frustration or conflict and the resulting anxiety did not exist or does not have importance, through mechanisms of denial, escape, or shift and substitution, such as exhibited in aggression, apathy, rationalization, displacement, repression, projection, and so on, and a new cycle commences.

Encountering Difficulties in Need Satisfaction

Homeostasis frequently is *not* achieved in the process of motivation. Difficulties in fulfilling needs can be encountered in the following areas.

Goal: the individual is unable to identify a goal that he or she sees as being related to the need.

Behavior: the individual may not be able to identify a form of behavior (method) to achieve a goal.

Performance: the individual may identify a behavior but is not able to successfully perform the behavior to accomplish the goal.

Need Satisfaction: the individual may achieve the goal but finds that it does not satisfy his or her need.

The Intensity of Needs Changes. At any time, an individual has a number of needs that exist at different levels of intensity. Under most circumstances most all humans experience simultaneous needs for food, water, rest, safety, shelter, attention, love, belonging, friendship, among others. The intensity of the needs that

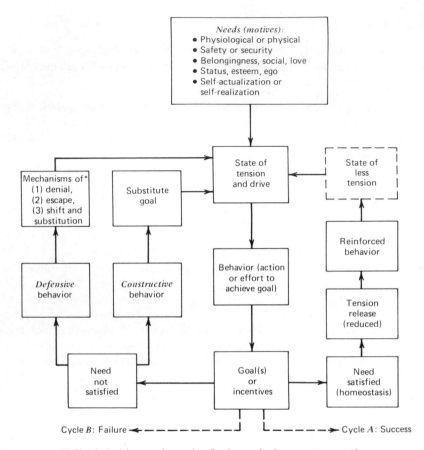

*1. Simple denial, repression, rationalization, projection, over-compensation
 2. Withdrawal, intellectualization, regression, developing physical ailments
 3. Displacement, compensation, sublimation, identification, etc.

Figure 9-1. A behavioral model of the motivation process for goal accomplishment. Cycle *A:* Success; Cycle *B:* Failure.

human beings experience is in a constant state of change as a result of some needs being satisfied and others increasing in intensity.

The Perception of Goals and Need Satisfaction

In previous chapters we have discussed both perception and the importance of goal setting as relevant to effective coaching, but we have not related this discussion specifically to motivation. The goals that humans select to satisfy needs depend on the following factors:

- The individual's perception of the expected satisfaction to be obtained from a specific goal.
- The availability of goals in the environment.
- The individual's estimate of his or her ability to achieve the goal(s).

An individual will attempt to select goals that can be achieved and that will provide the greatest need satisfaction. Almost any goal an individual chooses will satisfy some needs, while at the same time preventing the satisfaction of others.

The Law of Effect. In developing behavior patterns, individuals tend to choose goals they have found to be rewarding in the past, avoiding those goals they have found they were unsuccessful in achieving or have found unrewarding once achieved. This is known as the law of effect, as designated by Edward Thorndike in the early 1950s. Thorndike's laws of learning are discussed in the next chapter.

Goal selection is influenced by social norms, values, codes of behavior believed to be acceptable, and a number of other factors.

Goal-Directed Behavior

After a goal has been selected, a number of forms of behavior are available to achieve it. The particular pattern of behavior selected is affected by the individual's evaluation of his or her abilities, as well as an estimate of the most effective form of behavior in achieving a goal. When choosing behavioral patterns the law of effect tends to be a salient factor in the selection process.

Goal-directed behavior involves the following factors.

1. A single goal may satisfy many different needs, as illustrated in Figure 9-2.
2. Several different goals may satisfy the same need, as illustrated in Figure 9-3.
3. Several different behaviors can lead to the achievement of a goal, as illustrated in Figure 9-4.

CLASSIFYING HUMAN NEEDS

There are numerous systems and methods of classifying human needs, although there is *no one system* completely accurate or applicable to every individual or every situation. Most of the human needs systems are similar, with primary differences being the degree of detail and the number of categories used. There are differences of opinion among psychologists, sociologists, and others who have developed most

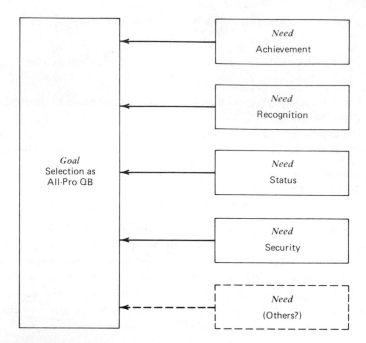

Figure 9-2. A single goal may satisfy several different needs.

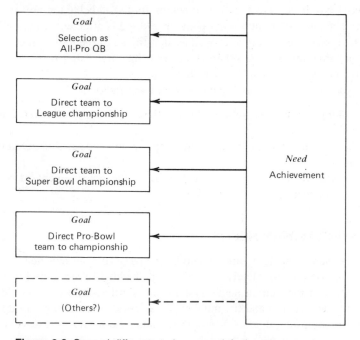

Figure 9-3. Several different goals may satisfy the same need.

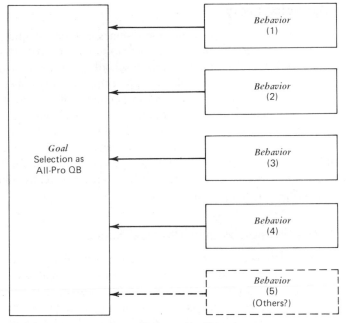

1. Work harder on improving skills than other QBs and teammates.
2. Study films to learn how to "pick" defenses and exploit opponents' weaknesses.
3. Study playbook to learn how to utilize offense effectively.
4. Learn strengths and weaknesses of teammates and their capabilities.
5. Other behaviors.

Figure 9-4. Several different behaviors can lead to the achievement of a goal.

of these theories and concepts, concerning the types of needs and the importance of various need categories. The basic classification of needs discussed is based on observable goals and behavior. Needs are grouped on the basis of similarity of goals rather than on the similarity of inferred needs, which is the most widely applied approach to motivation. Such an approach appears to be the most useful for coaches.

MASLOW'S HIERARCHY OF HUMAN NEEDS

Needs are the key to understanding motivation, and the most widely recognized, generalized approach to grouping and explaining needs is known as Maslow's Need Hierarchy. Dr. A. H. Maslow was a Professor of Psychology at Brandeis University when he developed his theory of motivation, which was first published in 1943 in *Psychological Review* and later in 1954, in his widely acclaimed book, *Motivation and Personality* (second edition, 1970). Maslow's need approach has served almost universally as the basis for modern theories of motivation.

A Holistic-Dynamic Theory

Maslow's personality theory is organismic and assumes that the potential for growth is contained within each person. *Humanistic psychology* is an offshoot of existentialism and phenomenology, and the humanistic school was started by A. Maslow and A. Sutich, who stressed the holistic approach and creativity. Maslow's holistic-dynamic theory is based on the innate goodness of human nature. The fundamental needs are good or neutral rather than evil. Human beings are made bad by adverse environmental factors. Maslow maintained that the underlying needs for all human motivation can be organized on five general levels, from lowest to highest. Within these levels there could be many specific needs. Figure 9-5 exhibits Maslow's hierarchy of needs, which frequently is diagramatically illustrated as building blocks, steps, or in a pyramid fashion.[1]

First Level: The Physiological or Physical Needs

The most prepotent of all needs are those that relate to one's physical well-being and include such needs as hunger, thirst, breathing, exercise, rest, and sex. It is for this reason that these basic and physiological or physical needs are the lowest in the hierarchy and for this reason that people concentrate on meeting these primary needs first before concerning themselves with higher-level needs. Certain physiological functions occur without motivation, but nearly all conscious behavior is motivated or caused. For the individual who is choking, behavior is directed toward the satisfaction of oxygen needs; for one who is starving, behavior is toward the satisfaction of food needs. Neither individual is concerned about higher-level needs.

Once physiological or physical needs are relatively well satisfied, although they are never completely satisfied, other needs become more dominant. Only the physiological needs function as relatively independent; that is, breathing air is independent of hunger or of status.

Second Level: The Safety or Security Needs

These needs involve physical safety such as being free from temperature extremes, assault, tyranny, fire, and other destructive forces. Maslow also implied that this level of needs involves psychological factors, such as the desire for an orderly, predictable environment and the desire of being protected from threat and injustice. In fact, individual motivation involves developing protection from a wide variety of threatening events, both physical and psychological in nature. Once the physical and safety needs are satisfied, the individual begins to concentrate on planning how to fulfill higher-level needs.

---

[1]Maslow, A. H. *Motivation and Personality.* New York: Harper & Row, 1954 (2nd ed., 1970). Copyright © 1970 by Harper & Row, Publishers, Inc. Reprinted with permission.

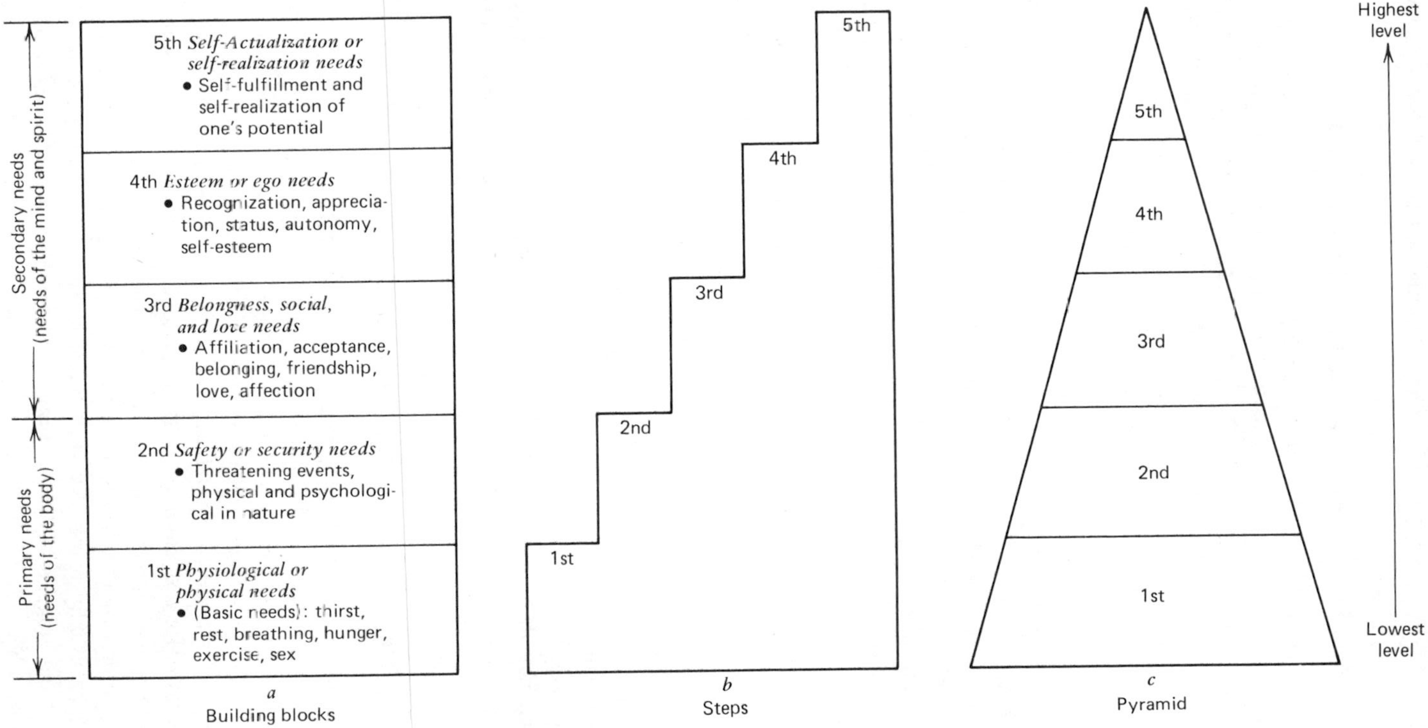
Secondary needs
(needs of the mind and spirit)
Primary needs
(needs of the body)
5th Self-Actualization or self-realization needs
• Self-fulfillment and self-realization of one's potential
4th Esteem or ego needs
• Recognization, apprecia-tion, status, autonomy, self-esteem
3rd Belongness, social, and love needs
• Affiliation, acceptance, belonging, friendship, love, affection
2nd Safety or security needs
• Threatening events, physical and psychologi-cal in nature
1st Physiological or physical needs
• (Basic needs): thirst, rest, breathing, hunger, exercise, sex
a
Building blocks
1st
2nd
3rd
4th
5th
b
Steps
5th
4th
3rd
2nd
1st
c
Pyramid
Highest level
Lowest level

Figure 9-5. Maslow's hierarchy of needs. (*Source:* From *Motivation and Personality*, 2nd ed., by Abraham H. Maslow. Copyright © 1970 by Abraham H. Maslow. Reprinted by permission of Harper & Row, Publishers, Inc.)

Third Level: The Belongingness, Social, and Love Needs

Maslow stated (1954, 1970), "If both physiological and the safety needs are fairly well gratified, there will emerge the love and affection and belongingness needs, and the whole cycle will repeat itself within this new center." These needs are probably the dominant ones in Western society. The social needs of affection, affiliation, companionship, belonging, and love are gained through contacts between individuals or individuals and groups. Most people are concerned about their social relationships and want to belong and be accepted by others.

In two areas where group dynamics occur, between the coaching staff and team members, where there should be cohesiveness for effective coaching, it is vitally important that individual and group social needs be met. Social needs can be met both within or outside of the staff and team activities. If an individual is prevented (excluded) from fulfilling social needs within the work-group (staff or team), he may become uncooperative, aggressive, and antagonistic toward other members and toward the head coach. Obviously when such a condition prevails, whether it be a disgruntled and discontented staff member or an athlete, effective coaching cannot take place.

Belonging to a group contributes to satisfying social needs. Individuals seek affiliation because they desire to have their values and beliefs reinforced by group members. Individuals who are deprived of social needs gratification will seek out this satisfaction as intensely as a thirsty person seeks out water to satisfy a physiological needs gratification. It is important for an individual in a leadership position, such as a head coach, to be cognizant of the intensity and the importance of belonging and of social needs.

Although the third, fourth, and fifth levels are identified as secondary needs, in terms of potency they are not necessarily secondary, since most major accomplishments of human beings have been the result of achievement and self-realization.

Fourth Level: The Esteem or Ego Needs

"With few pathological exceptions, all people in our society have a need or desire for a stable, firmly based, usually high evaluation of themselves, for self-respect, or self-esteem, and for the esteem of others" (Maslow, 1954, 1970). These needs are classified by Maslow into two subsidiary sets: (1) the desire for strength, achievement, adequacy, mastery, competence, confidence, independence, and freedom; and (2) the desire for reputation or prestige, status, dominance, recognition, attention, importance, or appreciation.

When autonomy and self-esteem needs are satisfied, feelings of independence and confidence usually result. Satisfaction of esteem needs involves the internal aspects of the individual's self-perception and the external aspect of acceptance and recognition by other individuals. The individual wants to be accepted for what he is rather than for what he can offer others. Satisfaction from esteem needs can result from gaining knowledge, developing abilities, and successfully accomplishing tasks. As individuals mature psychologically and as other lower-level needs are satisfied, persons attempt to attain higher levels of status and accomplishment. The failure to satisfy esteem needs can lead to feelings of inferiority and helplessness, which may lead to behaviors that are passive and apathetic.

Fifth Level: Self-Actualization or Self-Realization Needs

The term self-actualization, reputed to have been first coined by Kurt Goldstein (1939), is described by Maslow (1954, 1970) in detail in his book in a chapter entitled, "Self-Actualizing People: A Study of Psychological Health," and it refers to the human desire for self-fulfillment, namely "to the tendency for him to become actualized in what he is potentially." Behavioral psychologists interpret that Maslow's self-actualizing concept means "to become everything that one is capable of becoming." But in using this definition of the concept we can detect a shortcoming, because how can we determine and measure a human being's potential. Maslow maintained people have a restlessness for self-fulfillment that involves a constant striving to realize the potential of the self.

Two specific areas identified with self-actualizing needs are motivation for competence and achievement. The clear emergence of self-actualizing needs within a person usually rests on prior satisfaction of the physiological, safety, love, and esteem needs. Many people never become self-actualized because they are unable to adequately satisfy needs at lower levels.

While some authors use the term "a self-actualized person," others substitute the term self-actualizing, because there is always room for more development, as this fifth level of needs represents the "full flowering" of psychological health. People operating at the self-actualizing level have an accurate perception of reality, accept themselves and others, are creative, and are continually involved in self-development. Self-actualizers want to maximize all their capabilities and want to continue to grow and develop. Maslow pointed out, "The specific form these needs will take of course varies greatly from person to person. In one individual it may take the form of the desire to be an ideal mother, in another it may be expressed athletically, and in still another it may be expressed in painting pictures or in inventions."

Clarification of Maslow's Needs Hierarchy

For the individual who is learning about the need hierarchy for the first time, Maslow's theory is likely to appear to be relatively simple. One is apt to get the impression that an individual moves from one level to another as easily as the step-up illustration (Figure 9-5b) implies. To avoid confusion, several additional qualifying statements must be included so that Maslow's hierarchy is more accurately comprehended.

The Compositive Interaction of All Needs. Motives are highly complex, and no single motive affects behavior in isolation. As Maslow put it, "Behaviors always have more than one motivation." Needs, even those that are physical, are never completely fulfilled, and psychological needs are always in a state of tension—which reflects a need for higher fulfillment. Maslow (1943, 1954, 1970) postulated that "the average citizen is satisfied perhaps 85 percent in physiological needs, 70 percent in safety needs, 50 percent in love needs, 40 percent in self-esteem needs, and 10 percent in self-actualization needs."

All needs are active in affecting behavior, but the physiological needs are primary until a particular level of gratification is reached, after which the needs level of the next level becomes predominant. Therefore, although the five-way classification of needs is somewhat artificial because in a real-life situation all needs are interacting together within the whole person, it does provide coaches a convenient way of understanding which type of need is likely to dominate one's drive in a certain situation.

While all of the needs are always present, at different stages of psychological growth higher ones dominate the need hierarchy and the basic ones typically decline in importance over the passage of time for most individuals, as illustrated in Figure 9-6. Later in one's life span, however, the basic need may become dominant again. Initially physiological needs are dominant but, as a person develops, psychological needs have higher intensity. The peak of one set of needs must be passed before the next higher need becomes dominant.

Satisfying Lower-Level Needs First. There exists in every person a hierarchy of needs that requires, in general, that lower-level needs be partially satisfied before higher-level needs affect behavior. Although physiological needs are always present and some are never fully satisfied (we must always have oxygen in order to continue breathing to sustain life), varying minimal amounts of food, water, and sleep will gratify the physical needs of some people, and they may seek the satisfaction of higher-level needs. If an individual's lower-level needs are not satisfied, as occurs in many parts of the world, the individual will attempt to gratify these first before seeking higher-level needs.

An Illustration. Let us assume a young soccer prospect is being hazed and intimidated by several older squad members for whatever reason and the coaches are unaware of this. Also assume the youngster is physically unable to protect himself and is fearful if he "rats" either to his coaches or parents he will be assaulted by the bullies. At this point, the youngster's primary needs are security, safety, and protection, and he is more interested in satisfying these needs than he is in seeking higher needs gratification.

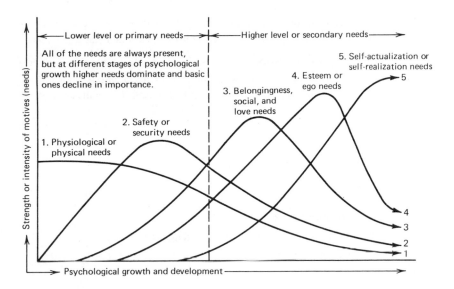

Figure 9-6. The relationship of needs to psychological growth. (*Source*: From *Motivation and Personality 2nd ed.,* by Abraham H. Maslow. Copyright © 1970 by Abraham H. Maslow. Reprinted by permission of Harper & Row, Publishers, Inc.)

A Satisfied Need Is Not a Motivator. When a need is satisfied another need emerges so that the individual always remains in a motivated state. A satisfied need is *not* a motivator.

An Illustration. Sleep is a motivating force when one is tired. "I am so tired I could sleep for a week" is the typical expression a tired person may make. After a night's sleep, the same individual might state, "I slept like a log. I feel great!" Since the previous physiological need has been satisfied, it is no longer a motivator.

Our example is carried a step further to reiterate the same point and to illustrate that an individual may operate at several need levels at the same time. After a restful night's sleep, our soccer prospect may report for the initial practice session rested, but in poor physical condition. After an extended period of running, our poorly conditioned prospect is gasping for air, sick to his stomach, and his legs and body are tired and weary. While his needs initially may have been achievement, status, self-realization, and fulfillment, his immediate needs now appear to be physical. Motivation? Should he stop? Walk off the practice field? Quit? Keep going? Stick it out? If he quits, he is attempting to gratify physiological needs; if he sticks it out, his behavior is motivated because he is attempting to gratify higher-level needs. If the strenuous pace continues, the prospect may be forced to make a decision as to need gratification. If the coach calls a halt to the practice session, permits the players to have rest and water, our soccer candidate may be able to satisfy both levels of needs. After his physical needs are partially gratified, higher needs may emerge.

Satisfaction of Higher-Level Needs. It is possible for individuals to satisfy higher-level needs in a greater variety of ways than lower-level needs, particularly in Western society. Davis (1977) pointed out the following characteristics of secondary needs:

1. They are strongly conditioned by experience.
2. They vary in type and intensity among people.
3. They change within any individual.
4. They work in groups rather than alone.
5. They are often hidden from conscious recognition.
6. They are nebulous feelings instead of tangible physical needs.
7. They influence behavior. It is said that ''we are logical only to the extent our feelings let us be.''

Davis also pointed out that, although human needs are classified as primary and secondary, this is for purposes of discussion only; Davis clarifies this point: ''The state of mind affects the physical body, and the state of the physical body affects the mind. In human beings the two are inseparable, which is the holistic concept.''

Healthy and Growing Individuals. Maslow's holistic-dynamic theory which is a humanistic approach is based on the motivation of healthy and growing people. For this reason many individuals prefer Maslowian psychology to other theories, since Maslow conducted and compiled research on psychologically healthy individuals. There are other psychologists who have formulated theories based on their research of psychologically ''sick'' patients. Therefore, Maslow's need hierarchy and his other theories of personality and motivation have much appeal for individuals in the coaching–teaching profession.

Limitations of Maslow's Need Hierarchy

Despite the fact that Maslow's need hierarchy has much merit, in that it is useful for understanding what motivates people *in general,* one must also recognize its limitations. For example,

- It cannot tell us what needs are motivating a given person at any given moment.
- It is dynamic in that an individual's position at any one need level is never fixed. However, at a given moment more than one need may be operating,

and the strength of each need varies, not only from individual to individual, but also within the same person.

- It does *not* itself indicate *how* to motivate people. It helps us to understand *why,* but it does not suggest specific ways of motivating people.

LEVEL OF ASPIRATION

Two other important psychological concepts are closely akin to our topic of motivation: self-concept and level of aspiration. Level of aspiration represents the long-run future goals and self-image of a person. If an individual aspires to be a successful coach or an outstanding athlete, he or she must be motivated to achieve this long-range professional and personal goal. If an individual does not aspire to do something, he or she does not try to put forth an effort.

Psychologists place feelings of success and failure in the context of a person's level of aspiration. The degree of satisfaction received from a reward depends on both the person's level of aspiration and the nature of the reward. Psychologist Kurt Lewin (1960) was one of the first to do major research on level of aspiration and described it as the "degree of goal difficulty a person sets for himself."

Factors That Influence Level of Aspiration

Lewin pointed out that level of aspiration is influenced both by the individual's stability, as he measures it through his past successes and failures, and by the standards of the group to which the person belongs. Success and failure of the individual's efforts result in raising or lowering the level of aspiration accordingly. However, this is not as dependent on the achievement itself as on the relationship between the achievement and the person's expectations.

It may be concluded that success and failure are forms of reward and punishment because they satisfy or deny certain social and ego needs. Such satisfaction depends on the individual's perception of his efforts, which in turn is closely related to the way other members of the group perceive such efforts and outcomes.

Raising or lowering levels of aspiration depends on past successes and expectations. Expectations in the sports world, however, are not clearly defined as success or failure when the numbers on the scoreboard determine the winner and loser. More often it is a matter of degree of success or failure rather than the complete measuring up or failing to measure up.

Congruence/Incongruence. If abilities and opportunities are consistent with the level of aspiration, an individual is well-adjusted. If his level of aspiration is lower than his abilities, his potential will not be realized. Conversely, if the individual's level of aspiration is beyond his capabilities and the opportunities that are available, frustration can result.

Many people never have the opportunity to discover their own capabilities. The satisfaction of their higher needs has been thwarted for such a long period of time that these needs cease to be an active source of energy. Maslow observed that people do not work to satisfy needs that seem impossible to satisfy.

Positive reinforcement is obviously a method a coach can use to get individuals to raise their level of aspiration. Adjusting a person's aspiration level is subject to the same unknowns and uncertainties as attempting to adjust the intensity of needs.

ACHIEVEMENT MOTIVATION

The need for achievement is one of many personality traits isolated by psychologists. Personologist H. A. Murray (1962) defined it as follows: "To accomplish something difficult. To master, manipulate, or organize physical objects, human beings, or ideas. To do this as rapidly and independently as possible. To overcome obstacles and to attain a high standard. To excel oneself. To rival and surpass others. To increase self regard by the successful exercise of talent."

Achievement: A Human Need

Harvard psychologist David C. McClelland (1961, 1962, 1965a, 1965b), and his associates (1953, 1969), studied achievement motivation extensively for more than a quarter of a century. Their research has led to the identification of human motivation as a distinct human need that varies in intensity among people. An extremely important contribution in this area of study has been the ability to measure the amount of achievement motivation possessed by individuals and its effect in specific situations. Research was conducted to discover which factors create or awake an individual's motivation by changing the way people think about themselves and their surroundings. Change how a person habitually thinks about his performance and you can change his actual performance, McClelland and his associates maintain.

Characteristics of Achievers. McClelland (1962) through empirical research found that the person with high achievement had the following characteristics:

1. . . . he likes situations in which he takes personal responsibility for finding solutions to problems.

2. . . . [he has a] tendency to set moderate achievement goals and to take "calculated risks."

3. . . . [he] wants concrete feedback as to how well he is doing.

Thus, high achievers choose goals that are both challenging and attainable; they are not gamblers, in that they prefer work situations where they can directly affect the outcome, and success is influenced heavily by the individual's ability and effort. They are more concerned with the achievement itself than with the rewards that result from their success; they desire specific feedback on how successful they are in attaining objectives. However, to be effective, the feedback must be objective, positive, and specific. Achievers also spend more time thinking about performing high-level accomplishments than do individuals with low achievement motivation; and high achievement motivation results in the individual's concentrating on higher levels of accomplishment and focusing behavior on reaching these goals.

Developing Achievement Motivation (n Ach)

McClelland (1965; McClelland and Winter, 1969) developed a theory of motive acquisition and designed a formal program for increasing human motivation in terms of some very practical problems. McClelland (1965) abstracted 12 theoretical propositions or guidelines for motive change. While the principles have evolved for a program designed to increase a particular motive, McClelland believes they should be applicable to the development of motivation dispositions in general.

IMPLICATIONS FOR COACHING

McClelland saw in the achievement motivation studies that he and his associates conducted distinct possibilities for self-help. Here are several specific suggestions for both coach and athlete:

1. Arrange for some "accomplishment feedback." This is the art of designing tasks so that participants succeed little by little, reaping a reward each time. Thus the desire to achieve more is strengthened. Success itself can condition success and "nothing succeeds like success."
2. Seek models of achievement. If one sees people around him succeeding, this will stimulate one's desire to succeed.
3. Modify your self-image. People with high achievement motivation seek personal challenges and responsibilities and require continual feedback on their success. They desire these experiences so much that it may be said they "need" them. It is possible to develop such needs by reconceptualizing oneself as someone who requires these things. As a first step, one should imagine himself as a person who *must* have success, responsibility, and challenge, according to McClelland.
4. Control your reveries (daydreaming). A person can be taught to change his motivation by changing his reveries; the individual can program his fantasies so that they constantly urge him on instead of blocking him.

McClelland's research has much merit for coaches since his studies have shown that a person's need to achieve can actually be created if certain environmental factors are present. One of the fundamental characteristics of an appropriate coaching strategy is that of creating a favorable environment that enables the athlete to achieve his own goals, including satisfying higher-level needs, which is best done by directing an athlete's efforts toward the team's goals.

Satisfy Needs and Achieve Goals

Many social scientists believe that the most productive organizations are composed of people who are satisfying personal needs while contributing to the achievement of organizational objectives. Such information is beneficial to coaches. The most effective head coaches undoubtedly make certain that subordinates, players, and others under their leadership have opportunities to satisfy their needs in their relationship to the team, squad, sport, and program.

Understanding motivation in an organization is difficult since individual behavior is affected by differing interactions that take place between people. Most coaches are dealing with smaller numbers and fewer individuals in groups, squads, and teams than a manager, for example, in a corporation. A coach dealing with a small squad or a team of several dozen players is not confronted with overwhelming numbers of individuals in attempting to resolve motivational problems. Regardless of the numbers involved, in order to gain an understanding of behavior, it is necessary to start with the individual as the basic producer of behavioral patterns.

Social scientists have reported that problems of employee motivation in an organization do not necessarily stem from lack of personal motivation. Motivational problems exist when behavior is focused either on goals other than organizational goals or at levels far below an employee's capability. These observations also apply to athletes and assistant coaches. Leadership positions in the coaching profession are very much like those positions in industry and government.

It was Douglas McGregor, Massachusetts Institute of Technology Professor of Management, who brought Maslow's need hierarchy to the attention of the business world. McGregor thought Maslow's description of human needs could help managers and supervisors better understand the behavior of their subordinates. Professor McGregor also felt that an understanding of the relationship between needs and motivation could help management create motivating work environments. Dr. McGregor's concepts gained attention first in an article entitled "The Human Side of Enterprise" (1957), based on a presentation he made before the Fifth Anniversary Convocation of the M.I.T. School of Industrial Management, and later in his widely acclaimed book (1960) of the same title. This book continues to be one of the most widely read books in the field of management theory and practice. In simple terms, by attempting to motivate others, a coach can try to "create" needs that are already felt and expressed by the individual. Therefore, it is important for a coach to understand the salient points of Maslow's need hierarchy, always mindful of the fact that individuals are not motivated by what they already have, but what they are seeking. The crux is that a coach must determine those needs that are relatively unsatisfied in order to motivate, mindful of the limitations of Maslow's theory as already outlined.

Dr. Bernard L. Rosenbaum (1978), President of the Management of Human Resources Division of the Personnel Services Center in New York, cited the following five psychological principles to be utilized to ensure performance:

1. Build people's self-esteem.
2. Focus on the problem, not personality. ✓
3. Use reinforcement to shape behavior.
4. Actively listen.
5. Set solid goals, keep communicating.

These principles are as applicable to the coach as well as to the supervisor or business executive.

Motivational Strategies

Since behavior is directed toward goals that will satisfy felt needs, the leader–coach has the following basic choices in attempting to motivate subordinates and players. (1) The coach can "create" felt needs within the individual(s); or (2) the coach can offer the possibility of satisfying needs already felt and expressed by the individual(s). A coach must be able to recognize and identify an individual's needs, to the best of his ability, and then provide the opportunity or situational environment so that those needs can be satisfied. For the coach this means getting to *know* his assistants and players, including their interests, desires, and goals.

Other than aiding an individual in fulfilling his or her needs, there is no single motivational strategy that can be utilized with the same degree of success by all coaches. Whatever is utilized is seldom effective and lasting if attempted on a group basis. It must be individualized because what "turns on" (motivates) one person may "turn off" another. Experience and research proves it is more effective and lasting to act on a one-to-one basis—coach and athlete interacting openly, genuinely, and honestly. Trust must be established. The more a coach knows about each of his players and assistants, knowing them as individuals and human beings, not just as athletes and subordinates, the greater the opportunities to motivate, and the more lasting the effects.

A highly successful approach (Rogerian psychology) is to give the individual personal regard without attaching any conditions to it. A coach should not be possessive of his or her athletes. Furthermore, to motivate successfully a coach must develop a genuine feeling of empathy and concern for each individual and try to recognize the athlete's and subordinate's frame of reference. This will provide an indication of where each "is coming from."

Once a coach is aware of the players' needs, he or she will have a better indication of what turns each "on" and "off" psychologically. Having some control over the environment and the situation, a coach is in the position to "make good things happen." A prudent coach will explain to his athletes and assistant coaches, and make them understand, that he does not control all factors in a situation; there are simply some things he cannot do or over which he has little or no control. Once the coach makes this clear, he can concentrate on those factors he can influence so that there is a positive interaction between the individual and the environment. A coach is considered part of that environment.

Other Motivational Methods and Techniques

Numerous methods of trying to arouse or motivate players have been used through the years. Many coaches have used, and some continue to use, fiery pep talks in order to try to ignite or spark their players to victory, although such a gimmick is seldom effective over the long run. As pointed out by Metz (1972), "The present day athlete is very perceptive and questions the status quo. He is not motivated by the Knute Rockne approach. He will not battle to exhaustion for the colors he wears."

Some coaches try to instill fear as a means of arousal. Not fear of an opponent, but fear of the coach. It is not unusual for many players to perceive their head coach as a father-figure or as another authoritarian figure. As a result many younger athletes, in particular, fear their coaches, although there is evidence to indicate that a number of the professional athletes, too, have been fearful of their head coaches. Respect for the head coach may also be a strong psychological factor which is coupled with fear; the athletes may be afraid *not* to perform well for fear of being censured and reprimanded by the head coach. A coach is most certainly aware of which members of his squad are more sensitive than others, and which are and are not fearful of him.

A second tactic where the coach is the object of motivation, and not the opposition, uses a version of the "hate and anger" method of motivational arousal. Such a ploy is dangerous, especially if it "psyches out" the players and the game is lost. Caustic, personal, and demeaning remarks directed by a coach at a number of the players individually may have the temporary effect of getting players aroused so that they play more aggressively and, one hopes, "over their heads," but it may have a more lasting effect, too. It may lead to a rebellion by the players, which is likely to get the coach fired. While a coach may be role-playing in an attempt to get his players "up" for a particular game, his players are not likely to accept personal "rip-ups" before the other squad members as a psyching tactic.

Other arousal methods are less dramatic, especially when coaches talk to their athletes of consistency, intensity, momentum, a defeatist attitude, being a "winner," and "paying the price." These terms all reflect definite psychological overtones.

Sometimes a coach can say little, or nothing, and he can arouse or motivate his players.

Axthelm (1974), a *Newsweek* reporter, discussed how Don Shula, Miami Dolphins' head football coach, motivates: "Shula uses an approach that is virtually unique in the tradition-bound, unimaginative pro coaching business: instead of motivating through fear or love or frenzied emotions, he treats all 47 Dolphins like the mature and intelligent athletes they are."

Jim Counsilman, Indiana University's highly successful swimming coach said, "I had to examine my philosophy concerning athletic motivation. I knew I could never be the type of coach who constantly chewed out his athletes or used fear to motivate. I decided that every coach had to acquire his own method of motivating athletes and that I had to develop my own style. That style had to be compatible with my philosophy and my personality."

Coach Counsilman (1977) developed the following list of needs that are basic to all humans in the context of the coach–athlete relationship:

love and affection	the group instinct
security	recognition
status	self-esteem
achievement	the role of challenge

According to Tuttle (1975), Lee Corso, head football coach of Indiana University, listed the following factors in successful motivation:

- A coach must have the respect of his players. This is not his due, but must be earned.
- The player must be taught to be a better man.
- The magic of believing must be emphasized. Then players must believe in themselves and the coach.
- A man must never be downgraded; he must be given his dignity.
- The coach must recognize the basic right of every player to be different.
- Discipline is a must, both as a team aspect and on an individual basis.
- No one but his family is more important to the coach than the team.

Coach Tuttle stated that Corso believes that the best combination of these factors is a well-disciplined team that believes in itself.

Motivation: A Positive Approach for Athlete and Coach. Fred Wilt (Wilt and Bosen, 1971), former NCAA and national AAU champion who has won international acclaim as a distance runner, stated

> *Internal motivation* is so vitally important to the champion athlete.... Only the individual athlete can provide his own personal, internal motivation. No one else can do it for him.... A coach can't put speed into the legs of an athlete, wind into his lungs, or courage into his heart. But he can alter faulty habits, correct his technique to improve his natural ability, train him to top physical condition, and build his confidence. However,

the athlete must always remember, from the very beginning, that the burden of physical effort and internal motivation are his exclusive responsibilities.[2]

Self-Motivation. Wilt and Bosen (1971) offered the following suggestions, which we have synthesized, on how an athlete can bring about his own internal and personalized motivation that is necessary for athletic success.[2]

1. Set definite, realistic, meaningful, and measurable short- and long-range goals, with deadlines for achieving them; review your goals and accomplishments daily.
2. Use positive imagination, maintaining a strong mental picture of yourself, as people tend to become precisely what they imagine themselves to be.
3. After listing all problems, difficulties, and obstructions between yourself and your goals, formulate a detailed, comprehensive daily, weekly, and monthly plan of action for overcoming all barriers within established deadlines for accomplishment.
4. Develop the desire and the will to achieve, using your step-by-step plan of action to achieve your goals.
5. Develop an iron-willed determination that reminds you that nothing will keep you from achieving your goals.
6. Avoid a negative mental attitude, and do not associate with negative-minded people.
7. Develop a positive mental attitude, and develop an affirmative, effervescent personality.
8. You must have self-discipline, since part of the price of success is hard work and clean living.
9. Utilize your time wisely, directing time and your efforts toward your plan of action which will lead to your goal-achievement.
10. Learn from your defeat or failure; temporary setbacks can often be valuable experiences.
11. Be enthusiastic by developing your own enthusiasm.

These suggestions are equally important for the coach, too. Highly motivated coaches produce both individual and team winners.

AROUSAL, ACTIVATION, ANXIETY, "PSYCHING," AND ATHLETIC PERFORMANCE

This discussion would not be complete without including the words arousal, activation, anxiety, and "psyching," all of which are used frequently and sometimes

[2]Wilt, Fred, and Bosen, Ken. *Motivation and Coaching Psychology*. Los Altos, Calif.: Tafnews Press, 1971, pp. 18–21. Reprinted with permission.

interchangeably with motivation and athletic performance, although all do not have the same meaning for everyone.

Frequently motivation is thought of and used in a positive sense, whereas emotional arousal may be thought of in a negative sense. In actuality both terms may be thought of and referred to under positive conditions, such as happiness, joy, elation, or under negative conditions of anger, hate, fear, embarrassment, or other similar terms. There is a great degree of overlap in both physical and psychological reactions, although different situations provoke the same or different emotional arousal states. There is a common motivation to participate in activities of any nature that may be classified as *eustress-seeking,* that is, seeking a pleasant type of stress associated with excitement, adventure, and thrilling experiences. Eustress ''psyches up'' or ''turns on'' an individual and, in the process, releases energy.

Psyching

In common jargon, a coach usually tries to ''psych up'' his players; or players ''psych'' themselves or each other; or a player is ''psyched out''; or one ''psyches'' another. *Psyche* is a Greek word that means (when not capitalized), ''soul, self, mind,'' as distinguished from the body; it is the mind functioning as the center of thought, feeling, and behavior. It is felt that if one ''psyches'' another one gains a psychological advantage or ''edge'' over that person, such as an opponent. An individual may think that he or she increases the probability of winning a competitive encounter by acquiring or adopting some attitude, tactic, strategy, or ploy. Although there is little scientific data to substantiate the theory that there is such a thing as gaining a ''psychological advantage'' in competitive athletics, since the beginning of sport coaches probably have used virtually every means imaginable to try to ''psych'' their players. Some have utilized, and continue to utilize, traditional, conservative, and conventional means of motivation; others have used unconventional, bizarre, and nontraditional means of psyching.

The tactic or ploy usually tries to intimidate, provoke anger, disrupt concentration, and/or destroy confidence, to adversely influence the performance of an adversary. If one is into the ''flow'' of his game, experiencing a ''high'' or ''rush,'' it would not be possible to disrupt his concentration, unless he acknowledged subconsciously or otherwise the competitor's psyching tactic. One may then become ''psyched out'' or ''choke,'' to use common jargon. Martens (1980) identified ''flow'' as a highly desirable psychological state of mind where the performer has it ''altogether,'' in mind, body, and performance; all is in control; all is put into playing the game. A player may literally become oblivious to anything a competitor does to try to psych him.

There are many types of psyches used by coaches and athletes, some of which may be labeled gamesmanship, although some tactics may border on being illegal, unethical, unsportsmanlike, unsafe, obscene, ''bush,'' without ''class,'' and questionable. Other tactics are acceptable. All are a ploy to gain a psychological advantage or "edge" over the opposition. Identifying and discussing "psyching" techniques and ploys is beyond the scope of this book. There is little doubt, however, that emotions are aroused if one "gets" to another, whether it is coach to athlete, coach to coach, or athlete to athlete. Tutko and Tosi (1976) have discussed "psyching" in book-length detail.

Arousal, Anxiety, Activation, and Athletic Performance

Briefly, when a player is "up" psychologically, there is emotional arousal and elevated anxiety; when "down," the player is not aroused, not ready for competition. He may have already participated in the competition and performed poorly because he felt he was not psychologically "up" to compete. *Arousal* refers to the degree of energy release of an organism varying on a continuum from deep sleep to high excitement (Duffy, 1957).

Every coach recognizes the importance of the mental aspects of athletic performance. Some coaches feel that it is impossible for a competitor to get "too high," or that the more "psyched up" or aroused a player gets the better he or she performs. Others feel to the contrary and make a concerted effort to calm down the athlete in order that he or she can perform more optimally during competition, being better able to cope with stress. It is a recognized fact that, if one can gain control over one's cognitive and emotional processes, one can perform better. While optimal performance requires that the athlete be physiologically aroused and "psyched up," too much tension can have an adverse effect by inhibiting concentration, impairing judgment, and causing premature fatigue.

Each Individual's "Hot Button".   Just as each coach has his own methods or tactics for getting his team ready mentally to compete, generally each athlete gets ready mentally in his or her own way. Many studies have been conducted, especially with championship performers in a variety of individual and team sports, where specific behavior patterns have been recorded. As might be expected, their range in scope was wide and diverse, so that opposite behaviors have been reported. For example, some performers were alert, nauseous, irritable, nervous, and displayed characteristics of high anxiety, while other performers displayed drowsiness, appeared to be very relaxed, and displayed other characteristics, indicating little or no anxiety. Plimpton (1978) recorded some of the mental gymnastics that a number of well-known professional athletes in various individual and team sports reputedly went through prior to their competing. Each had his or her own way of focusing on the game at hand, just as each had his own "hot button."

In some instances a performer does not need someone, such as a coach, to motivate him since he can get "up" on his own. In other instances, athletes may expect their coaches to try to get them aroused. However, many coaches try to motivate by appealing to the whole group, instead of individually.

The Inexperienced Athlete. While the experienced athlete frequently works through his own process in that he knows what gets him ready for competition, the inexperienced athlete who has not been exposed regularly to games and contests may not know how to get "up." Therefore, as a coach gets ready for a contest and strives to get his team "up," he must handle the inexperienced player with great care. Coaches sometimes do not recognize that they are not the only ones who are responsible for elevating the player's anxiety; parents, family, peers, cheerleaders, pep rallies, the media, rivalries, the competitive process, and the athlete himself, all affect motivation. Additional psyching or arousal by the coach places much pressure on the athlete and his ultimate performance. For the inexperienced athlete in particular, the culmination of these factors may cause him to be in such a high state of anxiety that his play is adversely affected. Or the athlete may try to give the false impression of being poised and relaxed, such as by singing or whistling in the locker room prior to a game, only to be censured by his coach for "*not* being serious about the game." While the inexperienced athlete may not be aware of the fact that his over-confident display of such lighthearted behavior is likely to incur the typical coach's wrath, covertly the athlete's anxiety level may be so elevated that he knows no other way to control his behavior. The pressure may be too great for him, and he tries to appease it by diverting his attention to something else other than the upcoming contest.

Conversely, the more experienced players tend to respond to the pressures, and their game performance tends to be superior to their practice performances. It actually depends on the individual athlete; some are "up" in every competitive situation, practice, or game, while others regulate their tempo and intensity to a lesser degree in practice, but are "up" and "always come to play" in an actual game or contest. Many coaches display similar behavior patterns.

"Up" Too High. While it is embarrassing to be the coach of a team that is "down" and lethargic in its play, there may be the possibility at halftime or during times-out to reorganize the players and correct their sluggish performance. While the players may be "down" because they are physically tired, usually lethargic play comes from mental tiredness, indifference, lack of confidence, or possibly even overconfidence, and lack of concentration. During the course of an athletic contest most of these can be corrected.

Being "up" too high for a contest, however, can be more embarrassing and may be more difficult to rectify. When a team is down, their play is merely sluggish and indifferent; they simply do not perform enthusiastically. When players are too high, at times it looks like a comedy of errors, and their performance may seem to get worse rather than better. Players literally trip over the painted lines on the court or those on the field, and the harder they try the more embarrassing it becomes. While with the "down" players it may look as if the team has had *poor* coaching, with the "up" players it may look as if they have not had *any* coaching. If timing and precision are involved, whether it be in an individual activity or a team sport,

218 THE PSYCHOLOGICAL DIMENSIONS OF COACHING

usually the ''up'' players are ''off,'' which destroys the execution of motor skills or the play. It is not that the athletes are not trying. On the contrary, when they are too high, generally they are trying too hard. First one player, then another, and then another, makes errors of execution, destroying the precision and timing, so that individual and team confidence may be destroyed and the entire team gets ''down.'' Once again, there is the possibility that during the course of the game a coach can calm down his players and get them to perform up to their potential expectations.

Keying or Pointing. Every team has a traditional rival, or in individual competition one performer he or she wants to defeat more than anyone else. In many leagues and conferences this one contest may be the *must win* or *job saver* game for the coach and team. The team that wins, regardless of the remainder of the schedule in terms of wins-losses, is successful, as is the coach who preserved his job if his team wins. In some instances the entire season is ''pointed'' or ''keyed'' toward this game. There is much pressure on players, and coaching staffs alike, when they engage in *must win* contests. Seldom does a team go into a foray of this nature being ''down.'' Often both of the teams are ''high.'' What occurs after the contest is another matter.

For the team that wins the big game, almost regardless of what they do thereafter, their season is a success. For the team that loses, almost regardless of what they do in their remaining games, not only will it be difficult to get the team ''up,'' but their season may be viewed as a failure. If the big game is the last one of the season, a coaching staff has months to prepare to get the team ''up'' to play again next year. When the traditional game is in early or mid-season and the team loses, it could be an avalanche of defeats thereafter, because in the minds of the players and boosters the most important game on the schedule has been lost and nothing after that matters. Such a coaching nightmare is the worst of any and is extremely difficult to combat. The battle is to ''capture the minds'' of the players anew in order to get them to believe in themselves.

Individual Differences

While a team is made up of individuals, each must *act* as a team member. Certain individuals, because of their psychological makeup, perform better at a lower level of anxiety and prefer to remain alone to think over and plan *their* own course of action. While other athletes might want to be ''emotionally aroused'' before a contest, the low-anxiety performer may well be ''turned off'' by this group-type approach.

A coach certainly does not have the time, nor perhaps the know-how, to work with each individual on the team to get him in the proper emotional state prior to a game. But the coach should at least try to take the individual differences of players into consideration.

The emotional stress involved in getting a team mentally and physically ready to play is not a task that can be approached half-heartedly. There is no one best way to get a team ready to play. Coaches have used some innovative and creative methods that have been effective in a given situation and yet proved to be ineffective on other occasions.

As Oxendine (1970) pointed out,

Changing arousal state in the desired direction requires an understanding of some basic principles of psychology and skill in using certain techniques. . The following techniques have been used in practical and experimental situations to raise the level of arousal in motor activities: competition (challenges), praise and reproof, rewards and punishment, "pep" talks, music, and hypnosis. . . .

It must be borne in mind that most of these techniques may be and have been used to heighten and to lower an athlete's level of arousal. For example, music played in the locker room prior to practice may be selected because it has a pronounced rhythmic beat with an increasing tempo and intensity so as to raise the athletes' level of excitement; or on game day the music selected may be soft and soothing so as to calm down overly excited athletes in an effort to lower the level of arousal. A coach needs to be cognizant of the fact that a technique to arouse everyone will increase the performance level of some athletes but decrease the level of performance of others.

Oxendine (1970) offered the following generalizations on the topic of arousal-performance, based on research evidence, scientific literature, and empirical observation:

1. A high level of arousal is essential for optimal performance in gross motor activities involving strength, endurance, and speed.

2. A high level of arousal interferes with performance involving complex skills, fine muscle movements, coordination, steadiness, and general concentration.

3. A slightly-above-average level of arousal is preferable to a normal or subnormal arousal state for all motor tasks.

It must be pointed out that not all physiologists, psychologists, and others who have conducted research in the area of emotional arousal and athletic performance agree implicitly with all of these generalizations. Dr. Oxendine's generalizations serve the practical purpose for which they were intended, however. As Oxendine (1970) pointed out, and his comment is as appropriate today as it was then, "A great deal of research is essential before refinement can be made in the use of these or other techniques for promoting the desired arousal level of athletic participation."

While a coach's objective is to motivate his or her athletes so they will perform better, there is empirical evidence that seems to indicate that high levels of arousal interfere with performance efficiency in certain activities. While this may seem contrary to the thinking and beliefs of some coaches, it has been found that the relationship between arousal and motor performance is a complex one and does not appear to follow a straight line. Current research on arousal and athletic performance clearly indicates that different individuals function optimally at different levels of arousal. Nor does the same technique arouse everyone the same; nor is the same individual always aroused by the same technique every time.

Coaching Guidelines

While a coach must be able to motivate individuals and know how to motivate a team, the coach must be careful of utilizing psychological concepts taken out of context or of taking any general theory of motivation and attempting to treat all individuals identically. A coach must be sensitive to individual differences. A human being is complex and it is difficult to offer a simple explanation of motivation. There are few "right" answers, and no magic formulas or "10 easy rules" one can use to explain human behavior or use in specific situations to resolve motivational problems.

Probably the most important lesson to be gained by a coach from a knowledge of motivation, and one of the most important guides relating to all human interaction, is that behavior can best be explained or modified through considering the human response to needs. Since all behavior is motivated by needs, the coach should concentrate on how his actions affect the need satisfaction of others.

The coach is not often successful in changing an individual's behavior by logical argument, which is the first impulse. More likely success will come through modifying the reward system, changing the environment, or otherwise taking actions that appeal to the needs of the individual.

Wayne Lanning has been a consultant to the United States Olympic Track and Field Development Committee and to collegiate basketball and track coaches and teams. He was a counseling psychologist at Indiana University and is now at the University of Wyoming. In his contributing article, "Applied Psychology in Major College Athletics," as reported by Suinn (1980), Dr. Lanning enumerated and discussed the following psychological implications for athletic programs:

1.   Each team and each program is unique.

2.   Each player on a team is different and must be treated differently.

3.   Coaches need to deal with their players as more than just athletes.

4.   In team sports, the interaction effect of the coach and the player is a most critical element in maximizing the team performance.

5.   Even the best coaches don't understand all the psychological implications of maximizing athletic performance.

6.   A psychologist or behavioral specialist can be a valuable and productive resource for coaching staffs.

William P. Morgan (1974), director of the Sport Psychology Laboratory at the University of Wisconsin, has worked with the United States Olympic and national rowing and wrestling teams. He has served as a consultant for the Institute on Aerobic Research and has been involved with world-class runners. In Dr. Morgan's (1974) article, "Selected Psychological Considerations in Sport," he identified and summarized the following concepts, familiarizing the reader with actual findings from important sport psychology studies:

1. Athletes from various subgroups differ on a variety of psychological states and traits.

2. High level performers in athletics are characterized by psychological profiles which generally distinguish them from lower level performers.

3. Attempts to elevate anxiety ("Psych-up") and reduce tension states should be used cautiously and employed on a personalized basis.

4. Mental health plays an important role in athletic success, and it is quite likely that "emotional first aid" following competition is just as important as physical first aid.

5. There is frequently a lack of congruence between the athlete's conscious and unconscious motives.

Dr. Morgan concluded, "The position which has been outlined emphasizes the totality of man and the necessity of coach, trainer, psychologist, physiologist, and physician working in concert as a multidisciplinary team."

Summary

While commonsense and trial-and-success methods will reveal to a coach successful motivational strategies, there is an abundance of psychological literature on motivation available for perusal. The motivational concepts and theories explained throughout this chapter should familiarize the reader with basic concepts. However, if one learns nothing else than that a coach must recognize needs and then aid the individual in fulfilling those needs, both coach and athlete will know enough to obtain successful results. Philosopher Goethe may have best summed up how to motivate when he said, "If we take people as we find them we may make them worse, but if we treat them as though they are what they should be, we help them to become what they are capable of becoming."

REFERENCES

Axthelm, Pete. "Why the Dolphins Jump." *Newsweek*. January 14, 1974, p. 71.

Carew, Rod. *The Sacramento Bee*. December 9, 1977, p. D-5.

Counsilman, James E. "A Philosophy of Motivating Athletes." *Summer Manual*. American Football Coaches Association, 1977, pp. 86–90.

Craig, R. E., Mehrens, W. A., and Clarizio, H. F. *Contemporary Educational Psychology: Concepts, Issues, Applications*. New York, John Wiley & Sons, 1975, p. 143.

Davis, Keith. *Human Behavior at Work: Organizational Behavior* (5th ed.). New York. McGraw-Hill, 1977, p. 42.

Deci, Edward L. *Intrinsic Motivation*. New York. Plenum Press, 1975.

Duffy, Elizabeth, ''The Psychological Significance of the Concept of 'Arousal' or 'Activation'.'' *Psychological Review*. Vol. LXIV, No. 5, 1957, p. 265.

Evans, R. I. *Konrad Lorenz: The Man and His Ideas*. New York. Harcourt, 1975.

Fulmer, Robert M. *Practical Human Relations*. Homewood, Ill. Richard D. Irwin, 1977, pp. 120–134.

Goldstein, Kurt. *The Organism*. New York. American Book, 1939.

Kagan, Jerome, and Havemann, Ernest. *Psychology: An Introduction* (3rd ed.). New York. Harcourt Brace Jovanovich, 1976, p. 559.

Kennedy, Ray, and Williamson, Nancy. ''Special Report: Money in Sports.'' *Sports Illustrated*. Vol. 49, No. 3, 1978, pp. 29–88.

Lewin, Kurt. *Field Theory in Social Science Selected Theoretical Papers*. Edited by D. Cartwright. New York. Harper, 1960.

Mann, Carol. ''Notes and Quotes.'' *The Sacramento Bee*. May 19, 1978, p. D-7.

Martens, Rainer, Staff Writer Tony Bizjak, quoting Dr. Martens, ''Psychologist Puts Kids' Sports in Proper Perspective.'' *Sacramento Union*. March 9, 1980. (From the lecture ''Competition in Youth Sports.'' American River College, Sacramento, Calif. March 8, 1980.)

Maslow, A. H. ''A Theory of Human Motivation.'' *Psychological Review*. Vol. 50, No. 4, July 1943, pp. 370–396.

Maslow, A. H. *Motivation and Personality*, New York, Harper & Row, 1954, pp. 89, 90, 199–234 (2nd ed., 1970, pp. 9–20, 89, 90).

McClelland, D. C. *The Achieving Society*, Princeton, N. J. Van Nostrand Reinhold, 1961.

McClelland, D. C. ''Business Drives and National Achievement.'' *Harvard Business Review*. July–August 1962, pp. 103–105.

McClelland, D. C. ''Toward a Theory of Motive Acquisition.'' *American Psychologist*, 1965a, pp. 20, 321–333.

McClelland, D. C. ''Achievement Motivation Can Be Developed.'' *Harvard Business Review*. Vol. 43, No. 6, 1965b, pp. 6–24.

McClelland, D. C., Atkinson, J. W., Clark, R. A., and Lowell, E. L. *The Achievement Motive*. New York. Appleton-Century-Crofts, 1953.

McClelland, D. C., and Winter, D. G. *Motivating Economic Achievement*. New York. The Free Press, 1969.

McGregor, Douglas. ''The Human Side of Enterprise.'' *The Management Review*. November 1957, pp. 22–28, 88–92.

McGregor, Douglas. *The Human Side of Enterprise*. New York. McGraw-Hill, 1960.

Mednick, S. A., Higgins, J., and Kirschenbaum, J. *Psychology Explorations in Behavior and Experience*. New York. John Wiley & Sons, 1975, p. 94.

Metz, Paul R. ''A Course to Build Player-Coach Rapport.'' *JOHPER*. April 1972, pp. 50–51.

Morgan, William P. ''Selected Psychological Considerations in Sport.'' *Research Quarterly*. Vol. 45, 1974, pp. 374–390.

Murray, Edward J. *Motivation and Emotion*. Englewood Cliffs, N.J. Prentice-Hall, 1964.

Murray, H. A. *Explorations in Personality*. New York. Oxford Press, 1938 (reprinted 1962), p. 62.

Oxendine, Joseph B. "Emotional Arousal and Motor Performance." *Quest XIII*. January 1970, pp. 23–32.

Plimpton, George. *Sports!*. New York. H. M. Abrams, 1978, p. 192.

Rosenbaum, Bernard L. "How Good People-Handlers Motivate Others." *Nation's Business*. March 1978, pp. 78–80.

Sage, George, "Sport as a Social Agent." Lecture at the California State University, Sacramento, Calif. 1977.

Skinner, B. F. *The Behavior of Organisms*. New York. Appleton-Century-Crofts, 1938.

Suinn, Richard M. *Psychology in Sports Methods and Applications*. Minneapolis. Burgess Publishing Company, 1980, pp. 364–367.

Tutko, Thomas A., and Tosi, Umberto. *Sports Psyching: Playing Your Best Game All of the Time*. Los Angeles. J. P. Torcher, Inc., 1976.

Tuttle, Steven C. "Motivating the Athlete." *Athletic Journal*. Vol. 56, No. 2, October 1975, pp. 76–78.

Wilt, Fred, and Bosen, Ken. *Motivation and Coaching Psychology*. Los Altos, Calif. Tafnews Press, 1971, pp. 18–21.

Zander, Alvin. "Motivation and Performance of Sports Groups." In *Psychology of Sport and Motor Behavior II,* Daniel M. Landers (Ed.), 1975.

SELECTED READINGS

Alderman, Richard B. "Incentive Motivation in Sport: An Interpretive Speculation of Research Opportunities." In *The Status of Psychomotor Learning and Sport Psychology Research*. Brent S. Rushall (Ed.). Dartmouth, Nova Scotia. Sport Science Associates, 1975, pp. 3.1–3.18.

Atkinson, J. W. *An Introduction to Motivation*. New York. Van Nostrand, 1964, pp. 188–197.

Clarke, C. "Psyching to Lose." *Runners World*. No. 13, 1978, pp. 56–57.

Fisher, A. Craig, *Psychology of Sport Issues and Insights*. Palo Alto, Calif. Mayfield, 1976, pp. 136–144.

Lowsley, James. "How to Manage Motivation." *Engineering and Services Quarterly*. February 1977, pp. 13–14.

Miller, Donna Mae. *Coaching the Female Athlete*. Philadelphia. Lea & Febiger, 1974, pp. 67–68.

Morgan, William P. (Ed.). *Contemporary Readings in Sport Psychology*. Springfield, Ill. Charles C Thomas, 1970.

Nideffer, R. M. *The Inner Athlete: Mind Plus Muscle for Winning*. New York. Crowell Publishing Company, Inc, 1976.

Oates, Bob. "Pardee and Vermeil Know A Secret: How to Motivate." *The Sporting News*. Vol. 190, No. 11, September 13, 1980, p. 19.

Steben, Ralph E., and Bell, Sam. *Track and Field: An Administrative Approach to the Science of Coaching*. New York. John Wiley & Sons, 1978, pp. 250–251, 273–274.

Straub, William F. (Ed.). *An Analysis of Athlete Behavior*. Movement Publications, 1978.

Suinn, Richard M. *Psychology in Sports Methods and Applications*. Minnesota. Burgess Publishing Company, 1980.

Takeda, Ken. ''Psychological Principles of Coaching.'' *Proceedings. American Football Coaches Association,* 1978, pp. 79–83.

Zander, Alvin. ''Motivation and Performance of Sports Groups.'' In *Psychology of Sport and Motor Behavior II,* Daniel M. Landers (Ed.), 1975.

10

The Psychology of Learning and Teaching – Coaching Effectiveness

In athletic competition, the athlete must usually coordinate eye, mind, and body, concentrating on affective and cognitive processes in the execution of motor skills for an effective performance. The intent of this chapter is to focus on the learning process as it relates to psychomotor or motor learning in athletics and sports. Since the learning of most skills is a thoughtful, active process, involving both mental and physical coordinations, many authorities use the term psychomotor in place of motor skills.

No attempt will be made to explain the learning process by discussing the physiological changes that are assumed to take place in the nervous system, such as advanced by Kappers (1917) and other psychologists, physiologists, and neurologists who have expressed theories regarding the structural changes that take place in the nervous system as a result of learning. Some theorists agree with Kappers, while others have proposed different kinds of structuring or more elaborate theories which describe learning as the growth of dendrites and axons in the area of the synapse in the nervous system of the individual.

THE FUSION KNOWLEDGE CIRCLE

Although a coach may possess a well-rounded philosophy and his coaching theory may be fundamental and sound, he may not enjoy coaching success unless he can convey his ideas and "know-how" to others. Therefore, he must have the abilities to teach and to communicate effectively. The methods or means he utilizes to convey his ideas and conceptions are important, as is *how* he teaches or coaches, which is "the art of coaching." A coach should always present his material and gear his instructions to the squad at their level of comprehension. His approach should be basic, his presentation clear and concise.

The coaching cliché, "It isn't what a coach knows, but what a coach teaches that is important," is only a half-truth with several implied assumptions. That most every coach knows more than he or she is capable of teaching is probably true in most instances, although many coaches try to teach too much. It is an erroneous assumption, however, to believe that athletes always learn what the coaches *attempt* to teach to them. If this were true, there would never be any broken plays, missed assignments, or the judgmental errors committed by players. However, all athletes do *not* learn because players do not intentionally commit such errors and mistakes. Therefore, a more accurate truism or corollary cliché is, "It isn't what a coach teaches, but what his or her players comprehend and *learn to execute correctly* that is the most important!" If there is to be effective learning, there must be effective teaching–coaching.

Coaching theory refers to the basic conception that each coach has as to how to play the game. For every theory that is advanced, there is another opposite in nature, so that frequently two theories are incongruent with each other.

Whether to teach and utilize the fast break or the slow break attack as one's basic style of play is an illustration of opposite offensive basketball theories. Or from a strategical and tactical standpoint, a coach's basic premise may be that of not playing to win, but first and foremost playing *not* to lose. While this may sound like an unusual point of view to the novice coach and the participants, there is a difference. When one plays to win, usually one is the aggressor, knowing his team will make mistakes, but he or she intends to outscore the opposition and thus win the contest. The contrary theory of *not losing* implies that the team is content to play a waiting game by minimizing its own mistakes, and letting the opposition make the errors and mistakes; thus winning is the result of the opposition defeating itself. Basically, this viewpoint is suggesting, "Before we can win, we must not lose by defeating ourselves." The salient point is that a coach's basic theory of play will determine the style he teaches and the strategy and tactics his team uses. Figure 10-1 conveys a circular fused effect, which describes the effects of coaching theory, methods, techniques, philosophy, and principles, all of which are influenced by a number of other variables.

The successful coach transmits his theory to his squad, securing adequate feedback from his players to determine whether or not they comprehend what he or she has attempted to teach to them. While contests presumably are *won* only on the game fields or courts, there are numerous instances where contests have been *lost* on the practice fields or courts because the players were not taught properly and did not comprehend the coach's objectives for victory.

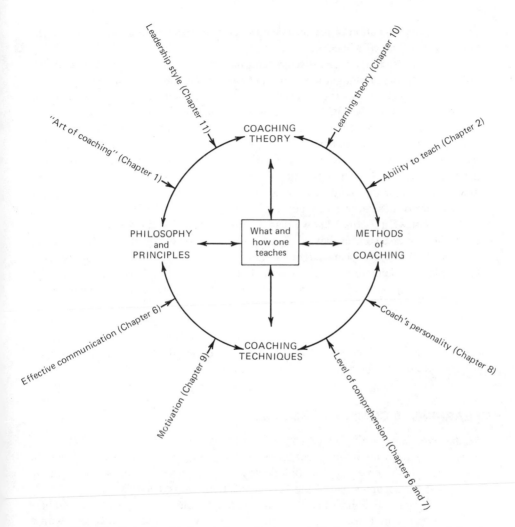

Figure 10-1. The fusion knowledge circle, and some variable factors that influence what and how one teaches-coaches.

Knowledge of the Subject Is Insufficient

While knowledge of the subject matter of the "science of coaching" obviously is important, a unique feature of coaching is that the ultimate evaluation of the teacher–coach generally is based on the performance of his or her players which is most frequently reflected in the final score of the contest. Therefore, while a coach may possess much knowledge and "know-how" about numerous aspects of the sport, if he or she is unable to convey this information and obtain feedback in terms of satisfactory execution or performance by the players, there is little likelihood the coach will be judged a success.

A coach can explain and discuss, and players can listen and comprehend, but unless the players are taught through repetitive practice under gamelike conditions the intricate aspects of the fast break, for example, they will be unable to execute the necessary motor skills with a high degree of success in an actual game. Some coaches merely verbalize or "tell" what to do, and conduct talk "seminars" on how it should be done, rather than adhering to the laws and principles of learning theories, which we will soon explain. While certain aspects of these theories are debatable and may even be refutable, all are more sound than merely instructing an athlete what he or she should do instead of placing the player in a learning situation to have him or her successfully accomplish the task.

It is not what a coach knows that is important, it is what he or she is able to teach the players, so that they may comprehend and execute through their motor skills what they have been taught. While we frequently recognize that too little knowledge is a dangerous thing, we do not always realize that too much knowledge has its limitations, too. The latter case is especially true in coaching where others must perform using their cognitive processes and motor skills by following what their coach has taught to them. Many coaches are good "students" of the game in that they study and learn much about the technology of their sport, but they are not effective teachers of the sport they coach because they do not successfully impart their knowledge to their players.

LEARNING: A COMPLEX PROCESS

To the layperson learning appears to be a relatively simple process. However, as we have already illustrated throughout the book, psychological constructs and proposed theories are both numerous and complicated, and the same may be said of learning theory, which occupies one of the central positions in psychology.

Learning is much more than what we are taught, although what we are taught is a simple theory of learning. Our intent is not to try to impress the reader with a number of complex theories of learning, but to cite various theories and to include information that will be useful to the coach. It is through the learning process, which includes communication, that the coach's goals for his program are transmitted to others. Therefore, each coach should understand *how* learning takes place. We will need to apply the research findings of psychologists to discover the learning process, the learner (athlete), and the conditions for learning. Once again, the reader should readily recognize the obvious, namely, that in a single chapter one can do little more than discuss superficially the subject of learning. The references and suggested readings at the conclusion of this chapter are mostly sources of book length that deal exclusively and extensively with the psychology of learning.

WHAT IS LEARNING?

Typically, learning is thought of as (1) a process through which we gain knowledge, or an understanding, or a skill by study, instruction, or experience; (2) it usually includes the memorizing of information and some form of teaching that informs; and (3) the process implies that we find out or ascertain something. The meaning of these definitions of learning bring to mind a baby who "learns" to crawl, walk, and talk, and to cry when hungry; or one who "learns" what is and is not acceptable social behavior; or one who "learns" to make decisions intuitively, or judgmentally, or by problem solving; or one who "learns" to "run to daylight," dribble and dunk a basketball, or drive a golf ball 250 yards off a tee—all of these are instances of learning. However, psychologists, who will concur with the layperson that in these examples something is "learned," will also agree that this definition is too limited; and it is very likely that most psychologists will disagree with the layperson as to *how* learning takes place, and for what reasons. An explanation of learning, agreed on by all, is an objective that psychology has not yet achieved.

Learning—The Result Is a Change in Behavior

It appears the majority of psychologists define learning in terms of a relatively permanent change in behavior as the result of an experience or a practice. Others may include the fact that learning is a process, and that the behavior is developed or altered (changed), but many include the change in behavior as the result of practice or experience. It may be concluded that for learning to have occurred there must be a relatively permanent change in the learner's behavior.

One may counter with the argument that the eye blink, knee jerk, and other similar behaviors are reflexive and are assumed to result from phylogenetic development, and thus that such behavior does not result from learning. While this assumption is correct, one "learns" from experience that if one places his hand on a hot surface he will get burned, and one "learns" from experience that when any foreign object enters the eye it causes irritation and usually pain, despite reflexive behavior which causes the individual to withdraw his hand quickly from the hot surface and to close (blink) his eye when a foreign object enters it. The change in behavior is of a permanent nature since one learns to avoid the painful acts or suffer the consequences, although many psychologists maintain that these acts are not learned; that is, they maintain that there are instances of reflexive behavior and that they are not learned.

TYPES OR FORMS OF LEARNING

Clearly, there is *no* unanimity among learning theorists as to the types or forms of learning, and only limited agreement on the topic prevails. There are still many questions in the minds of learning theorists. For example, one might be a skillful performer in certain sports that involve psychomotor activities, such as football, boxing, and wrestling, yet the same individual may be unable to perform basic dance steps or to learn how to play golf or basketball with any degree of skill; or one may be able to perform with ease the problems in geometry and calculus, but have great difficulty learning a foreign language, and perhaps greater difficulty learning to conform to acceptable social standards and mores. Discounting the fact that different learning processes are involved, as identified by Bloom et al. (1956), such as the psychomotor or motor domain, the cognitive domain, and the affective domain, all three of which are illustrated in our examples, even within the same "domain" of learning the answers are not clear. If one can ride a bicycle, should one be able to learn to ice skate immediately? If one can solve difficult mathematical problems, can one then learn a foreign language with ease? If one can dance, why can't one learn to perform acrobatic skills in gymnastics? Obviously different muscle groups may be employed in the different physical activities illustrated, but what we need to be concerned with is whether the learning process is similar or different in these examples. If one learns how to speak a foreign language, is it easier or more difficult to learn how to solve complicated mathematical problems or to learn how to become a skillful golfer? Or if one is a skillful performer in basketball, does one learn more readily or with greater difficulty how to perform with skill and grace acrobatic routines or how to speak a foreign language? The answers to these questions, and those of a similar nature, have much significance for all coaches and educators. In Figure 10-2, the theories of Bloom et al. and others who refer to types of learning as being motor or psychomotor, cognitive, and affective (domains) are illustrated. However, physical activity does not partake only of one "domain." Motor learning cannot be devoid of cognitive and affective processes, and as is indicated below, some theorists prefer not to employ the single word "motor" in conjunction with learning most physical skills because of its *implied* limited connotation. "Motor" learning will be explained in detail shortly.

Learning Theories Summarized

Figure 10-2 illustrates several types of learning, as theorized by different well-known authorities in the field. It may be noted in Figure 10-2 that there is no overall consensus among theorists relevant to the different types or forms of learning processes. Particularly in regard to motor skills, in which we are most interested, there are several conflicting views. Also note that it appears that some of the authorities seem to describe learning according to type of material learned, while other theorists emphasize the type of mental processes that are assumed to occur.

While most psychologists are convinced that not all learning involves the same basic processes, they do not agree how many processes there are. Behaviorists, for example, make operational distinctions among three types of learning pertaining to human behavior; yet many maintain in real life that most behavior is acquired and sustained by a combination of respondent, operant, and observational learning. Before discussing these three particular theories, mention should be made of the fact that, of the many theories of learning, some have greater impact on the field of education than others. Some belong to the association schools of learning or stimulus-response theories, and others are known as field or cognitive theories of learning.

The Association Schools of Learning. With their emphasis on stimulus, response, reward, and conditioning, this school views human beings as similar to machines; this group includes the behavioral theories or approaches. While it is recognized that humans really act as supermachines, more complex than the machine one may ordinarily visualize, these theories nevertheless state that man and machine operate on the same principles. Humans respond to their environment in a determined manner, and our cognitive nature, if it exists, is unimportant.

Field Theories of Learning. Other theories see human beings as demonstrating behavior that is obviously superior to and more complex than either mechanistic or animal activity. Humans are capable of creative expression and can solve problems, and this is done by a form of insightful behavior. One's insight into a problem is structured by a perception of the environment which surrounds the individual. However, humans are able to respond to the pressure of their environment in a creative fashion. The more we know of our environment or *field,* the more accurate is our perception of our problems and their solutions. Field theorists of learning maintain that human insight is sharper and that our learning is faster and more accurate than that of other animals.

ASSOCIATION SCHOOLS OF LEARNING, OR STIMULUS-RESPONSE THEORIES

Stimulus-response (S-R) theories have become major influences on education during the current century. S-R is used to indicate that a particular stimulus is connected or leads to a particular response. S-R theorists generally assume a direct cause-and-effect relationship, with the learner seeing a connection between the stimulus and the response. S-R theorists also emphasize the importance of reinforcement of this connection, or a stimulus-response bond. The bond psychology, or *Connectionism,* is so closely associated with the name of Edward Lee Thorndike that one has come to mean the other.

Thorndike's Connectionism and Laws of Learning

Many people feel that Columbia University's Professor Emeritus Edward Lee Thorndike has probably contributed more to our present understanding of learning

Figure 10-2 Several Types of Learning Summarized by Noted Learning Theorists

Kingsley's forms of learning (1946)[a]	Tolman's types of connections or relations (1949)[b]	Bloom's taxonomy of educational objectives (1956)[c]	Kingsley and Garry's types of learning (1957)[d]	Harris and Schwahn's variable processes in learning (1961)[e]	Gagné's types of learning (1965)[f]
1. Development of motor skills and habituation of action	1. Motor patterns—require simple conditioning	1. The psychomotor or motor domain	1. Perceptual motor learning	1. Reasoning—a rational approach to the solution of problem situations	1. Signal learning—rather "involuntary" conditioned responses
2. Problem solving	2. Cathexes—acquired relationship between drive and goal	2. The cognitive domain—development of intellectual abilities and skills	2. Problem solving—learner must determine solution to a novel situation	2. Aesthetic creativity—the application of creative or original thought in aesthetic production	2. Stimulus-response learning—voluntary responses to a discriminated stimulus
3. Development of attitudes and ideas	3. Equivalence beliefs—acquired relationship between drive and secondary or substitute goal	3. The affective domain—dealing with interests, attitudes, appreciations, and adjustments	3. Conditioning—both instrumental and classical	3. Conceptual learning—the interpretation of situations, signs, and symbols; and the representation of their meaning	3. Chaining—connecting a sequence of previously learned S-Rs
4. Development of understanding through observation, listening, reading, and generalizing	4. Field expectancies—learned signs or cues facilitate problem solving		4. Trial and error learning—refers to inefficiency of earlier behavior	4. Skill learning—the coordination of appropriate sensory and perceptual functions in motor performance	4. Verbal association—a type of chaining involving verbal materials
5. Memorizing ideas or verbal responses in fixed sequences	5. Field-cognition modes (of a higher order than 4)—innate capacities contribute to readiness to learn in several ways		5. Discrimination learning—judgment between two or more stimuli is required	5. Attitudinal learning—has to do with changes which involve a person's values	5. Multiple-discrimination learning—acquiring combinations of chains
6. Development of perception and	6. Drive discrimination—two modes of be-		6. Maze learning—learner must rely on	6. Group learning—learning in situa-	6. Concept learning—internal or symbolic

representation of environment

7. Principle learning—acquisition of the relationship between concepts
8. Problem solving—using two or more previously learned principles to develop new ones for specific purposes

tions in which interpersonal or social interaction plays a prominent role

memory of previous responses

7. Verbal learning

havior are learned, depending on the particular drive

improvement of observation

7. Modification of emotional reaction

Sources: Adapted from J. B. Oxendine, *Psychology of Motor Learning*, Copyright © 1968, pp. 10–11. Adapted by permission of Prentice-Hall, Inc., Englewood Cliffs, New Jersey.

[a] H. L. Kingsley, *The Nature and Conditions of Learning*, Copyright © 1946. Adapted by permission of Prentice-Hall, Inc., Englewood Cliffs, New Jersey.

[b] E. C. Tolman, "There is More Than One Kind of Learning." *Psychological Review*, 1949, pp. 56, 144–155. Reprinted by permission (public domain).

[c] Benjamin S. Bloom, Max D. Engelhart, Edward J. Furst, Walter H. Hill, and David R. Kratwohl, *Taxonomy of Educational Objectives, Handbook 1: Cognitive Domain*. Copyright © 1956. New York. David McKay Company, Inc. Reprinted by permission.

[d] H. L. Kingsley and R. Garry, *The Nature and Conditions of Learning*, 2nd ed. Copyright © 1957. Adapted by permission of Prentice-Hall, Inc., Englewood Cliffs, New Jersey.

[e] T. L. Harris and W. E. Schwahn (Eds.). *Selected Readings on the Learning Process*. Copyright © 1961. New York. Oxford University Press, p. 29. Reprinted by permission.

[f] From the *Conditions of Learning* by Robert M. Gagné. Copyright © 1965 by Holt, Rinehart and Winston, Inc. Reprinted by permission of Holt, Rinehart and Winston.

than any other individual, and his influence on American education has been monumental. For many years Thorndike's Connectionism was *the* leading theory of learning in American education, and his laws of learning were widely adhered to.

In his posited S-R theory, or Connectionism, Thorndike maintained that the connections were products of biological changes in the nervous system. A major tenet in his theory is that learning takes place as a result of trial-and-error, and he concluded (1913, 1931) from his research that all learning functions in accordance with his major laws of learning: readiness, exercise, and effect.

The Law of Readiness. Thorndike posited that learning will take place most effectively when the learner is ready or prepared to respond. To act when ready is pleasurable, while not to act when ready brings displeasure or annoyance. Although Thorndike did not discuss maturation as a factor of readiness, the concept of readiness has been extended to include the interaction of maturation, prerequisite learning, and motivation. Thorndike's law of readiness is closely linked to his law of effect, which he added after formulating his law of exercise.

The Law of Exercise. Before 1930, Dr. Thorndike felt that a "connection" was strengthened by practice, thus "practice makes perfect" was a fundamental tenet. Through the *law of use* the bond is developed and strengthened. Conversely, if practice is discontinued, the connection becomes weakened or lost entirely; this is sometimes referred to as the *law of disuse*. Thorndike seemed to indicate that learning was almost automatic with practice, and the more one practiced the more indelibly a subject was stamped into the nervous system. However, criticism was swift and devastating, and Thorndike, recognizing that repetition of an act did not ensure its permanence, after 1930 revised his original law of exercise as originally posited to include the law of effect.

The Law of Effect. To use Thorndike's (1913) own words, "When a modifiable connection between a situation and a response is made and is accompanied or followed by a satisfying state of affairs, that connection's strength is increased; when made and accompanied or followed by an annoying state of affairs, its strength is decreased."

Thorndike's law of effect is considered his most important one, the foundation of *connectionism;* basically it states that a bond is strengthened or weakened in accordance with the pleasure or pain that is associated with it. Controversy came from others of the mechanistic school who maintained that pleasure and pain were too subjective and too difficult to measure objectively. Although initially he had considered reward and punishment to have an equal and opposite effect, after further experimentation, Thorndike (1932) later reported that reward was much more potent in the shaping of behavior than was punishment; in fact, learning occurs because of positive afteraffects. He refuted the phase of his law of effect pertaining to punishment as a weakening of the bond, stating that an unpleasant experience might indeed be well remembered.

Thorndike's Influence and Effect. Thorndike also formulated several subordinate laws that were mainly designed to clarify and expand on his three basic laws of learning: effect, readiness, and exercise; but it is Thorndike's main laws that gave dimension and scope to his learning theory.

The educational implications of Thorndike's work have been far reaching. Many teachers and coaches exposed to the assumptions of associationist methods of instruction as undergraduate and graduate students adhere to Thorndike's learning theory today in the classroom and on the playing fields and courts, despite the recognized and admitted weaknesses inherent in connectionism. Thorndike also established the basis for early scientific approaches to educational problems. His assumptions gained popularity and wide acceptance because they were specific and could be investigated by scientific means. Most learning theorists used Thorndike's view as a reference point. Tolman (1938), in reflecting on the influence of Dr. Thorndike, stated:

> The psychology of animal learning—not to mention that of child learning—has been and still is primarily a matter of agreeing or disagreeing with Thorndike, or trying in minor ways to improve upon him. Gestalt psychologists, condition-reflex psychologists, sign-gestalt psychologists—all of us here in America seem to have taken Thorndike overtly or covertly, as a starting point.

Dissatisfaction with Thorndike's concept of pleasure caused many American psychologists to turn to the theory of conditioning. The impetus given to classical conditioning came primarily from the work of Ivan P. Pavlov, a Russian physiologist; and the impetus to operant conditioning came primarily from the work of B. F. Skinner, an American psychologist.

Behavioral Theories or Approaches to Learning

Psychoanalytic, dispositional, and *phenomenological* strategies for the study of personality were discussed in Chapter 8. The fourth strategy, the behavior strategy, for the study of personality as you recall is directly and ultimately concerned with overt behavior, which is learned. The basic assumption made by behaviorists is that behavior develops and is modified primarily, though not exclusively, in accordance with the principles of learning rather than by being acquired through heredity and determined biologically. Behavioral approaches or theories differ, however, with respect to the form of learning that is emphasized.

The Respondent Theory. The classical conditioning or respondent approach focuses on an organism learning new responses by coming to associate a set of circumstances that previously did not elicit a particular reaction with another set of circumstances that had already led to that reaction. The respondent approach focuses on the conditions that *antecede* and elicit behavior, as compared to the operant approach, which deals with the effects of *consequences* of behavior on its subsequent performance. Antecedent conditions refer to all stimuli that are present before the target behavior occurs, including situational, temporal, and interpersonal clues. Succinctly, respondent behavior is elicited by some identifiable stimulus, and thus derives its name from the fact that the subject *responds* to something. When reflexes occur, such as perspiring in response to heat or the knee jerking in response to a tap on the patellar tendon, these are examples of respondent behavior. Examples of respondents that have been learned through classical conditioning may include feeling nervous (perspiring, stomach queasy, difficulty breathing) before starting an athletic contest, feeling angry (set jaw, grim appearance, clenched fists), or feeling humiliation (blushing, downcast) when censured publicly before squad members for making a critical error in a game. In each instance, a stimulus serves as a cue for the response to occur. From the respondent viewpoint, behavior is elicited by its antecedents and not by its consequences.

Pavlov: Classical Conditioning. Most people in the field of education, and students of psychology, are familiar with the famous experiments on the conditioning of dogs conducted by Ivan P. Pavlov. Pavlov conducted experiments for a half century on the nature of classical conditioning, which is referred to as Pavlovian conditioning. Pavlov's (1927) historic experiment has had an enormous influence on the psychology of learning and the specific terms connected with the classical conditioning approach to learning.

Briefly, Pavlov's experiments in learning were concerned with reflex, which is an inborn, built-in response to a stimulus. Pavlov utilized sound (a bell, tuning fork, metronome), but the stimulus may be any form of energy capable of exciting the nervous system. Through learning, a reflex response can become attached to a stimulus that did not originally cause the response. Pavlov ''taught'' a dog to respond to sound by salivating; this reflex response originally was caused by the presence of food in the dog's mouth. Behavior that is a response to a definite stimulus is called *respondent behavior,* and Pavlov elicited this type of behavior in his historic experiments.

In summary, the salivary response produced (by the bell) is called a conditioned response (CR) because it had been learned upon presentation of a conditioned stimulus (CS); previously the conditioned stimulus (CS) was paired with the unconditioned (meat powder placed in the dog's mouth) stimulus (UCS). This pairing is referred to as *reinforcement.* When reinforcement (reward) is withdrawn, the conditioned response (CR) tends to disappear, and this process is called *extinction.* After a rest period, however, it tends to reappear, a process called *spontaneous recovery.*

Two additional terms pertaining to classical conditioning are *stimulus generalization* and *stimulus discrimination.* When a response in a subject has been conditioned to one stimulus, the response is likely to be aroused by a similar stimulus, and this process is known as *stimulus generalization*. Through further training, however, the subject can learn to respond to a particular conditioned stimulus but not to other stimuli even when they are similar, and this process is known as *stimulus discrimination*.

This type of stimulus-response learning situation can be observed in and outside of the field of coaching. The offensive starting count in football is a stimulus which cues respondents to react, as does the sound of the official's whistle which terminates play.

The Instrumental Learning Theory. According to the operant conditioning approach, or the instrumental learning approach, behavior is learned through the consequences which the organism receives when he performs the behavior. Consequent conditions refer to everything that happens *after* the target behavior is performed, including both the immediate and long-range consequences to the organism performing the behavior.

Credit for distinguishing between *operant* and *respondent* behavior is given to Skinner (1938). Operant refers to responses that an individual emits and that he is operating on his behavior. Such behavior is controlled by the consequences that follow its performance. Operant behavior is also called *instrumental behavior,* because the performance of the behavior is instrumental in producing some end result. The behavior is under the control of its consequences in the sense that if the consequences are positive, the behavior is likely to occur again; whereas if they are negative, the behavior is less likely to recur. Much of what we have learned has come to us via operant or instrumental conditioning.

Skinner: Operant Conditioning. In Skinner's (1938) operant conditioning, nothing is done by the investigator to elicit the response. It is the organism's responsibility to "operate on the environment," and should the subject respond in terms of the correct or particular behavior, the organism receives a reward that reinforces the subject's response or behavior. Skinner showed that a rat placed in a cage would eventually press a bar and a pigeon would peck a disc, each through its operant behavior, and then would learn to keep pressing the bar and pecking the properly designated disc if such action were rewarded with food. A simpler explanation is that the animal or human being must do the appropriate trick before receiving the treat in operant conditioning. Since manipulation of behavior is essential to Skinner's theory, the consequences could be startling.

Skinner's *Walden Two* (1948) illustrates operant conditioning, and his best-known book, *Beyond Freedom and Dignity* (1971), continues to be widely read, frequently quoted, and much debated. According to Skinner, people are not to blame for their failures, nor are they deserving of credit when they achieve. People are simply the creatures of their environments, and their behavior depends solely on the kinds of stimulus-response learning to which they have been subjected, particularly which of their actions have been rewarded and which have been punished. Other schools of psychological thought are moving in quite different directions from Skinner's S-R psychology.

The basic premise of operant conditioning is that operant behavior that is reinforced tends to be repeated, while operant behavior that is not reinforced takes place only at random intervals or is abandoned. Like classical conditioning, instrumental learning also follows the rules of extinction, spontaneous recovery, stimulus generalization, and stimulus discrimination, all of which were explained previously. The learning of complicated tasks through operant conditioning is called *shaping*, a process by which actions are built up, step by step, by rewarding simpler actions that lead to the final behavior.

In general, reinforcement is the process of assisting learning by pairing desired behavior with something the organizer finds rewarding. However, on occasion, reinforcement can be unpleasant or negative, and *operant escape* or *operant avoidance* is likely to be the result. In operant escape the organism learns through operant conditioning to get away or escape from an unpleasant form of reinforcement; in operant avoidance, one learns to prevent or avoid the unpleasant reinforcement by taking some kind of action before it occurs.

In most of Skinner's (1953) operant conditioning experiments (and it is Skinner who gave this name to the process of learning which he studied and distinguished from classical conditioning), the negative reinforcement is eliminated and learning is based on positive reinforcement alone. However, the principle of reinforcement infers both positive and negative reinforcers or reinforcing stimuli. In *positive* reinforcement, a stimulus is *presented* following an operant; whereas in *negative* reinforcement, a stimulus is *removed* following an operant. In either situation, if the stimulus event increases the likelihood that the operant will be repeated, *reinforcement* is said to have occurred. A simple example, with several variations, will illustrate the principle of reinforcement and the differences between positive and negative reinforcement.

An Illustration. In an athletic situation when an athlete is lauded by the coach for performing well and another athlete is censured for not performing well or for having disruptive behavior, each operant's behavior is being reinforced in a *positive* sense, although this is *not* the coach's intent with the censured athlete. Conversely, in the same situation, if the coach neither lauds the first athlete nor censures the second one, neither athlete's behavior is being reinforced since the coach has removed the stimulus. This is *negative* reinforcement, which is not what the coach intended for the first individual. In all situations, if the stimulus event increases the likelihood that the operant will be repeated, reinforcement is said to have occurred.

Although some fail to differentiate between *negative reinforcement* and punishment, most psychologists do not consider the two to be the same. *Punishment* involves applying *aversive* consequences to a response in order to reduce or eliminate the rate of occurrence of the response. Although in his original formulation of the law of effect Thorndike (1913) assumed that reward and punishment worked in "equal and opposite ways," he later concluded that punishment was relatively ineffective. It must be pointed out that the research that supports this conclusion is almost all based on the responses of nonhuman organisms. Clearly there are ethical and moral questions to be considered when *aversive* consequences may occur to human subjects.

From a coaching standpoint, "punishment" frequently means running laps or the stadium steps, or doing push-ups or some other activity of a similar nature. From a teaching standpoint, the coach wants a player to learn, not to foul up a play; thus, to reprimand the athlete who has fouled up a play may not be the best action to take. In fact, many educators and coaches maintain that punishment as a reinforcement is ineffective. Let us look at another illustration of positive and negative reinforcement in an athletic setting.

An Illustration. A linebacker performs well by making a number of assists and solo tackles, and he intercepts several passes. His performance is reinforced by his teammates and coaches with handshakes, embraces, pats on the helmet, back, and buttocks, and verbal comments, such as "nice going," "great interception," "good hit," and "fine job." In addition, the linebacker is awarded four oak-leaf clusters to affix on the outside of his helmet to denote "great plays." Obviously receiving such adulation, praise, and recognition will motivate the player to continue to perform well.

The linebacker's behavior and performance will also be shaped and affected if, despite the fact that he plays well, he seldom or never receives praise, or if he is criticized severely when he does not do as well as expected by his coach.

It is difficult to separate learning and motivation theories, as we have attempted to do for purposes of discussion, but not all coaches and others in leadership positions recognize the important link formed between learning and motivation. Reinforcement strengthens that link whether it be positive or negative reinforcement.

The Observational Learning Theory. While the previous two behavioral views of personality were based on the principles of operant and classical conditioning, which grew out of basic experiments in the laboratory and more or less traditional theories of learning, learning *by observation* makes unique contributions to human personality and social behavior. The observational learning, or imitation, approach considers learning to be a function of a person's observations of the behavior of others and the consequences of these behaviors.

Miller and Dollard (1941), Bandura and Walters (1963), Liebert (1972, 1973), and others have proposed various models since Tarde's (1903) initial treatise, *The Laws of Imitation,* on observational learning. Liebert and Spiegler (1974) defined the terms and meanings associated with *imitation* as follows: "Overall, our focus of interest is on *observational learning:* the process through which the behavior of one person, an *observer,* changes as a function of merely being exposed to the behavior of another, the *model*. . . . Modeling . . . refers only to the behavior or alleged behavior of the exemplar. . . .''

Cognitive psychologists maintain that learning through observation, also referred to as *learning by imitation* or *learning through modeling,* is the most common form of learning as well as the most important one. The organism learns by studying the behavior of a model organism. Motor skills in athletics are most commonly taught by coaches either demonstrating or having other performers demonstrate (model) skills and techniques prior to having team members perform (imitate) them.

The three behavioral approaches we have looked at are paradigms, or theories, of learning. Each theory can explain the same behavior in a somewhat different way, although all of the explanations involve learning. One should remember, however, that although the three theories can be useful, especially pedagogically, in real life most behavior is acquired and sustained by a combination of observational, operant, and respondent learning. Obviously there are limitations or liabilities in these behavioral strategies as there are in the psychoanalytic, dispositional, and phenomenological strategies.

COGNITIVE OR FIELD THEORIES OF LEARNING

''Cognitive'' school theorists have come to regard learning not so much as the establishment of stimulus-response (S-R) connections, but as the acquisition of *knowledge*. Cognitive psychologists maintain that, even in the respondent approach to learning when Pavlov experimented on conditioning the dog, it was not an S-R connection but a *cognitive pattern* that somehow informed or ''told'' the dog that food (reinforcement) would follow the sound. That is, the cognitive psychologist would say there is a learned *expectancy* that reinforcement (food in Pavlov's experiment) will follow. Others maintain that *motivation* causes such behavior. Cognitive psychology, as the name implies, stresses the importance of mental processes and is a derivative of the Gestalt psychology movement. Gestalt psychology will be explained after first discussing briefly the cognitive theory of learning.

William James (1890) viewed psychology as ''the study of mental life.'' About 1913, John Watson (1930) posited that, since ''mental life'' could not be seen or measured, it could not be studied scientifically. Thus Watson maintained that psychologists could study *overt* behavior, since these actions are plainly visible, and stimulus-response (S-R) psychology grew out of Watson's theories. Cognitive psychologists reject many aspects of behaviorism and question the importance of the conditioning process that Watson saw as the key to human behavior. Cognitive theorists maintain that behavior cannot possibly be explained in full by stimulus connections and that, indeed, the human mind is much more than the mere reflections that its possessor has encountered. Cognitive psychologists tend to think of the mind as operating as a sort of ''mental executive'' that actively makes comparisons and decisions, thus processing the information it receives into new forms and categories.

The cognitive psychologists tend to think of mental activity and human behavior in general as a pattern and a unity, regarding learning, for example, as a series of very complex but closely related activities that can be described as information processing. The processing steps include seeing and hearing, the organization of what one sees and hears into perceptual patterns, and the storing of what one has seen or heard into one's memory. One then has access to his memory, drawing on the information stored there, to solve problems, to make judgments, and to decide on appropriate behavior.

Cognitive theorists believe that all things derive their character from their relationships to other things. Stimuli from the environment are *not* discrete and independent from each other. Stimuli are observed against a background or *field*. The individual makes a psychological reality of all stimuli that come to him; therefore, the cognitive concept is not as scientifically exact as the S-R theory. The environment is dynamic, and the individual's process of interacting, adapting, modifying, and changing results in learning, according to Oxendine (1968).

The basic tenets of cognitive learning theory originated with the Gestalt psychologists in Germany during the 1920s and 1930s, and continued with the *sign-gestalt* work of Edward C. Tolman (1934, 1949) and the *topological psychology* theory of Kurt Lewin (1935, 1936). Tolman and Lewin need not be discussed further, since learning experiments in the tradition of cognitive theory have declined in the last three decades.

Gestalt Psychology

Gestalt psychology originated in Germany at about the same time John Watson's behaviorism was becoming influential in the United States. *Gestalt,* a German word that has no exact English equivalent, can be roughly translated as "pattern" or "configuration." However, the word "Gestalt" means something more than that.

The Gestalt school believed that, in studying any psychological subject, it was essential to look for a pattern and consider it *as a whole*. Gestalt theories frequently have been summarized as maintaining that "the whole is greater than the sum of its parts." Not only does Gestalt psychology stress the whole rather than the parts, but it also emphasizes the importance of the entire situation, or context, in which the "whole" is found.

A simple illustration will quickly clear up any confusion. Imagine one individual meeting another. Gestalt psychologists maintain one would *not* respond cognitively by saying, "I see a head, a body, two arms, two legs; therefore I must be looking at a person." Gestalt psychologists argue that learning often takes place by "insight," a creative thinking process, which is a contrary point of view expressed by those psychologists who believe in *introspection* and *behaviorism*. While Gestalt psychology has largely died out as a movement in its own right, many of its ideas continue to thrive in cognitive psychology and humanistic psychology, two very modern schools that grew out of Gestalt psychology.

CONSENSUS ON LEARNING THEORIES

As we observed previously in our discussions on personality and motivation and in discussing other psychological constructs and theories, there is no single theory of learning that is acceptable to all psychologists. It appears the only agreement among psychologists is that they agree to disagree, and for the person who is seeking simplistic solutions to complicated issues or problems this is disconcerting and confusing. However, the situation is not as chaotic as it may seem to the teacher-coach. An analysis of the theories by Dashiell (1935), McConnell (1942), and Hilgard (1956) revealed there are a number of principles that are characteristic of all learning theories. Dashiell, on the basis of his study, concluded that six points were apparent in each of the theories, and McConnell's five-point conclusions were similar to Dashiell's but were structured somewhat differently.

Dr. Ernest Hilgard, associated with Yale's highly creative Institute of Human Relations, a former president of the American Psychological Association (1949), and a Professor Emeritus of Psychology at Stanford University, after reviewing the theories of learning, established fourteen statements on which he believed most theorists would agree. These practical ideas Hilgard (1956) developed for the benefit of the teacher, but they are also useful to the teacher–coach:

1. Brighter people can learn things less bright ones cannot learn; in general, older children can learn more readily than younger ones; the decline of ability with age, in the adult years, depends upon what it is that is being learned.

2. A motivated learner acquires what he learns more readily than one who is not motivated. . . .

3. Motivation that is too intense (especially pain, fear, anxiety) may be accompanied by distracting emotional states, so that excessive motivation may be less effective than moderate motivation for learning some kinds of tasks, especially those involving difficult discriminations.

4. Learning under the control of reward is usually preferable to learning under the control of punishment. Correspondingly, learning motivated by success is preferable to learning motivated by failure. . . .

5. Learning under intrinsic motivation is preferable to learning under extrinsic motivation.

6. Tolerance for failure is best taught through providing a backlog of success that compensates for experienced failure.

7.   Individuals need practice in setting realistic goals for themselves, goals neither so low as to elicit little effort nor so high as to foreordain to failure. . . .

8.   The personal history of the individual, for example, his reaction to authority, may hamper or enhance his ability to learn from a given teacher.

9.   Active participation by a learner is preferable to passive reception when learning, for example, from a lecture or a motion picture.

10.   Meaningful materials and meaningful tasks are learned more readily than nonsense materials and more readily than tasks not understood by the learner.

11.   There is no substitute for repetitive practice in the over-learning of skills (for instance, the performance of a concert pianist), or in the memorization of unrelated facts that have to be automatized.

12.   Information about the nature of a good performance, knowledge of his own mistakes, and knowledge of successful results, aid learning.

13.   Transfer to new tasks will be better, if, in learning, the learner can discover relationships for himself, and if he has experience during learning of applying the principles within a variety of tasks.

14.   Spaced or distributed recalls are advantageous in fixing material that is to be long retained.

MOTOR LEARNING

From the point of view of sports and games, the typical person is likely to regard *motor learning* as the mere mechanical manipulation of some object, such as kicking a soccer ball, putting a golf ball, spiking a volleyball, shooting a basketball, passing a football. Unfortunately, this view is a widely accepted oversimplification of a vastly more complicated procedure. In the performance of the above-mentioned physical actions, if each were considered as a separate entity by itself and each did not occur in a competitive situation, they may appear to be relatively mechanical. However, the performance of a physical skill in athletics is seldom a separate entity unto itself, and the assumption that affective and cognitive processes are not occurring in the above illustrations is erroneous. For these and other reasons, many writers use other terms and words to identify motor learning, and this leads to some confusion. While there is disagreement as to the terms and labels, there is concurrence among professionals in the field of physical education and coaching that motor learning is perhaps the most neglected and underrated type of learning.

Motor Learning: Controlled Motor Behavior

In the numerous studies on patterned motion, different terms and names have been affixed to similar actions, which tends to confuse, on occasion, rather than to clarify. Here are some examples: motor learning, sensory-motor learning (sensorimotor, sensori-neuromotor); psychol-motor learning (psychomotore); menti-motor learning (ideo-motor); neuro-muscular learning (neuromotor); perceptual-motor learning (perceptuo-motor, visuo-motor, tactural-motor). There are probably others that have escaped our examination. However, as posited by Dr. Aileene Lockhart (1964), a well-known physical educator and author in the field of motor learning and human performance, the single term *motor learning* alleviates confusion, since

> ... this term refers to action instigated through the sense receptors, integrated through the nervous system, and modulated through the response mechanism, into controlled motor behavior. This name emphasizes organized motion, the executive expression of organismic activity (the end-result, not the means of getting there). ... There are many kinds of learning; the term motor learning simply designates the type of learning we are talking about: that manifested by controlled movement.

Lockhart (1964) further suggested that

> ... the term ''motor learning'' would include all studies aimed at understanding primarily those factors which have specific relevance to the motor function. (It is important to note the word ''primarily.'' This term—motor learning—seems restrictive enough to indicate the *primary task,* but open enough to admit all the constellations of complex inputs, integrations and interactions that most certainly are involved in the learning and performance of complex gross motor activities. ...

Psychomotor Skills, a Better Term. Noble (1968) stated that ''motor'' skills is a less satisfactory term than ''perceptual-motor'' or ''psychomotor'' skills; that is, this category of learning is *not* restricted to tests of strength, the predominance of hands, or reaction time skills. Noble classified *psychomotor skills* as those that require the identification and combination of stimulus-organism-response elements into coordinated spatiotemporal patterns of receptor-effector activity. The skill then becomes a joint function of pro-active repetitions and reinforcing feedback to provide success in acquisition, retention, and transfer in all aspects of the psychomotor domain.

Therefore, motor learning, which is within the overall definition of learning that was included earlier in this chapter, refers particularly to types of behavioral change that involve bodily movement, which is usually thought of as the acquisition of physical skills. Obviously the range of acquired responses varies widely.

Three Domains of Human Behavior: "Knowing," "Feeling," "Doing"

Renowned educational psychologist Benjamin J. Bloom, and his associates, categorized human behaviors into three domains of learning: the cognitive, the affective, and the psychomotor (column *C* in Figure 10-2) domains, which are included here for discussion purposes. Bloom's (Bloom et al., 1956) taxonomy of educational objectives, as it is commonly and widely known, was the first major publication on the topic (entitled *Handbook I: Cognitive Domain*). Krathwohl, Bloom, and Masia (1964) followed with a second publication on the taxonomy of educational objectives (entitled *Handbook II: Affective Domain*). Harrow (1971) followed with a book on the psychomotor domain, and physical educators Singer (1975), Cratty (1973), Oxendine (1968), Drowatzky (1975), and others have authored outstanding much-needed texts in the area of motor learning and human performance.

Each of Bloom's domains of learning is discussed briefly to illustrate the point that psychomotor or motor skills do not occur as separate actions devoid of cognitive and affective processes. As Lockhart (1964) pointed out, "those who would understand learning of any sort must remember that so far as is presently known the *ingredients of learning are intricate, multidimensional, delicately integrated and basically inseparable.*"

The Psychomotor or Motor Domain: "Doing." Objectives such as the development of strength, endurance, neuromuscular coordination, cardiovascular efficiency, and skill in body movement are located within the psychomotor or motor domain since they deal with physiological and motor skill development.

The Cognitive Domain: "Knowing." Cognition implies a mental process by which knowledge is acquired, and Bloom (1956) referred to the cognitive domain of learning as "the development of intellectual abilities and skills." The objectives of this domain emphasize recall or recognition of knowledge. *Cognitive psychology* is a school of thought that maintains that the mind does not merely react to stimuli but actively processes the information it receives into new forms and categories. Kagan and Havemann (1976) define the *cognitive theory of emotion* as, "The theory that an emotion is the cognitive interpretation of a change in level and quality of internal sensations in a particular context."

The Affective Domain: "Feeling." The area of "emotionally loaded learning" is referred to as the *affective domain,* which Bloom (1956) defined as "dealing with interests, attitudes, appreciations and adjustments." From the standpoint of the teacher–coach–educator, by being cognizant of the affective domain the main objective should be to foster the development of positive feelings regarding participation in athletics, including its concomitants. From the standpoint of the learner–athlete, within the hierarchy of the affective domain, each person goes through an internalization process which entails conceptualizing and organizing a value system.

Illustrations. In competitive athletic situations in particular, and not excluding the successful performance of physical activities in noncompetitive situations, all three domains of learning are active and have a direct bearing on each other and on the athlete's ultimate performance. If a basketball player does not comprehend the "give and go" concept, for example, he cannot execute playing skills successfully; nor can the basketball player who, after getting "picked," becomes angry and intentionally fouls the "picker" and forgets all about the player whom he was guarding initially, who is probably driving for the basket to score.

All domains of learning are interacting in a game situation. Imagine a situation in baseball when the bases are loaded, the score is tied, it is the bottom of the ninth, the leading hitter is at bat with a 3-2 count, and the pitcher knows all runners will be going on his next pitch and he, the pitcher, must either strike out or force the batter to hit out, or force out a base runner, in order not to lose the game.

Situational game skills are rehearsed and perfected during practice with the intent that they will be executed successfully in contests. The more skilled the movements, and the more challenging or competitive the situation, the more satisfying is the outcome to the successful performer. Each game or sport is a sequence of movements directed toward a specific goal. A participant cannot achieve success and satisfaction in the performance of a physical activity until he can integrate the various parts of the skill. As is illustrated in both of the examples cited, the learner–athlete must interpret and comprehend not only the nature of the skill he is performing, but also its relationship to the goal he is seeking, individually and as a team.

Arousal and Motor Performance

An individual's emotional state may range from the high activation of extreme excitation to the low activation of death, the two extremes on the continuum. Positive or negative *emotional* factors, such as hate, love, fear, happiness, anxiety, embarrassment, and *physical* factors, such as exercise and fatigue, and *chemical* factors, such as hormones and drugs, all cause a state of arousal. One's heart rate, blood pressure, muscle tension, respiration, galvanic skin response, and numerous other bodily functions are all sensitive to changes in emotional arousal. One's normal physiological functions are intensified when there is emotional arousal.

According to Cratty (1968), Hussman (1969), and Oxendine (1968, 1970), the optimum level of arousal varies with the particular motor task. That is, different tasks require different levels of arousal for most effective performance. In addition, the optimum arousal state varies from person to person, and even for the same person the optimum level varies somewhat from day to day depending on the individual's personality and motivation.

Changing arousal state in the desired direction requires an understanding of some basic principles of psychology and some skill in using certain techniques. Most textbooks on the psychology of behavior or teaching devote large portions to these psychological processes, several of which have already been included in other chapters. A *caveat,* however, is that a coach must be concerned about the psychological health of his players, and he should avoid anxiety-provoking methods. Not infrequently in competitive situations the arousal level of the anxious athlete is high, and the coach needs to lower the player's arousal level by reassuring and calming him. Coaches should always remember that athletes are not toys to be manipulated and that their state of arousal is often a reflection of their general emotional state. That is why physical exercise seems to be the safest way psychologically to improve performance. Researchers have conducted a number of studies on the effects of arousal on the learning and performance of motor skills, and the reader's attention is directed to the References and Suggested Readings at the conclusion of this and the previous chapter.

THE LEARNING OF MOTOR SKILLS

The learning of motor skills commences early in one's life, and depending on one's vocation or avocation one may continue to learn motor skills throughout one's lifetime. The adult who is studying to be a surgeon or a dentist, for example, often finds the development of a manual skill important, since he or she must learn to use instruments with skill and dexterity. The same may be said of the individual who later in life wants to learn to make jewelry, or do fine detailed lettering, or repair his own automobile, or weave or work carving figurines; all of these activities involves learning manual dexterity. If one wants to learn to draw or paint with skill so that one's work does not look too amateurish, it is obvious that perceptual-motor factors come into use. However, these motor skills are beyond the scope of this discussion since we are primarily concerned with learning motor skills applicable to athletics or physical activity. But let us look first at the beginning, rather than at the middle or later years, of one's contiuum of life.

Broad Categories of Motor Skills

Motor skills of the initial group are those developed early in life, and they are dependent on the maturation of the child, such as crawling, walking, speaking, and the general coordination of body movements. While parents and others may try to speed up the maturation process by exposing their child to special teaching at a very early age, maximal development of these skills will occur if the child is exposed to a favorable home and school environment, and if the child has the opportunity and receives the encouragement to learn.

Motor skills of the second group are those essential for achieving educational success in school, such as handwriting and reading; these will contribute to more advanced learning throughout one's life. The development of proficiency in these activities in the early school grades is most essential and, for this reason, the primary grade teacher is particularly concerned with this type of motor learning.

Motor skills of the third group are those taught for their own value, or for the benefits that are derived and are directly related to learning them. This category includes the vocation and avocation skills mentioned previously, in addition to recreational or sports skills one may learn at an early age. Generally the physical education teacher is responsible for developing these particular skills, as well as movement patterns and fitness levels essential for other specialized skill learning. However, motor learning is not restricted to the physical education class or to participation in individual and team sports, and in the typical educational environment teachers of a wide variety of subjects at the various scholastic and collegiate levels are often involved in the teaching of motor skills.

Types of Motor Skills. Learning a motor skill, such as putting a golf ball, diving, doing a back flip, driving for a layup shot in basketball, or "running to daylight" as a ball carrier in football, involves both mental and physical coordinations. The execution or performance of various motor skills requires different levels and amounts of mental functioning; for example, compare the physical skill needed in brushing one's teeth to the act of doing a half-gainer in diving. The learning of most skills is a thoughtful, active process, and one can readily deduce that not all motor skills are the same. Depending on the magnitude of the movement or skill to be performed, there are *fine* and *gross* motor skills. Fine motor skills involve little or minimal response, such as in handwriting or in the normal brushing of one's teeth. In gross motor skills, the magnitude of movement is much greater, such as swinging a golf club or kicking a soccer ball. In addition, movements may be described as *discrete, serial,* or *continuous.*

Discrete skills require a single exertion, such as shooting a foul shot in basketball or coming off the blocks from the "set" position in track, although some may interpret the track illustration as a serial skill and not as a discrete skill. A serial skill involves a series of movements, each of which must follow in a particular sequence, such as when one kicks off or attempts a point-after-touchdown kick in football, or when one gets possession of the basketball, dribbles while moving toward the basket, and then shoots attempting to score the basket (as compared to foul shooting). Continuous movements require repetitive actions, such as are evident in track and swimming.

Track and swimming are also illustrative of activities that are not like the other motor skills we have discussed, since they do not depend on vision as much as other sports, where there must be a coordination of eye, mind, and body in order to execute the perceptual-motor skill with any degree of success. Activities that involve hitting a golf ball, baseball, tennis ball, hockey puck, or the kicking of a soccer ball or football, or the catching of a football, baseball, or basketball, or almost any activity where a ball is involved in the sport, all require perceptual-motor skills.

Therefore, there are numerous methods of typing or categorizing motor skills. Which categories are used depends on the purposes of the discussion or the kinds of comparisons being made.

THE LEARNING PROCESS

In order for learning to occur, the following elements are necessary:

- A motivated individual
- An incentive that will lead to the satisfaction of motives
- Some sort of an obstacle that prevents or inhibits the individual from immediately attaining the incentive
- The individual must exert effort or activity in an effort to attain the incentive

Succinctly, incentives are central to learning since their attainment leads to the satisfaction of motives. Motivation arises from the individual's (organism's) desire to attain the incentive that would satisfy his need. If the individual attains his goal or incentive without too much difficulty, this is an indication that the learning has already occurred. If success is not immediate, and if the individual is sufficiently stimulated (motivated), most likely he or she will continue to make repeated attempts to attain the incentive. As the process continues, the more successful responses will be selected and repeated while the least successful ones and the failures will be gradually eliminated until learning occurs. Regardless of the nature of the learning task, the four essential elements listed above are the same.

Six Sequential Steps in the Learning Process

A brief discussion of the sequential steps in the learning process as viewed by Woodruff (1948) should clarify the overall topic of learning. Woodruff's sequential steps appear to be characteristic of all types of learning and his views seem to be consistent with the consensus on current learning theory. However, it should be pointed out that there does not seem to be any uniformity in the speed or ease with which individuals progress through the different steps or phases of the learning process. An individual may progress through a particular step quickly, only to encounter difficulty in getting through another step. The same is true with the degree of speed of learning the total task or the progressions, ranging from a relatively sudden start to a very slow process. As Woodruff (1948) pointed out, the speed of the learning process depends on the following three factors and their interaction: the capacity of the individual, his degree of motivation, and the nature of the task.

Woodruff's (1948) six-step process appears to be characteristic of all forms of learning:

1. Motivation within the learner makes him receptive to stimulation.

2. A goal becomes related to motivation.

3. Tension arises.

4. The learner seeks an appropriate line of action to reach his goal.

5. The learner fixes the appropriate line of action.

6. Inappropriate behaviors are stopped.

INSTRUCTIONAL CONSIDERATIONS FOR TEACHING–COACHING

In any teaching–learning situation, numerous external conditions are under the jurisdiction of the teacher–coach and can be controlled and manipulated depending on his or her expertise. Singer (1975) discussed in detail three major areas of consideration, display, practice considerations, and practice conditions, each with a number of subitems. Paraphrasing only Singer's list of "Practice Considerations," which are probably "old-hat" to psychologists, generally research indicates the findings we discuss below.

Massed Conditions Versus Distributed Practices

While organizing practice sessions and drill guides, each coach has to decide which procedures are best to utilize in developing proficiency, whether to use concentrated (*massed* conditions) practice periods, or *distributed* periods with longer intervals between sessions. The crux of the issue is whether, during a given period of practice, it is better to make one attempt to learn and act, or to repeat it often. What is the best amount of time to allow between practice periods?

For most skills, distributed practice exerts a more positive influence on performance than massed practice. Although immediate skill acquisition is favored under distributed practice, tests of retention demonstrate little difference in performance between massed and distributed practice groups.

Practice Sessions Must Be Made Meaningful

For learning to occur in practice sessions, which one hopes will be carried over to the actual contest, the participants must comprehend the "why" of what they are practicing. Otherwise the drills and activities have little purpose or meaning, and there is little motivation, attention, interest, and readiness to learn, since there is no actual correlation of practice to game assimilation. Therefore, practice alone is not sufficient for improvement. In fact, practices devoid of meaning, for all practical purposes, are probably a waste of time.

Overlearning

When one is exposed to learning what has already been learned (overlearning) through continual "polishing" of the skill or technique, providing boredom does not set in and the athlete is no longer motivated, the result is better retention of that which has been learned. The assumption is that the performer is practicing or "polishing" the skill correctly, not merely "putting in time" and "going through the motions" of performing the skill.

Environmental Conditions

Better learned skills are less prone to be disrupted by manipulated environmental conditions. Experiences in varying instructional or stressful conditions will contribute to high levels of skill.

Reinforcement

Reinforcement increases the probability that the desired act will occur; and random reinforcement is more effective than constant reinforcement.

Goals

While goals may be difficult, if they are realistic and attainable, one is more likely to be motivated and to produce a better performance than if there are easy goals or a general goal of merely "to do one's best."

Motivation

It is possible to be too highly motivated to the extent that it interferes, not aids, progress in complex tasks. Highest performance is attained by individuals with an intermediate level of motivation; and as tasks increase in complexity, individuals with moderate motivation do better. Evidently there is an optimal motivational level for each task.

Behavior

Behavior is influenced by previous experiences. There is a greater amount of *positive transfer* when there is a greater resemblance between task elements, and between their respective stimuli and responses. Factors that influence transfer include the amount of practice on the prior task, motivation to transfer skill, method of training, and the intent of transfer.

PART AND WHOLE METHODS OF LEARNING

To thoroughly understand the whole, its component parts must be known. It makes little difference whether it is an individual activity, such as the progressions an individual takes in throwing a discus or driving a golf ball, or the team concept of the fast break in basketball or a double play combination in baseball. While the two individual activities are not integrated into the team concept other than contributing to team scoring, the mechanics, fundamentals, and techniques of the fast break and of a double play must be broken down into component parts before they can be woven into the whole team concept. While a coach cannot teach the whole method or concept and expect comprehension by his team until he has presented the various components, the inexperienced coach is likely to make this glaring error. However, it is not reasonable to expect a basketball or baseball team to have a working knowledge and proficiency of team fundamentals until they have been taught and have an understanding of individual fundamentals.

A vast amount of research is available on the relative efficiency of the part and whole methods. The part method allows the individual to concentrate on one portion of the material, or one aspect of the skill, at a time. The whole method calls for an athlete to concentrate on the whole or the entire task.

Research indicates that parts are easier and more quickly learned, and the learner is more satisfied and confident when confronted with the whole. However, while he carries over some of the skills and knowledge to the learning of the whole, depending on the complexity of the skill, he may find he encounters difficulty in assimilating the learned parts together. An illustration is analyzing the separate components or parts of a golf swing, and then attempting to put the learned parts together to execute a coordinated golf swing.

If a person can adjust to the whole method and handle it properly, one can better learn through the whole method. However, one may save time using the part method if he cannot adjust himself to the magnitude of the task presented by the whole method. Some coaches most always begin teaching with the part method, probably going on two basic assumptions. (1) The athlete has little knowledge about the proper and correct execution of skills, techniques, fundamentals, and systems, so the coach teaches and builds on a sound base of fundamentals and parts woven into wholes. (2) The coach wants the athlete to learn *his* way or methodology, which he teaches by commencing with parts; the coach is not overly concerned with what the athlete has been taught previously by others.

Other coaches may commence with the whole problem, with a willingness to concentrate at any time on a part that presents difficulty to the learner. He or she builds on what the athlete already knows.

Field, Floor, and Court Coaching During Practice Sessions

Basic concepts and coaching theory should be presented at the simplest level. Effectiveness of performance is reduced if there is not complete player understanding of team aims and objectives. Not infrequently a coach will direct his remarks and focus his teaching primarily for the benefit of the regulars, and the "down-the-liner" substitutes receive little individualized teaching and instruction other than in their expected roles as bag holders, "go-fers," and scout team demonstrators. Since these individuals who are not regulars play an important role in the success of the team sport and group effort, their continued motivation is important, too. Not only should their roles and efforts be recognized so that they are aware that they, too, are contributing to team success, but substitutes also should be "brought along." Not only may a substitute be "thrown into the breach" sooner than planned, as the result of losing a regular performer unexpectedly and being forced to play an untried substitute in a game or contest, but often a highly motivated substitute has been waiting for the opportunity to prove he is capable of performing as a regular when given the opportunity to do so. Obviously, if the substitute has received practice instruction and experience, his opportunity to be successful is greatly enhanced because the theory of individual and team play is advanced primarily through practice drills and concentrated instruction.

Learn by Doing. While it is important that a player be instructed how to execute fundamentals, skills, and techniques, it is more important that the athletes be given the opportunity to perform these activities. Players learn by doing, not merely by being instructed what to do. Many coaches do too much talking, conduct on-the-field "seminars" with their players, and fail to give their players maximum opportunities to practice the skills, fundamentals, and techniques that have been explained. Also, a more total picture can be presented to the players through a physical demonstration on the field, floor, or court rather than merely explaining what and how the skills should be performed. The coach need not be the demonstrator and, on occasion, he should not even attempt to demonstrate certain motor skills. However, a coach should be able to analyze and explain thoroughly for the comprehension of his athletes the techniques, skills, and fundamentals of his specific coaching theory.

Use of Visual Aids in Teaching–Coaching

Other mediums are also necessary to advance coaching theory. The use of films, filmloops, closed-circuit television, videotape, speed sequence polaroid cameras, wall charts, and other similar visual aids are commonplace in current teaching–coaching methods. While theory is taught on the practice field or court, the opportunities for coaches and athletes to view applied coaching theory through other mediums cannot be overlooked. Several of these valuable teaching–coaching aids provide realistic feedback both to players and coaches and provide the tool for evaluating player and team performance and coaching effectiveness. Frequently, in watching and analyzing a film, for example, coaches discover athletes are not performing or executing as taught, and they may also discover their teaching is not only ineffective but incorrect.

Films. Probably more coaches have access to utilizing films than most any other medium, although closed-circuit television and videotapes are used quite extensively, too. Where participants have opportunities to observe their own performances in practice under gamelike conditions or in actual contests, the chances of correcting performance errors are much greater, and errors are corrected more rapidly, than if the players are merely informed verbally of their mistakes. Also, in a team sport, the importance of coordinated teamwork is dramatically portrayed. The individual in a team sport has an opportunity to better comprehend the total team objectives as the participant observes his part in the overall team effort. What has been theorized and taught in the practice sessions will be more clearly focused and comprehended by analyzing performance on films. They will not only increase the participant's knowledge of what he is trying to do and what he should be doing, but also what the player's team is trying to do. After the participant sees the "big picture" (overall team concept), the player's basic concept of the coach's theory will be clearer. It also follows that it will bring about a more effective team effort.

Films offer more to a coach than an examination of the application of the coach's practical theory. Film allows the coach and his staff to plan practice sessions more effectively to meet individual and team needs and goals.

OTHER MEDIUMS FOR TEACHING–COACHING

Since this is the age of the computer, it is possible to garner virtually any type of information a coach would care to secure on his own team or opponents. Since major colleges and universities have access to computers on their own campuses, many major college athletic staffs have access to computerized data. Professional teams also use computers for compiling data on personnel, scouting, strategy, among other things. High school teams that use computers for their athletic teams are minimal, although probably a number of scholastic coaching staffs use data hand card sorts for scouting. Many college coaches used the card sorts before computers were available to them.

Game Statistics. Regardless of how the data is compiled, much can be garnered from game statistics, whether a coach is analyzing his own team's or scouting the opposition's performance statistics. In fact, a danger of acquiring computerized data is that there tends to be too much information that may overwhelm the coaches working with it. Also, when one works with the data on card sorts or in some other manner in a manual sense, one tends to become more familiar with the data since the coach is entering, copying, and transposing figures in order to compile meaningful data. Obviously there are advantages to both methods, although the use of a computer by a coaching staff may not be feasible because of the prohibitive cost of buying computer time.

Drive Sheet. For the coach who does not have access to a computer, he should make every effort to secure this information manually. For example, securing information on how a team obtained possession of the football and on what part of the field, or what the team did before they surrendered the football, and how they did this, are all invaluable to the coach. The usual passes attempted/completed/intercepted/incompleted both from an offensive and defensive standpoint are also meaningful statistics.

Shot Charts. The basketball coach will find it necessary to acquire, compile, and analyze statistics. Who shot and from where, who got the rebound, what were the ball control errors, and categories of a similar nature are most meaningful information for both the coaching staff and the players, individually and for the team. Each has its relative value and can help improve performance.

Shooting percentages in basketball, for example, directly correlate to the offensive theory and the methods of teaching that a coach employs. Why does a coach use the fast break as his primary offensive weapon? The basic theory is that one wants to create the in-close high percentage shot and to allow for stronger rebounding. Also, it is theorized that a fast break team will get more shots, and a fast break offense weighs the advantage of obtaining an in-close shot before the defense masses at the risk of more ball control mistakes.

On the other hand, the patterned offensive sets up a high percentage shot within the opposition's massed defense. It is theorized that the patterned offense reduces the mistakes by more careful ball handling at the risk of shooting against a relatively heavy defense. To more fully comprehend the effectiveness of his team's efforts, a basketball coach should be guided and concerned with the statistics that are associated with both offensive styles of play.

Analysis of Data. Despite the statistics, charts, and performance percentages, a coach must still be careful not to accept this data as the sole criterion of performance. Many contingent factors tend to increase or decrease the percentages needed for winning. For example, with basketball statistics on ball-handling ability, rebounding, defensive ability, and scoring potential of the opponent, it is important to remember that other factors exert and influence the ultimate outcome of a game. A recognition of what are considered *norms* constitutes the basis on which the coach can accurately judge individual and team performance from a statistical standpoint. It is important that a coach recognize above average shooting, substandard shooting, excessive poor passes, strong or weak rebounding, violations, or inferior ball handling, as well as strong or weak individual defensive play. With the inclusion of these statistics in the method of approach, coaches are better equipped to correct and instruct.

Training Aids Should Be a Supplement, Not a Substitute

Although mention was made of the desirability of using different training aids or mediums for teaching–coaching, a coach must always bear in mind that they should be used as a supplement, not a substitute, for teaching. It is possible to overuse teaching aids, making them more of the end than the means; they may even become too time-consuming. The players may also find them boring or even detracting. It is always desirable to follow-up immediately, if possible, with court, field, or floor situations, so that the players are able to apply what they have seen or heard presented by their coach.

TEACHING–COACHING–LEARNING GUIDELINES AND SUGGESTIONS FOR IMPROVING PERFORMANCE

As we have indicated throughout this chapter, learning is closely associated with the concepts of perception and behavior. It is difficult to understand behavior without understanding learning, because it is through learning that behavioral changes take place. As we have seen from the commonly accepted definition of learning, unless a change in behavior is experienced, learning has not occurred. Such knowledge is vital to the coach, since learning is essential to effective coaching.

Hammer (1963), Lawther (1974), Drowatzky (1975), Butts (1976), and others have offered suggestions and guidelines for teaching–coaching motor skills in working with students and athletes in order to improve their performance. While learning encompasses too many concepts to be covered in detail in a single chapter, knowledge and the application of these concepts of learning, along with guidelines and suggestions, which we have gleaned from numerous sources on the psychology of learning, should prove beneficial to the teacher–coach.

Structure and Manage the Conditions or Environment of Learning

The arrangement of favorable and efficient conditions for the learning process to occur is known as the management of learning. A coach should attempt to arrange or structure the most favorable and desirable conditions so that optimal learning and effective coaching can occur. One must "manage" the environment for coaching success.

Guide and Monitor the Learning Process

Having definite lesson or practice plans that form a teaching progression of skills, techniques, offensive and defensive concepts, and tactics is beneficial to the learner because it aids in his or her learning. As a result, the athlete is able to find meaningful connections, grasp logical patterns, and organize the material into categories or other forms. In this way the coach guides and monitors the athlete's learning process.

Utilize Positive Reinforcement

The law of effect, cited previously, includes both positive and negative reinforcement. Learning is more rapid and more effective if positive reinforcement is utilized. The use of negative reinforcement and punishment may have a deleterious effect to the extent that the athlete ends up disliking the coach and/or the sport, and thus effective learning–coaching may not occur.

Capture the Learner's Attention

The learner's attention is necessary in all learning experiences. The coach should arrange the environment so that the learner–athlete can focus his attention on what the coach is teaching. Paying attention helps by transferring information from sensory memory to short-term memory, enabling the short-term memory to rehearse the information and transfer it to long-term memory. One theory of how we remember what we learn suggests that there are three systems of memory: sensory, short, and long term.

Acquire Feedback to Determine Effectiveness

Attention can be attracted by motivation, rewards, punishment, and feedback. All have been discussed in this and other chapters. Feedback is a primary ingredient in learning, since individuals require a knowledge of results so that they can modify their behavior. If an individual accomplishes his or her goal(s), self-satisfaction (intrinsic reinforcement) is likely to occur; should he or she receive praise, extrinsic reinforcement occurs. Such feedback (and reinforcement) is most effective if it is immediate. Rewards are reinforcers.

The Presentation of the Subject Matter Should "Make Sense"

How the material is organized and presented is important in the management of learning. Effective storage in long-term memory, where it can then be recalled when needed (retrieved), depends in large part on "making sense" out of new information and fitting it in with what is already known. Materials are easiest to organize in the learner's mind if they are meaningful, and when they can be learned by rule or by logic, instead of by rote. For example, some football coaches and others devise somewhat complicated numbering systems or affix names or colors to identify plays, formations, offenses, defenses, and so on, and frequently the terminology is not meaningful and does not "make sense" to some of the players. While "Brown Right" and its counterpart, "Red Left," may make sense to a professional football player, to the inexperienced player the logic that "brown" is the opposite of "red" in learning offensive formations is missed.

Cluster the Material

One method of organizing material for teaching is known as clustering, which means lumping together material that has some sort of affinity. For example, if the offensive backs are numbered on a football team so that the ''3 back'' is the player who lines up in the ''3 position'' four yards directly behind his quarterback, then on 30 Buck, 30 Trap, and 30 Pass, the ''3 back'' is involved in the plays. If the ''0'' hole is to the right of the offensive center, then the player in the ''3 position'' knows on 30 Buck and 30 Trap that he is carrying the ball at the ''0'' hole, and on 30 Pass, that he is faking receiving a hand-off from his quarterback, but runs directly at the ''0'' hole. This is clustering, since all three plays have an affinity and fit together in the offensive numbering/play series scheme.

Present New Information on a Solid Foundation

Learning builds on learning. In the example above, the ''3 back'' is taught 30 Buck, then possibly 30 Pass, which is a play action pass off the fake buck. The addition of ''Trap'' merely means to the ball carrier that instead of the blocking being straight man-on-man, as in 30 Buck, his left guard will be trapping, and the ball carrier will be breaking behind his left guard's trap block right. This not only ''makes sense'' to the ball carrier if he has been taught these plays in progressive sequence, but he learns his plays more quickly because the greatest possible aid to learning is the possession of prior knowledge or mediational units to which new information can ''stick.''

Do Not Merely Explain, But Have Learners "Do"

It is better for a coach to have the players ''do'' (practice performance) rather than for the coach merely to ''tell'' the players what to do. While coaching instructions are important, participation or actively ''doing'' is more important if the players have been properly taught what to do. Many inexperienced coaches, in particular, erroneously conduct ''talk shows'' or coaching seminars on the practice field where the coach does maximal explaining and the players are given minimal opportunity to perform or participate. For learning to take place, frequently there must be repetition of an action for it to become a permanent part of the athlete's frame of reference. Learning occurs rapidly at first when interest and attention are the highest, and then slackens off so that despite repetition learning does not continue indefinitely (learning curve concept).

Do Not Demand More Than Can Be Learned

Learning goals should be realistic and within the expectations of the individual. Also, if they involve new, challenging assignments, they will generally be more stimulating. A coach must use discretion and common sense in both the amount of new material and the rate at which he introduces it into his teaching plan. Otherwise, too much, too rapidly is likely to result in confusion, frustration, and poor performance, rather than being challenging and satisfying to the athlete. The coach's expectations of the players' learning goals may be unrealistic and beyond those of some of his players. To demand more than can be delivered physically, mentally, or emotionally is useless and grossly ineffective.

The Law of Primacy and Recency

Teaching and learning by the part method has certain advantages. One stems from the fact that the difficulty of learning increases disproportionately as the amount to be learned increases. The other stems from what some psychologists refer to as the law of *primacy* and *recency*, which summarizes the fact that in any series of items it is easier to remember the ones that come first or last than the ones in the middle.

Utilize Part and Whole Learning Separately and in Combination

Whole learning also has advantages, chiefly in making materials and information more meaningful and logical. (See the discussion on "clustering" above, and remember to make it "make sense.") Oftentimes a combination method, utilizing the advantages of both part learning and whole learning, is the most efficient and effective method.

Utilize the Overlearning Technique

Overlearning is an effective teaching method. The more time one spends continuing to learn, beyond the point where one can barely remember the materials, the longer one tends to remember, and this is known as overlearning.

Distributed Practice Versus Massed Practice

When the learning process is broken down into separate periods, which is known as distributed practice, generally this is more efficient than massed practice.

Understanding the Concept of Transfer of Learning

The old theory of general transfer of learning has been discredited. For example, it was once thought by some psychologists and many educators that the study of Greek and Latin disciplined the mind and made future learning easier. This theory has been disproved. However, there is positive transfer where learning Task 1, for example, makes it easier to learn Task 2. It occurs most often in situations where Task 2 calls for making the same response to a different stimulus; that is, the stimulus is different but the responses are the same. There are other situations where learning Task 1 makes it more difficult to learn Task 2, and this is called negative transfer. It occurs most prominently in situations where a new response must be made to an old stimulus; that is, both stimuli are the same, but the responses are different.

Understanding Retroactive and Proactive Inhibition

When new learning interferes with the memory for old learning, this process is called *retroactive inhibition*. It is called *proactive inhibition* when old learning interferes with the ability to remember new learning.

Understanding the Curve of Learning

The *curve of forgetting* shows that when one learns something new often he quickly forgets much of what he has been taught, but he remembers at least some of what he has learned for a long time. Some coaches, for example, on assuming a new coaching position, will introduce much of their "system" to their players knowing full well their athletes cannot fully comprehend all of what is being taught. The coaches have no intent of teaching "all" of their system, but they use the saturation method for several reasons. First, it gives the coaches an opportunity to evaluate personnel and to determine what the players can do best. Second, being cognizant of the curve of forgetting, these coaches know when they eventually introduce the major portion of their system which they have finally decided to use, the players are likely to recall at least some of what they were previously taught, and it is not then "new" learning for the first time.

Evaluate Teaching–Coaching Methods

Where teaching–coaching theory is involved, there are probably three methods, two of which are extremes and the other is in a middle ground. Some coaches teach few techniques. The best illustration may be professional football coaches who merely instruct defensive linemen to "Rush the passer," or defensive cornerbacks to "Cover the wide-out one-on-one to your side," but give no instructions on *how* to execute these individual techniques. Much teaching–coaching time may be spent on the overall team defensive concept. It may be presumed that every professional player already knows the individual techniques. If collegiate and scholastic coaches make this presumption, they have erred, as sometimes professional coaches do, too, in not teaching individual techniques. However, the environment or climate is different in professional athletics, and many aspects of professional coaching and professional athletics are *not* applicable to scholastic and collegiate coaching and sports.

The other extreme is the "overkill" of teaching–coaching techniques, which occurs more often at the scholastic and collegiate levels. Not infrequently a coach who is a "student" of the game, who has studied the techniques or some specialized area of the game for which he is accountable, arrives at *the one best way* for all players under his tutelage to execute their particular techniques. While it is highly laudatory to be competent and knowledgeable of one's subject matter, and this principle is not being criticized, a coach should take into consideration individual differences. Not everyone can perform in a robotlike manner, and it is a teaching–coaching error to try to insist that all performers attempt to do so. A coach should try to aid each of his players, not hinder their performance. If a player performs the task assigned, he should be evaluated on the end result *not* on the technique he used to accomplish the task or the end result. Some coaches are critical of the player's methods since they do not conform to the coach's. If an individual cannot perform the technique as taught by his coach, but he can perform it effectively in his own manner within the team concept, then the player should be permitted to execute the technique or skill in the manner most natural and comfortable to him. This is the middle ground approach between the two extremes. The teaching–coaching emphasis should be on results or performance efficiency, not on technique or style. If an athlete is not performing effectively, then the emphasis should be on perfecting his techniques and skills in order to improve his performance. If the athlete is performing effectively and a better or more refined technique will *not* improve his performance effectiveness, then a coach should not insist on the player trying to perform techniques just because the coach feels they are necessary.

An Illustration. A 20 percent foul shooter in basketball with an unorthodox shooting style should be coached to change his foul shooting techniques in an effort to improve individual performance and to increase his contribution to team goals. Conversely, regardless of how unorthodox the style of an 80 percent foul shooter, a coach should *not* attempt to alter this player's foul shooting style. The 80 percent shooter needs only to be reminded of the importance of concentrating on the task and should be given more opportunities to practice foul shooting, if his percentage is to be improved on. If the coach were to attempt to change the 80 percent foul shooting style to conform with what the coach considered better or more correct methods of foul shooting, the performer would probably shoot less than 80 percent. As such, this would probably be an "overkill" in teaching techniques.

Evaluating Techniques and Performance

When evaluating player performance and coaching effectiveness, techniques and performance should be evaluated and graded separately unless some sort of a bonus system is awarded to the player who carries out his assigned task utilizing all of the proper techniques to do so. For example, a player may utilize improper techniques or style in executing a particular skill, but he does his assigned task. The performer did what was required of him, although he used the wrong methods in performing the assigned task. While he may perform even better in the future if he is taught to execute the right or proper technique, he should not be penalized or graded down because he used the wrong methods of performing the required task. Grade the performance not the technique.

Conversely, an athlete could do everything correctly from a technical aspect, but fail at his required assignment or task. It is not logical that the athlete be graded favorably for a performance merely because he looked good in failing at his task or assignment.

Evaluating Potential and Performance

Films and videotape accounts of an athlete's performance can be a great help in evaluating the performance and learning process in order to improve certain skills. In track-and-field sports, the stop watch is a means of evaluating the performance; or one can take the measured distance of putting the shot or throwing the discus, or perhaps the measured height of a jump or pole vault. In dual sports the use of a ladder tournament can be used to determine who is the best performer, which can be accomplished prior to the actual contest.

Certain statistics in team sports can be used for measurement and evaluation, such as a batting percentage in baseball, number of times a ball carrier carried the ball and yards gained or lost in football, and shooting percentage in basketball. Basically this form of evaluation is as good a measure as a coach may expect. The difficulty arises in the team sports where the athlete cannot always be measured objectively, and precise individual evaluation is more difficult. In a team sport there are many factors that may affect a team's success or failure, and the value of the contribution of any one individual is more difficult to determine. Therefore, at times, a coach must make determinations based on his perceptions only of an athlete's potential, if little data is available on the athlete's performance. At best this method may be little more than a hunch by the coach since it is mostly intuitive. Therefore, every effort should be made to evaluate objectively as soon as possible the individual's performance so as to support or refute the coach's previous evaluation which was not supported by performance facts. Many inexperienced coaches in particular evaluate in terms of the potential of the athlete, and not on his actual performance.

Coaches are teachers; coaching is teaching; and teaching is the management or guidance of learning. Learning is an active process. Learning is the acquisition of new behavior patterns, or the strengthening or weakening of old behavior patterns as the result of practice. Since both the rate and degree or amount of learning and motivation are influenced greatly by the teacher–coach–leader, in the chapter that follows we will examine and discuss "What is leadership?" and leadership effectiveness in coaching.

Summary

While a coach may possess a well-rounded philosophy and sound coaching theory, he will not enjoy coaching success unless he can convey his ideas and "know-how" to others. A coach must have the ability to teach and communicate effectively. The methods or means he utilizes to convey his ideas and conceptions are important, as is *how* he teaches or coaches which is "the art of coaching." A coach should always present his material and gear his instructions to the team members at their level of comprehension.

The successful coach transmits his theory to his squad, securing adequate feedback from his players to determine whether or not they comprehend what the coach has attempted to teach them.

While knowledge of the subject matter or "the science of coaching" is important, a unique feature of coaching is that the ultimate evaluation of the teacher–coach generally is based on the performance of his or her players which is most frequently reflected in the final score of the contest. It is through the learning process, which includes communication, that the coach's goals for his program and his sport are transmitted to others.

Coaches are teachers; coaching is teaching; and teaching is the management or guidance of learning. Learning is an active process. Learning is the acquisition of new behavior patterns, or the strengthening or weakening of old behavior patterns as the result of practice. Psychologists have established the general laws of learning, and for effective teaching–coaching, one needs to apply the research findings of psychologists: coaches need to be knowledgeable about the learning process, the learner (athlete), and the conditions for learning.

REFERENCES

Bandura, Albert, and Walters, Richard H. *Social Learning and Personality Development.* New York. Holt, Rinehart and Winston, 1963.

Bloom, Benjamin S., Englehart, Max D., Furst, Edward J., Hill, Walter H., and Krathwohl, David R. *Taxonomy of Educational Objectives, Handbook I: Affective Domain.* New York. David McKay, 1956.

Butts, Dorcas Susan. *Psychology of Sport: The Behavior, Motivation, Personality, and Performance of Athletes.* New York. Van Nostrand Reinhold, 1976, pp. 137–141.

Cratty, Bryant J. *Psychology and Physical Activity.* Englewood Cliffs, N.J. Prentice-Hall, 1968.

Cratty, Bryant J. *Movement Behavior and Learning* (3rd ed.). Philadelphia. Lea & Febiger, 1973.

Dashiell, J. F. "A Survey and Synthesis of Learning Theories." *Psychological Bulletin.* Vol. 32, 1935, pp. 261–275.

Drowatzky, John N. *Motor Learning Principles and Practices.* Minneapolis. Burgess, 1975.

Hammer, Bill. *Football Coach's Complete Handbook.* Englewood Cliffs, N.J. Prentice-Hall, 1963, pp. 9–10.

Harrow, Anita J. *A Taxonomy of the Psychomotor Domain.* New York. David McKay Co., 1971.

Hilgard, Ernest R. *Theories of Learning* (2nd ed.). Englewood Cliffs, N.J. Prentice-Hall, 1956, pp. 486–487.

Hussman, B. F. "Sport and Personality Dynamics." Durham, N.C. *NCPEAM Proceedings.* January 1969.

James, William. *Principles of Psychology.* New York. Henry Holt & Co., 1890.

Kagan, Jerome, and Havemann, Ernest. *Psychology: An Introduction* (3rd ed.). New York. Harcourt Brace Jovanovich, 1976, p. 332.

Kappers, C. V. A. "Further Contributions on Neurobiotaxis." *IX Journal Comp. Neurology*. Vol. 27, 1917, pp. 261–298.

Krathwohl, David R., Bloom, Benjamin S., and Masia, Bertram B. *Taxonomy of Educational Objectives, Handbook II: Affective Domain*. New York. David McKay, 1964.

Lawther, John D. "Learning and Performance at the High Skill Level." In *Winning Edge*, Walter C. Schwank (Ed.). Washington, D.C. American Alliance for Health, Physical Education and Recreation, 1974, pp. 82–84.

Lewin, Kurt. *A Dynamic Theory of Personality*. Translated by Donald K. Adams and Karl E. Zener. New York. McGraw-Hill, 1935.

Lewin, Kurt. *Principles of Topological Psychology*. Translated by F. Heider and G. M. Heider. New York. McGraw-Hill, 1936.

Liebert, R. M. "Television and Social Learning: Some Relationships Between Viewing Violence and Behaving Aggressively." In *Television and Social Behavior. Vol. 2. Television and Social Learning,* J. P. Murray, E. A. Rubinstein, and G. A. Comstock (Eds.). Washington, D.C. U.S. Government Printing Office, 1972, pp. 1–34.

Liebert, R. M. "Observational Learning: Some Social Applications." In *The Fourth Western Symposium on Learning,* P. J. Elick (Ed.). Bellingham, Washington. Western Washington State College, 1973, pp. 59–73.

Liebert, Robert M., and Spiegler, Michael D. *Personality Strategies for Study of Man* (rev. ed.). Homewood, Ill. Dorsey Press, 1974, p. 384.

Lockhart, Aileene. "What's In A Name?" *Quest* II. April 1964, pp. 9–13.

McConnell, T. R. "The Psychology of Learning." *Yearbook, National Society for the Study of Education*. Vol. 41, Part II, 1942.

Miller, N. E., and Dollard, J. *Social Learning and Imitation*. New Haven, Conn. Yale University Press, 1941.

Noble, Clyde E. "The Learning of Psychomotor Skills." *Annual Review of Psychology*. Vol. 19, 1968, pp. 203–250.

Oxendine, J. B. *Psychology of Motor Learning*. Englewood Cliffs, N.J. Prentice-Hall, 1968, pp. 10–11, 36.

Oxendine, J. B. "Emotional Arousal and Motor Performance." *Quest* XIII. January 1970, pp. 23–32.

Pavlov, I. P. *Conditioned Reflexes*. Translated by G. V. Anrep. London. Oxford, 1927.

Singer, Robert N. *Motor Learning and Human Performance* (2nd ed.). New York. MacMillan Publishing Co., 1975.

Skinner, B. F. *The Behavior of Organisms*. New York. Appleton-Century-Crofts, 1938.

Skinner, B. F. *Walden Two*. New York. MacMillan Co., 1948.

Skinner, B. F. *Science and Human Behavior*. New York. MacMillan Co., 1953.

Skinner, B. F. *Beyond Freedom and Dignity*. New York. Knopf, 1971.

Tarde, G. *The Laws of Imitation*. New York. Henry Holt, 1903.

Thorndike, Edward Lee. *Educational Psychology. Vol. 2. The Psychology of Learning*. New York. Teachers College, 1913.

Thorndike, Edward Lee. *Human Learning*. New York. Appleton-Century-Crofts, 1931.

Thorndike, Edward Lee. *The Fundamentals of Learning*. New York. Teachers College, Columbia University, 1932.

Tolman, E. C. "Theories of Learning." In *Comparative Psychology,* F. A. Moss (Ed.). Englewood Cliffs, N.J. Prentice-Hall, 1934.

Tolman, E. C. "The Determiners of Behavior at a Choice Point." *Psychological Review,* 1938, p. 11.

Tolman, E. C. "There is More Than One Kind of Learning." *Psychological Review.* Vol. 56, 1949, pp. 144–155.

Watson, John B. *Behaviorism* (rev. ed.). New York. W. W. Norton, 1930.

Woodruff, A. D. *The Psychology of Teaching.* New York. David McKay, 1948, p. 59.

SELECTED READING

Bartz, Douglas. "Perceptual Motor Program: A Classification." *The Physical Educator.* Vol. 32, No. 3, October 1975, pp. 130–133.

Cermak, Laird S. *Psychology of Learning Research and Theory.* New York. Ronald Press, 1975.

Cratty, B. J. "A Three-Level Theory of Perceptual-Motor Behavior." *Quest* VI. May 1966, pp. 3–10.

Martens, Rainer. "Anxiety and Motor Behavior: A Review." *Journal of Motor Behavior.* Vol. 3, 1971, pp. 181–188.

Richardson, Elizabeth. "The Physical Setting and Its Influence on Learning." In *Environmental Psychology,* Harold Proshansky et al. (Eds.). New York. Holt, Rinehart and Winston, 1970.

Robb, Margaret. "Feedback and Skill Learning." *Research Quarterly.* Vol. 39, No. 1, March 1968, pp. 175–184.

Sage, George H., and Bennett, Bonnie. "The Effects of Induced Arousal on Learning and Performance of a Pursuit Motor Skill." *Research Quarterly.* Vol. 44, No. 2, May 1973, pp. 140–149.

Salmela, John H. "Sports Task Analysis: An Interface of Motor Learning and Sport Psychology." In *The Status of Psychomotor Learning and Sport Psychology Research,* Brent S. Rushall (Ed.). Dartmouth, Nova Scotia. Sport Science Associates, 1975, pp. 9.1–9.12.

Siedentop, Daryl. *Developing Teaching Skills in Physical Education.* Boston. Houghton Mifflin Company, 1976, pp. 163–277.

Williams, Ian D. "Necessary Conditions for Learning." In *Psychology of Sport and Motor Behavior II,* Daniel M. Landers (Ed.). Penn State HPER Series #10. The Pennsylvania State University, 1975, pp. 369–376.

Four

THE SOCIAL PSYCHOLOGICAL DIMENSIONS OF COACHING: SOCIAL INFLUENCE

11

Theories and Styles of Leadership Behavior and Coaching Effectiveness

There is growing recognition that perhaps the most critical determinant of organizational success—whether it be in business, education, government, athletics, the military, or other organizations, regardless of the goods or services they provide—is the presence of effective leaders. Much research on leadership comes from psychologists and others connected with the industrial world and the fields of management and business, but unfortunately most coaching texts are devoid of such research. Frequently the topical subjects of motivation and leadership are discussed together in a general and cursory manner, since motivation is most frequently thought of in terms of effective leadership provided by the coach. There is an implied assumption that a coach automatically will lead and motivate others. Merely because one is placed in a leadership position or has a title bestowed, implying that he or she is a leader, does not automatically make one a leader. Perhaps the most useful starting point is *not* ''What does a leader do?'' but rather to seek the answer to the question, ''Why does the follower follow?'' Central to the answer of this question are the concepts of motivation discussed in a previous chapter; suggestions were offered there of ways that influence could be brought to bear on an individual's motivation. This chapter builds on the previous chapters of motivation and personality.

Down through the centuries humans have been interested in obtaining the answers to such questions as, ''What is leadership?,'' ''What and who is a leader?,'' ''What makes a leader?,'' and similar queries dealing with the concepts of leadership and styles of leadership behavior. Since leadership is a phenomenon that concerns two or more individuals in a particular relationship, this chapter is concerned with how coaching leadership styles influence individual and group behavior in athletics and sports. Effective leadership will result in effective coaching.

FORMAL/IMPOSED AND INFORMAL/EMERGENT LEADERSHIP

When discussing leadership, much of the literature makes a distinction between formal/imposed or appointed leadership and informal/emergent leadership. The inference is that imposed leadership is determined by a superior authority, whereas informal leadership emerges as a result of internal group dynamics. However, these specific categories tend to relate more to the structure of the organization, which determines the pattern of authority, as each category's position of authority is different. For purposes of clarification and discussion, we too will follow these specified categories, cognizant of the fact that while the formal leader is bestowed with imposed or appointed leadership, he must "emerge" or come forth to be an effective leader. It is possible to "impose" or bestow leadership on a member of the group who appears to be the emergent leader, so that the terms as used in the subheading are not necessarily "pure" and synonymous with each other as implied. Our intent is not to confuse the issue, but to point out that while one may be in a leadership position the terms "imposed" or "appointed" and "emergent" are not rigidly fixed and static terms, and leadership implies more than a single element in the leadership process, whether it be the formal or informal structure.

Head Coach: The Organization's Appointed Formal Leader

Organization structure is primarily a system of A/B relationships in that A is the superior and B the subordinate in the line relationship. In athletics the appointed formal leader is the head coach, who is in a superior line position over assistant coaches and players. The discussion in this chapter will be limited in scope to the formal leader, although a superior line position in an organization's structure does *not* automatically guarantee that the head coach or any other individual in such a position will be an effective leader. The acceptance of his style of leadership by his followers and subordinates will determine his effectiveness as a coach and as a leader.

An appointed leader has organizational authority and can get performance solely on the basis of his "headship" or title position, although his leadership may be ineffective. Many people erroneously believe "headship" automatically guarantees effective "leadership." However, this is not the case, nor do the two terms headship and leadership mean the same, as will be discussed shortly.

The Group's Emergent Informal Leader

Informal structure differs from formal structure in that the informal one develops through social interaction. An emergent leader, who may emerge from within any group of individuals, has no official position of authority and must satisfy the needs of his peers to become the leader. For example, the emergence of an informal leader from a group of assistant coaches frequently occurs, going on the assumption that one of the assistants does *not* have the title of *assistant head coach*. Should the latter be the situation, then this would be an *A/B* relationship with the other assistant coaches and *not* the group's emergent informal leader, since the assistant head coach would also be a formal leader appointed by his head coach although their relationship would be *A/B* in the organization's structure.

A more typical illustration of emergent leaders comes from within the squad or team members, and such leadership is greatly encouraged. Winning teams usually have strong formal and informal leadership, although our discussion in this chapter focuses only on the head coach's style of leadership behavior. However, many of the suggestions, guidelines, and comments offered here for the appointed leader are also applicable to the individuals who emerge as the informal leaders of the group.

Power/Authority/Influence—The Acceptance Theory of Authority

While most everyone in any organization is familiar with the appointed leader's power and authority, in terms of the rewards and punishment system, the intent here is *not* to consider leadership in such a context. While position-based authority, such as the head track coach, permits one in a ''headship'' position to exercise power, the ''acceptance theory of authority'' holds that authority has no influence or force until it is accepted by subordinates. ''Headship'' does not automatically mean positive acceptance, although effective leadership generally results in the ready acceptance of such position-based authority.

The relationship between power and authority is that authority and power are both forms of influence. Effective leadership for maximal results entails *leading,* although some feel it also means the leader pulling others up to his level. However, in the context of this chapter, we are referring to formal leadership in terms of *influencing,* not controlling, others.

WHAT IS LEADERSHIP?

There are numerous points of view on the dimensions of leadership, as well as many misconceptions about theories of leadership. Frequently the terms leadership and leader are used together in everyday language, but there is a great difference in what is meant by the terms. There is not a clear understanding by everyone as to whether leadership is a position, a person, or a process.

In many organizations—whether profit-making, service, business, or volunteer—the erroneous idea prevails that promotion or appointment to a clearly defined position qualifies the occupant to lead and manage subordinates. The opinion is prevalent that given power or title, a coach, for example, can automatically lead. The conferring of ''headship'' is commonplace in government, industry, and enterprises of every variety, including coaching. However, too often the process of selecting someone to occupy a leadership role and position fails to take into account the necessity of *ascertaining* whether or not the candidate is thoroughly investigated as to technical competency as well as *human skills*. Leadership and headship too seldom occur together. To be made head of something does not make one a leader. Headship can be delegated, conferred, appointed. Anyone, regardless of other qualities, can be made head of a group or organization by outside authority, or even by the group itself. Not so with leadership, which is an interaction process, and is the indispensable ingredient in any successful, effective organization. Leadership is much more than "headship."

Leaders on Leadership

There is no agreed-on definition of what leadership is, and even less agreement on what it should be. The definitions of leadership range from short, general statements to detailed theories of leadership.

Phi Delta Kappa, a professional educational fraternity with its International Headquarters in Bloomington, Indiana, produced a fast-track audiotape cassette/filmstrip, "Leaders on Leadership" (1973), in which four well-known leaders from the fields of education, state and national government, and athletics (Al McGuire, who was then head basketball coach at Marquette University) were interviewed by Dr. Donald Robinson, Director of Publications, Phi Delta Kappa International, Inc.[1] The following are some of the responses, *in part,* that Dr. Robinson received to his opening question, "Would you like to make any kind of a general statement about leadership?"

- "Somebody out in front: very visible . . . repetition is the sign of a leader."
- "There has to be an informed followership. . . ."
- "A perception of the future . . . systematic diligence . . . skillful in the use of words. . . ."
- "A thick skin."
- "You've got to have compassion . . . careful research of the alternatives. . . ."
- "Willingness to risk . . . delegate authority. . . ."
- "Man is not meant for safe havens . . . recognize leadership on the other side of the table."
- "Self discipline . . . encourage participation and involvement. . . ."
- "There are a lot of bases to cover in this business."
- "There's no sin in not being a leader—the sin is not trying."

[1]Phi Delta Kappa Committee on Educational Leadership. "Leaders on Leadership." Audiotape cassette/filmstrip. Interviewer Dr. Donald Robinson, Phi Delta Kappa, Bloomington, Ind. Copyright © 1973, Phi Delta Kappa, Inc. Reprinted by permission.

Vincent Thomas Lombardi (1970) expressed his views on the subject in this way:

> Leadership is not so much leading as having the people led accept it. You know how you do that? You've got to win the hearts of the people that you lead. The personality of the individual has to do it. There's no hereditary strata in leading. They're not born; they're made. There has to be an inclination, a commitment, a willingness to command.

Coach Lombardi's viewpoint of leadership expresses, in part, a concept of leadership, one of several approaches to answering the query, "What is leadership?" His particular style of leadership behavior, well-known and probably emulated by numerous individuals in leadership positions, was distinctly different from others who effectively utilize different styles of leadership behavior.

One of the best definitions of leadership is that which President Dwight D. Eisenhower gave. He said leadership was the ability to get a person to do what you want him to do, when you want it done, in a way you want it done, because he wants to do it. Obviously this deals with motivation, too, which was discussed in detail in a previous chapter.

The objective of including the comments by leaders on the subject of leadership is to illustrate the point that the terms leader and leadership do not mean the same to everyone, including those individuals who have been identified and recognized as leaders by others.

Leader, Leadership

A layperson would probably define a *leader* as a person who leads or as a person commanding authority or influence; the first or principal performer of a group. For our intended purposes, this definition of leader is inadequate, since one can be in a position of authority but fail to be a leader. In such a situation, one may hold a headship, which by definition is the position, office, or dignity of a head. Leadership entails more than headship, just as leadership is only one dimension of coaching. However, leadership is an important one.

Smith and Kreuger (1933) surveyed the literature on leadership to 1933. Jenkins (1947) reviewed leadership studies with particular reference to military problems. Stogdill (1948) surveyed the literature for personal factors associated with leadership. Of the numerous definitions of leadership, such as those postulated by Young (1946), Stogdill (1950), Bennis (1959), Argyris (1976), and others, covering a span of three decades, 1946–1976, they are very similar in that a common thread runs throughout. Specifically, these authors found that leadership is a process whereby one individual, the leader, exerts influence over others, his followers. Stogdill's work is quoted most frequently in the leadership literature, as is his (1950) definition, "Leadership may be considered as the process (act) of influencing the activities of an organized group in its efforts toward goal setting and goal achievement."

The Dynamic Quality of a Relationship. Although by commonly accepted definition *management* is the accomplishment of predetermined goals and objectives through others, the leadership definition emphasizes the personal relationship through the word "influencing." Perhaps the leader is the one who "inspires" others, to work toward goals. Leadership has to do with the *dynamic* quality of a relationship, the action-reaction phase of motivating and influencing others, in a coaching context in our discussion, which would include managing others, too. Although much of managing is nonbehavioral, the behavioral part is a critical feature of leadership.

While a head coach can be readily recognized as an appointed leader by his position and title, he may not be able to "inspire" assistants, players, and others toward the successful accomplishment of common goals. Not all coaches are able to bring off the required dynamic quality of the personal relationship, the action-reaction phase of leading and managing others. As we discuss the ingredients or components of leadership, the reader will recognize why a formal appointed leader may be unable to induce or inspire others to produce some output or specific performance. When this occurs, frequently it is because the leadership process is incomplete.

The Work of Stogdill, Fiedler, and Their Associates

Dr. Ralph M. Stogdill (1948, 1950, 1974), along with his associates Carroll Shartle (1948, 1956), and Dr. Fred Fiedler (1967, 1969, 1974), and his associates (1976), have made significant contributions to the topical subject, "What is leadership?" Undoubtedly there are other authors on the subject, but the research of Stogdill and Fiedler is most prominent.

Ohio State University's Professor Ralph Stogdill, through the university's Research Foundation and as an Associate Director of the Ohio State Leadership Studies, has been involved in leadership research for more than three decades. The Ohio State Leadership Studies was a 10-year program of research on leadership problems in military, business, industrial, educational, and civilian governmental organizations.

Leadership research by Dr. Fred Fiedler, and his associates who were at one time or another associated with the Group Effectiveness Research Laboratory at the University of Illinois and the Organization Research Group at the University of Washington in Seattle, is also frequently quoted in leadership literature. Professor Fielder's (1967, 1974) contingency model of leadership effectiveness will be presented in the following discussion.

SELECTED THEORIES OR APPROACHES TO LEADERSHIP

There are at least two broad leadership theory categories: the traits theories, and the situational or contingency theories. Some refer to contigency theories as being part of the behavior approach to leadership, and others do not. Some refer to personal-behavioral theories as a third broad category because these deal with how the leader–manager (coach) carries out his job or the individual's style of leadership behavior. Our intent is to discuss concepts and styles of leadership behavior without rigidly fixing each in a specific category since there appears to be a recent trend toward integrating the numerous theories of leadership.

The "Great Man" Approach to Leadership

The earliest approaches to leadership concentrated on the particular characteristics of the individual, the leader, and the "great man" theory. The focus was on the hereditary backgrounds of great men of the times, well-known politicians, soldiers, statesmen, and others, in an attempt to explain leadership on the basis of inherited characteristics. It was posited that leadership, power, and influence were the result of inherited abilities. The basic assumption of the "great man" approach is that inherited characteristics determine whether a person will be a leader, thus "leaders are born, not made."

Most Prominent and Simplest Theory. The "great man" theory of leadership is not only the simplest, but probably more people believe this approach to leadership than any other. Throughout history, title and organizational structure have thrust many individuals into positions of power and authority, and they have become well-known as influencial leaders. Without taking into consideration other circumstances, the simplest approach to leadership is to believe that "leaders are born." If one is born with leadership characteristics, one can become a leader! If one never acquires a leadership position, then one never really possessed the innate characteristics to be a leader. If one acquires a leadership position and is ineffective, then the failures can be directly attributed to abilities that were *never* inherited.

The simplicity of the "great man" approach to leadership is its weakness; furthermore, research evidence does not support that leadership abilities are inherited. Therefore, despite its popularity by the masses, most social scientists reject the "great man," or "leaders are born," approach to leadership.

The Traits and Abilities Approach to Leadership

The identification of various personal traits of leaders as criteria for describing or predicting success has been used for some time. The traits and abilities approach is actually an extension of the "great man" approach to leadership. The concept is that there are certain characteristics that distinguish leaders from nonleaders.

Through the years efforts have been made to discover why leaders are successful by analyzing their personal characteristics. However, a comparison of leaders using various physical, personality, and intelligence traits has resulted in little agreement among researchers.

It is difficult, if not almost impossible, to correlate the "traits" studies on leadership in order to validate data. The number of traits in leadership studies varies from less than a dozen, to more than two dozen in number, and different methods of measurement and a variety of definitions are found for a given trait. For example, Stryker (1958) pointed out that, from 147 different descriptive statements utilized to identify the concept of "dependability," a list of 25 different definitions for the trait was compiled. The point is that there is a great deal of difference in the manner in which a trait can be identified, so that it is difficult to compile scientific data with any degree of validity and reliability. Also, the trait approach does not enable one to determine how much of a trait is needed for one to become an effective leader.

Trait Studies Have Not Produced Clear Results. The study of leadership traits has proven to be unsatisfactory as an approach to leadership theory. In addition to the cited limitations, a problem with the traits approach is that most of the traits that are associated with leadership are indications of expected behavior patterns of an individual in such a position. For example, a head coach is *expected* to possess "leadership traits" or specific patterns of behavior denoting leadership ability, because he is in the position of a head coach, whether he possesses them or not.

Jennings (1961), Davis (1972), and numerous others who have researched leadership traits have concluded that trait study has not produced clear results because it does not consider the whole leadership environment, and there is no sure connection between traits and leadership acts.

Research Findings. Despite the comments by Jennings and Davis, to the contrary, several researchers have reported favorable research findings, relevant to the trait theory and effective leadership. Ghiselli (1963) found that leaders who have the drive to act independently and are self-assured are successful in achieving organizational goals. He also concluded that an individual's intelligence is an accurate predictor of managerial success within a certain range. Ghiselli pointed out, however, that above and below this range the chances of successful prediction significantly decreased. Ghiselli (1971) studied eight personality traits and five motivational traits, and the following summary gives the results of his findings as to the importance of each personal trait to management success:[2]

Personality traits:

- Intelligence: of a verbal and symbolic nature (1)
- Initiative: the willingness to strike off in new directions (2)

---

[2]Ghiselli, Edwin E. *Explorations in Managerial Talent.* Pacific Palisades, Calif.: Goodyear Publishing Co., 1971. Copyright © 1971 by Goodyear Publishing Co., Inc. Reprinted by permission.

- Supervisory ability: the ability to direct others (1)
- Self-assurance: favorable self-evaluation (1)
- Affinity for the working class (2)
- Decisiveness (1)
- Masculinity–feminity (3)
- Maturity (2)

Motivational traits:

- Need for job security (2)
- Need for financial reward (2)
- Need for power over others (3)
- Need for self-actualization (1)
- Need for occupational achievement (1)

Key:

(1) Very important
(2) Moderately important
(3) Very little importance

Ghiselli's findings (1971), although well respected because of the scientific quality of his work, must be tempered because the traits are not totally independent of each other. However, they do provide some interesting pieces of information. Despite a slowly changing society where the "macho concept" still prevails to a large measure in some circles, according to Ghiselli's findings masculinity–feminity seems to have little to do with managerial success. Not surprisingly to many, intelligence and self-actualization are important to success; and power over others is not very important. However, the finding that power is not important in leadership may not be readily accepted by many because some think of leadership solely in terms of authority, power, and headship. Then, too, the limitations of the trait theory of leadership, as discussed previously, are also applicable to Ghiselli's findings, despite the fact that his work is one of the best available on the trait theory of leadership.

Stogdill (1948) analyzed several thousand sources of information in the field and found a relationship between leadership and traits, which he classified under five general headings. His conclusions were supported by 15 or more studies he reviewed where the person in the leadership position exceeded the average member of the group in the possession of the trait. Each trait as defined by Professor Stogdill involved a number of factors, as follows:[3]

Capacity (intelligence, alertness, verbal facility, originality, judgment)

Achievement (scholarship, knowledge, athletic accomplishments)

[3]Stogdill, Ralph M. "Personal Factors Associated with Leadership: Survey of Literature." *The Journal of Applied Psychology,* Vol. 25, 1948, pp. 64–65. Reprinted by permission.

Responsibility (dependability, initiative, persistence, agressiveness, self-confidence, desire to excel)

Participation (activity, sociability, cooperation, adaptability, humor)

Status (socioeconomic position, popularity)

Stogdill's findings are not surprising, since it is primarily by virtue of participating in group activities and demonstrating the leader's capacity for expediting the work of the group that one becomes endowed with leadership status. As Dr. Stogdill (1948) pointed out,

> A number of investigators have been careful to distinguish between the leader and the figure-head, and to point out that leader-ship is always associated with the attainment of group objectives. Leadership implies activity, movement, getting work done. The leader is a person who occupies a position of responsibility in coordinating the activities of the members of the group in their task of attaining a common goal. This leads to consideration of another significant fact. *Situation* (mental level, status, skills, needs and interests of followers, objectives to be achieved, etc.).

Stogdill, Davis, and many others refer to the *situational* approach to leadership, indicating there is more than merely the traits of the leader. In fact, the traitist theory of leadership ignores the subordinates, which is a major weakness, since the followers have a significant effect on the accomplishments of the leader and of the group goals or objectives. It became apparent that a study of leadership represents a study of relationships, of variables in interaction. According to Pigors (1935) a study of leadership must consider: (1) the leader, (2) the members as individuals, (3) the group as a functional organization, and (4) the situation. As early as the 1920s, however, there were those who felt that leadership involved more than the traits of the leader, and that the situation had much to do with the leadership process.

The Situational or Contingency Approaches to Leadership

Mary Parker Follett, a social worker and philosopher, recognized in the 1920s the "law of the situation." Metcalf and Urwick, as editors of *Dynamic Administration, The Collected Papers of Mary Parker Follett* (1942), in quoting Miss Follett noted that "there are different types of leadership" and that "different situations require different kinds of knowledge, and the man possessing the knowledge demanded by a certain situation tends in the best managed businesses, other things being equal, to become the leader of the moment."

Miss Follett was far ahead of her time, but the same theme was advanced again after World War II by other researchers on leadership. The traitist approach dominated leadership studies before 1945, but this theory of leadership was refuted by Stogdill's analysis of the leadership studies in 1948, showing the "law of situation" prevailed. Since that time the situational explanation of leadership has been one of the most common theories.

The Law of the Situation. As Stogdill (1948) pointed out,

> A person does not become a leader by virtue of the possession of some combination of traits, but the pattern of personal characteristics of the leader must bear some relevant relationship to the characteristics, activities, and goals of the followers. Thus, leadership must be conceived in terms of the interaction of variables which are in constant state of flux. . . . It is quite another matter to place these persons in different situations where they will be able to function as leaders. It becomes clear that an adequate analysis of leadership involves not only a study of leadership, but also of situations.
>
> The evidence suggests that leadership is a relation that exists between persons in a social situation, and that persons who are leaders in one situation may not necessarily be leaders in other situations. . . .

Diagrammatic Illustrations of Leadership Elements and Attributes. Authors utilize different diagrams to illustrate the elements and attributes of leadership: the *leader* and the *followers,* each with his or her own characteristics, including each person's own perceptions, motivations, and resources relevant to the attainment of the group's goals; and the *situation,* involving functions to be fulfilled, desired goals, and other conditions. Common to all these diagrams—whether illustrated by intertwining circles, a circle within a circle, a triangle, a diamond, or by some other illustrative diagram—are the interacting relationships between the elements and attributes in a situation of leadership.

The Leadership Fusion-Interaction "Triangle" and "Diamond" Illustrations. Figures 11–1 and 11–2 are two diagrams that may be utilized to illustrate the components or elements of the leadership process, taking into account the fusion and interaction of the leader, the followers or group members, and the situation. With this approach, in both diagrams, the most effective leadership style depends on the nature of the situation, the characteristics of the followers, and the abilities of the leader.

In Figure 11–1, the "triangle" of components are three in number, with goals and objectives being variables in the situational element.

In Figure 11–2, the "diamond" illustration, a common goal (goals and objectives) is considered by some theorists as the fourth component or element, although the variables are the same as those included in Figure 11–1.

The situational approach to leadership is more realistic than the "great man" and "traitist" approaches discussed previously and is extended further by Fiedler's contingency approach.

Fiedler's Contingency Approach to Leadership

Organizational psychologist Fred Fiedler (1967, 1974), and his associates (1976), demonstrated in their studies that a contingency approach to leadership, emphasizing the factors that make it effective or not, is superior to the generalized approaches of the past. In Fiedler's contingency model, effective leadership requires that the leader's style match the demands of the situation. Leadership effectiveness is defined in terms of group performance and how well the group accomplishes assigned functions. The effectiveness of the group depends on the relationship between the leadership style and the group situation.

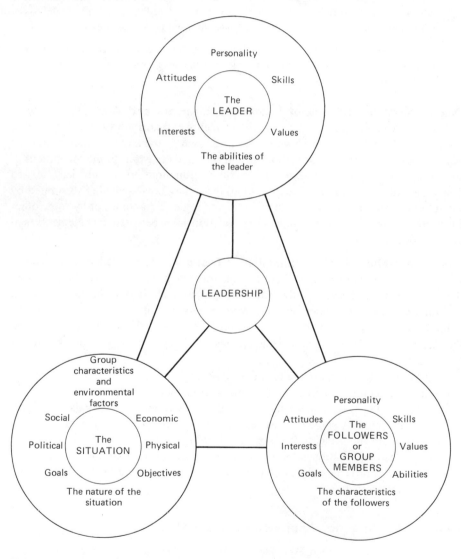

Figure 11-1. The leadership fusion-interaction "triangle" of elements and variables.

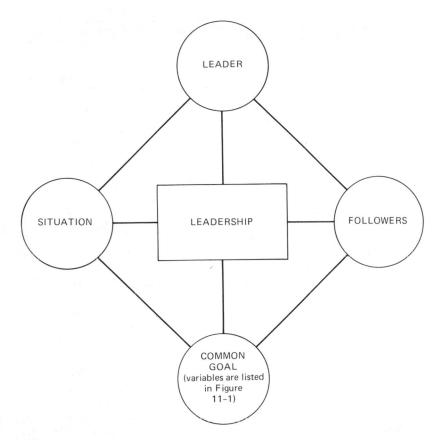

Figure 11-2. The leadership fusion-interaction "diamond" of elements. (The varibles are the same as those in Figure 11-1.)

Identifying One's Leadership Style. According to Fiedler's (Fiedler et al., 1976) leader match concept, one's attitude toward his least-preferred co-worker (LPC) will measure his leadership style.[4] Figure 11-3 illustrates the chart utilized for determining one's LPC.

The following scale is offered to identify two types of leadership styles:

- If one's score is 64 or above, one is considered a *high* LPC person, who is further identified as *relationship-motivated*.
- If one's score is 57 or below, one is considered a *low* LPC person, and is identified as *task-motivated*.

[4]Fiedler, Fred E., Chemers, Martin M., and Mahar, Linda. *Improving Leadership Effectiveness: The Leader Match Concept.* New York: John Wiley & Sons, 1976. Copyright © 1976 by John Wiley & Sons, Inc. Reprinted by permission.

Least Preferred Co-worker (LPC) Scale to Measure Leadership Style

										Scoring
Pleasant	—	—	—	—	—	—	—	—	Unpleasant	—
	8	7	6	5	4	3	2	1		
Friendly	—	—	—	—	—	—	—	—	Unfriendly	—
	8	7	6	5	4	3	2	1		
Rejecting	—	—	—	—	—	—	—	—	Accepting	—
	1	2	3	4	5	6	7	8		
Tense	—	—	—	—	—	—	—	—	Relaxed	—
	1	2	3	4	5	6	7	8		
Distant	—	—	—	—	—	—	—	—	Close	—
	1	2	3	4	5	6	7	8		
Cold	—	—	—	—	—	—	—	—	Warm	—
	1	2	3	4	5	6	7	8		
Supportive	—	—	—	—	—	—	—	—	Hostile	—
	8	7	6	5	4	3	2	1		
Boring	—	—	—	—	—	—	—	—	Interesting	—
	1	2	3	4	5	6	7	8		
Quarrelsome	—	—	—	—	—	—	—	—	Harmonious	—
	1	2	3	4	5	6	7	8		
Gloomy	—	—	—	—	—	—	—	—	Cheerful	—
	1	2	3	4	5	6	7	8		
Open	—	—	—	—	—	—	—	—	Guarded	—
	8	7	6	5	4	3	2	1		
Backbiting	—	—	—	—	—	—	—	—	Loyal	—
	1	2	3	4	5	6	7	8		
Untrustworthy	—	—	—	—	—	—	—	—	Trustworthy	—
	1	2	3	4	5	6	7	8		
Considerate	—	—	—	—	—	—	—	—	Inconsiderate	—
	8	7	6	5	4	3	2	1		
Nasty	—	—	—	—	—	—	—	—	Nice	—
	1	2	3	4	5	6	7	8		
Agreeable	—	—	—	—	—	—	—	—	Disagreeable	—
	8	7	6	5	4	3	2	1		
Insincere	—	—	—	—	—	—	—	—	Sincere	—
	1	2	3	4	5	6	7	8		
Kind	—	—	—	—	—	—	—	—	Unkind	—
	8	7	6	5	4	3	2	1		

Source: Fred E. Fiedler, Martin M. Chemers, and Linda Mahar. *Improving Leadership Effectiveness: The Leader Match Concept.* New York: John Wiley & Sons, 1976, p. 8. Copyright © 1976. Reprinted by permission of John Wiley & Sons, Inc.

Figure 11-3.

- If one's score is between 58 and 63, it is difficult to draw a clear-cut personality sketch, and Fiedler (1976) suggested the individual himself will have to determine in which of these groups he belongs.

The Leadership Situation. Before analyzing one's effectiveness as a leader as the result of the LPC scale (Figure 11-3), it is necessary to analyze the following three major components which primarily determine control and influence in the situation, according to Fiedler:

1. *Leader-member relations:* The degree to which the group supports the leader.
2. *Task structure:* The degree to which the task clearly spells out goals, procedures, and specific guidelines.
3. *Position power:* The degree to which the position gives the leader authority to reward and punish subordinates.

Neither the relationship-motivated style nor the task-motivated style of leadership can be considered effective in themselves. The effectiveness of the leadership style depends on the three situational factors in terms of the favorableness of the situation for the leader. The situation is considered favorable when the leader-member relations are good, pleasant, cooperative, and dependable; when the task structure is clearly defined, and goals and tasks are clearly spelled out; only then is the position power evident. However, Fiedler considers position power the least important of the three dimensions of situational leadership. If these three dimensions are high or favorable, then the leader can exercise a high degree of influence in his leadership. If the three elements are low or unfavorable in that the leader is disliked, or has little support from his group, or the task is not well-structured and is vague, and there is little position power, obviously the leader has low or little influence.

The Relationship-Motivated Leader. For the person who scores 64 or above on the LPC scale (Figure 11-3), *generally* this kind of leader is more concerned with interpersonal relations, is more sensitive to the feelings of others, and tries to avoid conflict. Such a person is better able to deal with complex issues in the interpersonal relations area and is able to take more factors into account when making personnel decisions.

Fiedler (1976) summarized *high* LPC leaders as follows:

[They] tend to acomplish the task through good interpersonal relations with the group in situations in which the group as a whole participates in the task performance. When their primary goal has been accomplished and things are under control, they may behave in a brisque, authoritarian manner which is seen as inconsiderate by subordinates. In a tense, anxiety-arousing situation, they may become so concerned with interpersonal relationships that they fail to accomplish the task.

The Task-Motivated Leader. For the person who scores 57 or below on the LPC scale (Figure 11–3), *generally* this kind of leader is more concerned with the task and is less sensitive to interpersonal relations. Generally he is eager and impatient to get on with the job. Usually he quickly organizes the job and has a no-nonsense attitude about getting the work done.

Fiedler (1976) summarized *low* LPC leaders as follows:

> [They] are strongly motivated to accomplish successfully any task [to] which they have committed themselves. They do this through clear and standardized work procedures and a no-nonsense attitude about getting down to work. Although they want to get the job done, they will care about the opinions and feelings of subordinates as long as everything is under control. But in low control situations, they tend to neglect the feelings of group members in an effort to get the job done, "business before pleasure!" For them there is no conflict between the esteem they get from subordinates and the esteem from their boss. They use the group to do the job, and when they feel that the situation is under control. they try to do it as pleasantly as possible.

Fiedler pointed out that whether a person is a "true type" or a combination of leadership types, *"Your effectiveness as a manager will depend on how well your individual personality and leadership style fit the requirements of your leadership situation and not whether you scored high or low on the LPC."*

For a more detailed explanation of this contingency model of leadership effectiveness, the reader is directed to the self-teaching guide bound in a soft cover, *Improving Leadership Effectiveness: The Leader Match Concept,* by Fiedler and his associates (1976).

STYLES OF LEADERSHIP BEHAVIOR

In our discussion an attempt has been made to isolate theories or approaches to leadership from the styles of leadership behavior. However, as we have seen in Fiedler's works, for example, one's attitude determines whether one is relationship-motivated or task-motivated, which in turn determines one's leadership style. Then, too, some authors refer to a third broad category as the personal-behavior theories of leadership, contending leaders may best be classified according to behavior patterns or styles. As an illustration of personal behavior (P-B) theories, we will discuss briefly Blake and Mouton's (1964) managerial grid, since it is applicable to coaching.

What Is Leadership Style?

Leadership style refers to the *qualities* in the *relationship* between the leader and the followers in a particular situation. The stylistic approach to leadership is concerned with how the leader acts toward the members of the group. Leadership style is concerned with what leaders do, rather than the personal characteristics they may possess. Authors have used numerous terms and models to describe the various styles of leadership behavior on a continuum ranging from the autocrat–dictator, the "coercing boss," who makes all of the decisions, to the "abdicrat," who takes no part in decision-making, remains aloof from the activities of the group, and is in effect no leader at all. Each is an extreme on the continuum of leadership behavior, and seldom is any one style practiced in a "pure" form all of the time.

Achieving the Best Results. One's basic leadership style is part of one's personality. Radically attempting to change one's style would be as difficult as suddenly trying to become a completely different person. However, through experience of trial-and-error or trial-and-success, individuals learn which leadership style achieves the best results. This does not mean that the leader is purposely manipulative, although Sage in "Machiavellianism Among College and High School Coaches" (1972) quoted sources making this allegation. However, at times a leader is forced to alter, modify, or temper his style of leadership behavior in order to lead effectively. For example, the leader may be too authoritative or too permissive, and his followers may have different expectations of their leader and one in his leadership position. Despite the leader's position and title, unless he modifies his style the "acceptance theory of authority" will not prevail, and mutually desired organizational and group goals will not be achieved. While his followers may be physically present, they are not motivated to perform optimally and the dynamic interaction of the leadership process will not take place. Not infrequently when a coach is dismissed, the reason cited is that he failed to provide leadership, which means he did not motivate his assistants and players or measure up to the perceived role expectations of his position.

Leadership Styles and Philosophies

Some of the traditional terms used in identifying leadership styles include autocratic, authoritarian, permissive, democratic, assignment, benevolent autocratic, participative, paternalistic, laissez-faire, and others, several of which are merely different terms to describe the same style of leadership. Also, several are a combination of different styles of leadership behavior. For our purposes, we will discuss Steben and Bell's (1978) five styles of leadership and their corresponding philosophies since they relate to coaching; thus we quote them at length.[5]

> *Laissez-faire—nondirection leadership.* This is not an uncommon style for authoritarians who have lost their touch and accepted defeat or who cannot function

[5]Steben, Ralph E., and Bell, Sam. *Track and Field: An Administrative Approach to the Science of Coaching.* New York: John Wiley & Sons, 1978. Copyright © 1978 by John Wiley & Sons, Inc. Reprinted by permission.

properly because of restraints. Quite often a beginner who prefers to avoid contact with people and problems will adopt this marginal philosophy. This person adheres to convention and follows rules of conduct in a passive, unenthusiastic manner. When conflict that requires a course of action occurs, he or she tends to remain neutral and rarely gets stirred up by any problems. The basic attitude seems to reflect personal survival within the system by assuming no position at all. Like driftwood, these people move with the current rather than selecting a direction of their own.

Paternalistic leadership. In this humanistic style of leadership, the coach discovers what the team members want and, by gentle persuasion and manipulation, helps to achieve the goal. Coaches are so intent on being accepted as ''good guys'' that they are inclined to accept the opinions, attitudes, and ideas of others rather than pushing their own. There is a looseness of organization, with any deviation usually being overlooked. The coach is patient, friendly, paternalistic, likable, and not apt to exert positive leadership. By setting general goals that everyone can support, the underlying attitude is one of joining a comfortable and friendly country club. In order to avoid social rejection, conformity to team atmosphere and work tempo is essential.

Compromise-democratic leadership. This pragmatic style leans heavily on precedent and established rules. To emphasize this, the approach to any conflict relies on finding what has worked best previously. These persons try to be firm, but are interested in obtaining a fair solution, equitable to as many people as possible. They rarely innovate and wait for others to test something before adopting it. Because this is a political kind of leadership, they are likely to eventually win some measure of security, status, and prestige since they support the status quo.

Autocratic-authoritarian leadership. These leaders are not only achievement oriented but are also impervious to criticism, feeling that nice guys usually finish last. Aggressiveness is characterized by doing things their way. They have great confidence in their ability to get things started and completed, interpreting facts to support their own views. There may be some substitution of quantity goals for quality performance. Although these coaches may not always be right, they are never wrong. Since they believe that any decision is better than none, they never doubt their actions.

Control leadership. This style is oriented toward finding the best and most effective solution to problems in given situations, not necessarily the traditional ''one best way.'' This coach has strong convictions, is not only a starter and finisher, but looks for a better way to reach the common goal of team success by working for and with the people involved. Open and candid communication allows any conflict to be dealt with by direct confrontation, out in the open where those involved can settle any differences honestly and rationally. Mistakes are not deliberately committed but are regarded as misunderstandings, which can be modified and corrected through teaching. No attempt is made to pressure, abandon, compromise, or buy effort to improve performance; instead the key is to make things happen through involvement and participation.

Although it is convenient to categorize coaches by their leadership qualities, very likely the majority of coaches will reflect characteristics of each of the coaching styles discussed. However, Steben and Bell (1978) felt that most of the coaches could be placed in the compromise-democratic category.

Cerutty's Two Categories of Leadership Styles

Percy Cerutty (1975) felt coaches could be categorized into two leadership styles: the prestige-seeking noncompetitor coach, and the coach who wins the respect of his players. The former, according to Cerutty, demands respect by exhortation. The prestige-seeking noncompetitor coach is prone to guess at some readily convenient workout schedule and insist that his athletes expedite it. The respected coach, however, wins respect from his athletes by demonstrating techniques and scientifically developing schedules, guiding the athlete to learn and develop an inquiring attitude and personal philosophy.

The Grid® Theory of Management-Leadership Styles[6]

Blake and Mouton (1978) postulated that leadership styles could be plotted on a two-dimensional grid, as illustrated in Figure 11–4.[7] This diagram is applicable to head coaches or anyone else in an *A/B* relationship in management.

Only five leadership styles are indicated in the managerial grid, as illustrated in Figure 11–4.

Point −1,1 *Impoverished Management* (lower left-hand corner). This style is very similar to the laissez-faire leader; this leader shows little concern for both people and production. The leader tries to avoid responsibility and decision making by remaining neutral and not raising any controversial issues. A minimum effort to accomplish the work is exerted by the leader.

Point −9,1 *Authority-Obedience Management* (lower right-hand corner). This style of this leader places major emphasis on getting the job done, on task efficiency, and has little concern for subordinates and others. People are viewed solely in terms of their contribution to achieving task-related objectives. The authority-obedience or task-centered leader places a high value on his making the decision, and group members have little input in the decision-making process. They are to follow orders. Problems of human relations are viewed as interferences in getting the job done and are seen as adversely affecting the efficiency of operations and output.

Point −1,9 *Country Club Management* (upper-left-hand corner). This type of leader has high concern for people and a low concern for production. This leader is

[6]Grid ® is a registered service mark of Scientific Methods, Inc.

[7]Blake, Robert R., and Mouton, Jane Srygley. *The New Managerial Grid.* Houston: Gulf Publishing Company, 1978. Copyright © 1978 by Gulf Publishing Company. Reprinted by permission.

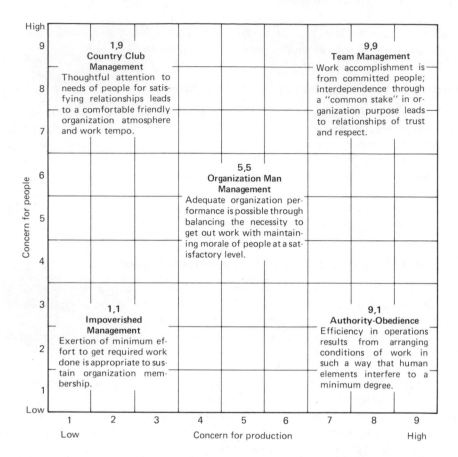

Figure 11-4. The Managerial Grid.® (*Source:* From *The New Managerial Grid* by Robert R. Blake and Jane Srygley Mouton. Houston: Gulf Publishing Company, 1978. Copyright © 1978. Reprinted by permission.® The Word Grid is a registered mark of Scientific Methods, Inc.)

the opposite of the task-centered (9,1) leader who has little concern for people. The Country Club leader focuses on being supportive and considerate of his subordinates. Task efficiency is not a primary concern of this easy-going leadership style. This leader prefers to accept the opinions, attitudes, and ideas of subordinates and group members and does not push for the acceptance of his personal points of view. Usually the country club leader is a warm and friendly person, and group harmony is very important to him.

    Point −5,5 *Organization Man Management* (middle square of grid). The middle-of-the-road leader has medium concern for people and medium concern for production. He attempts to get a harmonious balance, getting the job done and satisfying subordinates. The middle-of-the-road or the organization man leader works to avoid conflict since it would be disruptive to both production and personnel. His objective is to maintain a good, steady job pace without creating conflict or dissatisfied individuals. Adequate task efficiency and satisfactory morale are the goals of this type of leadership style.

Point −9,9 *Team Management* (upper right-hand corner). This type of leadership is the ideal, and one which every leader should be seeking. The team leader facilitates production and morale by coordinating the integration of work-related activities. It is the opposite of the impoverished leader (1,1), because the team or integrated leader has a high concern for people and also a high concern for production. While this type of leader may have strong personal convictions, he or she will seek out different opinions and ideas from subordinates. This type of leader is also not adverse to change as the result of objective, rational analysis of situations and problems. He emphasizes quality performance, accountability, responsibility, learning from past mistakes, self-control, and effective interpersonal relations.

This ideal style of leadership is desired and espoused by practically all coaches of all sports who have subordinates, but is seldom practiced in its "pure" form. However, by using the managerial grid we can see how the leader who is a (9,9) person would be the most effective leader. Coaches and other individuals should attempt to move toward a (9,9) style of leadership.

IMPLICATIONS FOR COACHING

There is no magic formula for becoming an effective leader. However, it is expected of one in the coaching profession, especially if a person is a head coach. The pressures of coaching can be fierce, one of a number of unique features indigenous to coaching that makes the job and the leadership function of the coach more difficult. All responsible leadership positions require many difficult decisions. Not all people, including some coaches, have the psychological or emotional makeup to be effective leaders. The business world, government, and athletics would benefit greatly if there were a formula available for the identification of effective leadership success, but presently no such formula exists. The generalized statements that follow are not formulas, but merely suggestions or guidelines from numerous sources as to effective leadership behavior.

Be Yourself

Observational learning or imitation influences our behavior greatly since the observer is exposed to the behavior of the exemplar, and frequently the observer tries to imitate that which he sees. Coaches and would-be coaches are not an exception, and there is no way of knowing how many have tried or are trying to emulate highly successful, well-known coaches. Every successful coach has his own particular coaching and leadership style, and the aspiring or inexperienced coach should not try to emulate or imitate others since each person's style and personality are unique. You can only be yourself, not someone else. It is not difficult for others to detect the actor or role-playing coach. Usually he or she is labeled a "phony" or fake, and the leadership one had hoped to provide is ineffective as a result of the coach trying to emulate some other individual's behavior or leadership style. Probably the best advice for any person is to "know thyself"; the individual's behavior will take care of itself.

Choose Your Own Leadership Style

While this is an extension of the previous suggestion, the philosophy that a coach adopts has a direct bearing on the coach's leadership style. Is it the "I'm the boss, you-do-as-I-say" autocratic attitude that you convey to subordinates and players? Or is it the "I'm the head coach and the head coach is never wrong" attitude? Or is the head coach genuinely concerned about subordinates and players and sees they are not treated as subjects and inferiors? In the autocratic style, the emphasis is on production, output, and high-stress performance, with the threat of a demotion or discharge hanging over the assistant or athlete who does not do his job; the attitude is "those are your tasks and responsibilities and if you can't do the job, I'll get someone else who can do it!" We are not implying that production and output should not be stressed, but that the nature of coaching is stressful enough without having a head coach providing additional stress through threats and negative psychology.

However, a more human-oriented leadership style will not automatically produce the highest productivity. Subordinates and others may misconstrue this approach as weak leadership, although it is "how" the coach achieves production and output from assistants and players that is most important. If the leadership style provides motivation and opportunities for individuals to fulfill their needs, then output and production performances are likely to be high. If the coach displays "I am the head coach and demand it" behavior, and this attitude is overtly or covertly perceived by players and assistants, effective coaching results are unlikely to be achieved.

Rewards Versus Punishment Approach in Leadership. People will perform quickly to avoid psychological, physical, and financial punishment and pain, but threats of punishment induce only minimal compliance. It is like the KITA (kick in the "tail") approach to motivation, which does get the individual moving, but motivation is not sustained. A rewards approach, which some may erroneously misinterpret as the "dangling carrot" approach to motivation, will have a longer benefit run than a punishment approach. Rewards, if they are intrinsic motivators, are pleasing and thus have benefits beyond the immediate performance since they affect expectations positively and carry over to other areas of compliance. The approach one uses to motivate suborbinates depends on one's leadership style, and frequently his attitude toward others.

Create and Maintain a Favorable Environment

The importance of creating and maintaining a favorable environment for coaching success cannot be minimized. Many industrial psychologists, faculty members who teach management courses at colleges and universities, and authors who publish in the professional journals and write management textbooks stress the importance of creating and maintaining a wholesome work environment—physically and psychologically—for employees. Here we are primarily concerned with the wholesomeness of the psychological environment. Psychologists McGregor, Maslow, and others have suggested that the leader can change, influence, or create the environments that will be supportive and reinforce the behavior desired. By creating the right kind of climate, coaches can have a definite impact on the achievement motivation of their subordinates. They can present these individuals with new sources of satisfaction and new opportunities to achieve, thereby arousing achievement motivation. Dr. David McClelland's extensive research focusing on a human's need to achieve was discussed previously in Chapter 9.

Behavioral research reveals that when authoritarian methods are impractical to motivate, much of the answer lies in *creating an environment* in which individuals may satisfy their own particular goals, while at the same time continuing in a responsible manner to the attainment of organization objectives. While one really cannot "make" an assistant or players perform in a desired manner, he can certainly *influence* their performance by his communication skills and the style of leadership he exercises.

Suggestions for Creating a Favorable Environment. Ohio State's Professor Robert Miljus, in "Effective Leadership and the Motivation of Human Resources" (1970), discussed eight important steps one could use in creating and maintaining a meaningful work environment, which we outline and summarize here:

1. Determine realistic objectives.
2. Provide necessary resources.
3. Make expectations known.
4. Provide adequate reward structure.
5. Delegate authority and invite participation.
6. Remove barriers to effective performance.
7. Appraise performance and communicate results.
8. Show consideration for employees

In a head coach's leadership role, and in the interaction with assistant coaches in particular, creating a *supportive* environment in which individuals can satisfy their various needs, while contributing to the attainment of organization objectives, provides more effective utilization of human resources than an autocratic environment or one which neglects human needs.

Negative Motivation is Ineffective. Since coaching tends to be somewhat of a "nomad" profession in that most coaches expect to move for career advancement purposes, and many do make frequent coaching changes for numerous reasons, many subordinates would *not* remain for an extended period under a head coach who displays an autocratic-authoritarian style of leadership. Behavioral research in the field of industrial management reveals that autocratic supervision, threats, and other forms of negative motivation have little relevance in today's work environment. Employees have higher educational attainment, generally oppose authority, are aware of alternative employment opportunities, and are willing to shift employers if necessary to avoid dissatisfying situations.

Although coaching has many "pitfalls", for numerous coaches who have been in the profession for an extended period coaching is still a most rewarding and satisfying experience, and financial remuneration is not the main reason for their remaining in the coaching profession. Poet Carlyle must have been thinking about a coach when he penned the following lines: "Blessed is he who has found his work; let him ask no further blessedness. He has a work, a life-purpose; he has found it and will follow it! Labor is life."

If the opportunities for self-fulfillment and self-satisfaction are not present, which is likely to be the situation under a head coach who is an autocratic-authoritarian leader, it is likely subordinates will either seek another coaching position or leave the profession and make their livelihood in another manner outside the field of coaching.

Four-Factor Theory of Leadership. Bowers and Seashore (1969) suggest that four factors have emerged from various research studies pertaining to leadership and that they are something the leader–manager does in order to become effective. They proposed that leadership behavior should do the following:[8]

1. Create support—this behavior will let others feel that they are of worth and importance.
2. Facilitate interaction—this behavior will encourage members of the group to develop close, positive, warm, and satisfying relationships.
3. Emphasize goals—this behavior will stimulate an enthusiasm among people to meet the performance goals of the group.
4. Facilitate work—this behavior is related to goal attainment and includes scheduling, coordinating, planning, and providing technical knowledge, tools, and materials.

[8]Bowers, David G., and Seashore, Stanley E. "Predicting Organizational Effectiveness with a Four-Factor Theory of Leadership." *Readings in Organizational Behavior and Human Performance,* L. L. Cummings and W. E. Scott, Jr. (Eds.). Homewood, Ill.: Irwin-Dorsey, 1969. Reprinted by permission.

Apply the Golden Rule

Research reveals that many leaders and managers have tended not to treat subordinates and others as they themselves would want to be treated. Many times people in leadership positions have described their subordinates in uncomplimentary, derogatory terms and feel their own insights constitute a law of human nature. At times these same managers and leaders have been amazed, surprised, and embarrassed when they find that their superiors describe them in the same way; and should they query their subordinates they are likely to find similar responses, including the opinion that subordinates do not respect them as leaders. The challenge to the person who wants to fulfill the leadership function and become an effective coach and leader is to recognize the dual and complementary objectives of both getting a job done and getting it done through other people.

While a manager must manage, a coach must coach, and a leader must lead, the latter function is not automatic merely because one is in a managerial position such as a head coach. As the late Vince Lombardi (1970) stated, "The strength of the group is the strength of the leader. Many mornings when I am worried or depressed, I have to give myself what is almost a pep talk, because I am not going before the ball club without being able to exude assurance. I must be the first believer, because there is no way you can hoodwink the players."

Help Others Fulfill Their Needs

In the last resort, a coach must use his skills and human insight, as does an orchestra leader, to capture individual satisfactions in the common enterprise and to create fulfillment that holds assistants and players to their part. No collection of cute tricks, of enticement or showmanship, can do that for the coach.

Leadership, despite what some people think, consists of a lot more than just "understanding people," "being nice to people," or "not pushing people around." Democracy is sometimes thought of as implying no division of authority, or to imply that everyone can be his own boss, do his own thing when he wants to do it, or not do it. This is nonsense, especially in athletics, as it would be in business or in an orchestra. But coaching leadership can be democratic in the sense of providing the maximum opportunity for growth to each subordinate and player without creating chaos and anarchy.

In fact, the orderly arrangement of functions and the accurate perception of a leader's role in that arrangement must always precede the development of the leader's abilities. A leader's job is to provide that recognition of roles and functions within the group, assistants, players, and team that will permit each member to satisfy and fulfill some major motive or interest.

Leadership usually begins to be learned early in life: in preschool days in the neighborhood, on the playground, even in the family; in school years on teams, in student body activities, in clubs, and possibly in the classroom; in later years in heading up work teams, from participating in conferences, from being on staffs, in societies and clubs, and sometimes in religious organizations. The basic relationship of leadership is not power and authority, but the influential interaction between the leader and the followers within a particular organization and environment. It is the composite influence of all the situational variables in the environment that determines the effectiveness of leaders and the styles they implement.

Evaluation of Your Leadership Style

As has been pointed out in this and other chapters, the role expectation of a head coach is that he or she be a leader and motivate others. Therefore, a head coach would do well to self-examine and carefully analyze, on other than a cursory basis, his or her leadership style in terms of relationships and the performance of assistants, players, and other subordinates. Regardless of whether a head coach is an inspiring leader or a coercing "boss," subordinates will evaluate their leader and his or her leadership style frequently. Although it may be informal, evaluation is critical, especially if the leader's style of influence and behavior are different from the subordinates' expectations of the role set and their individual perceptions of leadership. When the diversity becomes too great, usually there is a rebellion (which may be incorrectly identified as "disloyalty") within the squad or the coaching staff. The typical solution for trying to resolve the problem is for management to remove the head coach.

Leadership has to do with the dynamic quality of a relationship, the action-reaction phase of influencing others. And team effort and a spirit of cooperation are the necessary ingredients. The highest form of leadership is one that inspires personal commitment and involvement on the part of the followers. When people are approached in such a way that they provide momentum (motivation) from within themselves, leaders are able to do more leading and less pushing. Not everyone, including some coaches, recognizes this and works toward this end of motivation and leadership.

Summary

Down through the centuries, humans have been interested in obtaining the answer to questions such as, "What is leadership?," "Who is a leader?," "What makes a leader?," and similar queries dealing with the concepts of leadership and the styles of leadership behavior. Since leadership is a phenomenon that concerns two or more individuals in a particular relationship, we were concerned with how coaching leadership styles influence individual and group behavior in athletics and sports.

There is no agreed-on definition of what leadership is, and even less agreement on what it should be. President Dwight D. Eisenhower gave one of the best definitions of leadership when he said it was the ability to get a person to do what you want him to do, when you want it done, in a way you want it done, because he wants to do it. The earliest approaches to leadership concentrated on the individual characteristics of the individual, the leader, and the "great man" theory. The basic assumption of this approach is that it is inherited characteristics that determine whether a person will be a "great man," and thus "leaders are born, not made."

The identification of various personal traits of leaders as criteria for describing or predicting success has been used for some time. The traits and abilities approach is actually an extension of the "great man" approach to leadership. The concept is that there are certain characteristics that distinguish leaders from nonleaders.

Leadership styles refer to qualities of the relationship between the leader and the followers in a particular situation. The stylistic approach to leadership is concerned with how the leader acts toward the members of the group. Leadership style is concerned with what leaders do, rather than the personal characteristics they may possess.

One's basic leadership style is part of one's personality. Radically attempting to change one's style would be as difficult as suddenly trying to become a completely different person.

Some of the traditional terms used to identify leadership styles include autocratic, authoritarian, permissive, democratic, assignment, benevolent autocratic, participative, paternalistic, laissez-faire, and others, several of which are merely different terms to describe the same style of leadership.

There is no magic formula for becoming an effective leader. Every successful coach has his own particular coaching and leadership style, and the aspiring or inexperienced coach should not try to emulate or imitate others since each person is unique. One cannot be something he or she is not.

REFERENCES

Argyris, Chris. "Leadership, Learning, and Changing the Status Quo." *Organizational Dynamics*. Winter 1976, p. 29.

Bennis, Warren G. "Leadership Theory and Administrative Behavior: The Problem of Authority." *Administrative Science Quarterly*. December 1959, p. 261.

Blake, Robert R., and Mouton, Jane Srygley. *The New Managerial Grid*. Houston. Gulf Publishing Co., 1978, p. 11.

Bowers, David G., and Seashore, Stanley E. "Predicting Organizational Effectiveness With a Four-Factor Theory of Leadership." In *Organizational Behavior and Human Performance,* L. L. Cummings and W. E. Scott, Jr. (Eds.). Homewood, Ill. Irwin-Dorsey, 1969, pp. 599–615.

Cerutty, Percy. "Coaches and Coaching, World Roundup." *Track Techniques*. Vol. 62. December 1975.

Davis, Keith. *Human Behavior at Work* (4th ed.). New York. McGraw-Hill, 1972, p. 102.

Fiedler, Fred E. *A Theory of Leadership Effectiveness*. New York. McGraw-Hill, 1967.

Fiedler, F. E. "Style of Circumstances: The Leadership Enigma." *Psychology Today*. Vol. 2, 1969, pp. 38–43.

Fiedler, F. E. "The Contingency Model—New Directions for Leadership Utilization." *Contemporary Business,* 1974, pp. 65–79.

Fiedler, Fred E., Chemers, Martin M., and Mahar, Linda. *Improving Leadership Effectiveness: The Leader Match Concept*. New York. John Wiley & Sons, 1976, pp. 8, 11–12.

Ghiselli, Edwin E. "Managerial Talent." *American Psychologist*. October 1963, pp. 631–641.

Ghiselli, Edwin E. *Explorations in Managerial Talent*. Pacific Palisades, Calif. Goodyear Publishing, 1971.

Jenkins, W. O. "A Review of Leadership Studies With Particular Reference to Military Problems." *Psychological Bulletin*. Vol. 44, 1947, pp. 54–79.

Jennings, Eugene E. "The Anatomy of Leadership." *Management of Personnel Quarterly*. Autumn 1961, p. 2.

Lombardi, Vince. "Lombardi on Youth Unrest." As quoted by Murray Olderman. *San Francisco Examiner & Chronicle*. May 10, 1970.

Metcalf, Henry C., and Urwick, L. (Eds.). *Dynamic Administration, The Collected Papers of Mary Parker Follett*. London. Harper & Brothers Publishers, 1942, p. 277.

Miljus, Robert C. "Effective Leadership and the Motivation of Human Resources." *Personnel Management*, January 1970, pp. 36–40.

Phi Delta Kappa Committee on Educational Leadership. "Leaders on Leadership." fast-track audiotape cassette/filmstrip, interviewer Dr. Donald Robinson, Director of Publications, Phi Delta Kappa International, International Headquarters, Eight and Union, Bloomington, Ind. 47401, 1973, Appendix A, p. 7.

Pigors, Paul. *Leadership or Domination*. New York, Houghton Mifflin, 1935.

Sage, George H. "Machiavellianism Among College and High School Coaches." *Proceedings NCPEAM*. January 1972, pp. 45–59.

Smith, H. L., and Kreuger, L. M. "A Brief Survey of the Literature on Leadership." *Bulletin School of Education*. Indiana University, Vol. 9, No. 4, 1933.

Steben, Ralph E., and Bell, Sam. *Track and Field: An Administrative Approach to the Science of Coaching*. New York. John Wiley & Sons, 1978, pp. 4–5.

Stogdill, Ralph M. "Personal Factors Associate with Leadership: Survey of Literature." *The Journal of Applied Psychology*. Vol. 25, 1948, pp. 64–65.

Stogdill, Ralph M. "Leadership, Membership and Organization." *Psychological Bulletin*, Vol. 47, No. 4, January 1950, pp. 1–14.

Stogdill, Ralph M. *Handbook of Leadership*. New York. Free Press, 1974, pp. 63–64.

Stogdill, Ralph M., and Shartle, Carroll L. "Methods of Determining Patterns of Leadership Behavior in Relation to Organization Structure and Objectives." *Journal of Applied Psychology*. Vol. 32, 1948, pp. 286–291.

Stogdill, Raph M., Shartle, Carroll, L., and associates. *Patterns of Administrative Performance*. Columbus, Ohio. Bureau of Business Research. The Ohio State University, 1956, Sec. 1U.

Stryker, Perrin. "On the Meaning of Executive Qualities." *Fortune*. June 1958, p. 189.

Young, Kimball. *Handbook of Social Psychology*. London. Routledge and Kegan Paul, Ltd., 1946.

SELECTED READINGS

Cribbin, J. J. *Effective Managerial Leadership*. American Management Association, Inc., 1972.

Fiedler, F. E. "Validation and Extension of the Contingency Model of Leadership Effectiveness: A Review of Empirical Findings.'' *Psychological Bulletin*. Vol. 76, 1971, pp. 128–148.

Fiedler, F. E. *Leadership*. New York. General Learning Press, 1971.

Jacobs, T. O. *Leadership and Exchange in Formal Organizations*. Alexandria, Va. Human Resources Research Organization, 1971.

McClelland, David C. ''That Urge to Achieve.'' In *Organizational Psychology,* David A. Kilb, Irwin M. Rubin, and James M. McIntyre (Eds.). Englewood Cliffs, N.J. Prentice-Hall, 1971, pp. 123–130. And in *Behavioral Concepts in Management* (2nd ed.), David Hampton (Ed.). Belmont, Calif. Dickenson Publishing Co., 1972, p. 78.

McGregor, Douglas. *Leadership and Motivation, Essays of Douglas McGregor,* Warren G. Bennis and Edgar H. Schein (Eds.). Cambridge, Mass. The M.I.T. Press, 1966, pp. 5–6 (''Theory 'X' '') and p. 15 (''Theory 'Y' '').

Prentice, W. C. H. ''Understanding Leadership.'' *Harvard Business Review*. Vol. 39, No. 5, September/October 1961, pp. 143–151.

Urwick, L. F. *Leadership in the Twentieth Century*. New York. Pitman Publishing Corporation, 1958.

CHAPTER 12

The Psychology of Group Behavior and Coaching Effectiveness

The coach who is a consistent winner is one who optimizes the competencies and proficiencies of his or her available personnel, including assistant coaches as well as players. More often than not, however, this is seldom accomplished, especially in optimizing the available talents of assistant coaches.

Aligning, assigning, organizing, orientating, and coordinating the coaching staff, and utilizing their individual and joint efforts collectively, cannot receive cursory attention or be on a hit-and-miss basis if one desires to build a successful, winning program. Assistant coaches must be motivated, too, and the head coach's leadership style will have a direct bearing on the productivity and creativity of assistants. For a coaching staff as a group to be highly effective, there should be a common bond of affinity and cohesiveness. Therefore, a head coach needs to comprehend the differences between individual behavior and group behavior within the coaching staff, as well as on the squad or team.

Despite all other factors that affect the climate for building a successful, winning program, in the final analysis a coach wins with players. There have been coaching situations with no or few assistants, poor facilities, inadequate equipment and funding, and possibly even inferior player personnel; yet winning results have been achieved. Conversely, the opposite has been true, too, where some apparent ''good'' situations cannot win. While no team is stronger than its personnel, the chances of winning greatly diminish regardless of the available personnel if there is not affinity and cohesiveness within the group of players and among the coaches.

There have been numerous situations where coaches have lost with good personnel, and other instances where coaches have won with mediocre material. Numerous reasons could be hypothesized why each occurred. However, it is most likely that the missing ingredients included group cohesiveness and clearly identified group goals.

Most everyone everywhere is interested in groups, perhaps because each of us spends so much time in them. The social psychologist is interested in groups because they epitomize social situations and social behavior. Clinical psychologists are interested in groups because many personal problems are rooted in one's interaction with other human beings. Anyone, such as a coach, a manager, or others, who accomplishes his or her professional goals, and many personal goals, through group action needs to know and be aware of the most effective way to help the group achieve their goals. It seems that almost everyone has some reason to want to know about the dynamics of groups, although this single chapter cannot meet the needs of everyone who may have some interest in groups.

Our discussion will focus on group behavior, specifically the dynamics that occur within a team, among players and their coaching staff. The available literature reveals much about head coaches, but little about assistant coaches and coaching staff relationships. While group relationships will be discussed overall, in terms of players within their group, coaches within their group, and player–coach group relationships, special attention will be given to coaching staff relationships. Ways to achieve staff cohesiveness and to minimize staff conflicts will be discussed.

SOCIAL AFFILIATIVE RELATIONSHIPS

History is replete with instances of individual accomplishments. Sports history is not an exception. The most meaningful work, however, is not accomplished by persons singularly, but by people working together toward achieving common goals. In any formally structured organization, as discussed in Chapter 5, people are placed in formal, structured relationships with specific areas of authority and responsibility (as illustrated in Figure 12–1a).

Within every formal organization structure, whether it be in industry, business, government, education, or sports, there exists a social order of the members of the informal or emergent organization. In athletics, team or group members, whether they be players or coaches, interact and relate with each other in performing their assigned duties as designed by the formal authority structure, and they establish relationships with their own group members in order to satisfy affinity and achievement needs (as illustrated in Figure 12–1b). Out of this interaction of group members, social relationships and patterns of behavior that tend to be perpetuated are developed. While some of these relationships are formerly prescribed by the A-B (Superior-subordinate) relationship, such as a head coach to his or her assistant coaches, and all coaches to squad or team member participants, a significant

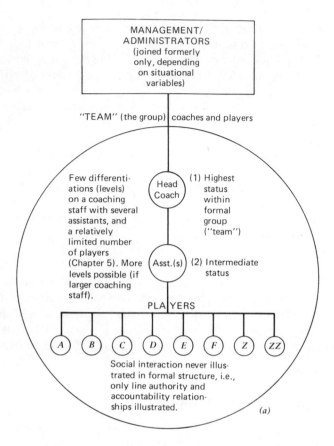

Figure 12-1. (a) A segment of a *formal* organizational structure within a "team" (group). (b) A hypothesized *informal* or emergent organizational structure within the peer groups. (The outer enclosed circles represent the "team"—players and coaching staff members.)

number of relationships evolve merely from the interaction process itself within each of the groups. Communication channels are established, status differences within the group(s) develop, and a set of practices and techniques unique to the emergent organization of players or coaches becomes accepted. Each group has its own internal life that tends to reject those individuals who are not a member of that particular group, condoning the behavior of its own members.

Informal relationships develop in every formal organization because members are on the same "team." These relationships are derived from friendship, physical proximity, common interests, common goals, or similar values. Individual behavior is largely shaped by group identification and by personal interaction with others. Human behavior is social behavior and is comprehensive only in the context of the

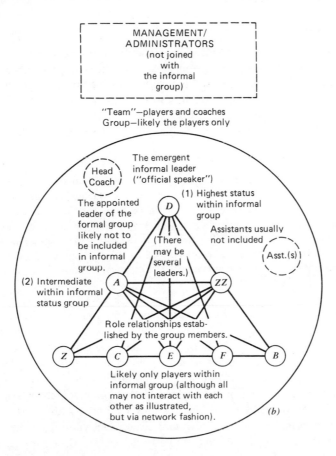

Figure 12-1—*Continued*

family, firm, school, peer group, athletic team, or other units comprising an organizational set. All organizations include both formal as well as informal groups, and many times the informal group welds the formal organization into a cohesive force if the informal group ties are strong.

On the other hand, groups within larger groups may form cliques and may be divisive and counterproductive because of their own vested interests. Each group has its own goals, behavior system, norms, rules, relationships, communication network, and other characteristics. If a coach is cognizant of this information in relating to his group or squad, he can coach more effectively. An understanding of the group process is very important in dealing with human behavior in an athletic team. The interpersonal relationships that develop within groups are extremely complex and are never completely understood. One can never truly understand people without considering their group.

Group Dynamics

The informal or emergent organization is spontaneous and dynamic. It has been stated that the social system that emerges from the group members within the organization provides the ''grease'' that lubricates the formal authority structure. The emergent organization converts the formal organization structure into a living, functioning, goal-directed group. Most coaches would refer to this end result as *teamwork* and *morale*. As Dr. Alvin Zander (1975), University of Michigan, Center for Group Dynamics, pointed out,[1]

> Since the beginning of history people in positions of authority have valued coordinated effort in a group, especially in athletic teams. . . . Nowadays, cooperation among members of a team is so widely respected that invocation of the idea through such terms as teamwork, team spirit, unselfish desire, clicking or precise execution, are uttered in a reverent tone; they are especially precious virtues (next to cleanliness) in the eyes of the priests for athletics, the sports reporters. Such concepts about teamwork and the nature of group-oriented motivation are familiar and practical matters to athletes, coaches, and spectators. . . .

Not all teams and coaching staffs have coordinated teamwork and good morale. Some are merely a collection of individuals, not a cohesive group of players and coaches psychologically aware of each other. The difference between the two types of ''groups'' will be discussed shortly. As Zander (1975) pointed out in his article, ''Motivation and Performance of Sports Groups,'' there is a difference between individual and group motivation. In the former, each individual is only concerned with how well he performs, or how well each individual works to improve his own skill and his own rewards. Group motivation, on the other hand, deals with pride and satisfaction in team performance, the desire for group success, and the desire to avoid group failure. With group motivation, success gives the player a disposition to experience pride and satisfaction with the group when it successfully accomplishes a challenging task; if the group fails, the player experiences embarrassment or dissatisfaction with the group.

While this chapter builds on the previous ones, in which the focus was on understanding the individual and his motivation, personality, perceptions, and behavior, the focus here will be on the psychology of the group or on team behavior.

GROUP VERSUS INDIVIDUAL CHARACTERISTICS

Groups have many of the characteristics of individuals and other living organisms. Groups are adaptive and experience stages of growth. A group, however, unlike an

---

[1]Zander, Alvin, ''Motivation and Performance of Sports Groups.'' *Psychology of Sport and Motor Behavior II*, Daniel M. Landers (Ed.) University Park, Penn.: The Pennsylvania State University Press, 1975. Reprinted by permission.

individual, does not have a will of its own. Group action is directed by the consensus of the dominating element of the group and consists of individuals interacting in a common social context. However, as might be expected, individual perceptions and those of a group often are vastly different, and research reveals that the individual's norms and values are rarely identical with those of the group.

When people perceive themselves as a psychological group, as compared to a collection of individuals who are identified as a group merely because of numbers only, a set of composite needs evolves which typifies group behavior. While these needs are only motivational in that they meet the needs of the individual members, they result in group reaction and group interaction. For example, a group has both affiliative and achievement needs. Individuals function in groups by combining to thwart external threats, acting to maintain consistency, and attempting to expand group power. Also, as Zander and Medow (1963) pointed out, there is even a group-aspiration level that rises when the group is successful and falls when the group experiences failure. However, even though groups have an internal life of their own that strongly modifies the behavior of its members, this internal life is created, modified, and subject to destruction by individuals.

Understanding Group Processes

It is not unusual for a coach to view the members on the squad strictly in a limited sense of belonging only to *his* team or to *her* group of players. A coach should realize that all individuals, including the players on the squad, probably belong to a number of different groups, and each group makes demands of its members. In a scholastic or collegiate environment, squad members are likely to belong to a number of the following diverse groups: church, family, social, study, dating or married, recreational, civic, fraternal, work, and possibly other groups, in addition to being a member of an athletic group or team. Some coaches try to impose restrictions on their squad members by limiting their activities in other groups or organizations to the extent that their participation in a particular sport is first and foremost, and all other activities or group memberships are to be limited or even terminated. When one considers the fact that probably most people spend the majority of their lives involved with most of the groups listed, one can see the futility of a coach trying to impose unreasonable restrictions on squad members to limit their involvement only to athletic participation or membership.

Group Membership Affects Individual Behavior. A coach should understand that groups have a major effect on individual behavior while the individual is interacting in the group. The effect carries over when the individual is outside the group, but it is very likely an individual will behave differently when functioning outside the group. Since many individuals belong to at least several groups, one can readily envision the complexity of understanding the behavior of an athlete who may change behavior patterns when involved in different groups. Obviously the greater the number of athletes in a group, and considering the fact there are likely to be groups within larger groups on some athletic squads, one can see the complexity of trying to understand the individual behavior of each of the squad members. Most people, including coaches and athletes, probably underestimate the degree to which their behavior is affected by the groups to which they belong.

A SYNERGISTIC EFFECT

Every head coach's job in a team sport is to mold the individual talents and skills of players *and* assistants into a synergistic effect. When a group of individuals, players, or coaches are working together and focusing all their energy on a common goal, they are said to be *synergistic* and the quality they are displaying is *synergy*.

Through the proper functioning, integration, and interrelationships of the individuals on the squad and coaching staff, a total effect (synergy) is achieved that is greater than the sum of the effect of the skills of all of the players and coaches functioning in an unrelated or independent fashion. Instead of each individual doing his or her own "thing," the major goal is to get all individuals collectively to do the group's or team's "thing." Synergy is always induced by leadership, which may have been appointed, elected, or simply emergent. In athletics the synergy-producing leadership can be the coach, the elected captain, or members on the squad without recognized leadership status. Synergy means that through interrelating parts a unified effect can be achieved that is not possible otherwise. When a coach can lead and motivate individual "stars" to accept the team concept, such is effective coaching. Synergy is actually a pooling of energy that was basically present in the individual all the time. Every team is potentially synergistic, and a team of players or coaches *can* become synergistic if charismatic leadership is present and the individual members perceive themselves as a psychological group. The social structure of every group has definite characteristics or features.

Forces Affecting an Individual Entering a Group. Before examining group variables, one should have a comprehensive knowledge and a thorough understanding of individual human behavior, as discussed in Part Three. One's individual needs, attitudes, values, aspirations, emotions, frame of reference, self-image, perceptions, personality, motivation, and so on, enter the group with the individual, commingling with each of the other individuals' traits. Since each person is different, obviously this commingling of psychological components causes forces and pressures to arise from within the group. Conversely, as depicted in Figure 8-1, Factors Affecting Behavior: Individual Personality/Environmental Stimuli, there are the same external forces exerting pressure and affecting the behavior of each of the group's members and the group collectively. These and additional forces are described here and in other chapters. However, people in a *group* are more likely to react or behave differently than as individuals.

While a head coach is attempting to attain group cohesiveness and a synergistic effect, it would be well for him or her to take into consideration the emotional tendencies and biological and psychological needs of each athlete on the squad and each coach on his staff. These affiliative and achievement needs have been discussed in detail previously. Many times the needs of assistant coaches are completely over-looked by a head coach, and as a result the coaching staff lacks cohesiveness and its members function almost individually, not as coaches of an effective group or team.

A Circular Relationship: Cohesiveness, Success, Satisfaction

Social psychologist Festinger (1950) defined *cohesiveness* as "the resultant of all the forces acting on members to remain in the group," which is probably the most common nominal definition of group cohesiveness. The most prevalent approach for measuring group cohesiveness has been to assess the degree of interpersonal attractiveness between members of a group, which is only one force or component of the nominal definition.

Gross and Martin (1952) have postulated against the attempt by researchers to measure only one component of cohesiveness and, then on the basis of the results obtained, make inference to the total concept of cohesiveness. Gross and Martin suggested it is better to assess cohesiveness by questioning directly each member of the group regarding the cohesiveness of the group.

Researchers Martens and Peterson (1971) maintain that Gross and Martin's argument for direct assessment of cohesiveness has merit. However, in their article, "Group Cohesiveness as a Determinant of Success and Member Satisfaction in a Team Performance," Professors Martens and Peterson postulated that their results suggested a circular relationship among the variables satisfaction, cohesiveness, and success, as illustrated in Figure 12-2.

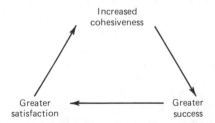

Figure 12-2. Relationship among cohesiveness, success, and satisfaction. (*Source*: From "Group Cohesiveness as a Determinant of Success and Member Satisfaction in Team Performance" by Rainer Martens and James A. Peterson. *International Review of Sport Sociology*, Vol. 6, 1971, p. 58. Reprinted by permission.)

The relationship among cohesiveness, success, and satisfaction is explained by Martens and Peterson as follows:[2]

> Those teams who are more cohesive are more successful, and teams which are successful have greater satisfaction from participation than unsuccessful teams. Greater satisfaction, in turn leads to higher levels of cohesiveness, thus maintaining a circular relationship. It must be borne in mind, however, this cause-effect triangulation is bombarded with a number of other important factors that may influence this sequence of events.

It should be obvious that cohesiveness is not the primary determinant for success in sports since there are too many other variable factors, namely player personnel and coaching. However, we concur with the findings of Martens and Peterson (1971) that suggested that higher levels of cohesiveness are associated with greater success and satisfaction.

Losing with Good Material and Winning with Mediocre Personnel

There are coaches year after year who have superior material from which to mold their teams, but they do not win consistently. From the point of view of personnel, they may have a number of "stars" individually superior to their opponents, but collectively they are unable to achieve the desired synergistic effect of playing together as a cohesive group. They may win the games and contests they are expected to win merely because they have superior personnel, but not infrequently they fail to win when their opposition's personnel is equal to or superior to theirs. Frequently the coach is accused of being unable to win the "big" one or to defeat anyone other than the inferior teams. While ultimately the head coach is held accountable, it could be that members within the team are unintentionally, or possibly even intentionally, working against themselves and others. The latter inference may appear to be far-fetched to some individuals, but one should constantly bear in mind that without question a human being is the least predictable element of any organization. While two soccer fields, two catcher's mitts, or two hockey pucks are essentially identical, two individuals are not. Not only are any two people different, but even the same person experiences at least slight changes in moods from day to day. Individuals tend to be relatively predictable on a group basis, but quite unpredictable on an individual basis, especially when compared with other nonhuman resources.

An Illustration. While many illustrations could be cited in sports of losing with players who were outstanding and skillful, or winning with a group of players who

---

[2]Martens, Rainer, and Peterson, James A. "Group Cohesiveness as a Determinant of Success and Member Satisfaction in Team Performance." *International Review of Sport Sociology,* 1971. Reprinted by permission.

had lesser athletic skills but possessed team unity and cohesiveness, probably the classic example occurred in the 1980 Winter Olympic Games when the United States ice hockey team won the "gold." In defeating Russia in the semifinal contest, the United States' team avenged an earlier loss when the Russian ice hockey team had defeated the Americans badly. The overall consensus was that the Russians would win the gold because they had superior personnel, and the United States team with less skilled personnel would be fortunate to win the bronze or even fourth place. After their stunning victories a newsreporter wrote, "And now, the world calls them champions, this United States Olympic hockey team, a rag-tag melange of peach-fuzz kids and knockaround minor leaguers who beat Finland 4–2 and won the hockey gold medal of the 13th Winter Olympics . . . two days after their staggering 4–3 victory over the mighty Soviets. . . ." (Shapiro, 1980).

Sports' history is replete with stories of undermanned, "underdog" teams that have had few or no established "stars," but have won because of their spirited, cohesive play.

Maximizing All Available Material

The art of coaching is getting every athlete to optimize his or her individual potential. If it is a team sport, each individual must fully comprehend if the team is to gain a synergistic effect; each player's skills and talents must be molded into the team concept. The effective coach is able to "sell" the team concept, the "we" approach, to his players, including the "stars," who will want to adhere to the "I" approach in order to achieve individual glory and recognition. Part of the art of coaching is that the squad members "buy" the "we" approach and come to realize that the rewards, recognition, and benefits that are derived through team effort are greater than those a player can attain individually.

WHAT IS A GROUP?

There is a distinct difference between people who constitute a psychological group, and a group of people who may be together because of a common interest but who do not get to know each other or have any meaningful social interaction with each other. At an athletic contest, for example, there may be hundreds or even thousands of spectators in attendance, and in common usage it would not be incorrect to refer to them as a group of spectators. While they may have a common interest in the particular athletic contest, it is unlikely they would all get to know each other or have any meaningful social interaction with each other. Since it may be impractical for all of these spectators to become psychologically aware of each other, or since they choose not to interact with each other to achieve common goals, in the true sense of the word as used by social psychologists and sociologists they are *not* really a group. Numbers have little to do with the use of the term *group* as there could be as few as two people, or many people, and they may or may not be considered a group. Coaches must work to mold a psychological group, not merely have a collection of individuals who may have a common interest. The achievement of group cohesiveness is a necessity for a winning program and effective coaching.

Group Cohesiveness

Lewin (1935) reputedly first introduced the technical term "group cohesiveness," and in 1941 gave it its definition, dividing the psychological force imposed on group members as follows: the force keeping members with the group, which he called "group cohesiveness," and the force which drove members from the group.

Lewin's concept of group cohesiveness has been developed through experiments with groups, and many different concepts have been presented, such as Schachter's (1951), Cartwright and Zander's (1953), among others.

Schachter (1951) wrote, "Cohesiveness has been defined as the total field of forces acting on members to remain in the group." Cartwright and Zander (1953) stated they thought group cohesiveness was related to (1) attraction to the group, (2) morale, and (3) coordination of the efforts of members. These writers added, "The cohesiveness of a group is the resultant of all the forces acting on all the members to remain in the group." Cartwright and Zander (1953) tried to prove their definition by describing the driving force *to* the group and the force restraining the members *from* leaving the group.

Niwa (1968) reported terms such as pride of the group, group solidarity, group loyalty, team mind, and team work. The meanings of these terms have been defined clearly from the viewpoint of attraction to the group. Hirota (1963) also made a significant contribution to group study. Above all, he discovered that group cohesiveness, from the viewpoint of attraction to the group, has a close relationship to important group phenomena such as communication within the group, social effect change of opinions, function of group standard, the group's pressures of uniformity on its members, and so on, giving the concept of group cohesiveness an important role when dealing with dynamics within the group.

Two Persons Can Form a Group

The characteristics of *dyads,* groups composed of only two individuals, have been described in detail by sociologist George Simmel (1950). For example, two people, such as two athletes within a particular team or from different teams, could form a group (Figure 12–3a). However, should one individual leave the group for whatever reason, neither the dyad nor the group would continue to exist.

A Group with Many People

There are numerous civic, religious, professional, fraternal, social, and political organizations, some national and international in scope, with many members, and not infrequently these are referred to as groups. All generally have a common interest indigenous to the members of that particular organization, but it is impossible for all to know each other. For example, it is impossible for all coaches of a particular sport such as football, gymnastics, or swimming to know, much less to have a psychological awareness of, all the other members in their particular sport's organization.

Other Definitions of a Group

Numerous social psychologists, sociologists, and others stress that a group exists only when members are psychologically aware of each other and each individual has some distinct impression about each other person in the group. Revising slightly the previously mentioned illustration of the hundreds or thousands of spectators viewing the athletic contest, some writers would maintain these spectators could be formulated into a psychological group quite easily. Let us assume many of the spectators become irate at the head coach, organize a "goodbye" campaign, and work for the coach's removal. They have a common goal, and it is very likely many would form distinct impressions of each other depending on the intensity of their campaign and their involvement. Many people could be involved and, while some would consider this as a group, others would not.

Interpersonal Interaction with Two or More People. Sanford (1973) defined *group* as "a relatively small number of people which engage in interpersonal interaction frequently." By this definition, it would appear that, if many of the above-mentioned spectators got together to organize a "goodbye" campaign to oust the head coach, this might not fulfill all of the criteria of a group. Very likely other writers would consider this involved group as a group within a larger group of spectators, since all would not be involved in the interpersonal interaction. The same distinction would apply to the political, fraternal, and religious groups and organizations. Therefore, a more inclusive definition is needed, and Myers and Myers' (1973) definition is best for our purposes.

Criteria of a Group. According to Myers and Myers (1973), a group can be defined as two or more individuals: (1) interacting with some or all group members on an individual network basis; (2) sharing one or more goals; (3) governed by a normative system of behavior and attitude; (4) maintaining stable role relationships; and (5) forming subgroups through various networks of attraction and rejection.

The definition by Myers and Myers is broad enough in scope to include groups with few and many members, such as a large football or track squad. Since it is

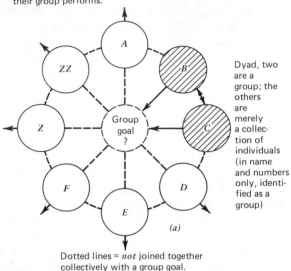

Other than the dyad of individuals *B* and *C*, who are the only two concerned about the group goal(s), the others are concerned possibly only about their own individual performance and their "I"-"me"-"my" goals; not necessarily how well their group performs.

Dyad, two are a group; the others are merely a collection of individuals (in name and numbers only, identified as a group)

(a)

Dotted lines = *not* joined together collectively with a group goal.

Figure 12-3. (*a*) Group or team circle—a collection of individuals (lacking a clearly identifiable common group goal, cohesiveness, psychological awareness, and other *group* qualities and attributes. (*b*) Psychological group or team cohesive fusion circle (with a clearly identifiable

awkward to always refer to it as a *psychological* group, the word *group* will continue to be used throughout although the reader should be cognizant of the fact that we are concerned only with the psychological groups within the context of athletic squads or teams.

Qualities of a Group.   Neither theorists nor writers in the field of group dynamics agree completely on what distinguishes collections of individuals that are groups from those that are not. Most of these disagreements, however, probably stem from a difference in emphasis and terminology, since most do agree that in general two or more people are in a group when they are identifiable by name or type, they perceive unity or group consciousness and act in a unitary manner because they have a common identifiable (group) goal, they interrelate and interact with each other and influence one another, and they need the help of each other to accomplish their own satisfaction of needs for which they joined the group. Figure 12–3*a* illustrates a collection of individuals drawn together for some common reason, but without the qualities of a cohesive, unitary, goal-oriented group; Figure 12–3*b* illustrates a psychological group having the qualities listed above.

As one can envision by comparing the two diagrams, each is identifiable as a

All are group-oriented and goal-directed players.
Pride and satisfaction in how well the
group performs collectively. A desire
for group success, and a desire to avoid
group failure. Synergy is induced by leadership. A "we"-"our"-"us" (team) concept.

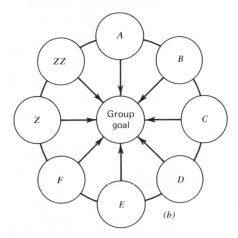

Solid lines = joined together psychologically, with a single goal.

common group goal, psychological awareness, and other qualities and characteristics that constitute a *group* and result in a synergistic effect).

group, but the differences are as follows: Figure 12-3a exhibits no commonly
identified group or team goal, individuals are possibly only concerned with how
well he or she performs individually, that is, the desire for individual success
outweighs desire of group success, and probably an "I", "me", or "my" concept
of goals is present; Figure 12-3b illustrates the synergistic effect (induced by
leadership), it shows group-oriented ("we", "our," "us" concept) motives, pride
and satisfaction in how well the group performs, the desire for group success and the
desire to avoid group failure, the common group goal is clearly identified, there is
cohesiveness in that all members want to be a part of the group, and each is
psychologically aware of the other members.

BASIC CHARACTERISTICS OF A GROUP

Coaches should be ever mindful of why individuals group, which includes common
interests, values, and personal need fulfillment, as well as other reasons. All individuals have certain sociopsychological needs which can only be fulfilled through
group membership.

Interpersonal Interaction

While one-to-one relationships are highly desirable, many times in larger groups interaction occurs as a result of a network system. For example, a large group of track and field participants on the same team performing different techniques and skills at different times both in practice and during track and field meets may not really have the opportunity to interact with each other. While they are likely to have a common team goal, and wear the same ''colors,'' in actuality each may be so busy practicing and doing his or her own ''thing'' that most of the individuals never really get to know each other through face-to-face in-depth contacts. In such situations, interaction typically occurs in network fashion with each individual making an impact on a limited number of other individuals.

Awareness. The awareness of others influences interaction patterns, and this signals the formation of a psychological group. Since such awareness can normally be best attained through face-to-face contact, it means that groups that are small in size have greater opportunities of achieving this objective. A dyadic group does require that the two individuals involved interact with each other. A 10-member basketball or gymnastic team or a 3-person coaching staff, for example, are almost certain to interact on a face-to-face basis, since the group is small enough in number to allow personal interaction. It would not be valid to set a specific number of people, such as less than two dozen, as a break point at which a unit becomes effective or ineffective because the erroneous inference would be that more than two dozen members could not cultivate an awareness for each other and would be an ineffective group. Beyond *some* number, however, a large unit becomes a deterrent if group structure and processes are to be highly effective. Therefore, retaining a 100-member football squad, for example, could be counterproductive in terms of achieving group cohesiveness and a psychological awareness among group members. Furthermore, on a large squad, it might be impossible for all to fulfill their affiliative and achievement needs.

Differentiation. When groups are small, they offer greater opportunities not only for personal interaction but also for need satisfaction. Also, small groups enhance interpersonal participation and understanding, which result in more internal cohesion and commitment to the group. Knowledgeable of this information, a coach with many squad members can formally structure his squad into smaller groups with varying numbers of members so that all individuals have opportunities to derive maximal benefit from their subunits which they might not derive in one large squad of players. When a coach *differentiates* structure in this manner, he must make certain all of the players do not lose sight of the *team* goals.

A typical football squad is likely to have at least 50 players, and in some situations more than twice this number may be on the squad. By breaking down the large squad into offensive and defensive linemen and offensive and defensive backs, linebackers, flankers, and similar units, and by assigning an assistant coach to each group for teaching and coaching purposes, unit goals can be readily achieved. Since the subunits are smaller in number, the individuals in each group have opportunities to interact with each other. A head coach will want to make certain these units do not interact exclusively with each other to the extent they do not actually know the squad members in the other units.

COMMON GOALS

The importance of setting goals, especially in terms of creating and managing a favorable climate for coaching success, has been discussed. While there are both personal and professional goals that every coach and his staff should be seeking, there are also team goals that the coaches and players should seek jointly. In all probability virtually all of the goals that are sought by the squad members and the coaching staff, if they are to be achieved, will be done jointly through the sports program or activity. In athletics the sport is the vehicle or medium through which goals are achieved. It is for this reason that it is tremendously important that players and coaches *know* the common goals they are seeking. Many do not! When this occurs, members may be a group physically, but not psychologically.

An Internal Governance System of Behavior and Attitude: Norms and Rules

Informal group requirements for attitude consistency are known as *norms,* and the group whose norms a person accepts is a *reference group.* Rewards and penalties that a group uses to induce persons to conform to its norms are *sanctions.* Nonconformers may be harassed or ostracized from the group until they capitulate or leave. There are many reasons why participants drop off a squad, one reason being that certain team members may force a nonconforming member to quit. Other team members may sanction this action of conformity by their silence. A coach would do well to query every squad member who quits the team, to determine the true reason why he or she did so.

For a group to survive, there must be an understanding of the rules of behavior of the group. While a coaching staff may set down formal rules of behavior or codes of conduct for the group, the informal group also has its own rules that may be explicit or implicit, formal or informal, popular or unpopular, but they always exist within a group. Every member of the group must follow the norms and rules of behavior if he or she is to remain in good standing with the other members of the group. By social control, which is both internal and external, members are made to conform. Internal control is directed toward making members of the group conform to its culture, whereas external control is directed toward those outside the group, such as management or administration, the coaches if they are *not* considered as members of the group (Figure 12–1b), or other informal groups. The informal group may exert stronger pressure for conformity via social control than the formal organization or group.

Maintaining Stable Role Relationships

While individual personality characteristics play a part in role formation, social factors are probably more important in maintaining stable roles. Coaches may (or may not) be members of informal groups of squad members, and a coach may even be the informal leader of a group, despite the fact that the head coach is also the formal appointed leader. The group decides, *not* the coaches, whether or not a coach will be accepted into their group as one of their members. Also, it may be virtually impossible to determine the extent of the head coach's influence on the group as an informal leader, since he is already the formal leader. It is almost inevitable that the members of the group or team will *not* display the same behavior in the head coach's presence as they display when he or she is not present. Therefore, despite excellent player–coach relationships and good rapport between a coach and his or her squad members, a coach is probably deluding himself if he feels he is the informal leader or perhaps even an accepted member of the informal group.

Within a typical group it should be recognized that each member has a particular role (Figure 12-1*b*). The group members determine the role of each other by what they will permit or sanction. They may permit one member to play the role of the jester or clown, while another member is the "official speaker" for the group. Should the former try to assume the latter's role, group members are likly to "put down" the "clown" because he is out of character for his role. Conversely, if the spokesperson for the group attempts to clown around, he, too, may be put down because he is out of character for his perceived role. Once role relationships become stable, it is difficult for a person to change his or her role in a group. The formation of stable roles in a group is another way that groups maintain themselves. When members tend to overstep their limits or perform functions outside their normal range of expected behavior, the relationships within the group tend to become unstable. Large groups, such as a 75-member football squad, display many complex role relationships.

More Than One Leader. A group of most any size can have several leaders. There may be appointed leaders, such as a head coach appointing X game captains, or they are selected by the squad members. It is always interesting to observe which players are selected, especially if the choice of the game captains is different from that of the coaching staff. Even if a coach appoints a formal leader of the informal group, the group may have their own informal leader to whom they look.

A group may have two or more strong informal leaders whereby give-and-take each knows his own role and the other's too, and they function in this manner together for the good of the group or team. The group knows where to look for leadership, and there is no instability or incongruency in having several acceptable leaders. Where there are several strong leaders within a group, a coach should scrutinize role structure and group stability carefully as there may be fighting for dominance to the detriment of team goals and objectives. While ideally it would be good to have several strong leaders in equal-but-different roles, in reality this is difficult to achieve because of one individual's desire for the dominant role over the group, including the other leaders. A coach would do well to try to determine the group's leader, try to give him or her the opportunity to display leadership ability, and seek the informal leader's input from the group or team.

Networks of Attraction and Rejection

Myers and Myers' (1973) basic group characteristic, "forming subgroups through various networks of attraction and rejection," is analogous in principle to Thorndike's law of reinforcement which was discussed in a previous chapter. A system of "networks" means we like some people and dislike others, and we tend to associate with the former and to reject the latter. Also, if A and B like each other, and B and C also like each other, it is very likely A and C also will like each other.

Within every group, such as participants on an athletic team or squad, there are those we like and dislike, although these relationships may not always remain constant. While first impressions are very important, and many times lasting, through group interaction over a period of time it is possible to learn to like someone whom a person disliked initially. Obviously the opposite can also occur. Social psychologists have discovered that people tend to like the people with whom they interact most frequently. Since people most often rely on first impressions when joining groups, and these impressions not only include the development of some friendships but the exclusion of others, familiarity can often overcome poor first impressions. While they may seem obvious, many coaches may not be knowledgeable of these findings.

The "networks" also work in another manner in terms of securing information, although the principle is the same as the likes-dislikes characteristic. It is likely A will ask B for information if he likes him, but not C if he dislikes him. Conversely A and B will share information, but in all probability they will not share it with C. They may share it with C if he asks A or B, but it is unlikely A or B will share the information on a voluntary basis with C.

For the coach who is trying to build team unity and cohesiveness, he or she can see the implications of understanding group structure. Players may be members of the same team or large group, but there may be several subgroups within the same team. Obviously a coaching staff should make every effort to unify the subgroups into one cohesive unit. The size of the squad makes little difference, since two groups could form within a 10-member gymnastics or basketball team or within a 75-member football or track squad.

Competition and Cooperation. In her classic, *Cooperation and Competition Among Primitive Peoples* (1961), world-renowned anthropologist Margaret Mead noted that three basic components of behavior operate in any society to give an overall indication of that society's general tendencies: cooperative, competitive, and individualistic behaviors. Obviously, contemporary Western society is not devoid of these three components. It is normal and important, too, to be competitive for success, especially in athletics. Yet within the realm of competitiveness, there must be cooperation in order for the team or unit to achieve success. The nature of group dynamics must be understood in any cooperative-competitive venture.

Church (1968) made a distinction between cooperative and competitive situations, as the former implies that two or more of the individuals have an opportunity to share in the "payoff" through their *joint* behavior, whereas in the latter situation the payoff or reinforcement depends on the individual's performance *relative* to the performance of one or more other people. Within this general framework, Alderman (1974) stated the following: "an acceptable or workable definition of *competition* is any situation in which two or more individuals struggle for the complete or larger share of a particular goal, and in which the success of their performance is relative to each other."

According to Sherif (1976), "Competition consists of activities directed more or less consistently toward meeting a standard of achieving a goal in which performance by a person or by his group is compared and evaluated relative to that of selected other persons or groups. . . ."

Martens (1976) defined competition as "a process in which the comparison of an individual's performance is made with some standard in the presence of at least one other person who is aware of the criterion for comparison and can evaluate the comparison process." Prior to defining competition, however, Professor Martens made an interesting observation; namely, because of the failure of theory to guide research on competition, this phenomenon as a concept has not been defined rigorously. He pointed out that what one scholar would consider as competition, another scholar might consider as rivalry, a third might consider as cooperation, and perhaps a fourth would consider it as noncompetition. The significance of this statement is that it need not relate specifically to scholars since some athletes are likely to have different concepts of competition, too.

Although it is sometimes assumed that competitiveness among humans is an inborn characteristic, it is likely that much of our competitive spirit is learned. Such is especially true in our American way of life. In fact, competition is not the way of life in some societies where competitiveness may be regarded as an abnormality.

In our society, people will compete for rewards (external motivators) when they (the rewards) are limited in number; yet people will also compete just for the sake of winning (internal motivation). In the latter situation when the competition is for the sake of winning, it is likely providing the rewards of status, self-esteem, or some other ego need satisfaction. But in actual competition there are losers as well as there are winners and, if one gains social need satisfaction, others must lose it. There is a danger, then, that competition will produce not only need satisfaction and raised levels of aspiration, but also need deprivation and lowered levels of aspiration.

In some organizations, whether it be in the business world or in athletics, some organizations' common goals are not always shared by all groups within the organization. Nor are they always shared by all individuals within a particular group.

An Illustration. Within an institution's overall athletic program or organization, the subgroup members and teams made up of those participants or coaches of the "major" sports may have little concern for those in the "minor" sports; or those in the revenue-producing sports will have little concern for the nonrevenue sports; or men will have little concern for the womens' program; and vice versa. Where such a situation prevails, this means that all of the subgroups within the institution's athletic organization do not share common goals indigenous to the *entire* overall program, and members within each sports group may share only their own group's goals. In specific sports groups the members' values, sentiments, and frames of reference are generally more compatible, whereas in the entire organization they are not. Groups develop a subculture of their own that is constantly monitored by face-to-face relationships, whereas groups within an entire athletic organization may be so large that individuals within groups either do not have the opportunity for intimate contacts or prefer not to engage in them. It may not be detrimental to the overall athletic program if the swimmers do not interact with the wrestlers, who may not communicate with the basketball players, who may not associate with the track performers. However, if the athletes within a specific group do not interact with each other and have face-to-face relationships, the coach of that sport has a dysfunctional group of individuals and is likely to have numerous morale problems on his squad.

While competition among players for positions within a squad is highly desirable, a coach must cultivate *cooperation* among competing squad members, too. Such does not occur at all times because the player who does not play regularly may lose sight of team goals and think only of his own personal goals. The coach must be mindful of cliques that form within various groups, among those players who are playing regularly, and those who are usually substitutes. Regulars may exclude the substitutes, but regulars are not likely to be disgruntled since they are playing regularly. Cliques not only become a morale problem, but they may become uncooperative and even disruptive in their behavior as selfish personal goals supplant team goals. A coaching staff should check the "down-the-liners" regularly as to their morale. Frequently this is not done and it is the "apples at the bottom of the barrel" (group) that cause the others to "spoil."

Social scientists have long noted that the characteristics of the members of a group will have an effect on how the group performs. Eitzen (1973) examined the effects of homogeneity on selected social characteristics as they contribute to the success of athletic teams, not discounting the fact that nonsociological variables such as athletic skills, injuries, coaching ability, the length of time the players have practiced together as a unit, and "tradition" have an affect on an athletic team's performance. From his study, "The Effect of Group Structure on the Success of Athletic Teams," Etizen (1973) concluded:

> This study has demonstrated that the social composition of athletic teams is related to their goal of winning games despite the many factors which are generally assumed to affect the outcome of athletic contests. The data showed that team homogeneity on selected social characteristics was moderately related to goal attainment. The explanation for this relationship was found in the presence or absence of cliques. The presence of cliques on an athletic team reduces the chances of winning.

A coach must be especially vigilant for the formation of cliques among assistant coaches as well as players, since members of cliques usually are interested in their own well-being to the exclusion of others. It is difficult for effective coaching and leadership to prevail under such circumstances because individual interests supplant team goals.

GENERAL PRINCIPLES FOR UNDERSTANDING GROUP BEHAVIOR

Knowles and Knowles (1972), Myers and Myers (1973), Shaw (1971), and other writers and theorists on group dynamics have produced some generalizations or laws of cause and effect that make it increasingly possible to understand, predict, and improve group behavior. Obviously these principles have pertinent implications for the coach, or any other individual whose success or accomplishments are measured or evaluated in terms of group achievement that he or she directs or is held accountable for.

Group Attractiveness

A group tends to be attractive to a person and will command his loyalty if the group satisfies the individual's needs, aids him in achieving goals that he perceives are compelling, provides the individual with a feeling of acceptance and security, and has a membership that is congenial to him; the group is also attractive if it is highly valued by outsiders.

Decision Making or Goal Setting Within the Group

Each person within a group tends to feel committed to a decision or goal of the group to the extent that he or she has participated in determining that goal or is involved in that decision. Therefore, much individual involvement results in more commitment and little or no involvement results in a similar degree of commitment.

A group is an effective instrument for change and growth in individuals when the following conditions prevail: when there is a strong sense of belonging to the same group, when the attraction of the group is greater than the discomfort of the change, and when the members of the group share the perception that change is needed. Furthermore, theorists and writers on group dynamics have found that change and growth occur to the extent that information relating to the need for change, plans for change, and consequences of change are shared by all relevant people; the group provides an opportunity for the individual to practice change behavior without threat or punishment; and the individual is provided a means for measuring progress toward the changed goals. Since every force tends to induce an equal and opposite counterforce, the preferred strategy for change is the weakening of forces resisting change rather than the addition of new positive forces that favor change.

The research of London and Oldham (1977) indicates that membership in informal groups may affect achievement motivation. In some instances, belonging to high-achieving groups may tend to raise individual standards. In cases where group norms are below individual standards, the group may reduce the effects of achievement on the individual.

Group Improvement and Effectiveness

Feedback is necessary for group improvement and effectiveness, as is inferred from the research of London and Oldham (1977), and others cited above. A group is able to improve its ability to operate as a group to the extent that it consciously examines its processes and their consequences and experiments with improved processes.

The determinants of group effectiveness include the following: the ever-present clarity of a goal; the degree to which the group goal moblizes energies of group members behind group activities; the degree to which there is agreement or conflict among members concerning which one of several possible goals should control the activities of the group; the degree of agreement-conflict as to the means that the group should use to reach its goal; the degree to which the activities of different members are coordinated in a manner required by the group's tasks; the availability of needed resources, whether they be economic, material, legal, intellectual, and so on; and the degree to which the group is organized appropriately to its task and stage of development.

Conformity

The strength of pressure to conform is determined by factors such as the strength of the attraction of a group on a person, the importance to the individual of the issue on which conformity is requested, and the degree of unanimity of the group on requiring conformity. Furthermore, the better an individual understands the forces influencing his or her own behavior and that of a group, the better the individual will be able to contribute constructively to the group and, at the same time, preserve his own integrity against subtle pressures toward conformity and alienation.

IMPLICATIONS FOR COACHING

Considering the role and function of the informal group as has been discussed, for the coach to view a participant solely as a singular individual, without taking into consideration the group in which the athlete operates, is a fallacy and a grave error of misjudgment. Not infrequently, however, coaches view players solely in terms of their individual skills and attributes of height, weight, size, speed, and their ability to jump, throw, dribble, shoot, pass, kick, hit, or in terms of other particular skills the coach is seeking for the sport he or she coaches. While the coach generally thinks of "team," as in team unity and cohesiveness, the athletes may perceive these entities differently than the coach. Probably a vast majority of coaches are not knowledgeable of how the group process operates, although he or she may have a basic understanding of why individuals join groups. Unfortunately many coaches forget about personal need satisfaction, feeling the team benefits that the sport offers are sufficient for every participant to fulfill those needs. To sustain interest and participation in the activity, a player must perceive some value to himself or herself, but *not* necessarily value to the coach or the team. If group ties and interaction are strong, a player may be reluctant to quit the team because he or she does not want to "let down" the group or team. For the most part, a player who wants to quit the squad may not have the same strong feeling for the coach despite the fact he or she may genuinely like the coach. Undoubtedly the strongest feeling for remaining as a squad member probably is for personal fulfillment, coupled with the fact that humans as social animals have a strong need to "belong" and tend to choose group membership carefully in terms of their own self-interests.

Let us now examine coaching staff relationships and their group behavior, since their unity and cohesiveness is vital for team success.

COACHING STAFF RELATIONSHIPS: FORMAL AND INFORMAL

Coaching staff relationships include those between a head coach and his or her assistants in an *A-B* vertical organizational structure, and those between assistants in their own peer group as a result of horizontal design structure. If the staff are all classified as assistant coaches, the structure may be identified as a *B-B* relationship within the peer group of assistant coaches, providing one or more assistants are not placed in the vertical structure over other assistants. Should this latter situation occur, then *within* the group of assistants in the formal structure there is another

A-B relationship, although all are subordinate to the head coach who is at the apex of the organizational pyramid of coaches. Organizational structure will define formal working relationships, and the informal group structure will determine social relationships.

Know the Organizational Structure

While most coaches are not likely to be too overly concerned or knowledgeable about organizational structure terms, such as vertical, horizontal differentiation, and horizontal integration, each should comprehend the formal and informal organizational structure under which he or she works. Most do not see all of the details, and others are uncertain. The failure of a head coach or an administrator to define specifically the formal organizational structure or design will result in confusion, conflict, and inefficiency.

While there may be functionalization, if there is no actual differentiation, theoretically all assistants have equal input directly to the head coach. While this cannot be considered as wrong, there may be a lack of clarity within the staff. If there are offensive and defensive coordinators, for example, it is very likely other offensive and defensive coaches give their input directly to their respective coordinators, who in turn may give it to an assistant head coach or even directly to the head coach. Organizational structure is more rigidly fixed in the last situation. Detailed staff orientation by the head coach will alleviate many potential problems that might arise otherwise in interpersonal relationships. The formal structure also has a bearing on the informal structure within a coaching staff.

Historically—"An Athletic Family"

Historically, society has thought of an athletic team as being akin to a family; the "old man," the patriarchial head coach, in the paternalistic "father surrogate" role in relation to his players, and frequently to his assistant coaches as well. While the assistants in the hierarchial sports structure are above the players, the head coach is over all.

More often than not, head coaches demand the sole right to decide who will and will not be their assistant coaches. Frequently executive management or administrators do not always heed a head coach's demands. Considering the hazards of coaching, this particular demand does not appear to be unreasonable since the success-failure win-loss record of the team is attributed directly to the head coach, not to the assistants. Difficulty does arise when head coaches demand total autonomy in a monarchical-authoritarian sense over players and assistants by trying to impose values and standards. A head coach may not be right in what he attempts to impose, but typically a head coach feels he has the right to impose his values and standards because he *is the head coach.*

If he has the authority to fire an assistant for failure to comply, the head coach is likely to exercise that right should he perceive that the assistant is defying his authority. If the head coach does not have this authority, typically he perceives this as a real threat to his position since the symbolic head of the family cannot discipline an errant member. Also, the other members of the family, the players and other assistant coaches, in time are cognizant of the fact that the head coach cannot fire the assistant who does not conform. While this is exceptionally difficult for most head coaches to accept, within their own families they may not be able to get their own child or children to adhere to their postulated standards and values. A head coach may identify the errant assistant as being disloyal; yet not think of using the same word to identify his own nonconforming child. Loyalty is a word that has much credence in athletics and coaching circles, although it frequently is used without a clear interpretation of its meaning and tends to be employed as a catchall and in an all-inclusive sense. As will be discussed and illustrated shortly, this can create tension and strain in coaching staff relationships.

Group Dynamics and Coaching Staff Cohesiveness

Within a good coaching staff, there should be group dynamics and cohesiveness. *Dynamics* means the study of the relationship between motion and the forces that produce motion and change in any field or system. The assumption, for our purposes, is that the results are of a positive nature; that is, they are *synergetic*. *Cohort* means a group or band united together in some common struggle. *Cohesive* means the process or condition of cohering; the mutual attraction by which elements of a body are held together. There are some coaching staffs that are held together in name only, in which an individual's competitive aspect and self-serving goals may overshadow the organization's cooperative aspect of group dynamics and, for various other reasons, the staff only pays lip service to the common struggle.

Maintain Trust and Respect. While a harmonious relationship between staff members is highly desirable, it is not mandatory as long as there is trust and respect and all coaches strive for unified, common goals. However, when personal and professional jealousies between staff members occur and become disruptive to the unity of the staff, it may be difficult for all of the coaches to keep their attention and efforts focused on the sport's ultimate program. A head coach must not only be cognizant of what is occurring, but he must take immediate remedial action to attempt to correct the situation. Unfortunately, the head coach unknowingly could be the one causing the problem. Should he do nothing, going on the erroneous assumption that the problem will go away, it will only get worse. Should the problem not be resolved, effective coaching is impossible.

Philosophical and Operational Differences: A Fire Preventer Or a Fire Fighter? When two individuals have a close relationship with each other, whether it be in the formal work force or in an informal social sense, it is not unusual that eventually there are disagreements, and a degree of tension and possibly stress may enter into their relationship. The greater number of individuals who are involved in this structural relationship, such as an eight-man coaching staff as compared to a three-man staff, the greater the possibilities for disagreements to arise and for tension and stress within the group to multiply.

Within the peer group of assistants, it is likely more tension and stress will arise than will surface in a head coach-assistant coach relationship. In the latter relationship disagreements are likely to be resolved more quickly because of the superior-subordinate (A-B) relationship, whereas within the peer group (B-B relationship of assistants, disagreements may smolder over a period of time and not come to the attention of the head coach until there is literally a behavioral explosion involving several assistant coaches.

From a head coach's standpoint in maintaining harmony and cohesiveness within his staff, it is better to prevent something of a correctable nature from occurring in the first place, rather than waiting until it has occurred and then attempting to correct it. The analogy is similar to a fire preventer and a fire fighter. It is better to prevent a fire from occurring in the first place, rather than waiting until a fire occurs and then working to put it out. Conflict within an organizational group is common and inevitable. Some can be avoided; other conflicts can be minimized. But they must be managed. Suggestions for preventing the "fire" from occurring in the first place will be offered. Other suggestions for containing the "fire" will be offered. Finally, if it appears the "fire" is getting out of control, drastic measures for a head coach to take are suggested.

CAN AND WILL DO PERFORMERS: ATHLETES AND COACHES

The essential qualities of a "good" coach were discussed in a previous chapter, and these characteristics or qualities are the same whether one is a head or an assistant coach. Most head coaches at the collegiate and professional levels of coaching have been assistant coaches earlier in their careers and have moved "up" through the ranks. Many have been assistants, and then head coach, at the scholastic level prior to moving into the collegiate or professional ranks of coaching.

Whether a head coach is selecting an assistant for the coaching staff, or evaluating an assistant coach, or selecting an individual or team performer, a head coach's primary job is to select those who can *and* will perform optimally, to the best of that individual's ability. To be successful a coach must "surround" himself with as many of those can *and* will do performers as possible. Some performers, whether coaches or players, may be labeled as being capable or *can do,* but they do not or will not for whatever reason. On the other hand there are *will do* performers in that they are willing to try to do most any task, but they may not possess the expertise or skills to perform, so that realistically they cannot do the required task satisfactorily. The can do person may lack motivation to perform optimally, whereas the will do performer does not lack motivation but lacks know-how or skills. Therefore, a head coach is seeking the *can and will do* performer, an individual who possesses the skill or expertise and who delivers the best performance.

Conversely, while a coach may be reluctant to separate from the program those individuals, whether they are players or assistants, who *will not* or *cannot* perform well and contribute optimally to their own individual and the sport's success, at some point he will have to limit the extent of his time and attention to their well-being, hoping for improvement. Most coaches tend to give preference to the *can do* individual who has displayed performance competencies in the past, because he has a proven track record despite the fact that the individual may not be performing presently. If team goals are to be realized, it is a mistake to stay with the unwilling too long, hoping the individual can be convinced and motivated to produce. The individual may be motivated to perform, but simply cannot produce, possibly because the tasks now are too difficult and demanding, or competition is more intense, or other situation variables may enter the picture. Motivation is a very personal thing. Most coaches believe they can motivate others. However, the issue is standard of performance; the individual may be incapable of performing the required tasks, and at some point there must be a realistic assessment of what he or she can produce.

A greater mistake is not to give the willing, already motivated individual opportunities to acquire additional skill or expertise so that he can become a can do performer. While it is extremely difficult to win consistently with players and coaches who have limited ability and competencies, the individual with the willingness and desire to perform, to do the best to his or her ability, is a better team member than the one who is not motivated to perform. Also, the individual who is motivated to learn, despite the fact he presently has limited skills, may be a "comer" and can make a contribution to the team in time. The individual who has the ability to perform, but does not or cannot, may be content merely to be a member of the squad or coaching staff for his own reasons of motivation; he may have no intention of trying to perform to the best of his ability. Since most individuals in the coaching profession are competitors, they cannot comprehend much less acknowledge the fact that a person may be a member of an athletic team but does *not* really wish to compete. Yet there are coaches who remain in the profession who have lost their motivation and enthusiasm for coaching and are no longer can and will do performers.

STAFF ORIENTATION

In an effort to create and manage a favorable environment for coaching success, it is extremely important that a head coach take the time to orient his assistants as to his philosophy, principles, and coaching theory. Not infrequently head coaches will plunge into coaching techniques, tactics and strategy, without laying a solid foundation of their philosophy and principles. At some point an assistant coach may unknowingly violate a basic tenet of his head coach because he has never been oriented as to his head coach's philosophy and principles.

An Illustration

Relevant to philosophical differences, a head coach, for example, may not believe in negative motivation such as having players run laps as punishment when they foul-up in some manner. From a personal point of view, an assistant may believe in this manner of "motivation," or he may have been on another coaching staff where assistants were "chewed out" by the head coach if they did not dole out laps or punishment when a player fouled-up. It is not a matter of who is right or wrong, but a matter of philosophical differences. If a head coach waits until an assistant does something the head coach is opposed to before he informs the assistant of this opposition, the situation is analogous to the fireman whose philosophy is that he is a fire fighter not a fire preventer. It would be better for a head coach to prevent an unpleasant situation from occurring over which he has control, such as by orienting assistants as to philosophy and basic principles, rather than waiting until the "fire" occurs and then being forced to try to rectify something that could have been avoided through proper orientation.

A Priority Item of Business

A high priority item of business is for the head coach to reaffirm his personal philosophy and theory of coaching to his staff since this serves as a review and reminder for assistant coaches who have been on the staff and as guidelines for the new assistants. Regardless of the number of coaches, the program and the team will reflect the head coach's philosophy. It provides the coaches with a sense of direction in everything they do, in carrying out their duties, and in fulfilling their responsibilities and obligations. Understanding the head coach's beliefs also is important in that it provides perimeters within which each coach must work, specifically in regard to coaching the athletes under their tutelage, the attitude toward winning and losing, the way the program will be conducted, and how coaches should conduct themselves at practice and during games. Once this is accurately delineated, each coach can then determine how best to carry out his or her responsibilities within the framework and specifics set down by the head coach.

COACHING STAFF CONFLICT

In a previous chapter, person-role, intrarole, and interrole conflicts were discussed, pertaining to one individual. Here the focus is on interpersonal conflict within the group or among coaching staff members, in one form or another, whether it be between the head and an assistant coach or between two or more assistant coaches. *Conflict,* from a coaching standpoint and within this context, may be defined as a disagreement between two or more coaches resulting from an incompatibility of goals, interests, perceptions, or values.

Disagreement or Conflict Continuum: Mild to Intense

The range and degree or intensity of interpersonal conflict if placed on a continuum would be low to high, depending on each individual's goals, interests, perceptions, and values, which would be influenced by each's background, personality, age, expertise, experience, and other factors. For example, low or mild conflict may occur between two staff members who feel some rivalry over goals and interests, but the disagreements are of a mild nature; common organizational or program goals predominate, and the parties remain friendly toward each other. Such conflict is healthy.

The high end of the conflict continuum is when the head coach has let the situation get out of control and the elements are disruptive and destructive to group cohesiveness. The coaches perceive each other as threats and adversaries, so that each tries to "defeat" the other, selfish personal goals may supplant team and program goals, and there is a complete breakdown in interpersonal relationships because of lack of trust and respect. There have been instances, one on a major college coaching staff, where two assistants got into fisticuffs with each other during a practice session in front of their players. The coaches' dismissals were immediate. There is no way of knowing the number of times this type of overt behavior has occurred in the past in the scholastic, collegiate, and professional coaching ranks. Staff meetings can become quite "heated" where there are many issues discussed of a controversial nature, but as long as trust and respect prevail and the differences of opinion are not "aired" with others outside of the staff room, it is not likely to be destructive to staff unity. The assistant who "goes outside" with staff matters creates problems for himself and others.

Conflict Must Be Managed.   Between these two extremes on the conflict continuum there are various shades of disagreement: clashes of interests or ideas, and interpersonal relationships within the coaching staff group that are tense. It should be recognized that conflict is common in most organizations and, in reality, conflict is inevitable. Therefore, a head coach must manage conflict, which depends initially on how he perceives conflict and then how he manages it.

Perceptions of Conflict

While one is more likely to think of conflict strictly in a negative sense, one can envision that not all conflict is bad and there are some positive benefits to be derived as long as common organizational goals continue to predominate throughout the encounter. There are drawbacks in conflict since it can become damaging and destructive. There are different types and sources of conflict and not all are managed the same. Being aware of this information, how conflict is managed depends on the head coach's personality, style of leadership behavior, experience, and his philosophical and managerial views of coaching.

Some topical subjects that are likely to cause encounters, if never permitted to be introduced into the discussion at staff meetings, can alleviate affective conflicts from occurring. Some head coaches may prefer to handle *every* possible conflict in this manner, going on the erroneous assumption that by suppressing debatable issues he can eliminate the probability of encounters and confrontations. Should the head coach dominate in this manner and suppress differences of opinion, it is likely conflict will occur anyway outside of the head coach's presence. Also, the staff and head coach will not derive any of the benefits of conflict.

Types and Sources of Conflict

Obviously conflict can be brought on by the inherent pressures in coaching and as a result of the lack of adequate consideration and understanding by management and administrators. The setting of unrealistic goals in terms of winning, yet not having adequate facilities, equipment, funding, and coaching personnel to effectively con-duct a winning program, having poor organization structure, and having low coach-ing salaries, all become sources of conflict. Undesirable situations and inequities in any organization will cause dissatisfaction and ultimately conflict. Since each coaching situation is different, such a discussion is beyond the scope of this book. However, relevant to interpersonal group conflict, basically there are two types: *interest* conflict and *affective* conflict. Most staff disputes are likely to involve a blend of both types, since seldom can conflict be attributed directly to one source. An exception would be personality clashes between individuals, as this may be more in the affective realm.

Interest Conflict. When individuals engage in an encounter where the intent is personal gain, either material or in terms of power and status, this is an interest conflict. On every coaching staff there are ambitious individuals who are motivated by their own self-interest and by the need for status recognition or achievement. As such, this in itself is not bad, providing the head coach and possibly other staff members recognize that, because of one's self-interests and their pursuit, there will be conflict when these interests are at cross purposes with those of others.

An Illustration. Imagine there are two assistant coaches on a basketball staff, each with equal input in presenting their ideas on devising a game plan to the head coach before the plan is finalized. One assistant favors a "run-and-gun" fast break attack, trying to out-run, out-condition, and out-score the opposition. The other assistant believes the way to win is by utilizing a slow, deliberate, patterned offense, working for the high percentage shot and playing tough defense. Strategically, their proposals for winning are opposite from each other.

After some questions, answers, rationale, and explanations, the head coach agrees basically with the first assistant's proposal in that the emphasis will be to fast break at every opportunity. What occurs from this point forward depends on the low to high conflict continuum. The important point relevant to the interest conflict, however, is that the head coach *know each of his assistants, and "where each is coming from."* As long as the disagreement is mild, although it may become significant and this would not be dangerous, if all maintain *"our* goal is to win," it makes little difference which coach is "right." In terms of the individual assistant coach's own status and ego, and perhaps in terms of his importance to the coaching staff, it would make a difference; but if the common goal is to "win," then no staff member is concerned about who gets the credit for proposing the "right" game plan. It is likely that if there is cohesiveness in the staff, it would be "we" won or "we" lost, not "I" won and "you" lost. When the latter occurs, as it does on some coaching staffs, group unity and cohesiveness is lost and this presents a problem for the assistant who verbalizes the *"I* won/*you* lost" behavior!

Affective Conflict. When the encounter between individuals is the result of different opinions, values, and norms and is philosophical and attitudinal in nature, involving basic personality differences, this is identified as *affective* conflict. *Affective* means relating to, arising from, or influencing feelings or emotions. If the subject matter deals with politics, religion, or race, for example, there will be disagreement when people with different points of view interact. Since none of these topical subjects are germane to coaching athletics, affective conflicts of this nature can be avoided by not permitting them to be introduced into discussions at staff meetings. When two individuals argue about political, religious, aesthetic, or philosophical differences, there is typically no interest to be gained other than the satisfaction of one's ego and the unlikely predominance of one's views. The more dogmatic the individual, the more likely conflict will occur. Basic personality differences relating to diverse frames of reference, biases, attitudes, and values will inevitably spawn disagreement when people interact. Basically, conflict arises within a coaching staff when individuals seek the advancement of their interests or the predominance of their views. Sometimes it may be difficult to separate one type of conflict from the other, although it is not absolutely necessary to do so.

An Illustration. The previous illustration implied it was an interest conflict where the "fastbreak" coach wanted to have his proposal of the game plan accepted, the inference being he would gain personally in terms of status and influence within the staff. However, the same illustration may be used to illustrate philosophical and attitudinal points of view and personal opinions. The more strongly one believes in something, for whatever reasons, the more likely conflict will occur when these attitudinal or philosophical views are challenged by others.

Group identification contributes to this perceptional distortion. Within an institution a basketball coaching staff may feel they are more effective, more competent coaches, and harder workers than the track and field coaching staff. Or within the same coaching staff, in baseball, football, or basketball, offensive-oriented coaches are likely to have different attitudes and philosophical viewpoints toward the sport they are coaching than the defensive-oriented coaches. The conflict, either interest or affective, may come from within members of the same unit on a coaching staff. Coaching strategy, tactics, methods, techniques, all are all facts subject to debate and conflict. Some conflict is good; some damaging.

Advantages and Benefits of Staff Conflict

There are certain advantages and benefits to be derived by a coaching staff when the head coach encourages and permits "open" discussion, which may lead to staff conflict. However, the head coach can avoid much affective conflict, in particular, if he permits only those subjects to be introduced at staff meetings that relate directly to some aspect of the sport, program, or participants.

By permitting every staff member to have his "say" should he wish to do so *before* decisions are made and plans are finalized, the staff should gain the benefits from the encounters. If the head coach manages the conflict, perhaps acting as a facilitator to keep the dialogue focused on the point or subject being discussed, the following benefits are likely to occur:

- Conflict is actually a form of competition and that is a well-known motivator.
- It causes all of the staff members to become knowledgeable about all aspects of the program, not for example, only the offensive coaches discussing offense and the defensive coaches only discussing defense.
- It is likely to "shake up" an apathetic staff.
- It is of value when coaches become too content, and mediocrity, instead of the pursuit of excellence, becomes the norm.
- It encourages creativity and innovativeness.
- It serves as one of the prerequisites to change.
- It can lead to improved interpersonal relationships within the staff.
- It can dissuade assistants from becoming "yes" men because each enjoys the freedom to "speak up" and be heard.
- External conflict (perceived or real threats or criticism from individuals or groups outside the coaching staff) generally results in internal group cohesion.

Disadvantages and Drawbacks of Conflict

When encounters between staff members are *not* managed by the head coach, especially if the intensity of the conflict is at the high end of the continuum, the following are deleterious effects:

- It is likely to cause hostility, not cohesiveness, among staff members.
- It is likely to polarize individual staff members, or even units (offensive coaches versus the defensive coaches), and cause cliques.
- Warring factions tend to enlist support for their arguments, and attention tends to become focused on the disputes and encounters instead of on winning games.
- It is difficult for some individuals to "forgive and forget," so that reconciliation between staff members may be impossible.
- It is likely there will be less cooperation among staff members, instead of more cooperation, because of a breakdown in interpersonal relationships.
- If perceived as a win-lose situation, individuals may resort to any means or tactics to win (malicious personal attacks).
- Personal goals are likely to supplant program and team goals.
- Some members will become "yes" men or not express their views, rather than get involved in "rip-up" conflicts.

Typically every member on a staff has his own ideas about strategies, tactics, methods, techniques, practice schedules, drills, coach–athlete relationships, and other aspects of a particular sports program. Most coaches tend to express what they believe, especially if encouraged to do so by the head coach. However, if the conflict is unmanaged by the head coach, probably few benefits and most of the drawbacks of conflict will be realized, which is not what is being sought by the good coach. Several suggestions have already been offered for managing conflict; others follow.

Monitoring or Controlling Staff Conflict

So that program goals and effective coaching may be realized, the following are methods a head coach may utilize to manage conflict:

- Orient the staff, as discussed above.
- Redesign the coaching staff structure, if necessary, to minimize conflict.
- Specifically define duties, responsibilities, and authority, so that each assistant knows what is expected of him in terms of his work (one may get into another assistant's designated areas of expertise and responsibility, which the assistant may perceive as an infringement and a threat).
- Remove the issue or condition that is generating the conflict (some may be outside the scope of the discussion; and some problems probably cannot be

solved at the coaching staff level of discussion, for example, lack of funding, inadequate equipment, poor facilities, etc.).

- Possibly acting as a third party, the head coach can force a confrontation meeting between the coaches so that they must try to "talk out" their differences and smooth over hurt feelings (but the source of the conflict may still be unresolved).
- If assistants will not "shape up" and resolve their conflicts and it adversely affects their work and the program, they should understand they will be removed from the coaching·staff.
- Get to know your assistants as persons and their strengths, weaknesses, motives, desires, goals (which is probably the most important suggestion pertaining to interpersonal relations).

Assistant Coaches and Head Coach Conflict

Frequently, an assistant coach's ideas and beliefs will not be in accord with the head coach's, and tension may emerge since there is incongruity of interests. The assistant's job is to try to "sell" the head coach on what he believes, presenting his ideas or concepts objectively in a sound, rational, articulate manner. The head coach does not expect the assistant to do less and would probably not consider the subordinate a contributor to the coaching staff if the assistant were to back off and agree quickly with the head coach just because the latter indicates it is contrary to his beliefs. Eventually the head coach accepts or rejects the subordinate's proposal. If he rejects it, the assistant should have the good sense to stop trying to "sell" it. While the assistant may try to "sell" the head coach on the same concept on another occasion, he must use discretion in doing so. If the assistant ever states, especially to outsiders, that his proposal would have won the contest had it been used, or the game would not have been lost had his proposal been accepted, it is likely he will be dismissed from the staff.

An Illustration. An assistant football coach who believed in coaching a four-deep secondary joined a major college staff where the head coach's philosophy was three-deep. After the assistant's initial presentation, the head coach indicated he wanted a three-deep secondary. The assistant persisted in his efforts week after week, trying to "sell" four-deep secondary play. Finally, the head coach relented and the four-deep was installed. The team lost badly, and the head coach decided to go back to the three-deep secondary play. The assistant agreed reluctantly, but still persisted the four-deep secondary was better. Reportedly staff meetings became tense and stressful, and little was accomplished as four-deep versus three-deep philosophical discussion took up much of the time. Eventually the assistant expressed his viewpoint that the team would not be losing if they played four-deep, and the head coach fired him. It is not known whether the assistant coach was fired for "second guessing" (disloyalty) the head coach, or whether he was fired so the staff could get on with their other work which was impossible to accomplish because one assistant usurped all of the staff's time trying to "sell" his four-deep secondary philosophy.

When the Conflict Involves Two Assistants. Where two assistants are involved in arguing about the "best" way, while tension may arise there is little threat of censure since they are peers, providing they stay on the subject and within the perimeters of good judgment. In time the head coach will be forced to accept one coach's proposal and possibly reject the other's. From that point forward, should the assistant whose proposal was rejected not be supportive of implementing fully the idea that was approved, he runs the risk of being fired also. Should he indicate outside of the staff room that, if his proposal had been accepted the team would not have lost, his chances of remaining on the coaching staff are slim.

Loyalty—Disloyalty. In terms of coaching staff relationships and the attributes sought in coaches, *loyalty* is mentioned the most often. By definition, to be *loyal* means to be faithful to a private person to whom fidelity is held to be due; it is showing loyalty, being faithful to a cause, ideal, or custom. No effort will be made here to identify loyal and disloyal acts, but for one entering the coaching profession he or she should be aware of the fact that at some point one is likely to work on a staff where his or her personal philosophical beliefs are incongruent with the head coach. It is suggested that the individual have a firm handle on what he believes and why he believes it, and then decide whether or not he wishes to compromise his own beliefs. If he "crosses this bridge" in his own mind and *decides beforehand* what his course of action will be should incongruent interests arise, if and when he is placed in such a situation where he is asked to sacrifice or compromise basic beliefs, he has already reached his decision. He may not wish to remain loyal to another person's beliefs if they are contrary to his. There are only three alternatives: compromise, try to change the other person's beliefs or course of action, or resign. If he really feels strongly about the issue involved, he should probably resign first and then try to bring about change. Others would disagree, saying one should not resign but try to force change from within. In coaching, since loyalty-disloyalty is such a strong issue, if one were to try to force change openly from within, he would probably be dismissed for disloyalty.

An assistant would do well to find out specifically what a coach includes under loyalty and disloyalty. It is conceivable that some head coaches may mean by disloyalty, "If an assistant *disagrees with me.*" Obviously a head coach would not want his assistants to agree with him all of the time on all matters, and it is recognized that in some situations under some conditions, disagreement with the head coach would be tantamount to disloyalty. One would do well to learn the situations and conditions where one may be labeled as disloyal, in order to avoid them. Rather than an assistant seeking these answers, however, it would be better for the head coach to orient all of his staff.

Loyalty Is a Two-Way Process. There are coaches who *demand* loyalty, whereas one actually *commands* loyalty through his relations with his subordinates. It is questionable whether, if loyalty has to be demanded, it will be genuine and lasting. If one helps subordinates to meet their needs, loyalty need not be demanded. A partial list of desirable behavior by a head coach toward his subordinates is as follows:

- Fair and equitable treatment for each individual.
- Aid each subordinate in maximizing his potential.
- Give each assistant the responsibility he can handle.
- Give each assistant credit and recognition for his contributions and accomplishments.
- Aid assistants in moving up their career ladder in securing better positions.
- Make every effort to secure for the assistant coaches the best possible financial compensation and fringe benefits.
- Be ethical, moral, professional, and an example of a truly outstanding coach and human being for your assistants to emulate.

If a head coach does not display loyalty, he cannot expect to receive loyalty. Sometimes it is the head coach who is the errant party in the two-way process. When this occurs, it is impossible to build strong esprit de corps within the staff. Pride, morale, and loyalty are highly desirable attributes that must be nurtured and are readily evident in successful, winning programs. If there is lack of trust and respect within a staff, especially if it is the head coach who is perceived as displaying disloyalty to his assistants, harmonious staff relationships cannot prevail and it is impossible to build a winning program.

PERTINENT QUESTIONS PERTAINING TO INTERPERSONAL RELATIONSHIPS

There are hundreds, possibly thousands, of sources available in books, professional journals, and magazines in the field of management and business that give guides, suggestions, and "do's" and "dont's" for any individual in a managerial position who needs information pertaining to interpersonal relationships. Surprisingly, little information is available in coaching texts, although a head coach is in the same position in his relationship with assistant coaches since he, too, is a "manager." Concentrating on the area of improving interpersonal relationships in order to build stronger, more humanistic staff relationships so that the end result will be more effective coaching, we have gleaned from diverse sources more than three dozen supervisory principles, have modified them so they are applicable to coaching, and have turned them into pertinent questions as a means of self-examination for anyone in a head coaching position, as illustrated in Figure 12–4.

In Figure 12–4 the questions are listed randomly and deal with goals, attitudes,

Figure 12-4 Self-Examination Questions Pertaining to Interpersonal (Staff) Relationships[a]

- Does each coach know his job and what he is supposed to do?
- Have I oriented my assistant coaches so that each knows my philosophy and coaching theory?
- Do I keep my staff posted on policies, procedures, changes?
- Do I take sufficient time to explain the "why" of our coaching and operation?
- Am I a person of my word? Any unfulfilled promises to any staff member at present?
- Do I have staff loyalty because I am the head coach, or because I inspire it (demand versus command)?
- Do I put my own personal interests ahead of the interests of my staff?
- Do I accept full responsibility for staff mistakes, or do I blame them?
- Do I "blow up" when a staff member "fouls up?"
- Do I become irritable when a coach does not live up to my expectations?
- Do I have well-defined, attainable goals for myself?
- Do I have well-defined, attainable goals for my staff? Are all staff members aware of these program goals?
- How well do I know each coach's family members?
- Am I aware of the personal goals of my staff members?
- Do I have empathy?
- Am I the leader because of "headship," or do I lead and have followers?
- Do I lead by example, or by telling assistants what to do?
- Are we working together as a staff, or are they working for me?
- Am I ever unreasonable in my work demands on an assistant?
- Am I supportive of each assistant?
- Do I work as hard as my assistants?
- Am I "open" to suggestions?
- Am I impatient and stubborn about accepting input from any staff member?
- Do I treat all of my assistants fairly or do I have favorites?
- Do I indulge in arguments with staff members, or perhaps with some assistants more than others?
- Do my personal feelings affect my manner of dealing with the staff?
- Do I lose my temper with subordinates?
- Do I avoid sarcasm?
- Am I objective, or do I become subjective?
- Do I allow personal likes and dislikes to influence my decisions?
- Am I impartial under all circumstances?
- Do I make all staff assignments fairly, or do I assign most of the unpleasant work to one or two staff members?

continued

Figure 12-4—*Continued*

- Do I criticize privately, impersonally, objectively, and fairly?
- Do I always give credit and praise publicly?
- Do I criticize the mistakes and the method, or the person?
- Do I ''go to bat'' for all of my assistants?
- Do I set high standards, both personal and professional, for my staff?
- Am I a ''fire preventer'' or a ''fire fighter?''
- Do I really know what makes each subordinate ''tick?''
- Do I listen and really hear what each assistant has to say?
- Do I delegate to subordinates, or do I try to do most everything myself?
- Do I admit when I have made a mistake?

[a]By substituting ''athlete'' for ''staff'' many of the same questions may be used for self-examination to determine a coach's relationship with his or her athletes.

loyalty, staff organization and orientation, delegation, communication, criticism, praise, and other behavior patterns of the coach. It is suggested that one read each question and respond ''yes'' or ''no,'' although one could set up a continuum and attempt to evaluate himself or herself in terms of high, medium, and low, instead of in terms of absolute yes or no. The list of questions is by no means complete, and the reader may wish to evaluate himself further by posing additional questions.

Previously it was suggested that one should get to ''know thyself.'' The advice has not changed, only here the emphasis is on getting to ''know thyself'' in one's relationship to other staff members. While these questions are directed to the head coach, if each staff member were to examine and answer the questions that relate to him or her, this would likely improve interpersonal staff relationships. Also, by substituting ''athlete'' in place of ''staff,'' many of the same questions in Figure 12-4 may be used for self-examination in order to determine a coach's relationship with the athletes on his or her team.

Summary

Within every formal organization structure, whether it be in industry, business, government, education, or sports, there exists a social system of the members of the informal group or emergent organization. In athletics, team or group members, whether they be players and/or coaches, interact and relate with each other in performing their assigned duties designed by the formal authority structure; they then establish relationships with their own group members in order to satisfy affinity and achievement needs. The emergent organization converts the formal organization structure into a living, functioning, goal-directed group.

Group characteristics consist of common goals, norms, reward and punishment systems, informal leader(s), role status relationships, communication networks, decision-making processes, and a unique organizational climate. These roles and norms of the group strongly influence an individual's actions. The individual's willingness to conform to the group's roles and norms is based on the rewards received from the position and group identification; these rewards are primarily security, acceptance, and status.

Conflict, consisting of a disagreement between two or more people resulting from an incompatibility of goals, interests, perceptions, or values, is commonplace in virtually all formal organizations even though the persons involved are members of the same company, group, or team. Although conflict is inevitable, it must be managed or it could become destructive and self-serving. Not all conflict is detrimental; some is good. Some competition between groups or individuals may be beneficial and stimulating, as long as the common goals predominate. When conflict turns into hostility, involving malicious actions against team or group members who are perceived as opponents or the enemy, it is obviously damaging and will destroy any team unity or cohesiveness if it is not minimized. It is important for a coach to understand the psychology of group behavior, how groups are structured, and how they function for effective coaching to occur.

REFERENCES

Alderman, R. B. *Psychological Behavior in Sport*. Philadelphia. W. B. Saunders, 1974, pp. 73–74.

Cartwright, D., and Zander, A. (Eds.). *Group Dynamics: Research and Theory*. New York. Row Peterson, 1953, pp. 77–78.

Church, R. "Applications of Behavior Theory to Social Psychology." In *Social Facilitation and Imitative Behavior*, R. A. Samuels et al. (Eds.). Boston. Allyn & Bacon, 1968.

Eitzen, D. Stanley. "The Effect of Group Structure on the Success of Athletic Teams." *International Review of Sport Sociology*, 1973, pp. 7–17.

Festinger, L., Schachter, S., and Back, K. *Social Pressures in Informal Groups: A Study of a Housing Project*. New York. Harper and Bros., 1950, p. 164.

Gross, N., and Martin, W. E. "On Group Cohesiveness." *American Journal of Sociology*, 1952, pp. 546–554.

Hirota, K. *Psychology of Group*. Tokyo. Seishin-Shobo, 1963, p. 391.

Knowles, Malcom, and Knowles, Huda. *Introduction to Group Dynamics*. New York. Association Press, 1972, pp. 60–64.

Lewin, Kurt. "Psycho-Sociological Problems of a Minority Group." *Character & Personality*. Vol. 3, 1935, pp. 175–187.

London, Manuel, and Oldham, Greg R. "A Comparison of Group and Individual Incentive Plans." *Academy of Management Journal*. Vol. 20, No. 1, March 1977.

Martens, Rainer. "Competition: In Need of a Theory." In *Social Problems in Athletics*, Daniel M. Landers (Ed.). Urbana. University of Illinois Press, 1976, pp. 9–17.

Martens, Rainer, and Peterson, James A. "Group Cohesiveness as a Determinant of Success and Member Satisfaction in Team Performance." *International Review of Sport Sociology*, 1971, pp. 6, 49–60.

Mead, Margaret, *Cooperation and Competition Among Primitive Peoples*. New York. McGraw-Hill, 1961.

Myers, G. E., and Myers, M. T. *The Dynamics of Human Communication*. New York. McGraw-Hill, 1973, pp. 125–127.

Niwa, Takaaki. "A Methodological Study on the Group Cohesiveness of Sport Group Based on Sociometry." *International Review of Sport Sociology*. Vol. 3, 1968, p. 58.

Sanford, Aubrey C. *Human Relations: Theory and Practice*. Columbus, Ohio. Charles E. Merrill Publishing Co., 1973, p. 84.

Schachter, S. "Deviation, Rejection, and Communication." *Journal of Abnormal Social Psychology*. Vol. 46, 1951, pp. 190–207.

Shapiro, Leonard. *The Washington Post*. As reported in *The Sacramento Bee*. "Miracle of Squaw Upstaged: Golden Ending for US Icemen." February 25, 1980, p. C-1.

Shaw, Marvin E. *Group Dynamics: The Psychology of Small Group Behavior*. New York. McGraw-Hill, 1971, pp. 189–232.

Sherif, Carolyn W. "The Social Context of Competition." In *Social Problems in Athletics*, Daniel M. Landers (Ed.). Urbana. University of Illinois Press, 1976, pp 18–36.

Simmel, George. "The Dyad and the Triad." In *The Sociology of George Simmel*, Kurt H. Wolff (Ed.). Glencoe, Illinois. The Free Press, 1950.

Zander, Alvin. "Motivation and Performance of Sports Groups." In *Psychology of Sport and Motor Behavior II*. Daniel M. Landers (Ed.). University Park, Penn. The Pennsylvania State University Press, 1975, pp. 26–35.

Zander, Alvin, and Medow, Herman. "Individual and Group Levels of Aspiration." *Human Relations*, 1963, pp. 89–105.

SUGGESTED READINGS

Aykens, Paul. "Making a Staff Team." *Interscholastic Athletic Administration*. Vol. 2, No. 4, Fall 1976, p. 26.

Cratty, Bryant J. *Social Psychology in Athletics*. Englewood Cliffs, New Jersey. Prentice-Hall, 1981.

Fuoss, Donald E., and Troppmann, Robert J. *Creative Management Techniques in Interscholastic Athletics*. New York. John Wiley & Sons, 1977, pp. 156–163.

Gammons, Peter. "New Coach, Same Old Success." *Sports Illustrated*. Vol. 48, No. 5, January 30, 1978, pp. 42–43.

Hall, Jay. "What Makes a Manager Good, Bad or Average?" *Psychology Today*. August 1976, pp. 52–54.

Landers, Daniel M., and Luschen, Gunther. "Team Performance and Cohesiveness of Competitive Coaching Groups." *International Review of Sport Sociology*. No. 9, 1974, pp. 57–69.

Melnick, Merrill J., and Chemers, Martin M. "Effects of Group Social Structure on the Success of Basketball Teams." *Research Quarterly*. Vol. 45, No. 1, May 1974, pp. 1–8.

Petrie, Brian M. "Social Psychology of Sports: An Assessment of Present Status." In *The Status of Motor Learning and Sport Psychology Research*, Brent S. Rushall (Ed.). Dartmouth, Nova Scotia. Sport Science Associates, 1975, pp. 14.1–14.13.

Snyder, Eldon E. "Variations in Team Status and the Coach's Influence on High School Athletics." *The Physical Educator*. Vol. 29, May 1972, pp. 2, 96–98.

Yanke, Paul. "Organizing the Staff." *Athletic Journal*. Vol. 55, No. 7, March 1975, pp. 38, 62.

Index